Tatsuki Fujimoto

I love *Séance!*

Tatsuki Fujimoto won Honorable Mention in the
November 2013 Shueisha Crown Newcomers' Awards for
his debut one-shot story *Love Is Blind*. His first series,
Fire Punch, ran for eight volumes. *Chainsaw Man* began
serialization in 2018 in *Weekly Shonen Jump*.

CHAINSAW MAN

8

SHONEN JUMP Manga Edition

Story & Art **TATSUKI FUJIMOTO**

Translation/AMANDA HALEY
Touch-Up Art & Lettering/SABRINA HEEP
Design/JULIAN [JR] ROBINSON
Editor/ALEXIS KIRSCH

First published in Japan in 2018 by SHUEISHA Inc., Tokyo.
English translation rights arranged by SHUEISHA Inc.

Printed in Italy

Published by VIZ Media, LLC
P.O. Box 77010
San Francisco, CA 94107

10 9 8 7 6 5 4 3 2
First printing, December 2021
Second printing, December 2021

VIZ MEDIA
viz.com

SHONEN JUMP

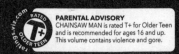

8

Super Mess

Tatsuki Fujimoto

CHARACTERS

Denji

A young man-slash-Chainsaw Devil who carries his partner Pochita inside him. He's always true to his desires. Likes Makima, the first person to ever treat him like a human being.

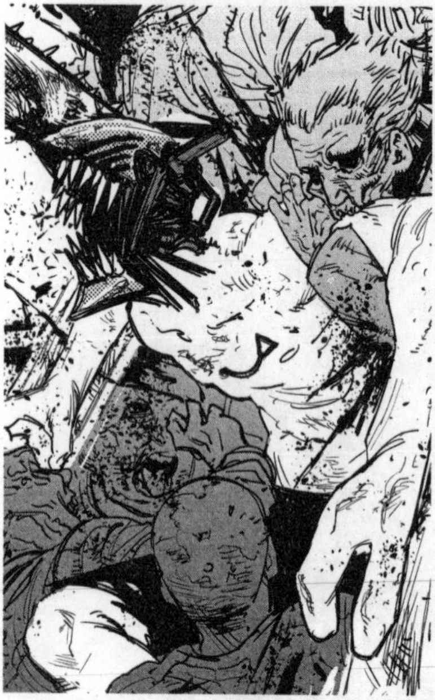

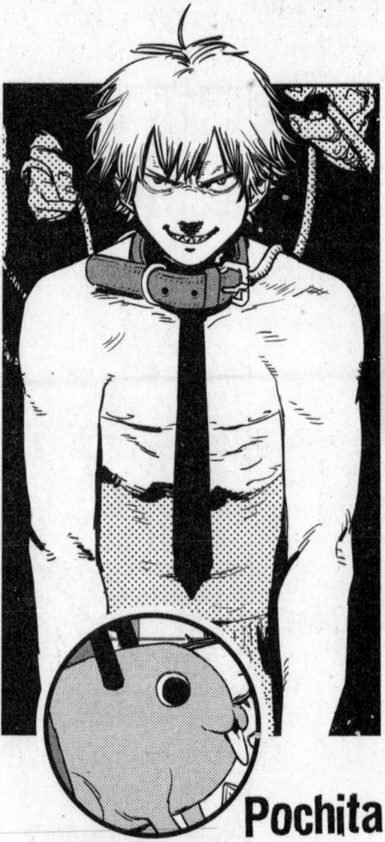

Pochita

Chainsaw Devil. Gave up his heart to Denji, becoming part of his body.

Makima

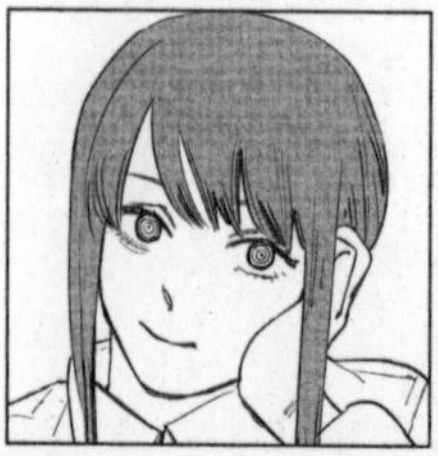

The mysterious woman in charge of Public Safety Devil Extermination Special Division 4. Can smell devil scents.

Aki Hayakawa

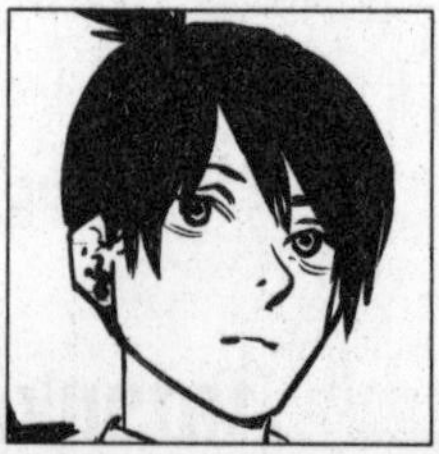

Makima's loyal subordinate and Denji's senior at Public Safety by three years. Devil Contracts: Future Devil, Curse Devil.

Angel Devil

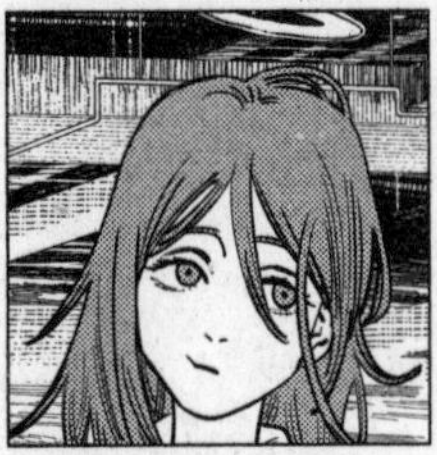

Though not hostile to humans, anyone who touches this devil directly will have their life span siphoned off. Special Division 4 agent.

Power

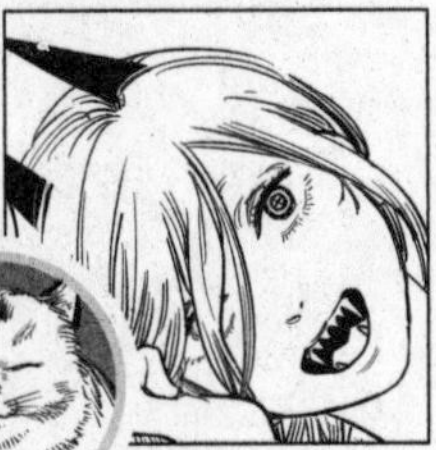

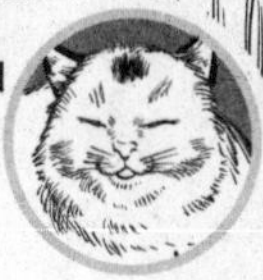

Blood Devil Fiend. Egotistical and prone to going out of control. Her cat Meowy is her only friend.

The Puppeteer

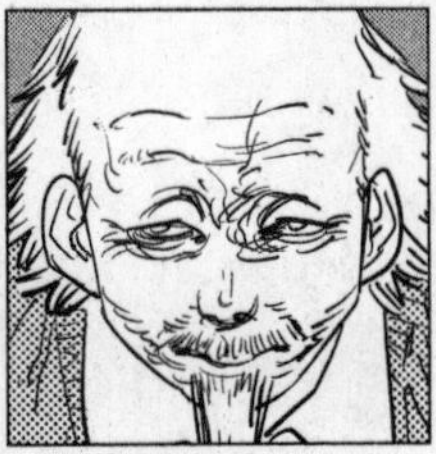

Uses the Doll Devil. Turns humans into dolls. Anyone touched by the dolls suffers the same fate.

Quanxi

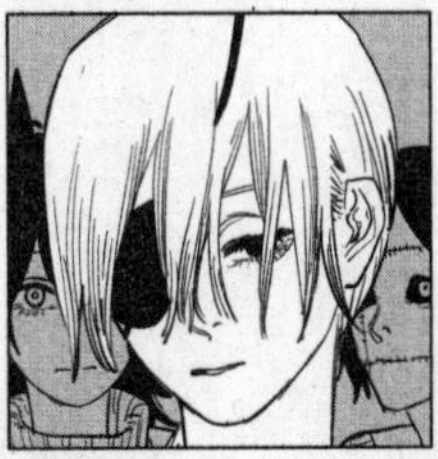

Assassin from China. Kishibe's ex-buddy and supposedly the strongest humanity has to offer. Accompanied by four female fiends.

Tolka

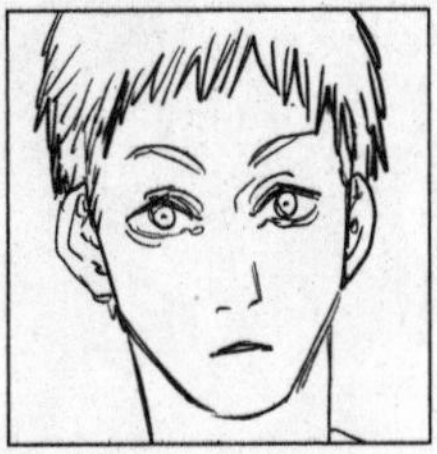

A young man training under Master. Won't hesitate to take a life.

Master

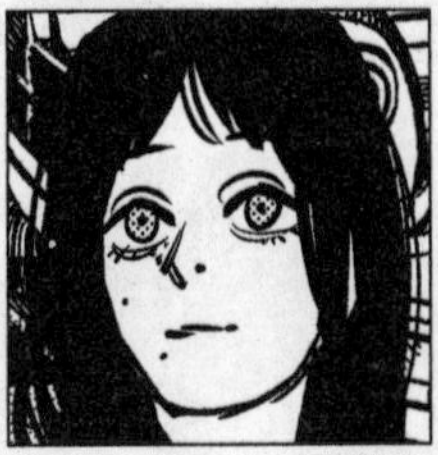

A Devil Hunter who has a contract with the Curse Devil. Only has six months left to live. Tolka's master.

STORY

Denji is a young man who hunts devils with his pet devil-dog Pochita. To pay off his debts, Denji is forced to live in extreme poverty and worked like a dog, only to be betrayed and killed on the job without ever getting to live a decent life. But Pochita, at the cost of the pooch's own life, brings Denji back—as Chainsaw Man! After Denji buzzes through all their attackers, he's taken in by the mysterious Makima, and begins a new life as a Public Safety Devil Hunter.

When Denji makes the TV news as the "Chainsaw Devil," the entire world suddenly knows he's in Japan—and governments across the globe are sending assassins to get their hands on the valuable human-devil hybrid! As Quanxi from China, Santa Claus from Germany, three Devil Hunter brothers from America, and more converge on Tokyo, Public Safety gets all hands on deck for a plan to protect Denji. But things spiral out of control when a doll army unleashed by an elderly man using the Doll Devil drives Denji and his bodyguards inside a department store. Quanxi joins the fray, and all seems lost until Kishibe's arrival turns the tables. Using Quanxi's companions as hostages, Kishibe offers her a deal...if she'll help him kill Makima. When Kishibe is caught off guard for a single instant, though, will he lose the upper hand?

CONTENTS

Chapter 62: Super Mess

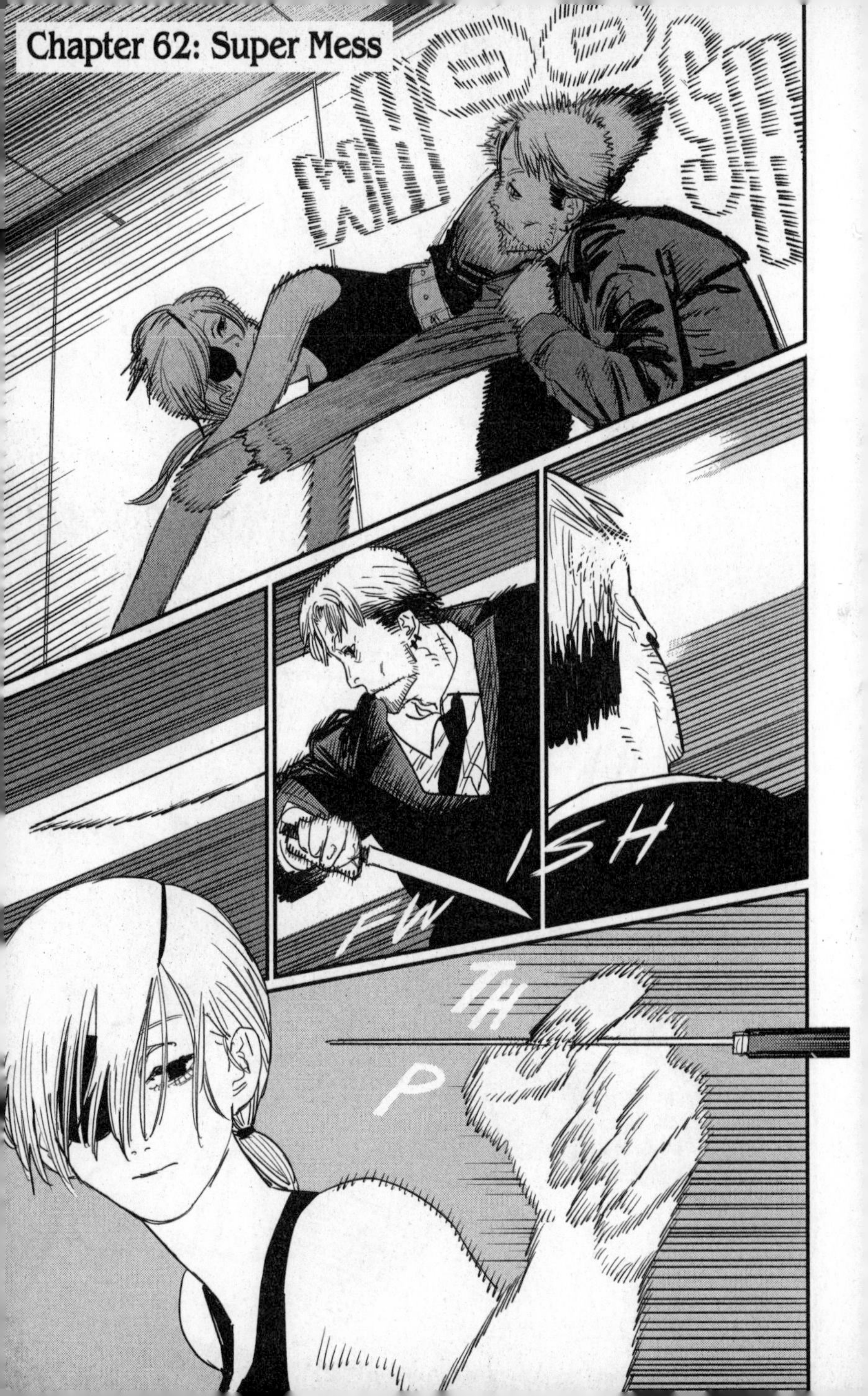
WHOOSH
FWISH
THP

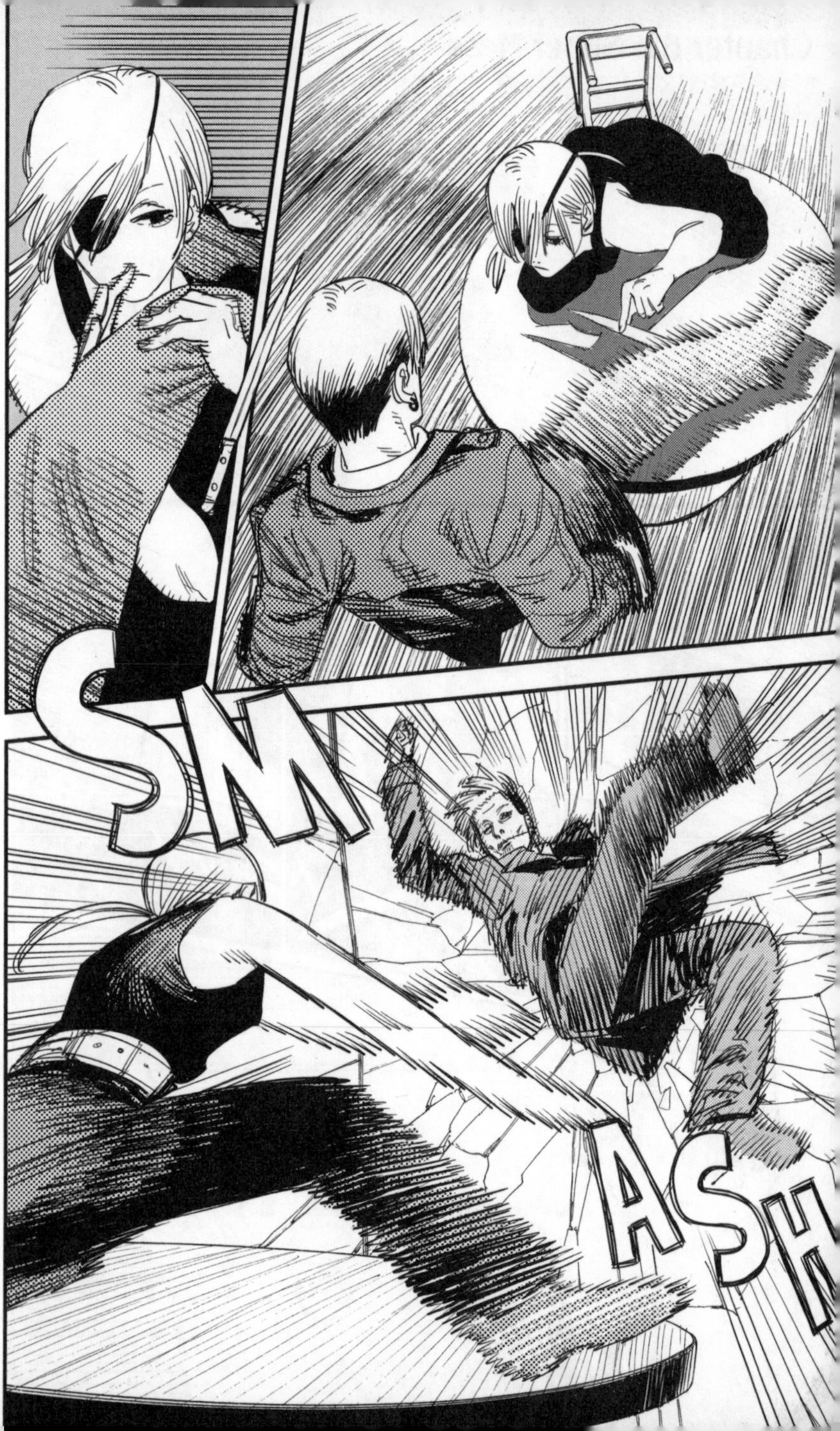
SMASH

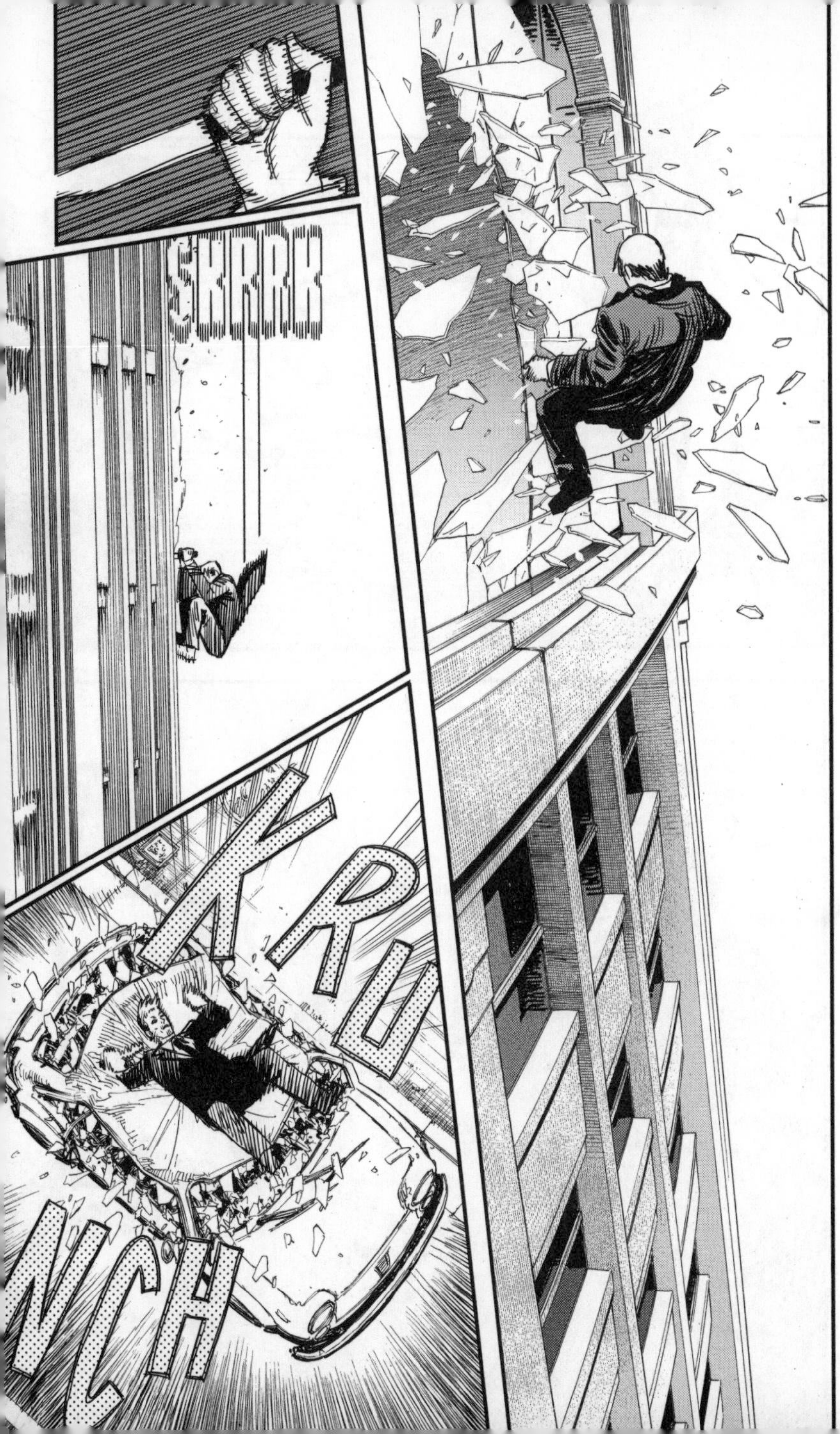
SKRRK
KRUNCH

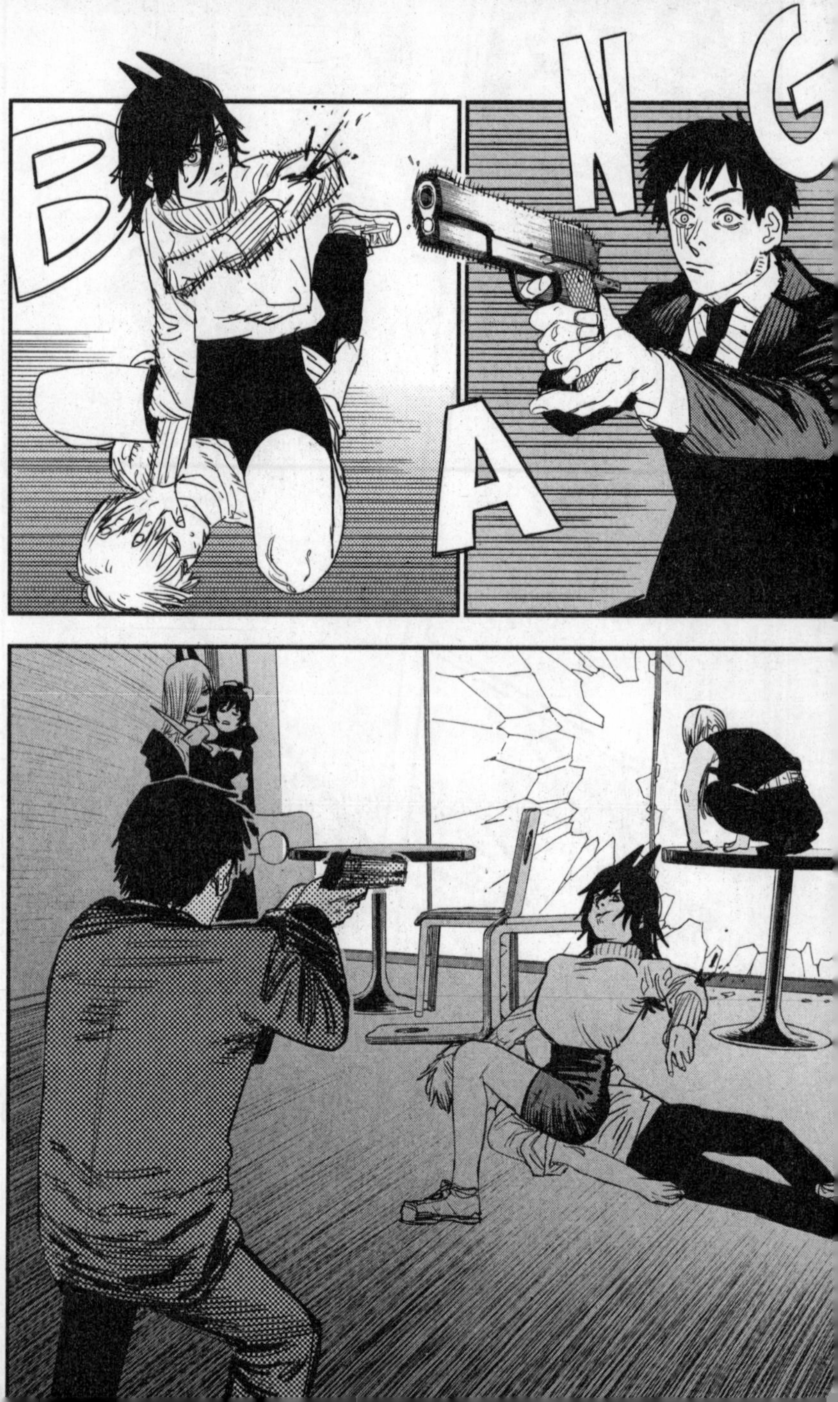
BANG

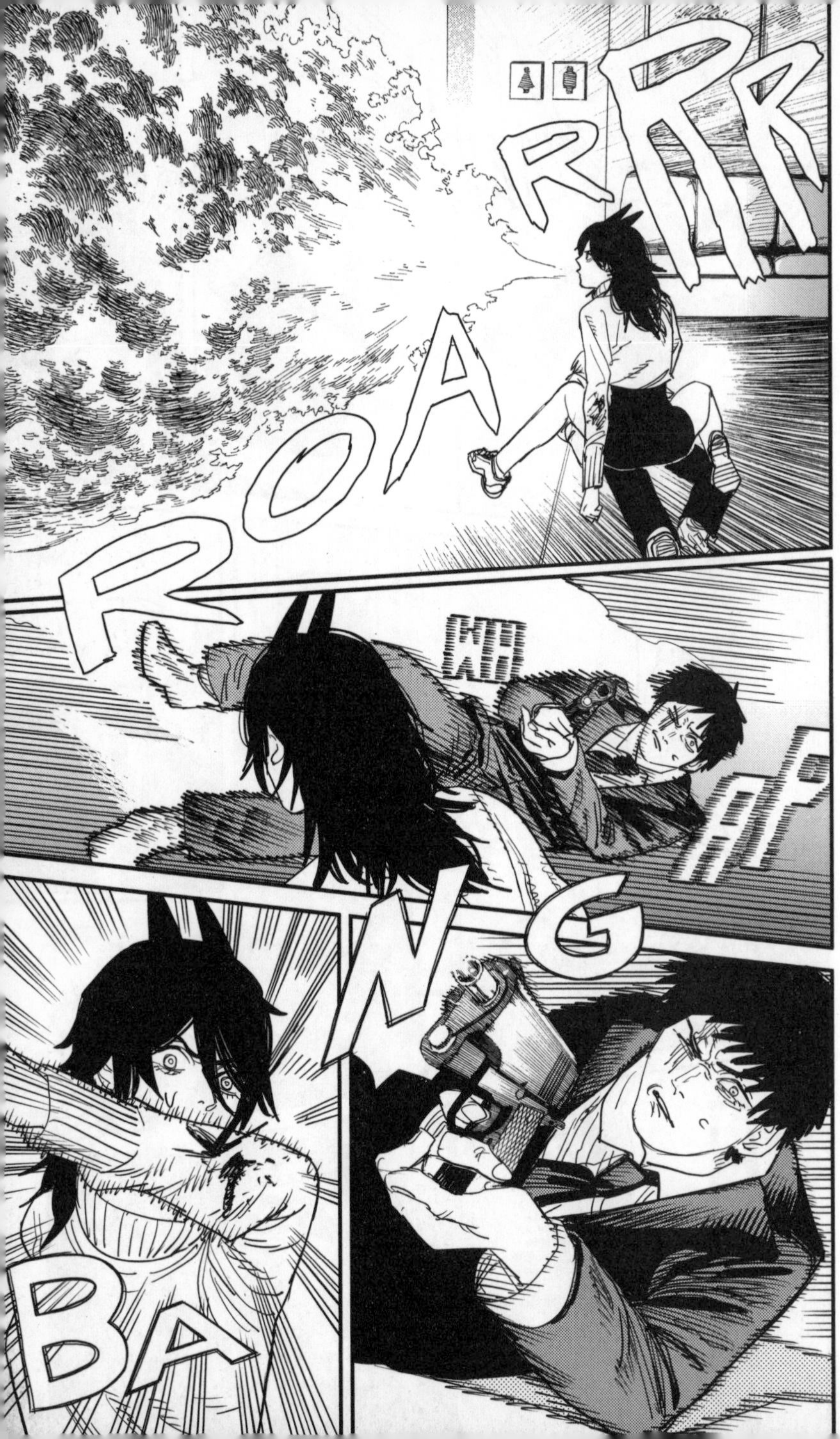
ROARRRR
BANG

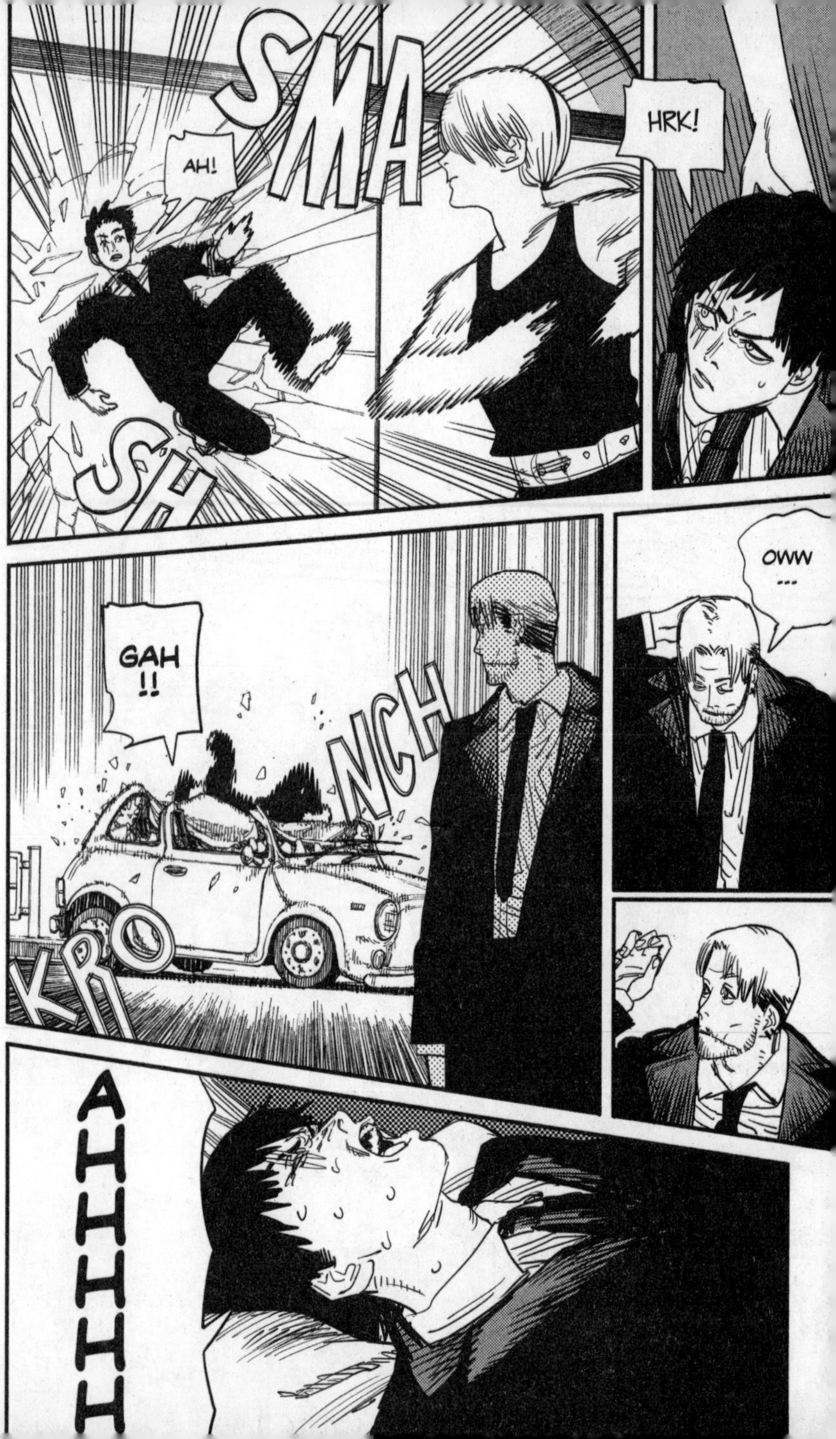
HRK!
SMA
AH!
SH
OWW ---
GAH !!
NCH
KRO
AHHHHH

MUH...

MUH...
M...
MY
CAR...

MY
CAR—

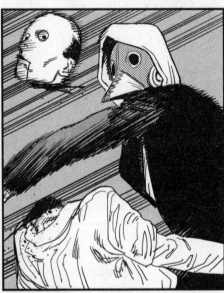

YOU ALL
GOOD
OVER
THERE,
KOBENI?

13

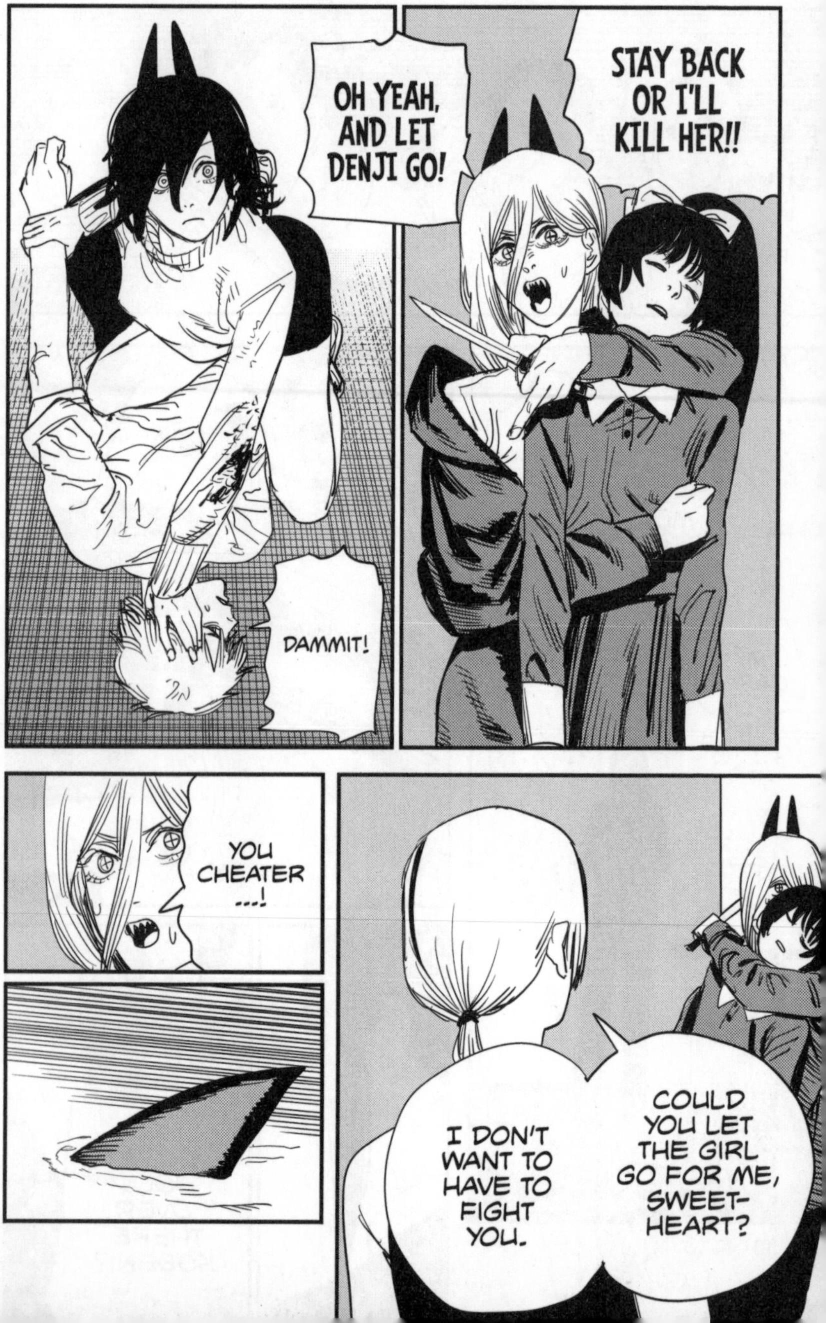
STAY BACK OR I'LL KILL HER!!
OH YEAH, AND LET DENJI GO!
DAMMIT!
COULD YOU LET THE GIRL GO FOR ME, SWEET-HEART?
I DON'T WANT TO HAVE TO FIGHT YOU.
YOU CHEATER ...!

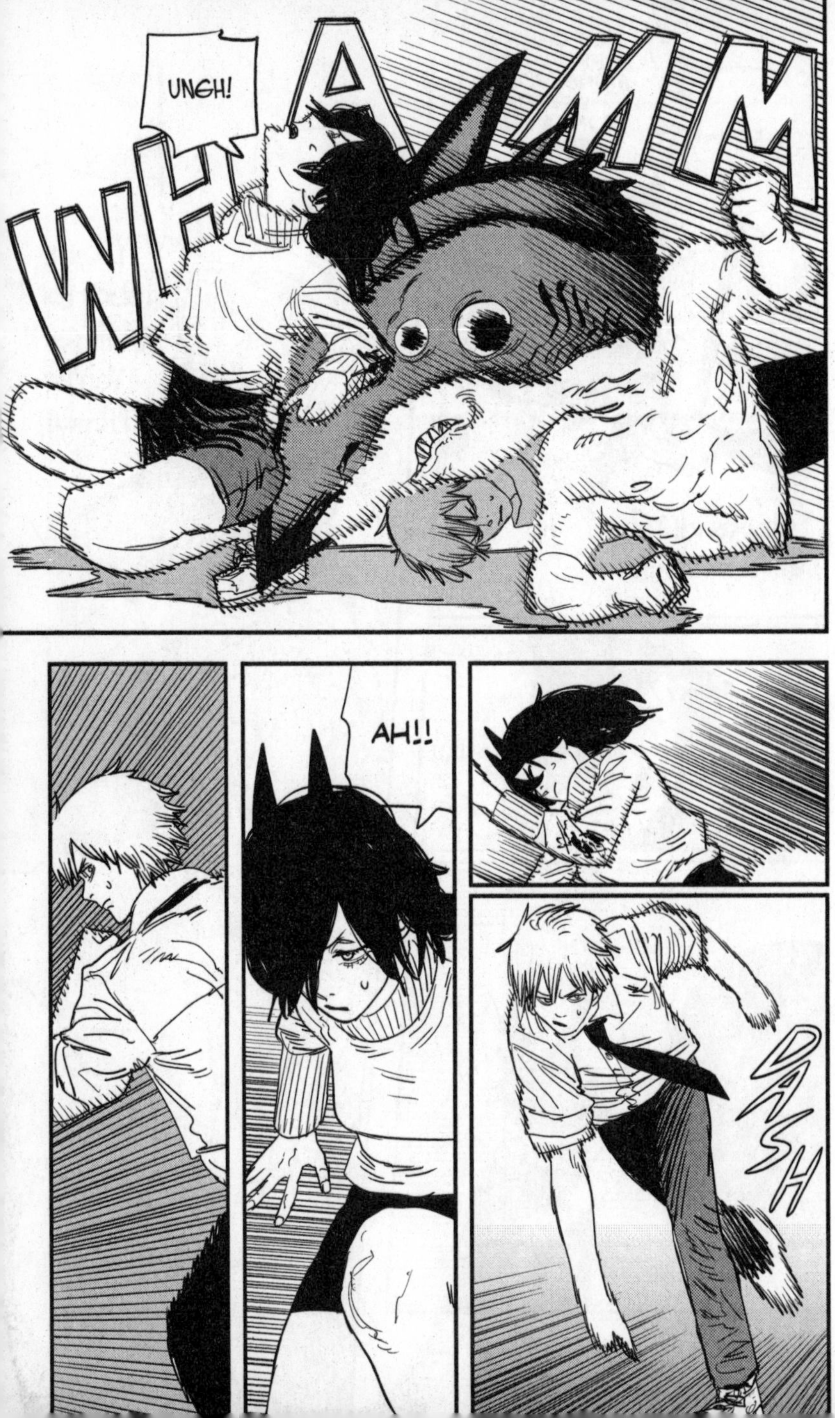
WHAMM
UNGH!
DASH
AH!!

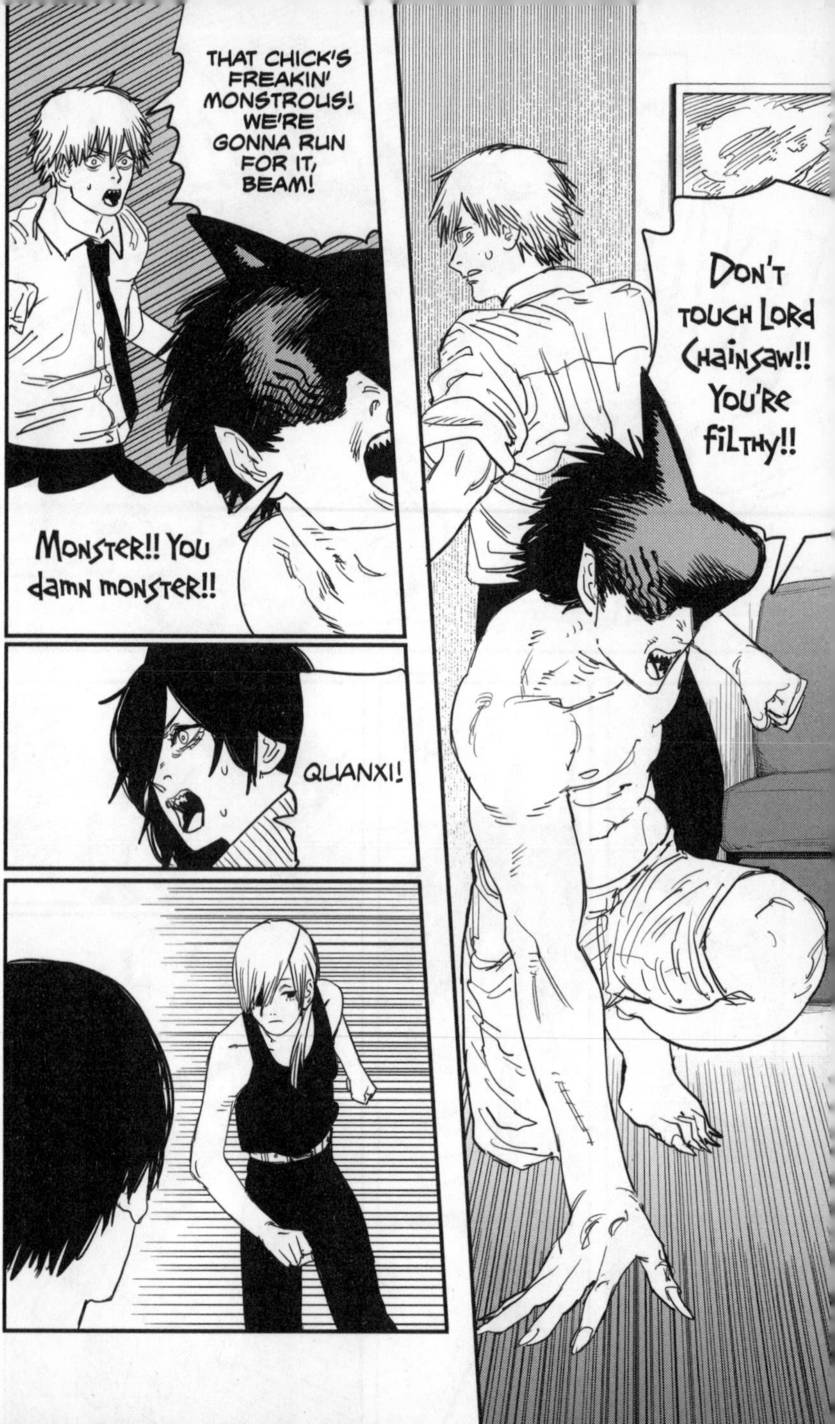

Don't touch Lord Chainsaw!! You're filthy!!
THAT CHICK'S FREAKIN' MONSTROUS! WE'RE GONNA RUN FOR IT, BEAM!
Monster!! You damn monster!!
QUANXI!

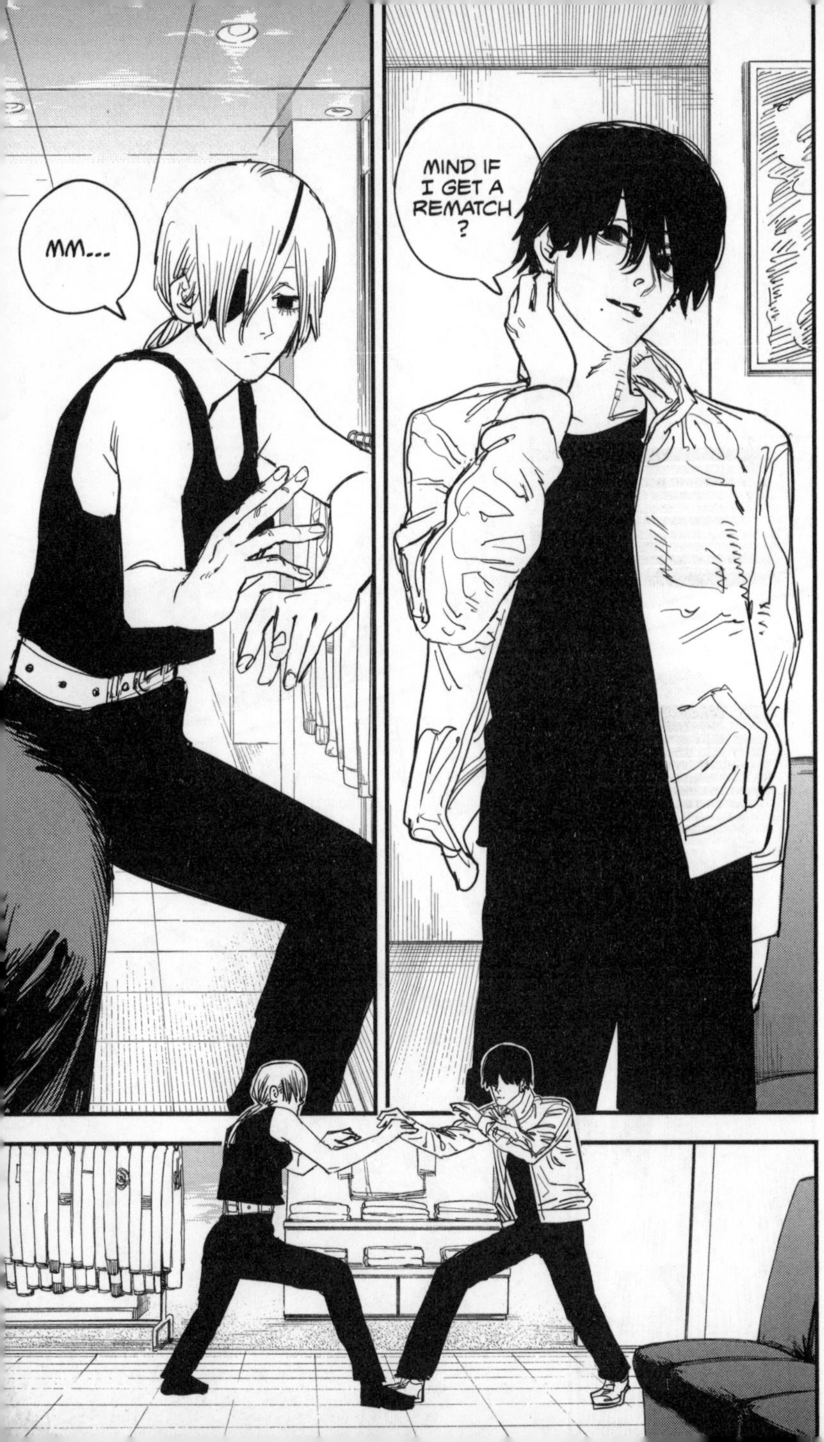
MIND IF I GET A REMATCH?
MM...

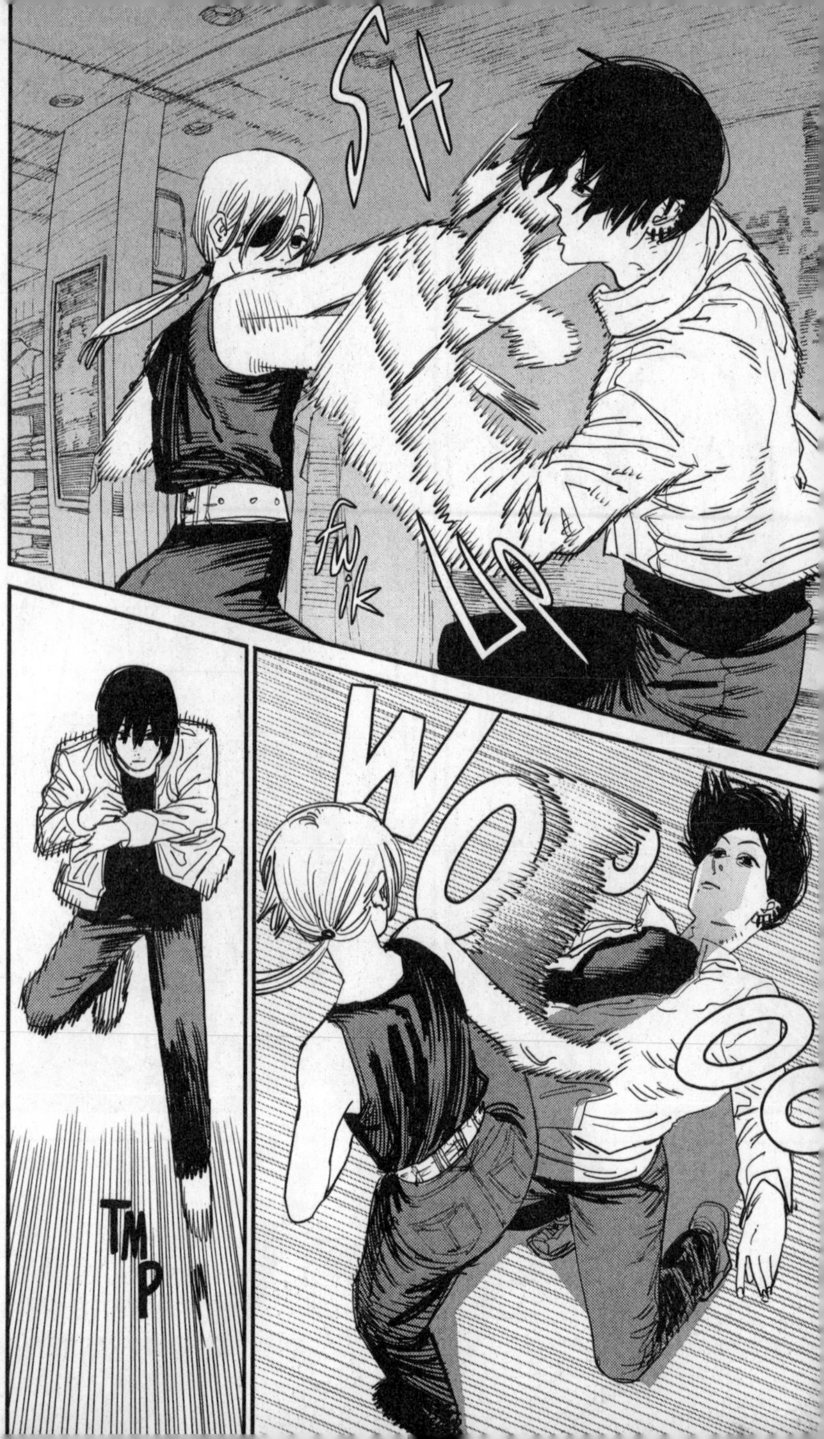
SH
fwik
WOOOO
TMP

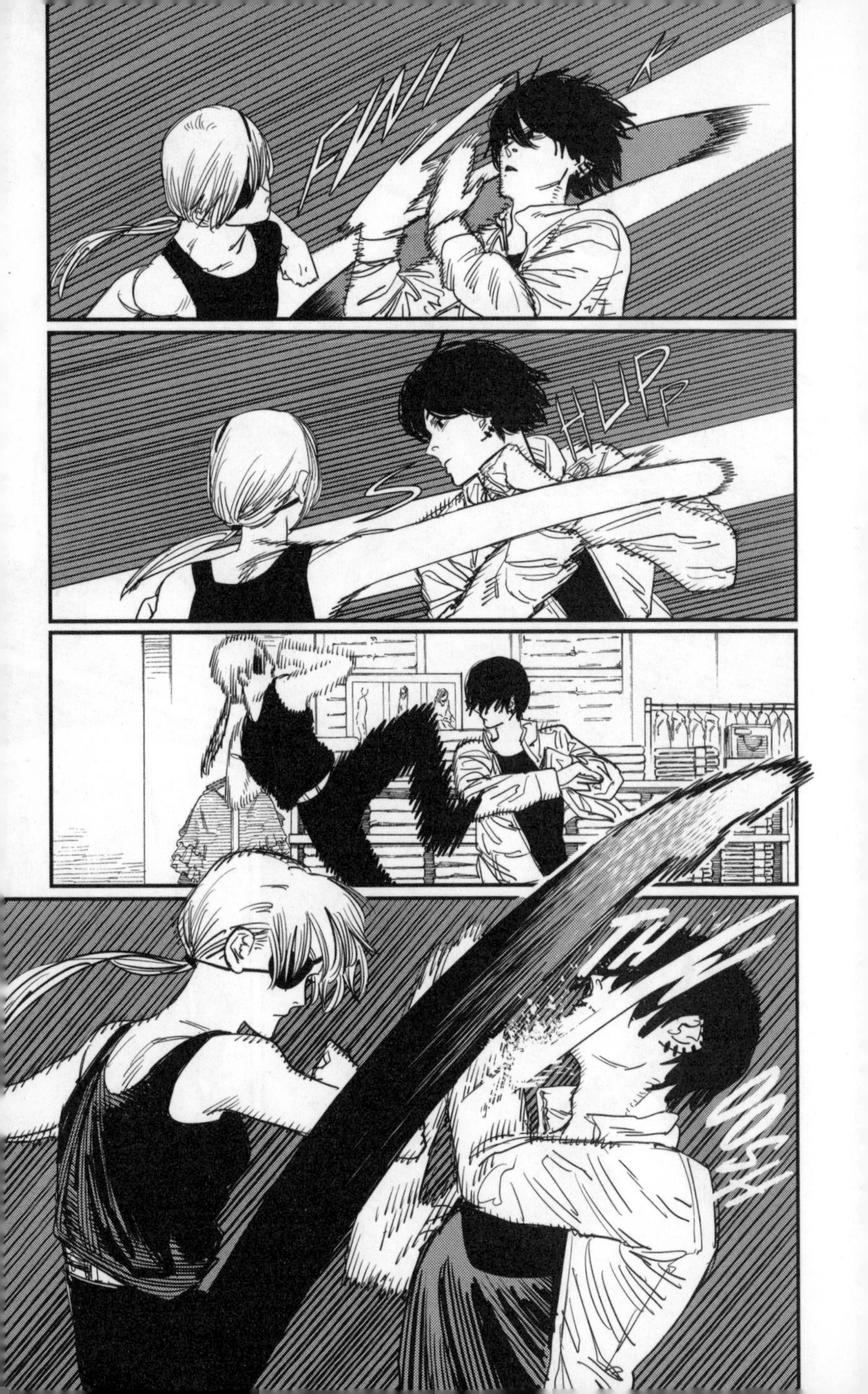
FWIIK
SHUPP
THWOOSH

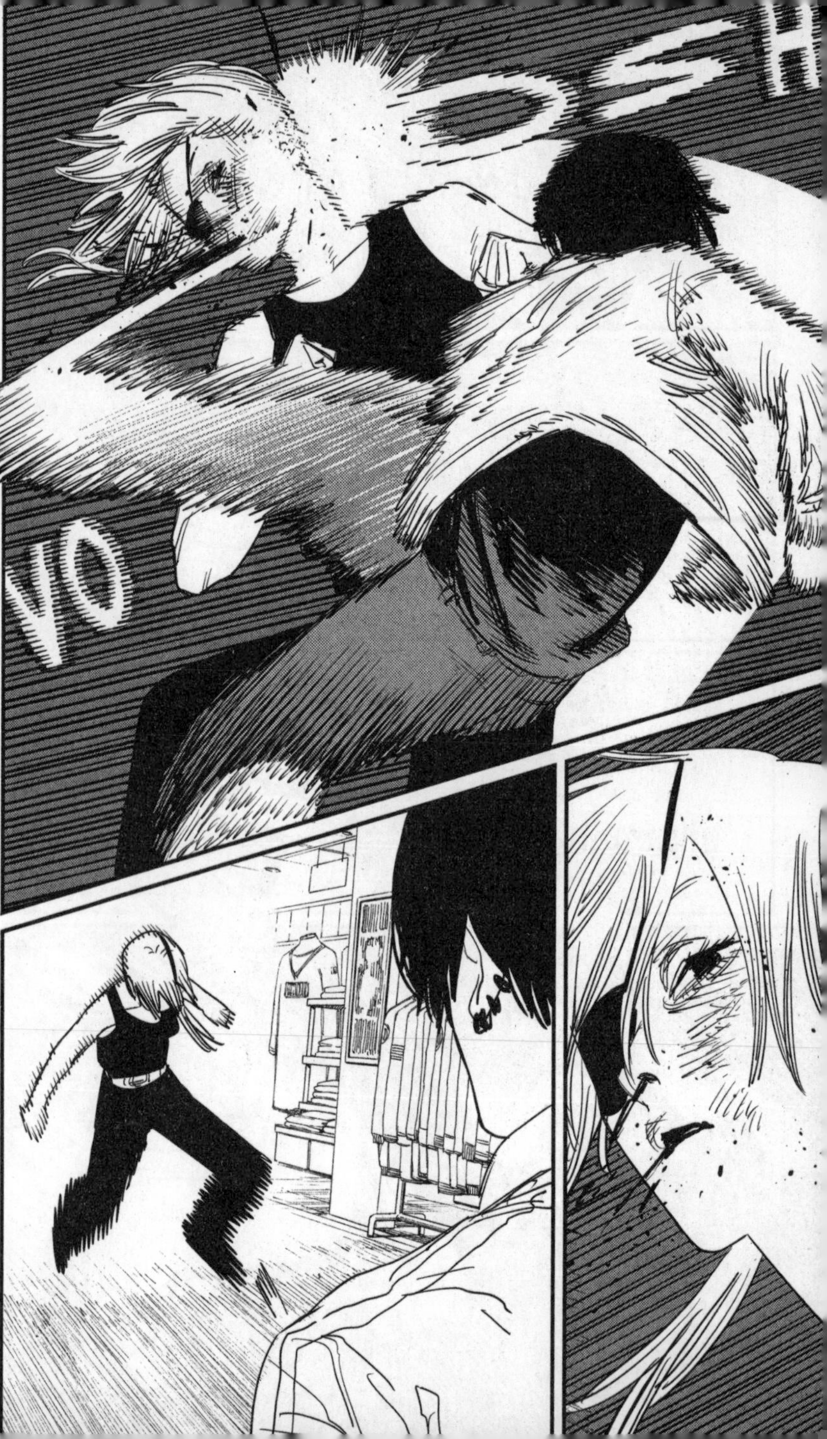
VO
OSH

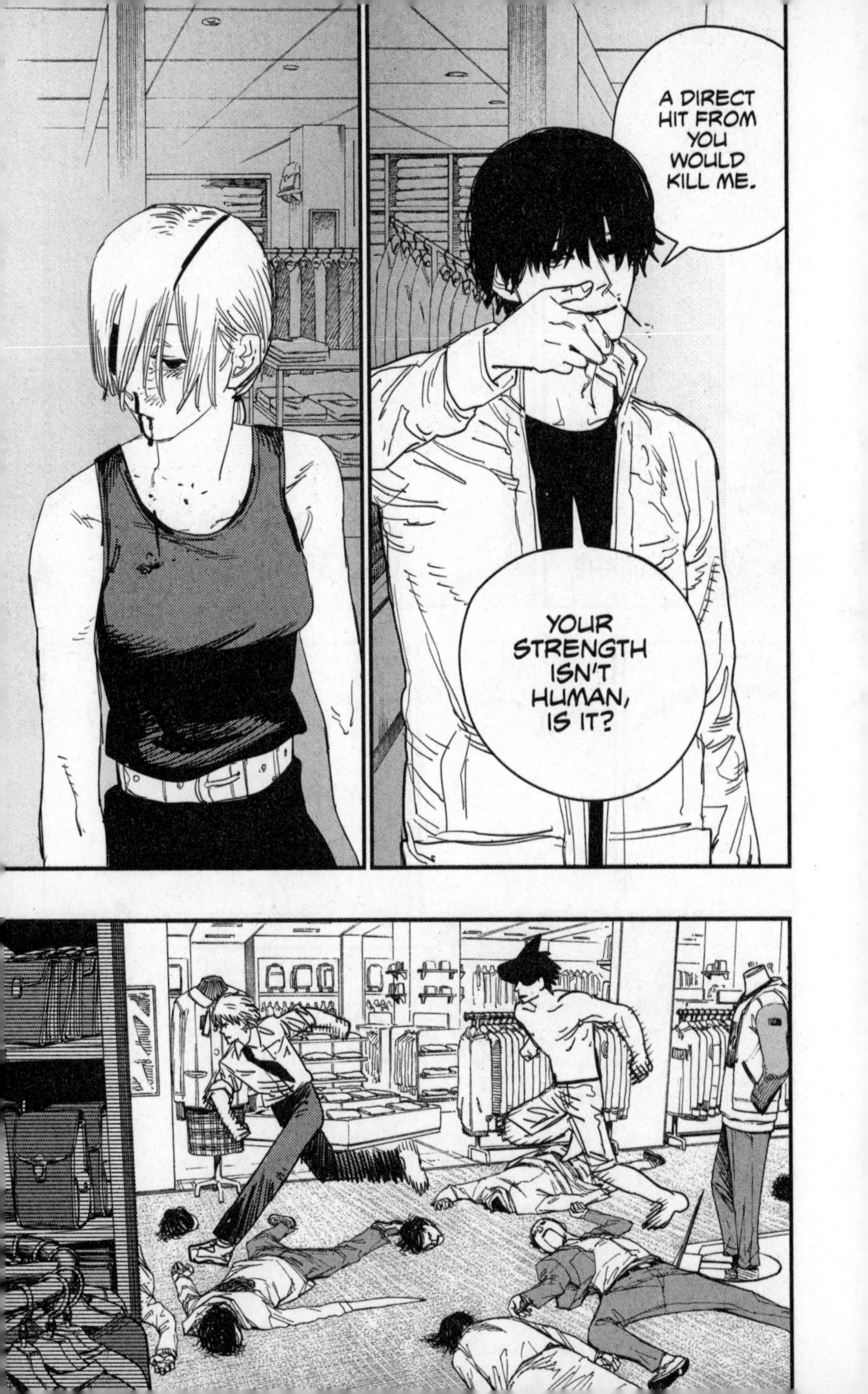
A DIRECT HIT FROM YOU WOULD KILL ME.
YOUR STRENGTH ISN'T HUMAN, IS IT?

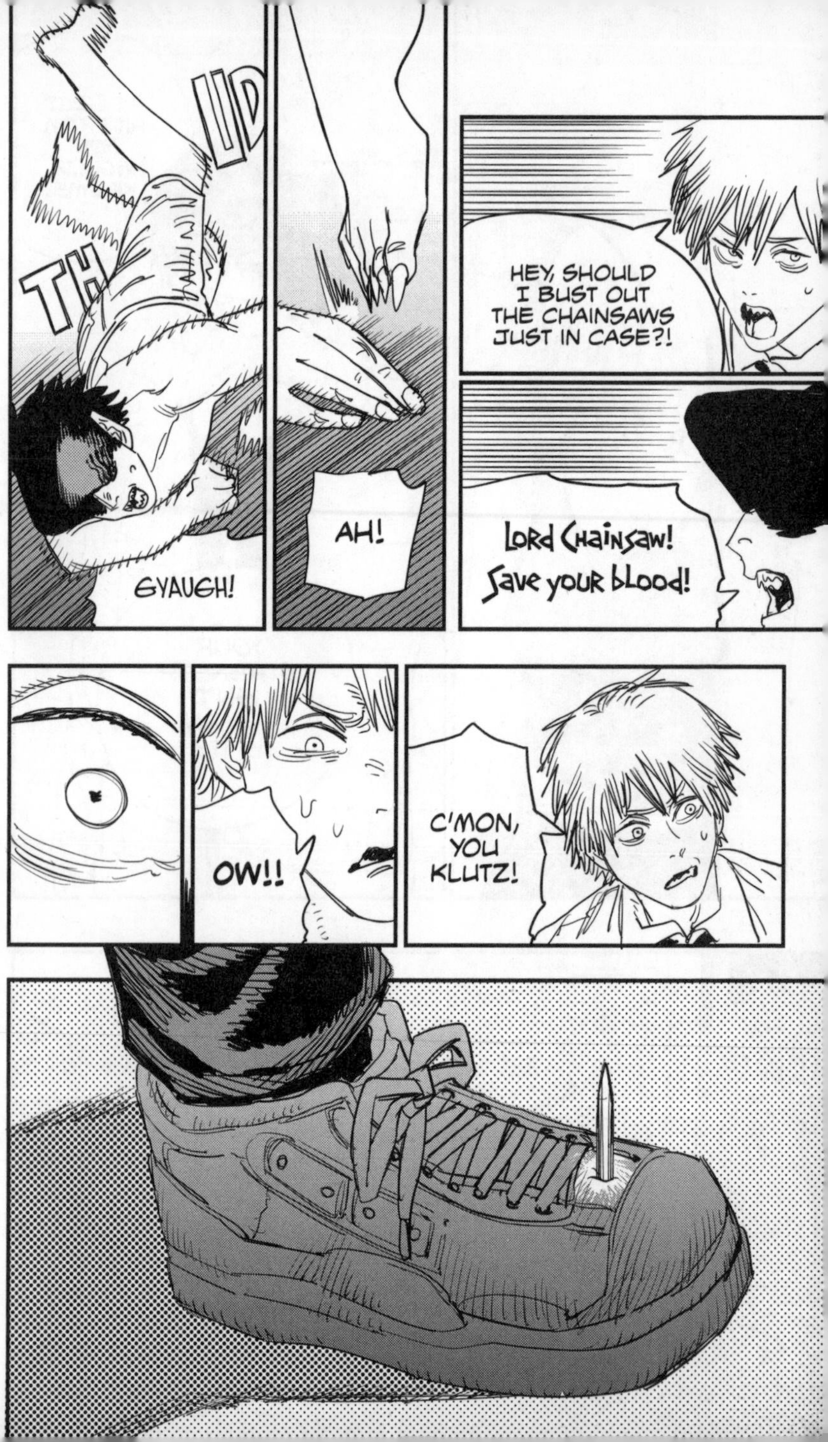
HEY, SHOULD I BUST OUT THE CHAINSAWS JUST IN CASE?!
Lord Chainsaw! Save your blood!
AH!
THUD
GYAUGH!
C'MON, YOU KLUTZ!
OW!!

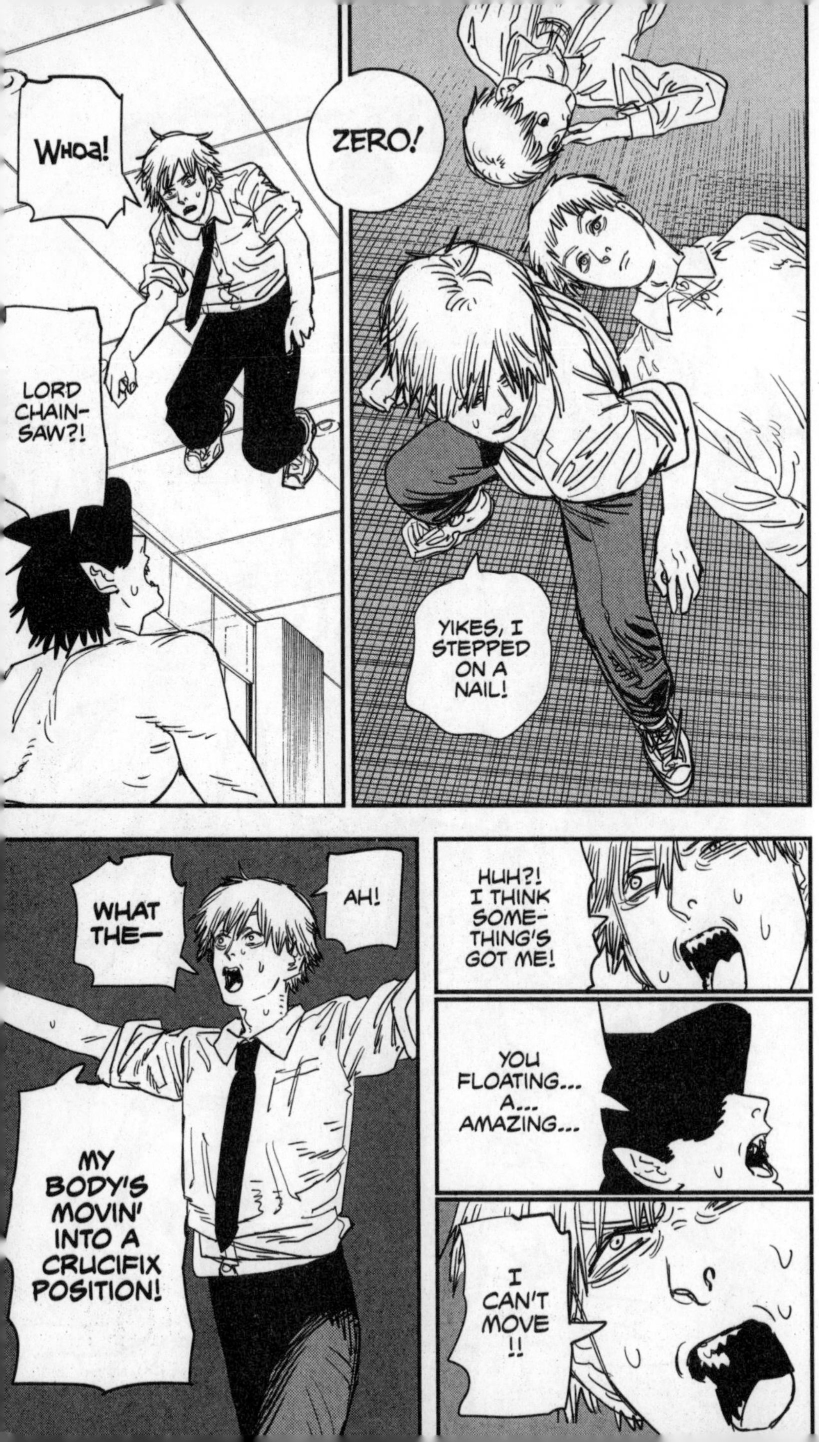
ZERO!
YIKES, I STEPPED ON A NAIL!
Whoa!
LORD CHAIN-SAW?!
HUH?! I THINK SOME-THING'S GOT ME!
YOU FLOATING... A... AMAZING...
I CAN'T MOVE !!
AH!
WHAT THE—
MY BODY'S MOVIN' INTO A CRUCIFIX POSITION!

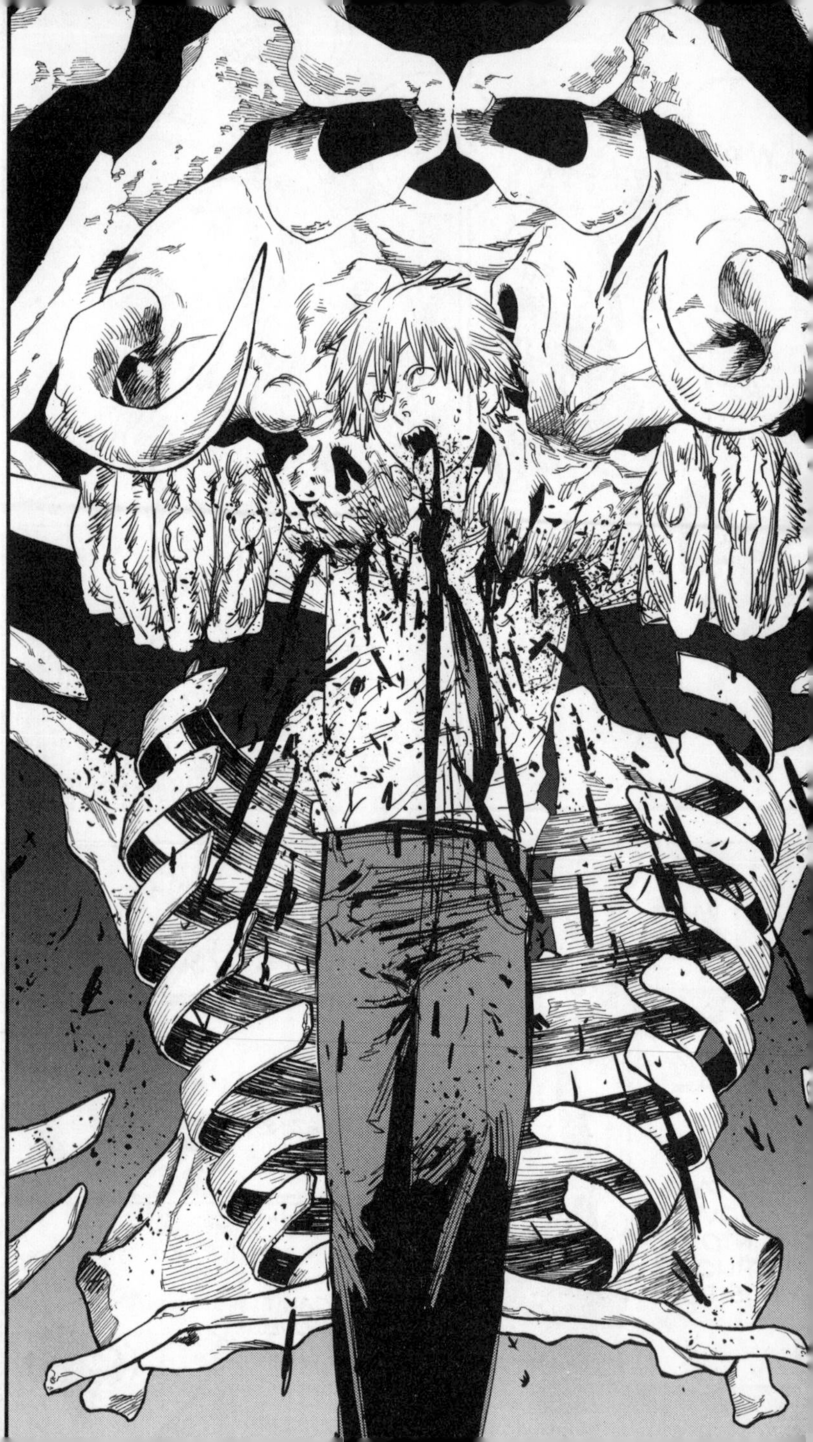

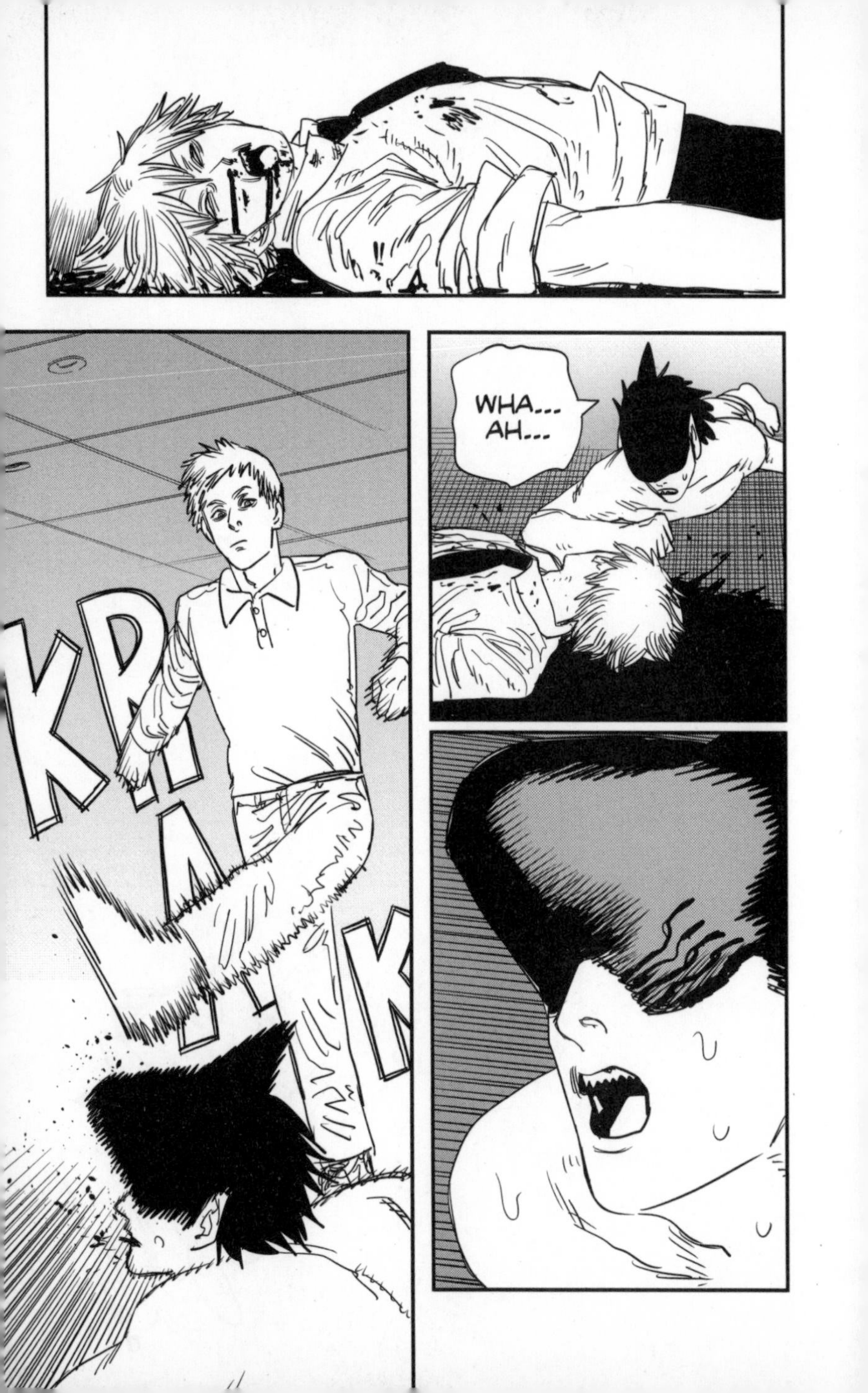
WHA...
AH...

Chainsaw man

Chapter 63: Trip to Hell

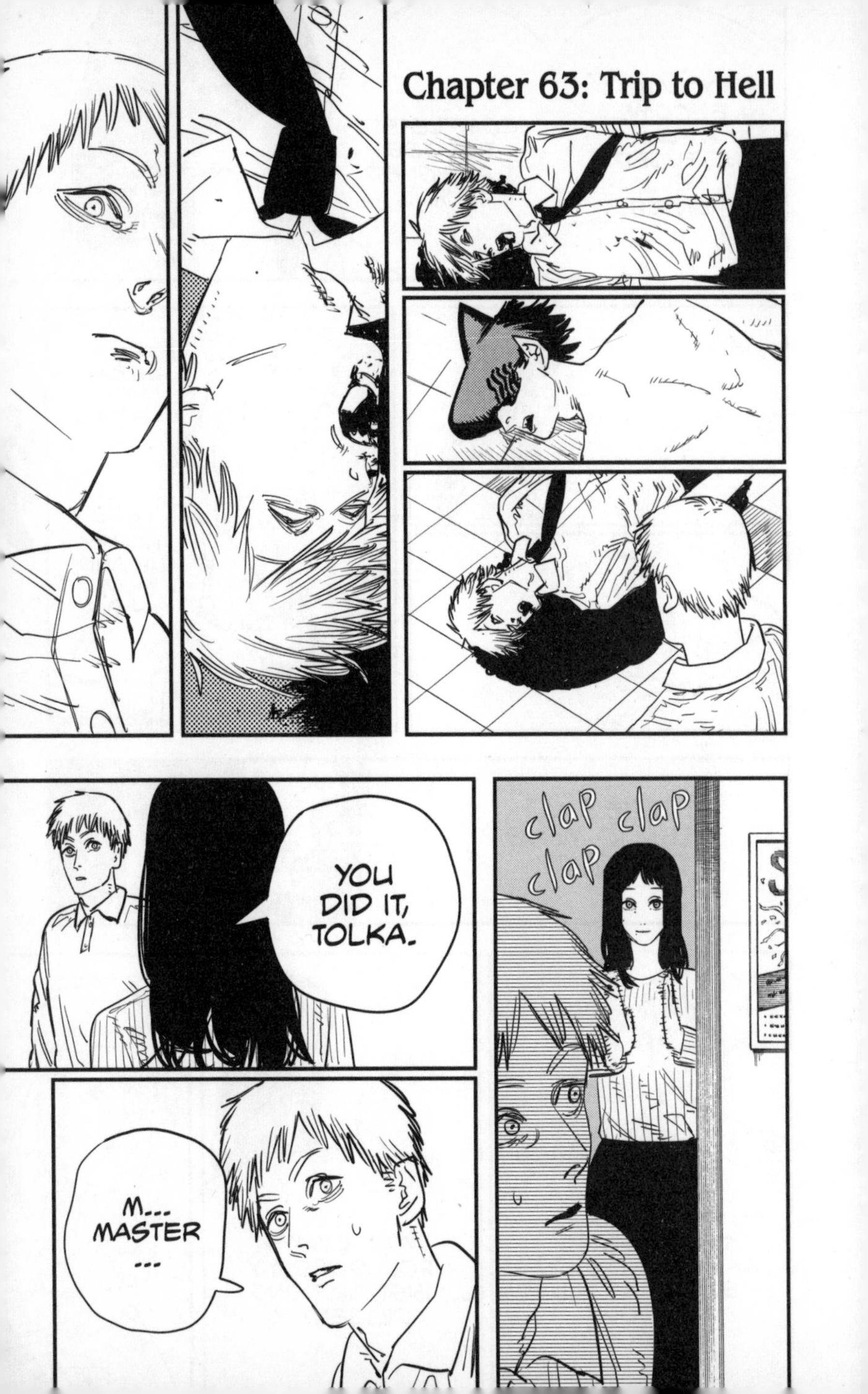
clap clap
clap
YOU DID IT, TOLKA.
M... MASTER ...

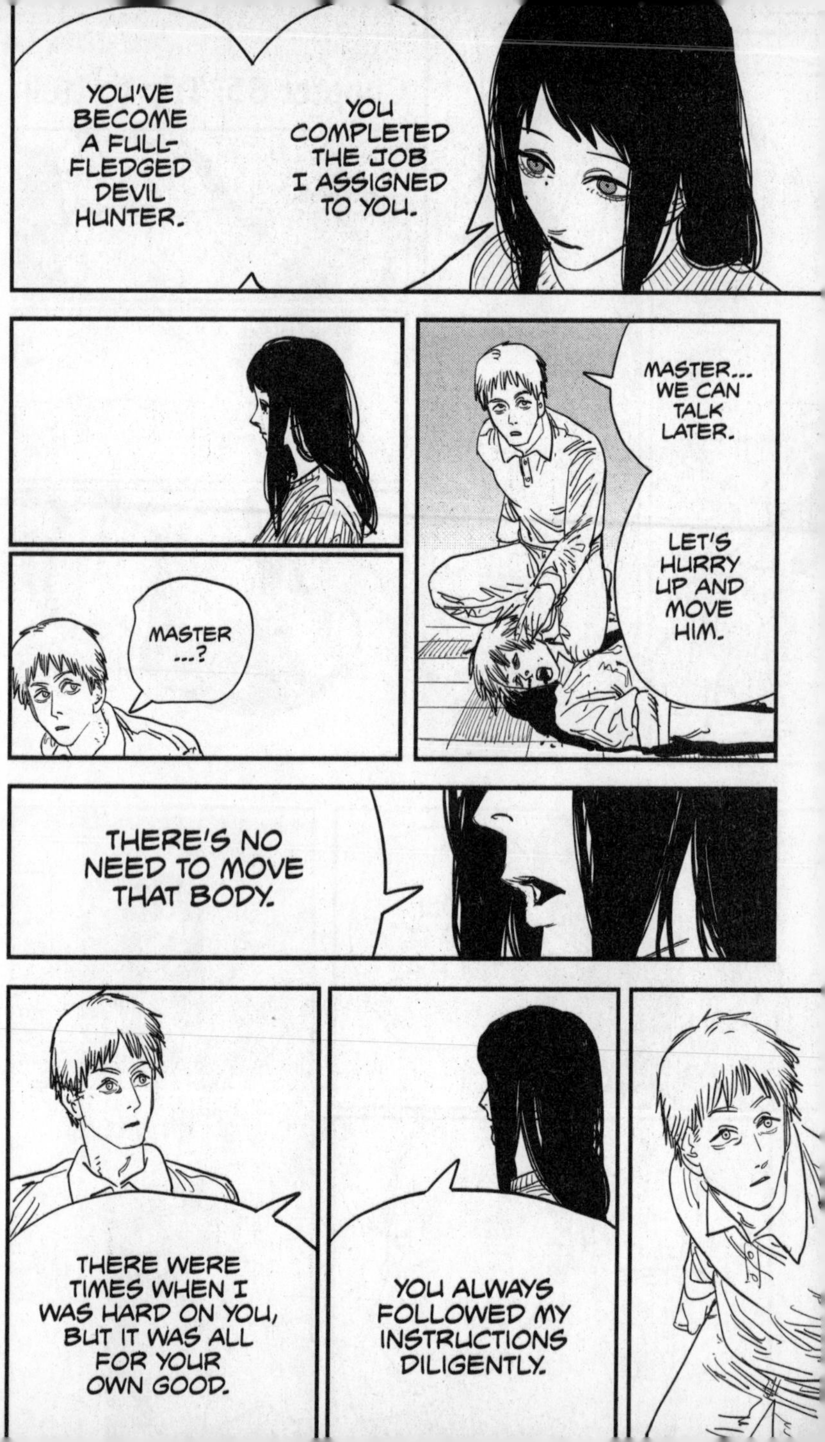
YOU COMPLETED THE JOB I ASSIGNED TO YOU.
YOU'VE BECOME A FULL-FLEDGED DEVIL HUNTER.
MASTER... WE CAN TALK LATER.
LET'S HURRY UP AND MOVE HIM.
MASTER ...?
THERE'S NO NEED TO MOVE THAT BODY.
YOU ALWAYS FOLLOWED MY INSTRUCTIONS DILIGENTLY.
THERE WERE TIMES WHEN I WAS HARD ON YOU, BUT IT WAS ALL FOR YOUR OWN GOOD.

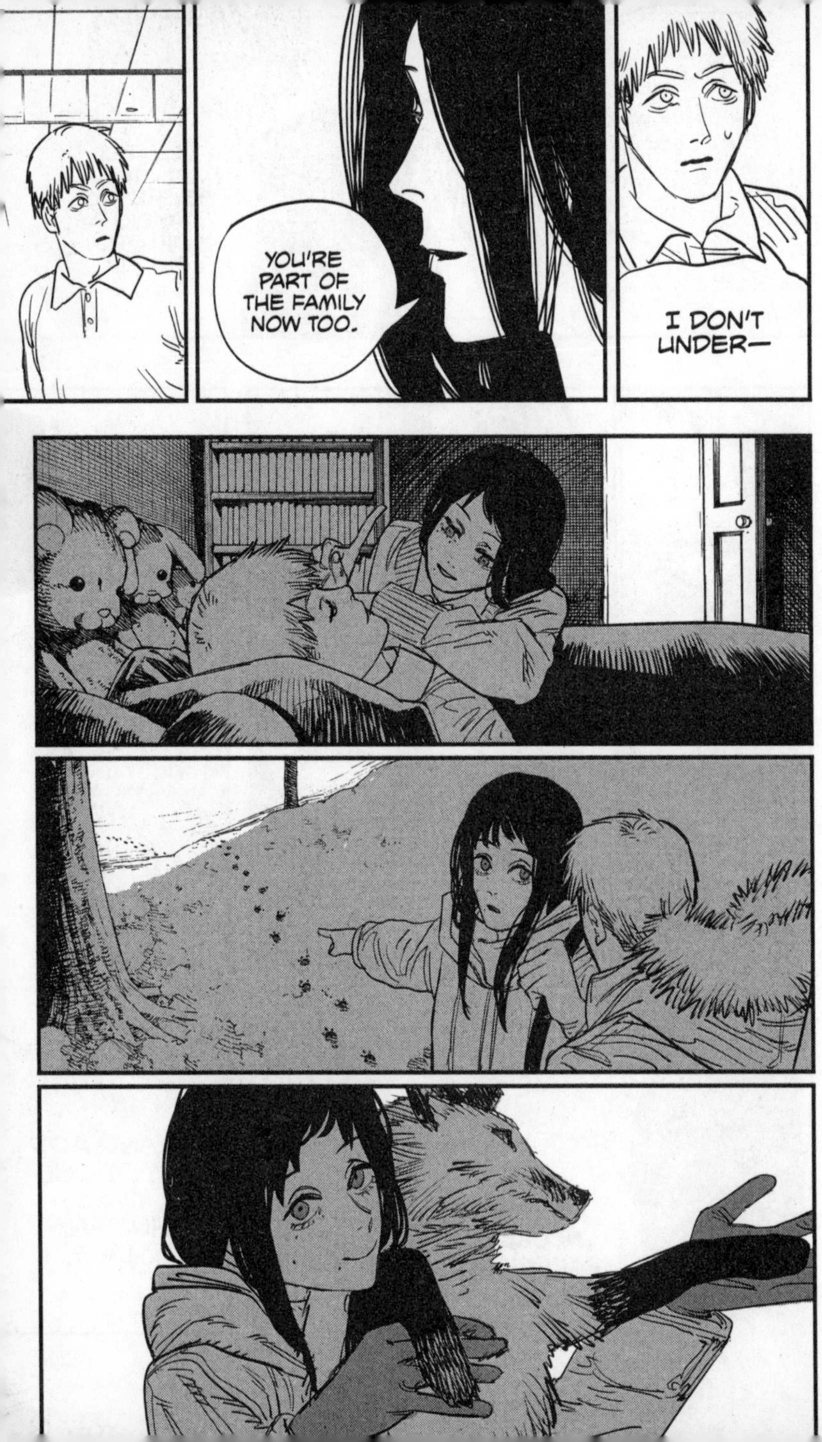
I DON'T UNDER—
YOU'RE PART OF THE FAMILY NOW TOO.

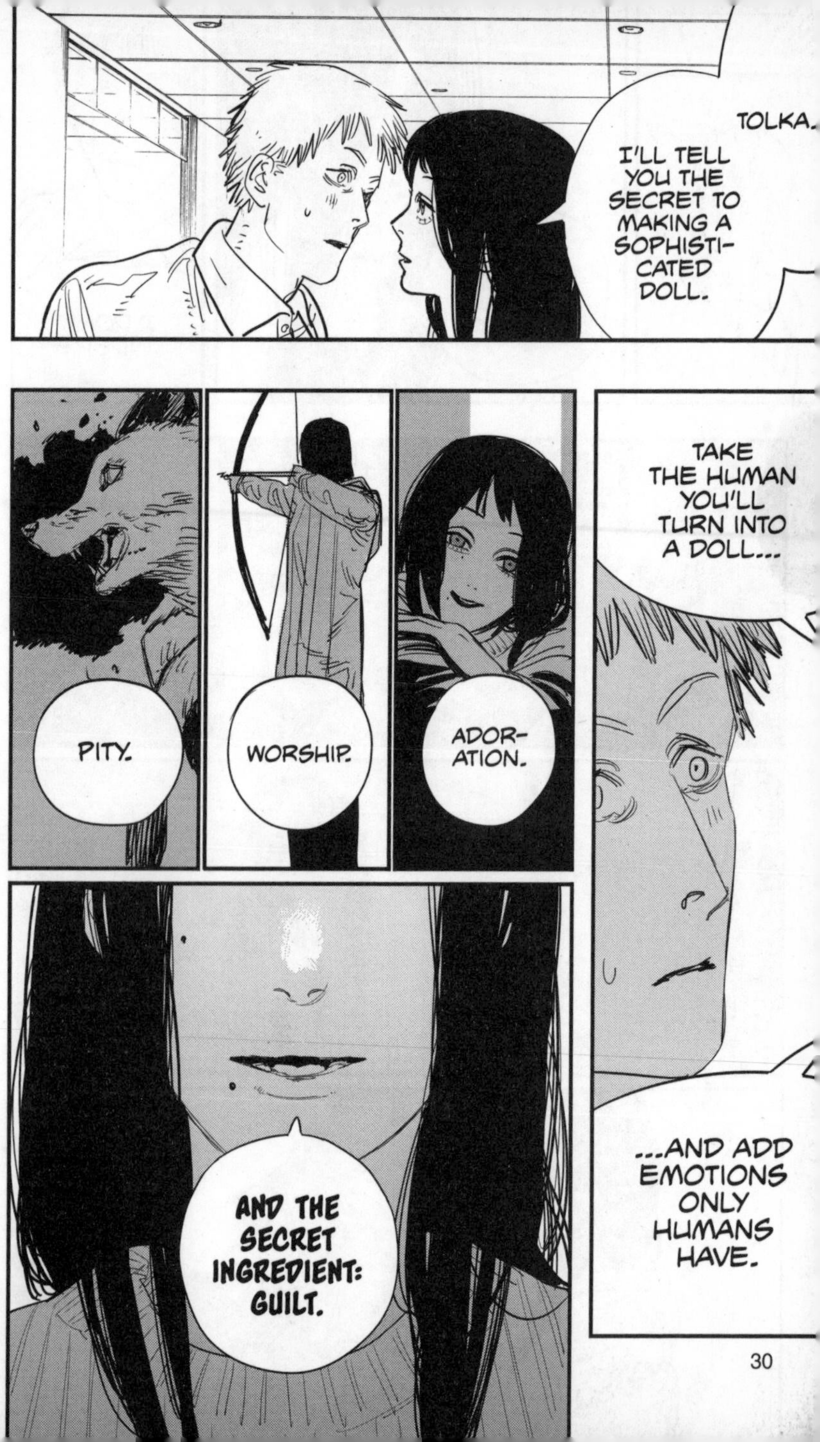
TOLKA.
I'LL TELL YOU THE SECRET TO MAKING A SOPHISTICATED DOLL.
TAKE THE HUMAN YOU'LL TURN INTO A DOLL...
...AND ADD EMOTIONS ONLY HUMANS HAVE.
ADORATION.
WORSHIP.
PITY.
AND THE SECRET INGREDIENT: GUILT.

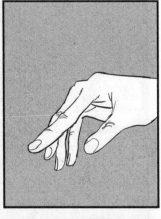

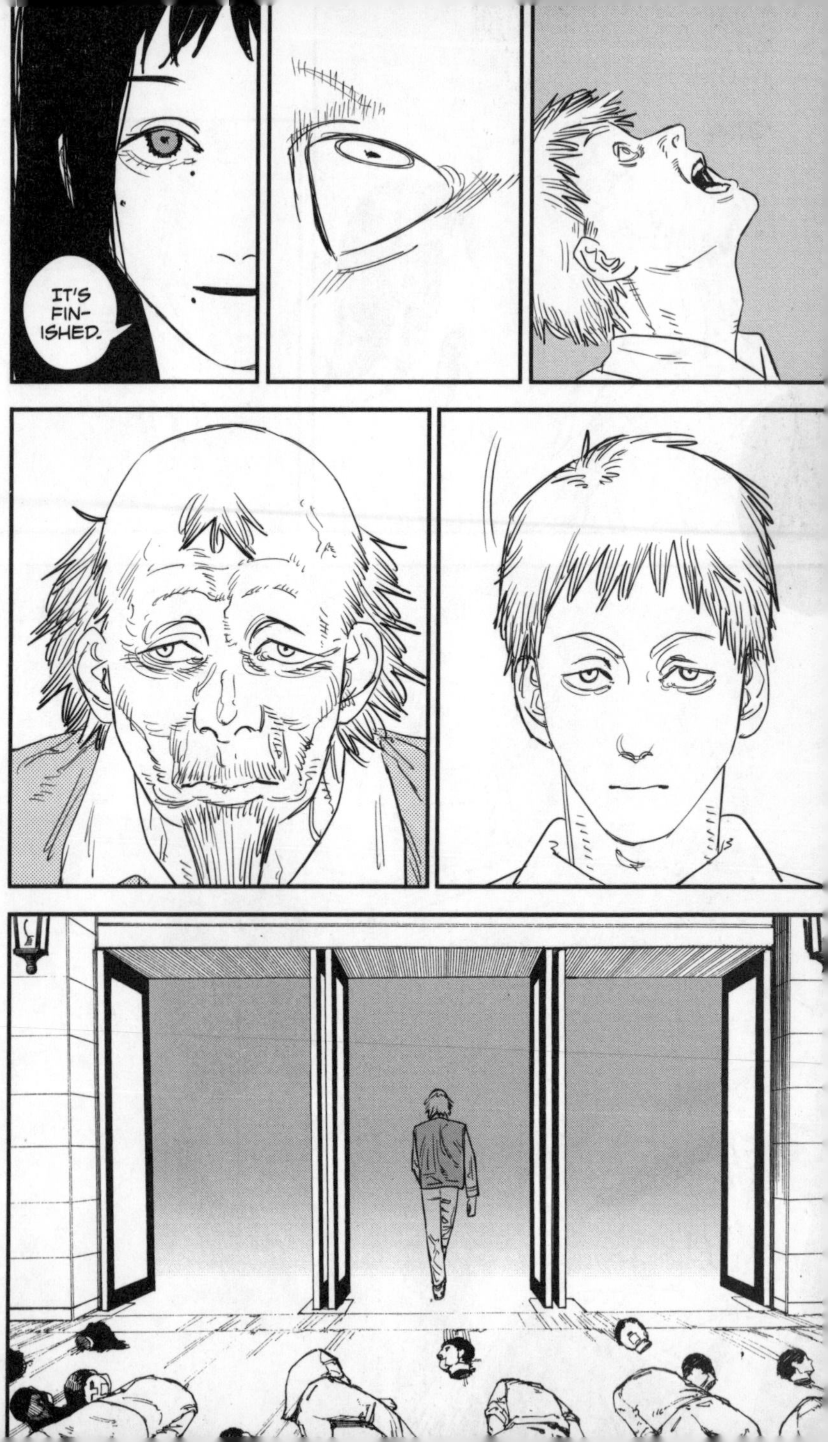
IT'S FIN-ISHED.

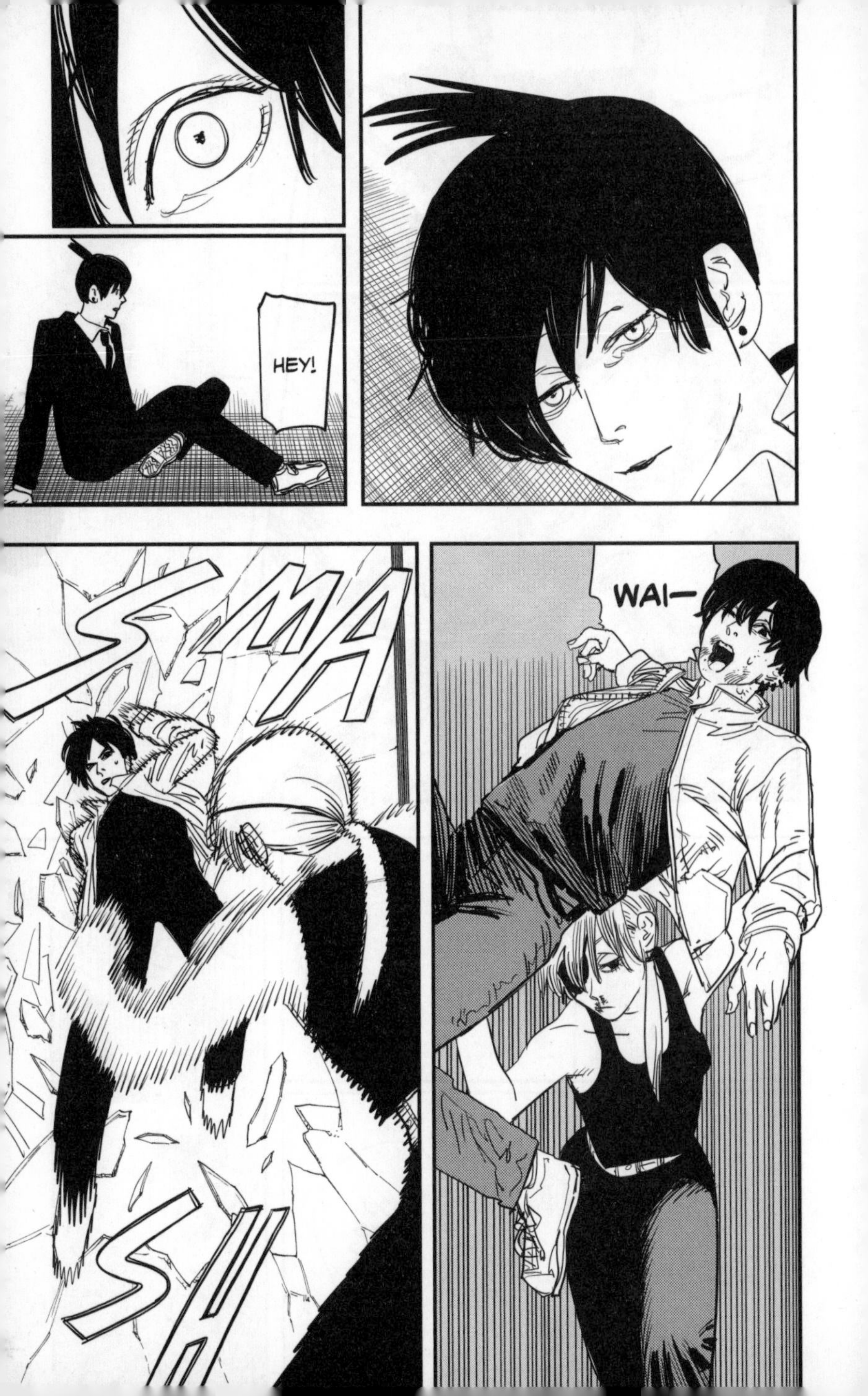
HEY!
WAI—
SMASH

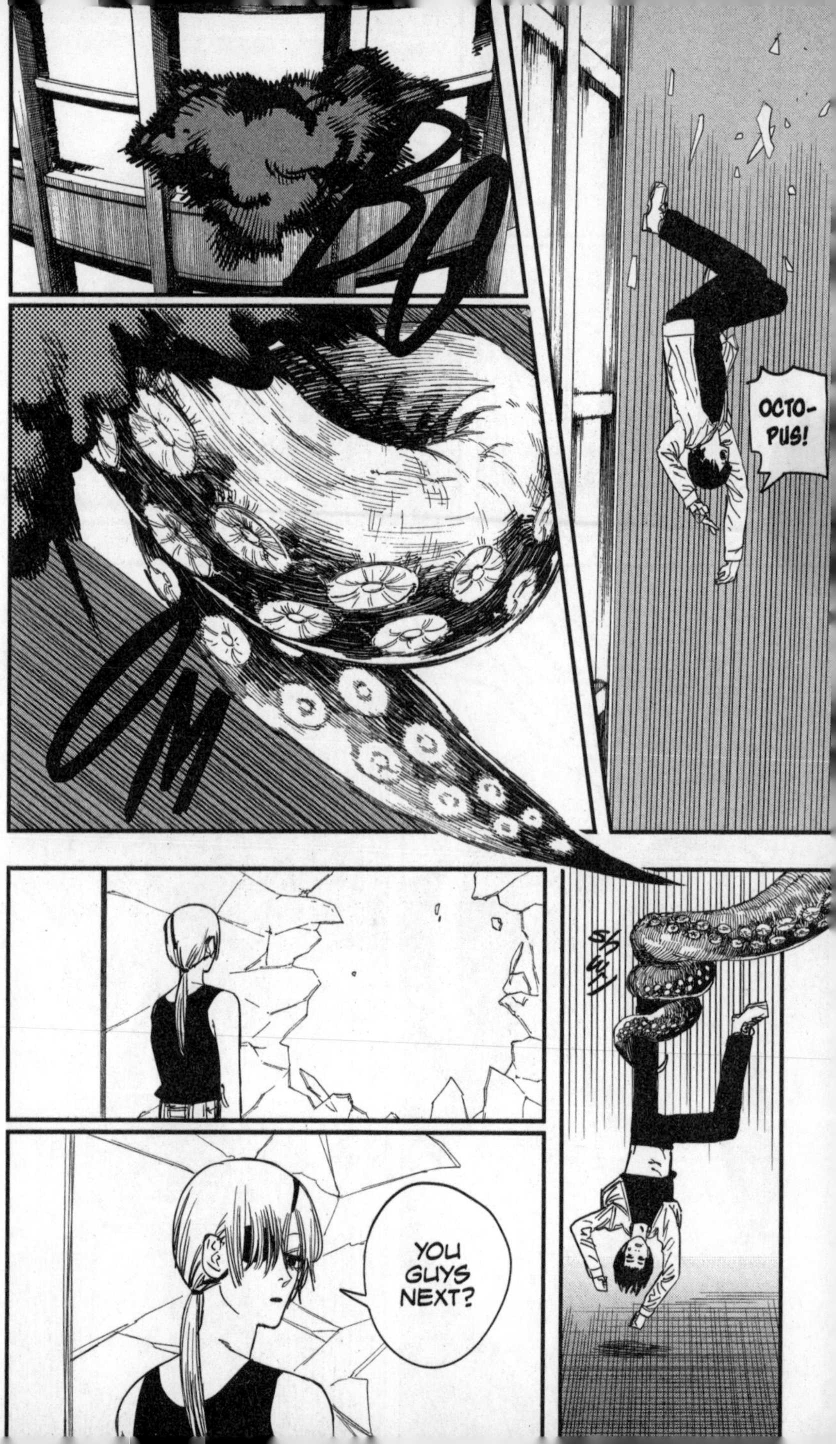
OCTO-PUS!
YOU GUYS NEXT?

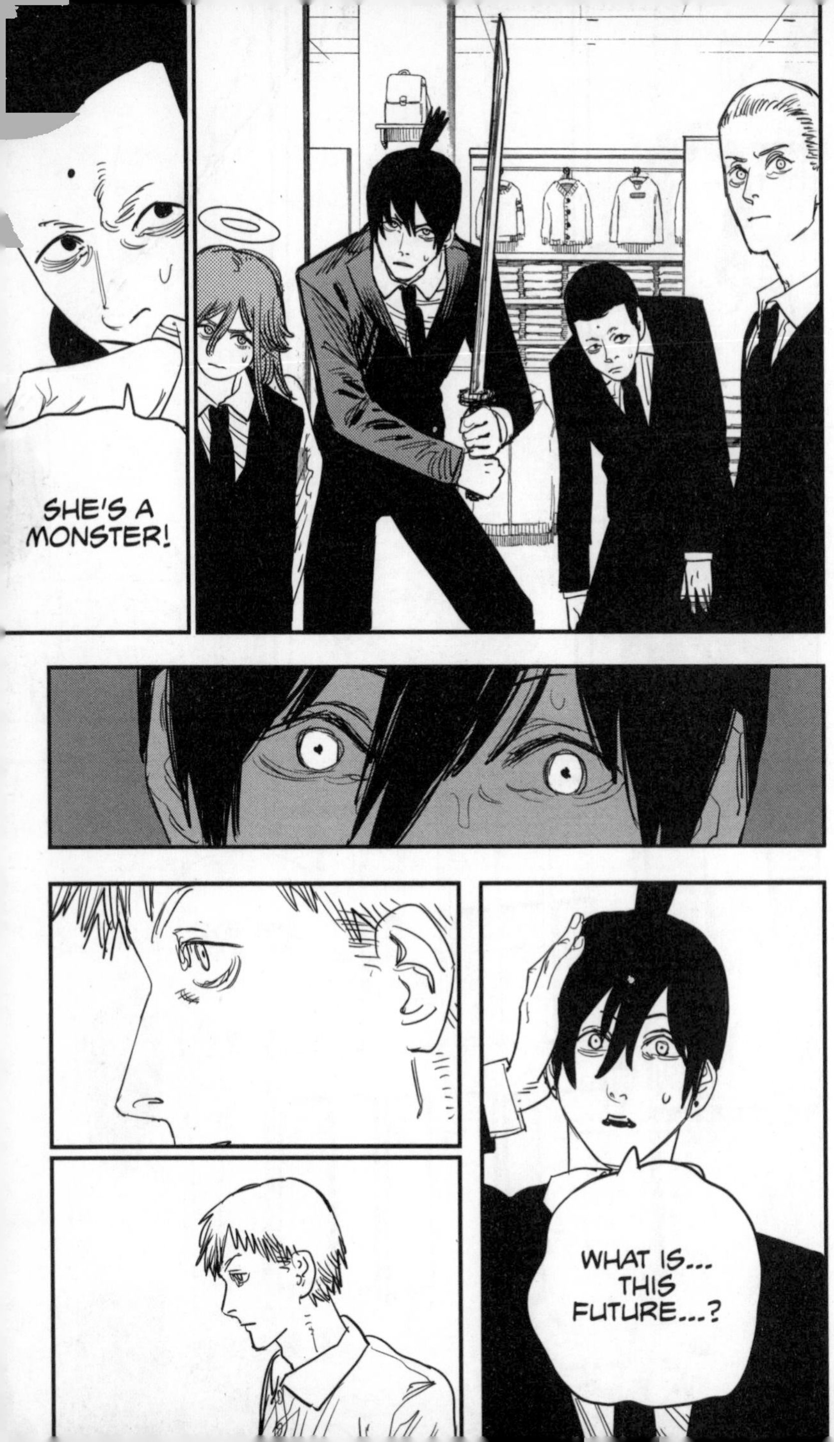
SHE'S A MONSTER!
WHAT IS... THIS FUTURE...?

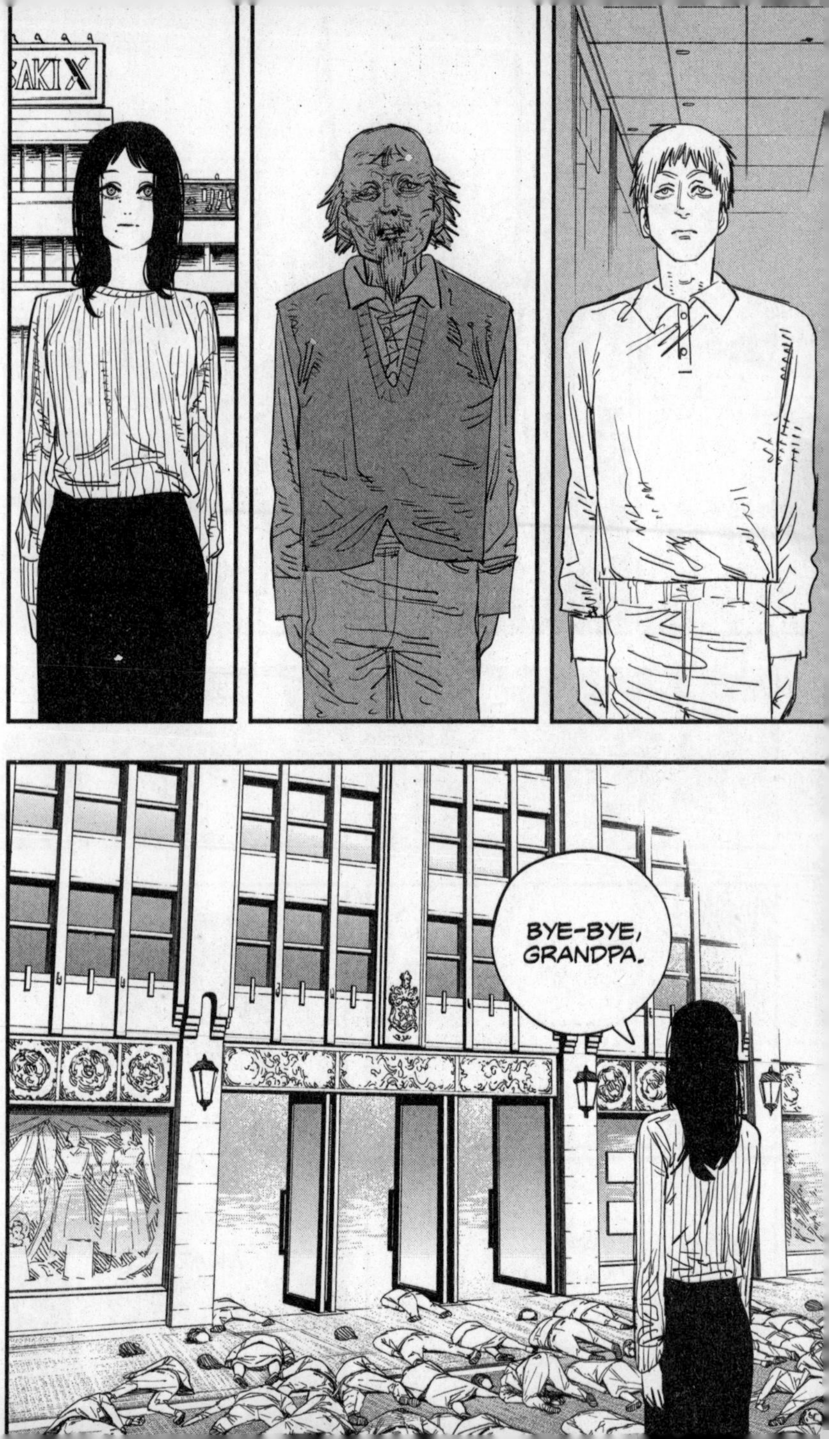
BYE-BYE, GRANDPA.

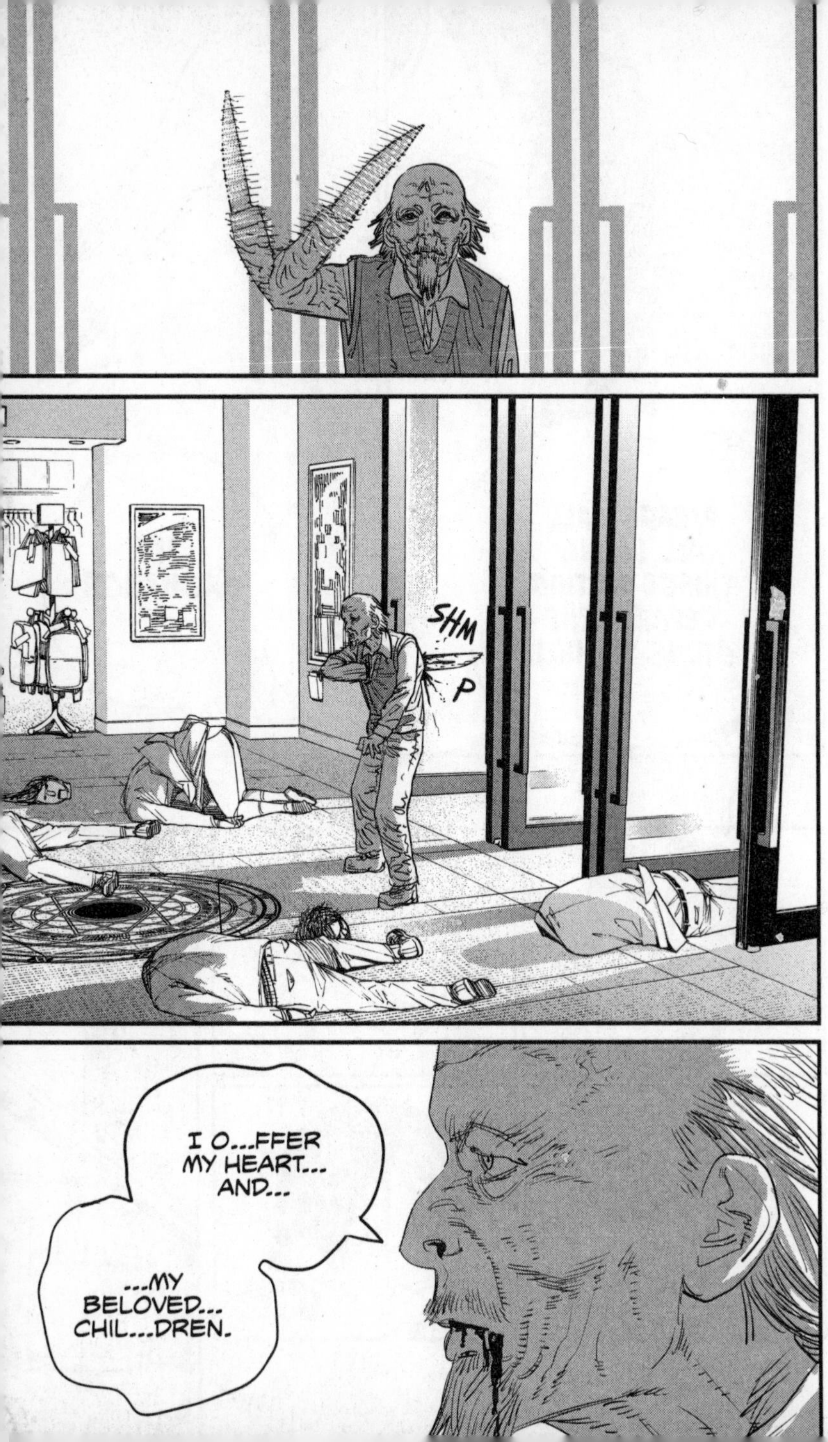
SHMP
I O...FFER MY HEART... AND...
...MY BELOVED... CHIL...DREN.

PLEASE CALL ALL LIVING THINGS IN THIS DEPARTMENT STORE TO HELL.

HELL DEVIL...

IN EXCHANGE...

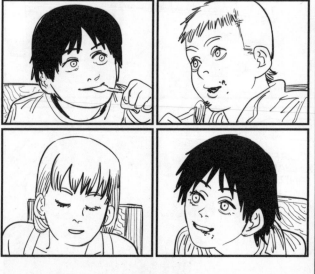

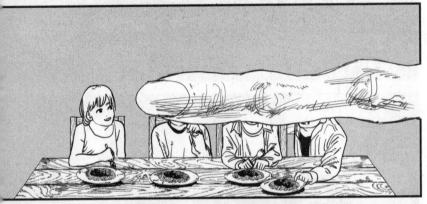

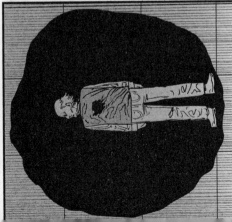

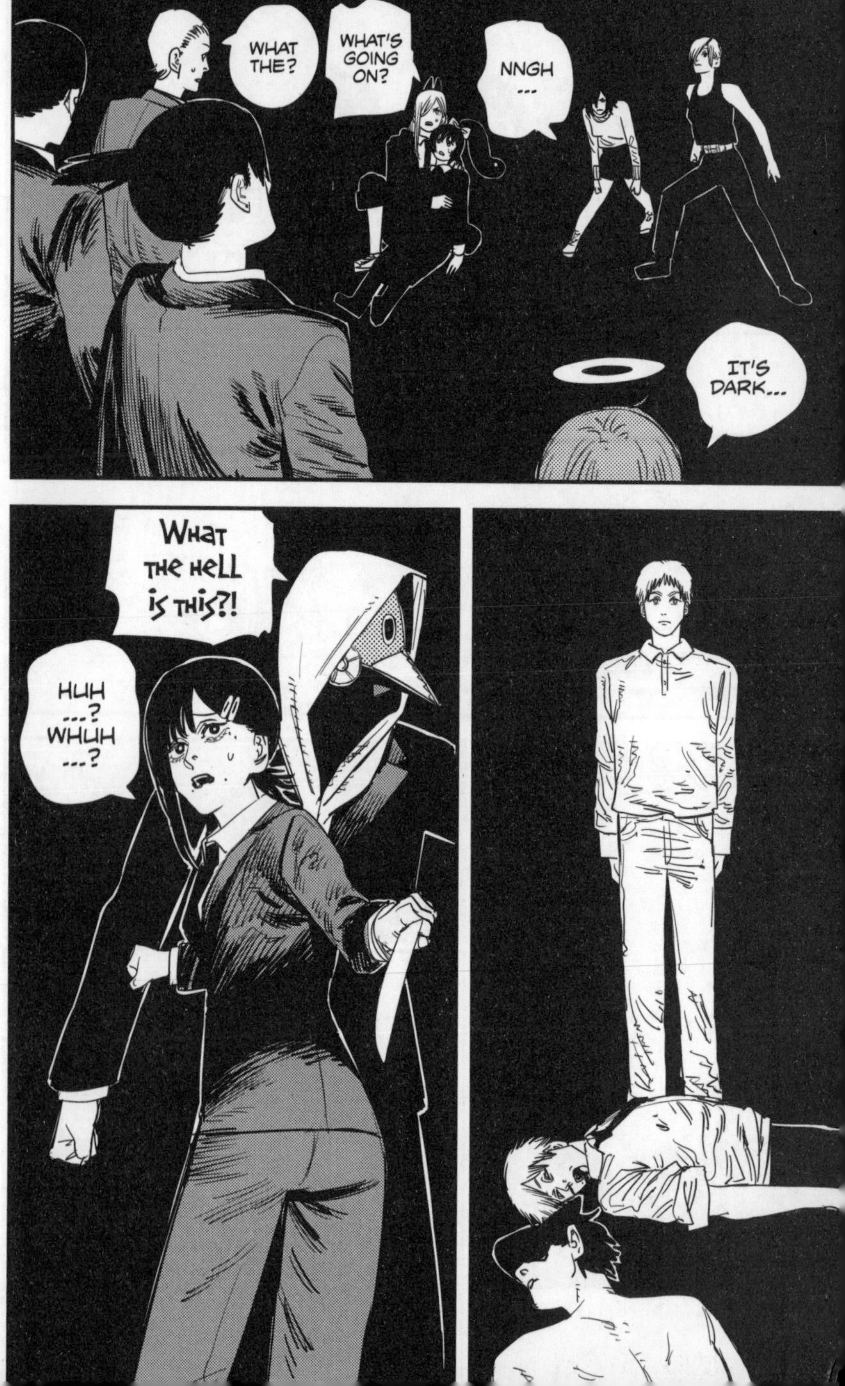
NNGH ...
WHAT'S GOING ON?
WHAT THE?
IT'S DARK...
What the hell is this?!
HUH ...? WHUH ...?

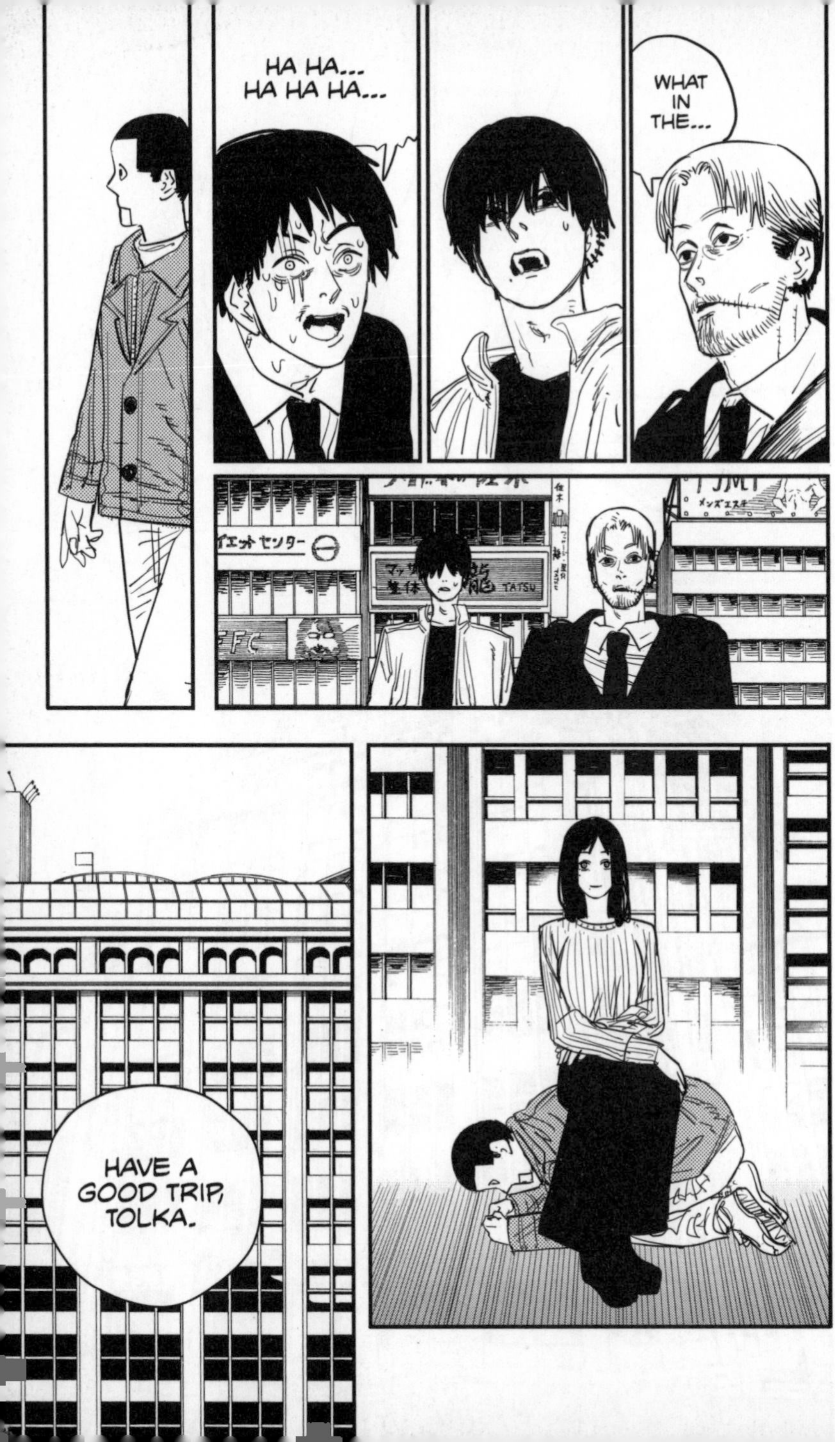
WHAT IN THE...
HA HA... HA HA HA...
HAVE A GOOD TRIP, TOLKA.

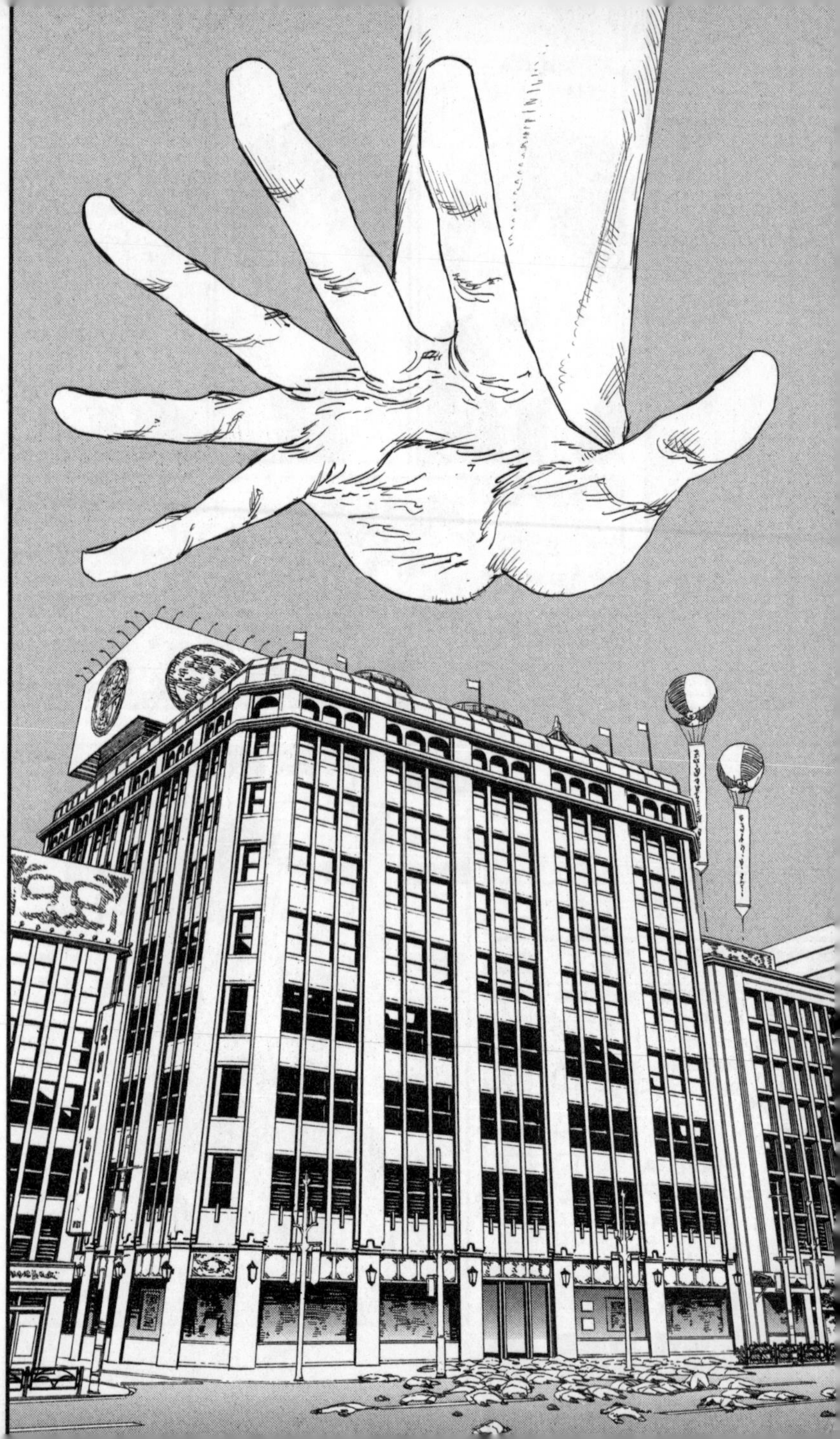

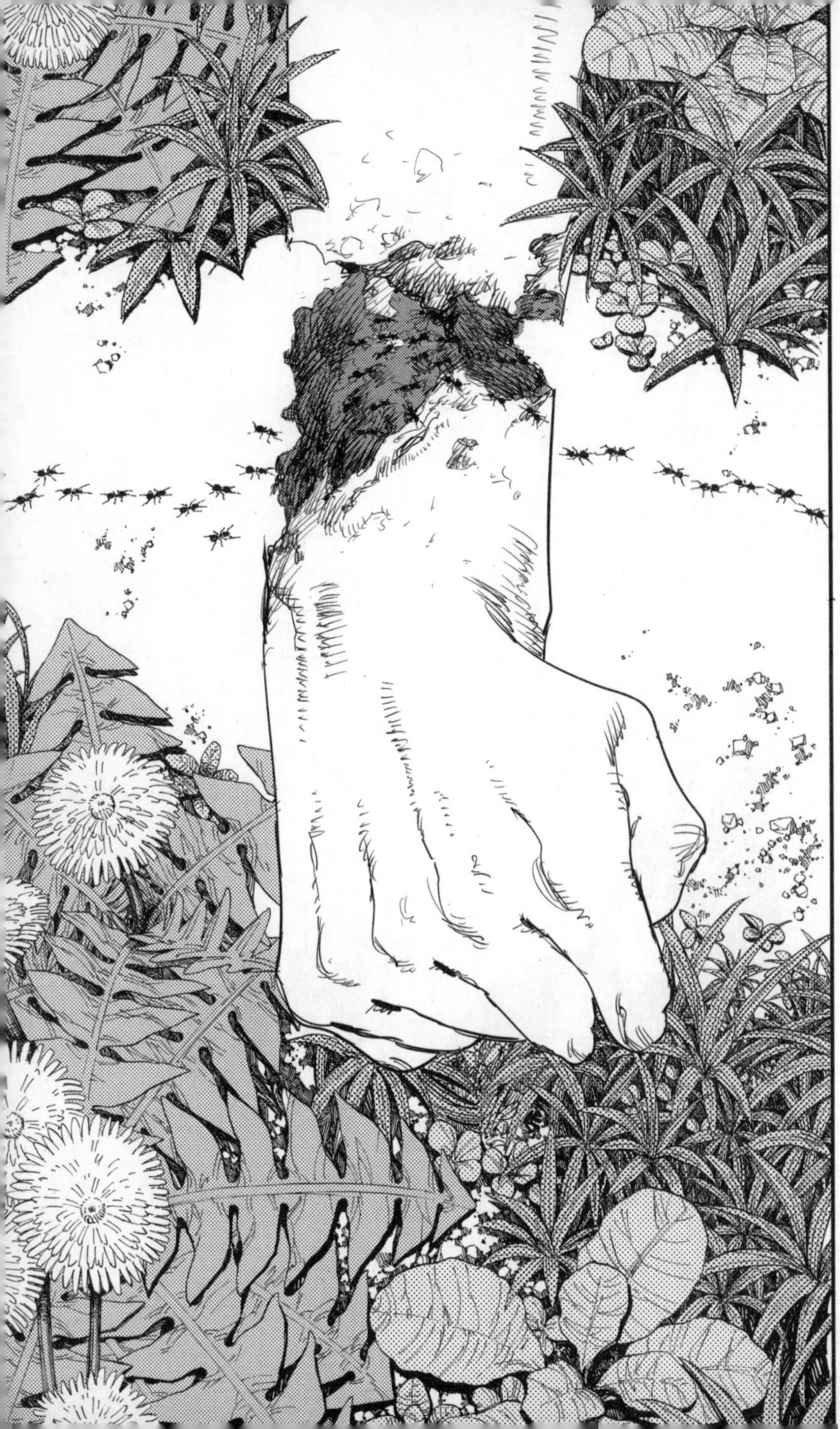

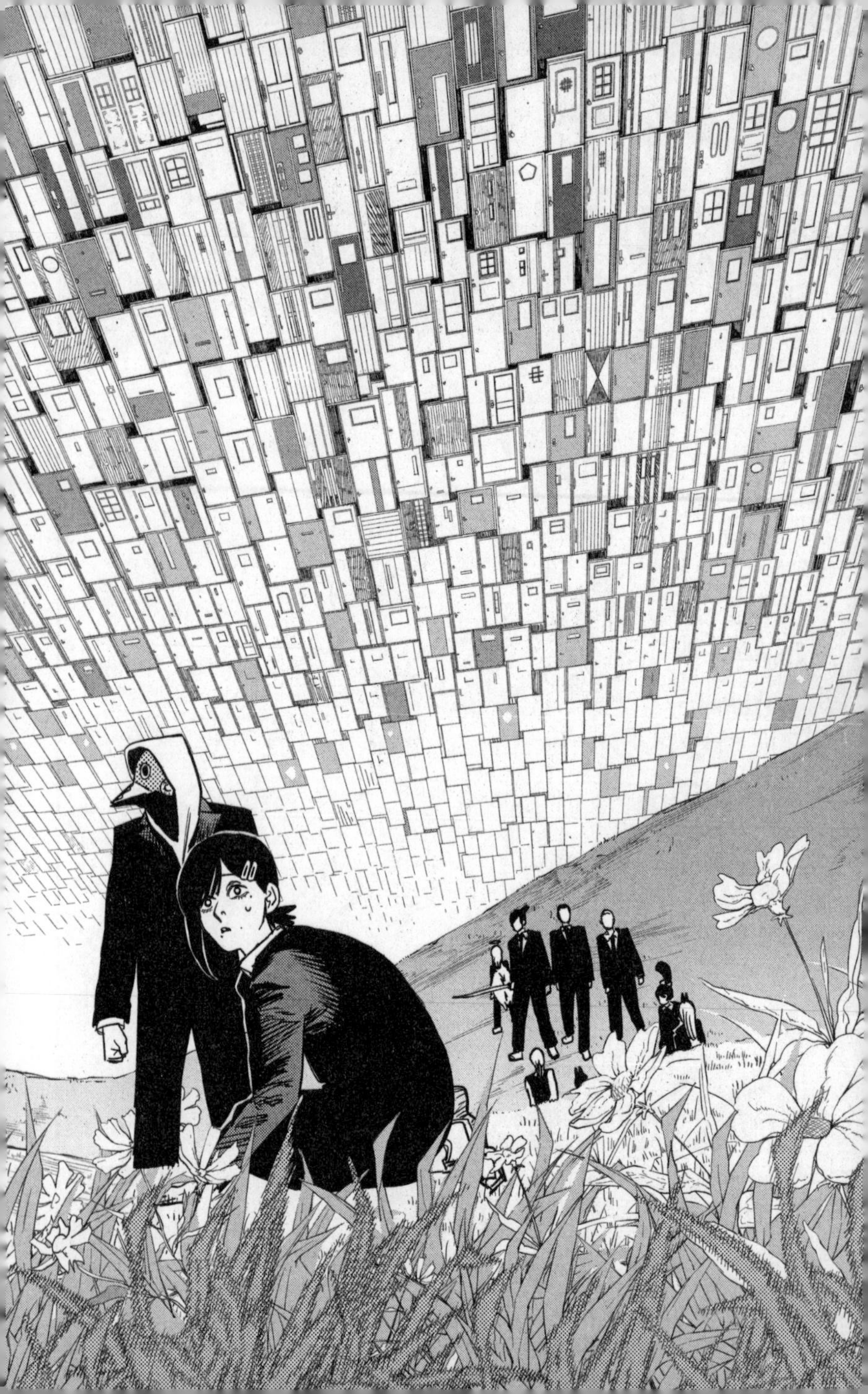

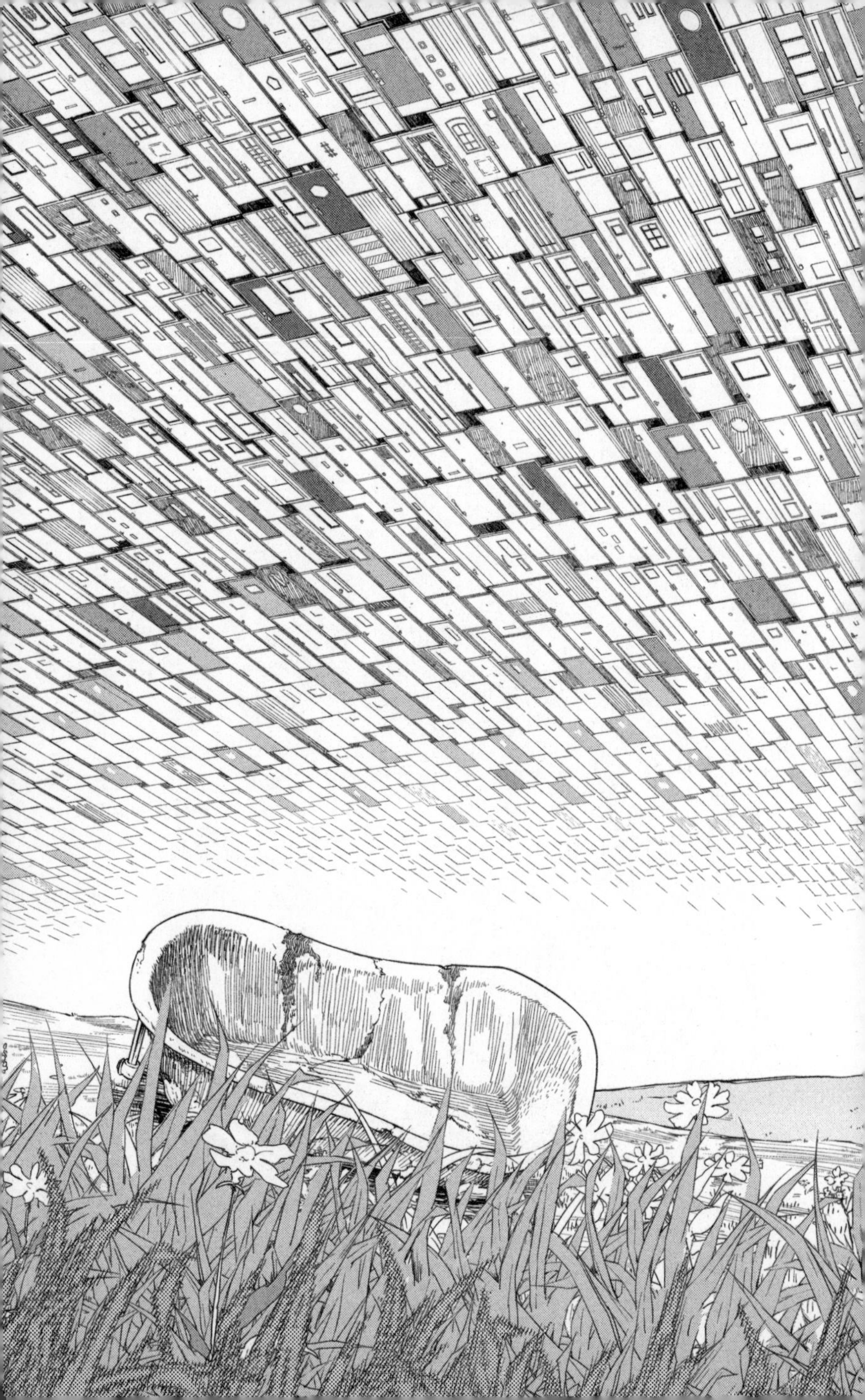

Chain saw man

Chapter 64: Welcome to Hell

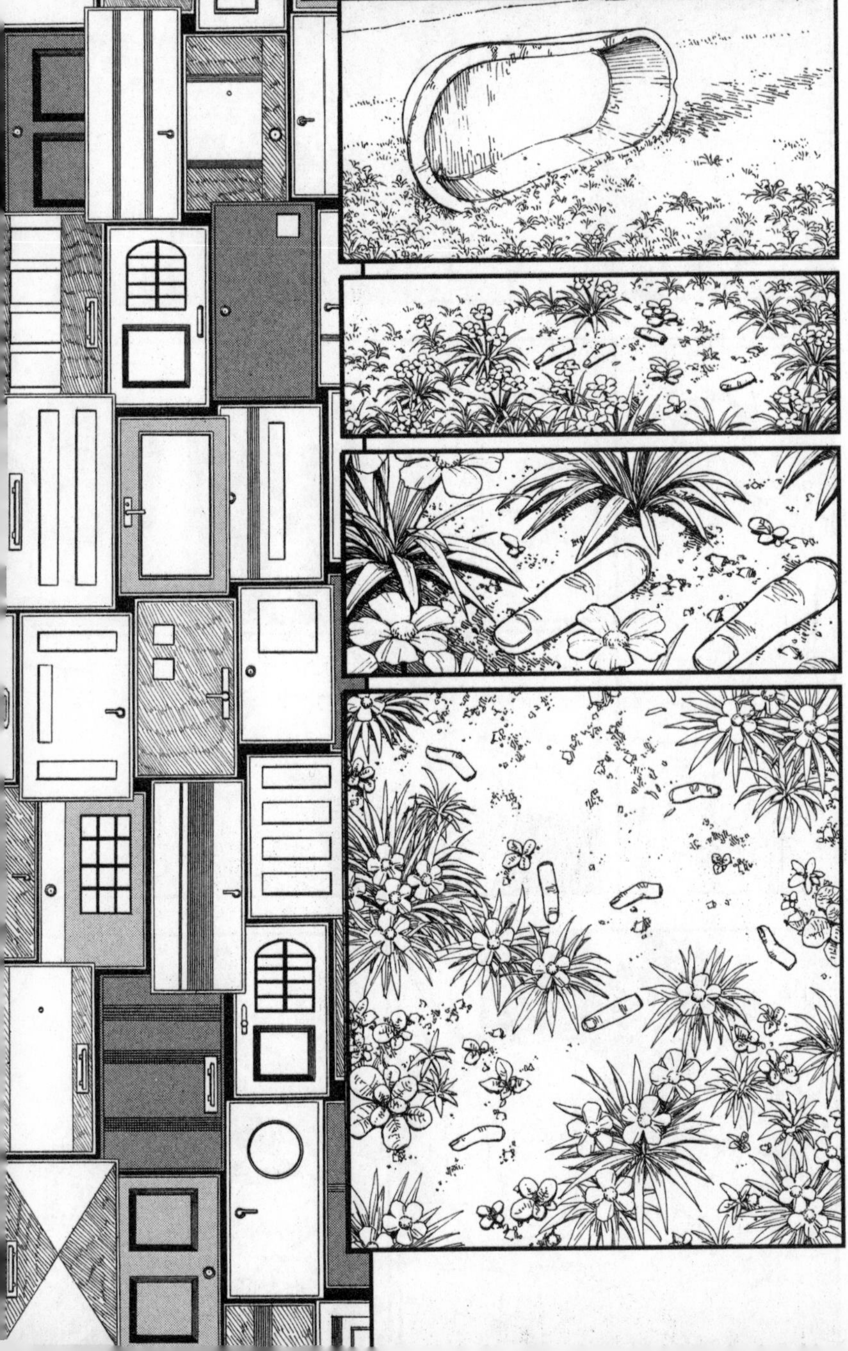

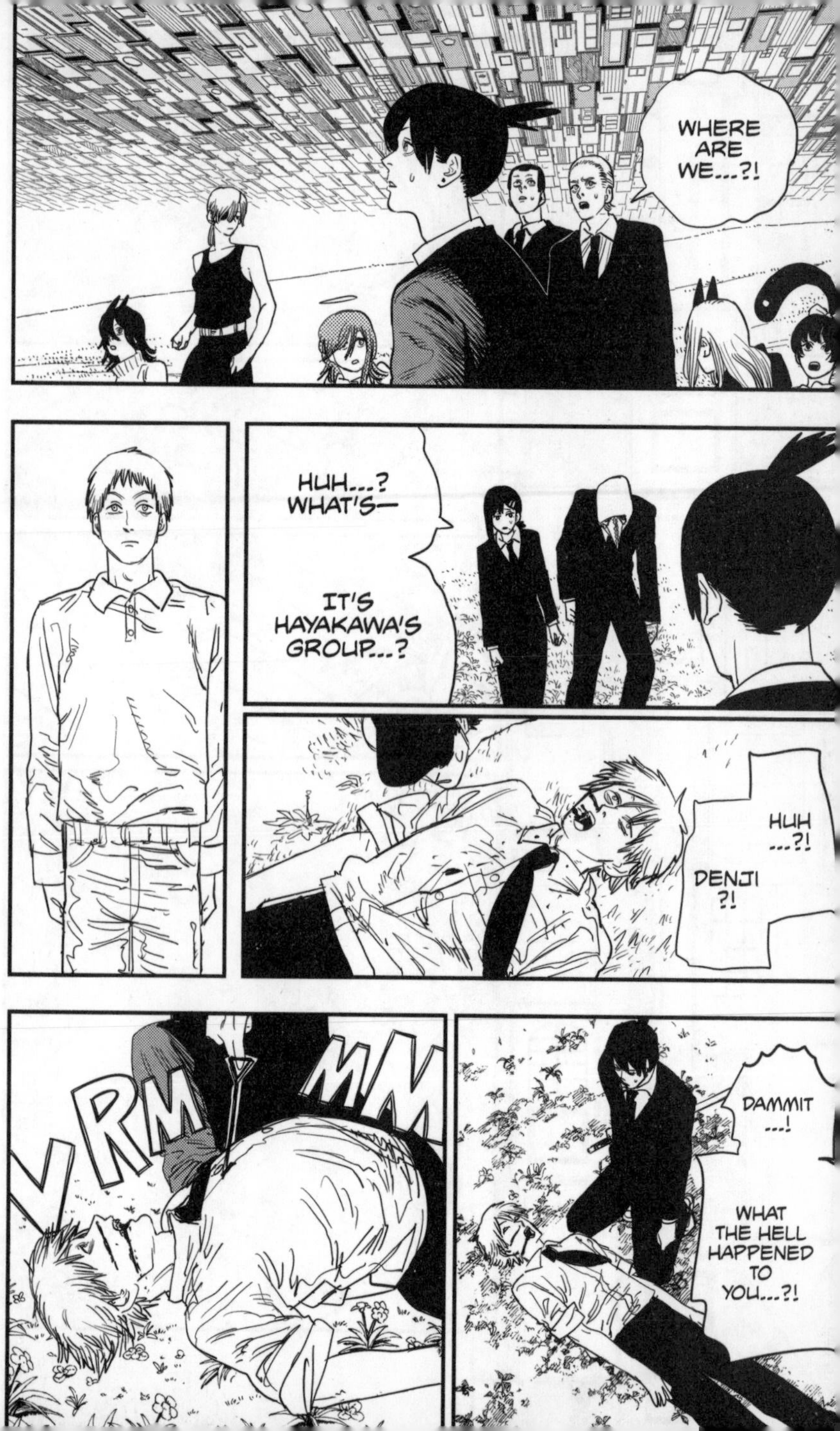
WHERE ARE WE...?!
HUH...? WHAT'S—
IT'S HAYAKAWA'S GROUP...?
HUH...?!
DENJI ?!
DAMMIT...!
WHAT THE HELL HAPPENED TO YOU...?!
VRMMM

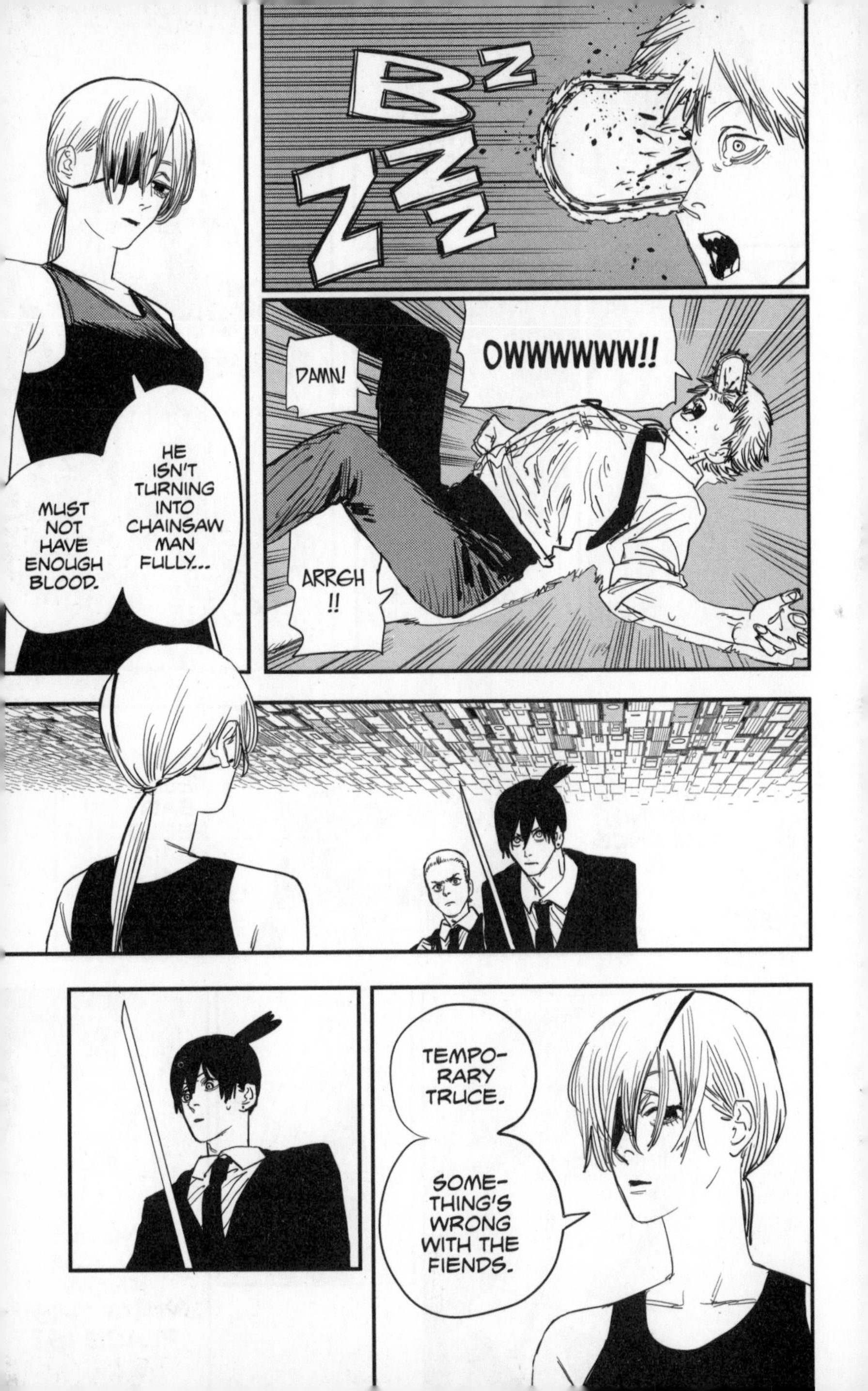
BZZZZZ
OWWWWWW!!
DAMN!
ARRGH!!
HE ISN'T TURNING INTO CHAINSAW MAN FULLY...
MUST NOT HAVE ENOUGH BLOOD.
TEMPORARY TRUCE.
SOMETHING'S WRONG WITH THE FIENDS.

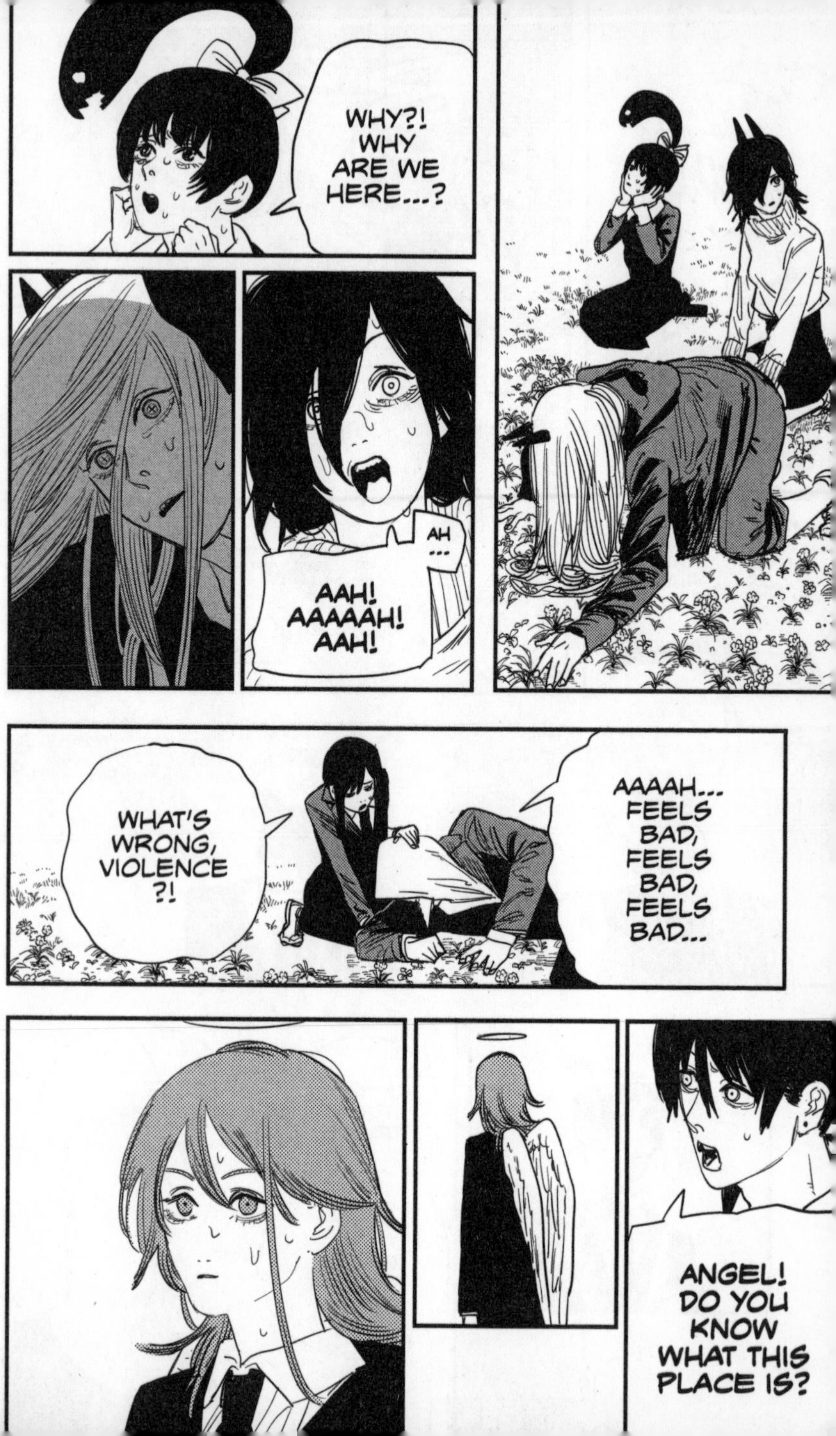
WHY?! WHY ARE WE HERE...?
AH...
AAH! AAAAAH! AAH!
AAAAH... FEELS BAD, FEELS BAD, FEELS BAD...
WHAT'S WRONG, VIOLENCE?!
ANGEL! DO YOU KNOW WHAT THIS PLACE IS?

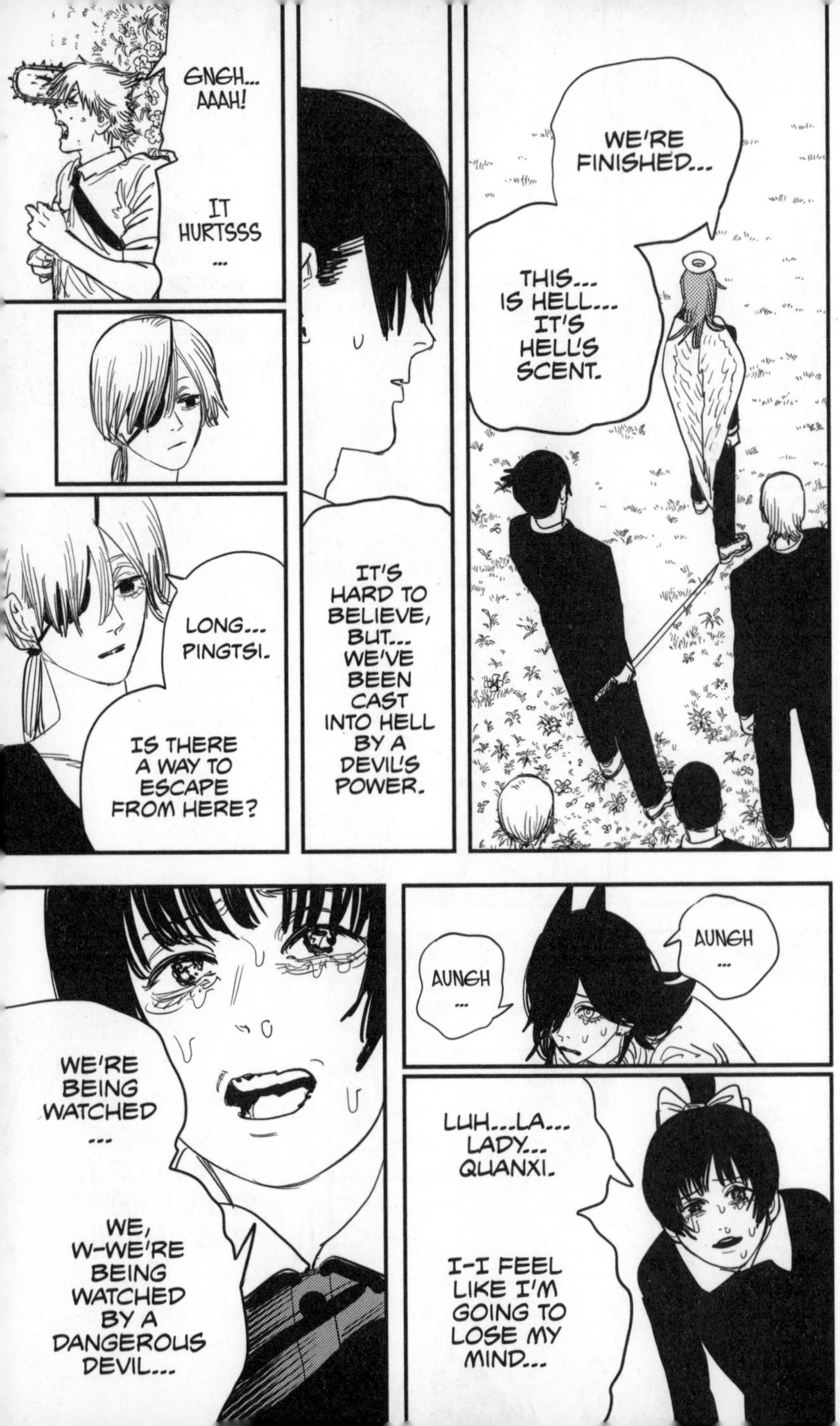
WE'RE FINISHED...
THIS... IS HELL... IT'S HELL'S SCENT.
IT'S HARD TO BELIEVE, BUT... WE'VE BEEN CAST INTO HELL BY A DEVIL'S POWER.
GNGH... AAAH!
IT HURTSSS ...
LONG... PINGTSI.
IS THERE A WAY TO ESCAPE FROM HERE?
AUNGH ...
AUNGH ...
LUH...LA... LADY... QUANXI.
I-I FEEL LIKE I'M GOING TO LOSE MY MIND...
WE'RE BEING WATCHED ...
WE, W-WE'RE BEING WATCHED BY A DANGEROUS DEVIL...

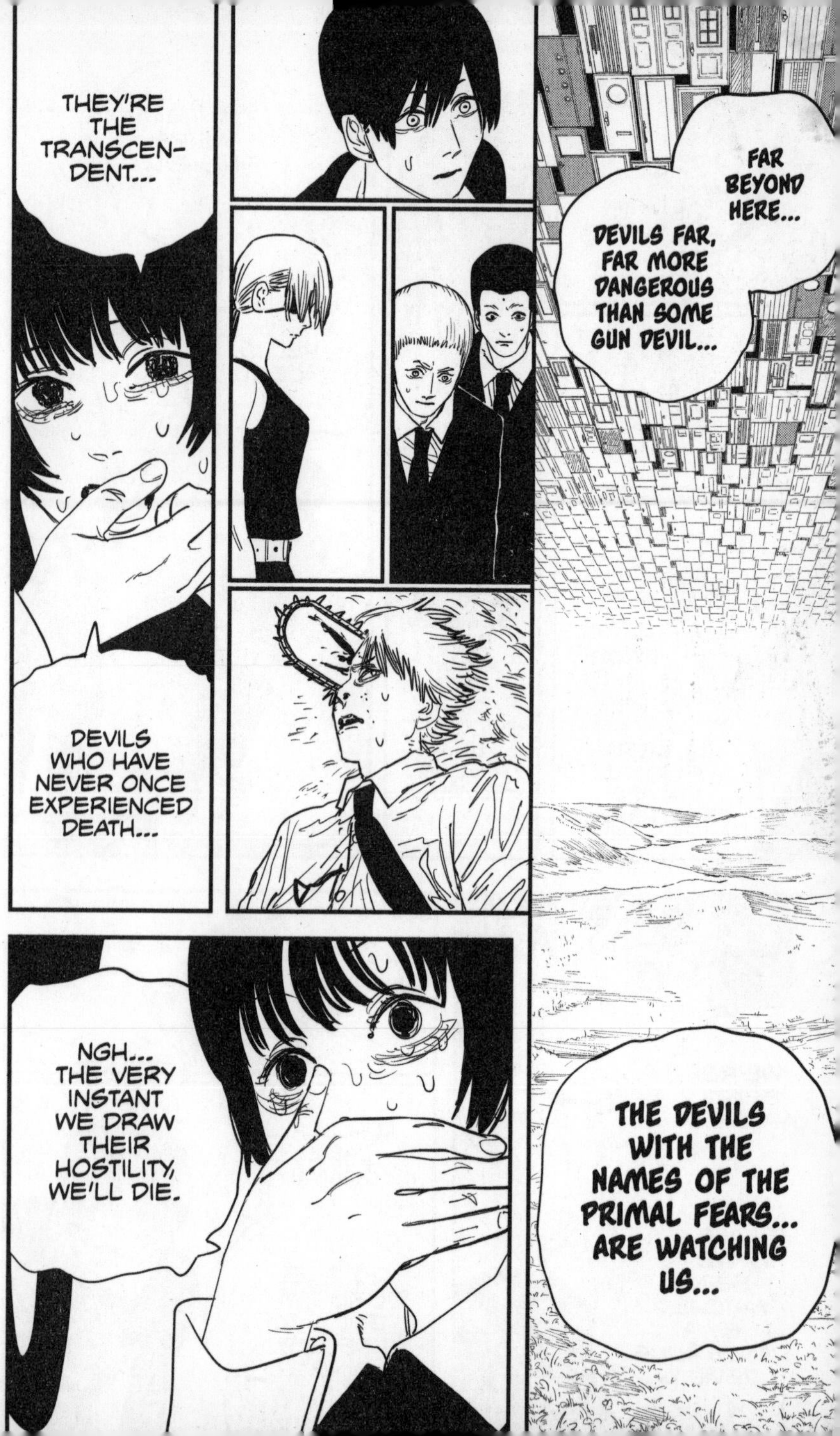
FAR BEYOND HERE...
DEVILS FAR, FAR MORE DANGEROUS THAN SOME GUN DEVIL...
THE DEVILS WITH THE NAMES OF THE PRIMAL FEARS... ARE WATCHING US...
THEY'RE THE TRANSCEN-DENT...
DEVILS WHO HAVE NEVER ONCE EXPERIENCED DEATH...
NGH... THE VERY INSTANT WE DRAW THEIR HOSTILITY, WE'LL DIE.

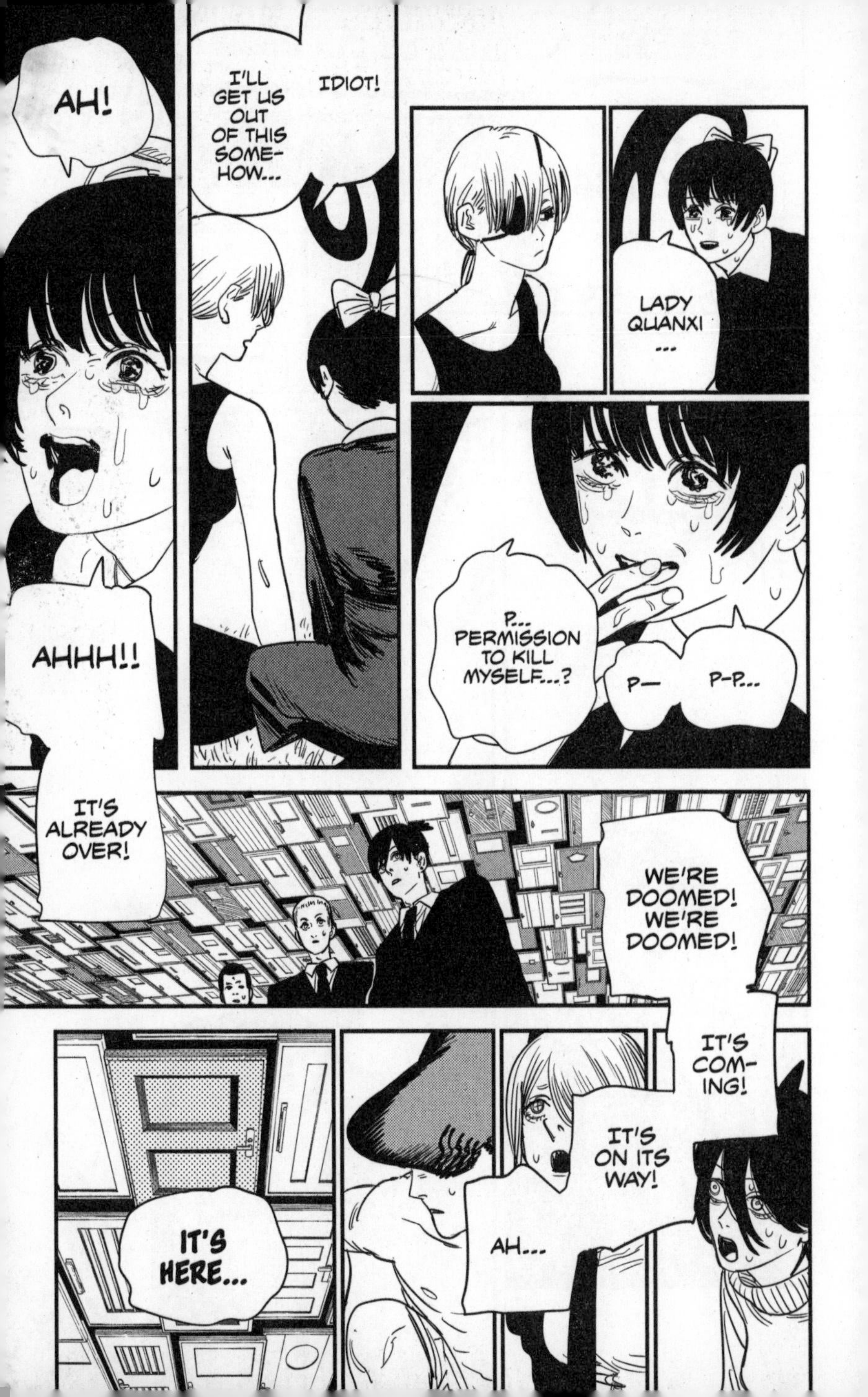
LADY QUANXI ...
P—
P-P...
P... PERMISSION TO KILL MYSELF...?
IDIOT!
I'LL GET US OUT OF THIS SOME-HOW...
AH!
AHHH!!
IT'S ALREADY OVER!
WE'RE DOOMED! WE'RE DOOMED!
IT'S COM-ING!
IT'S ON ITS WAY!
AH...
IT'S HERE...

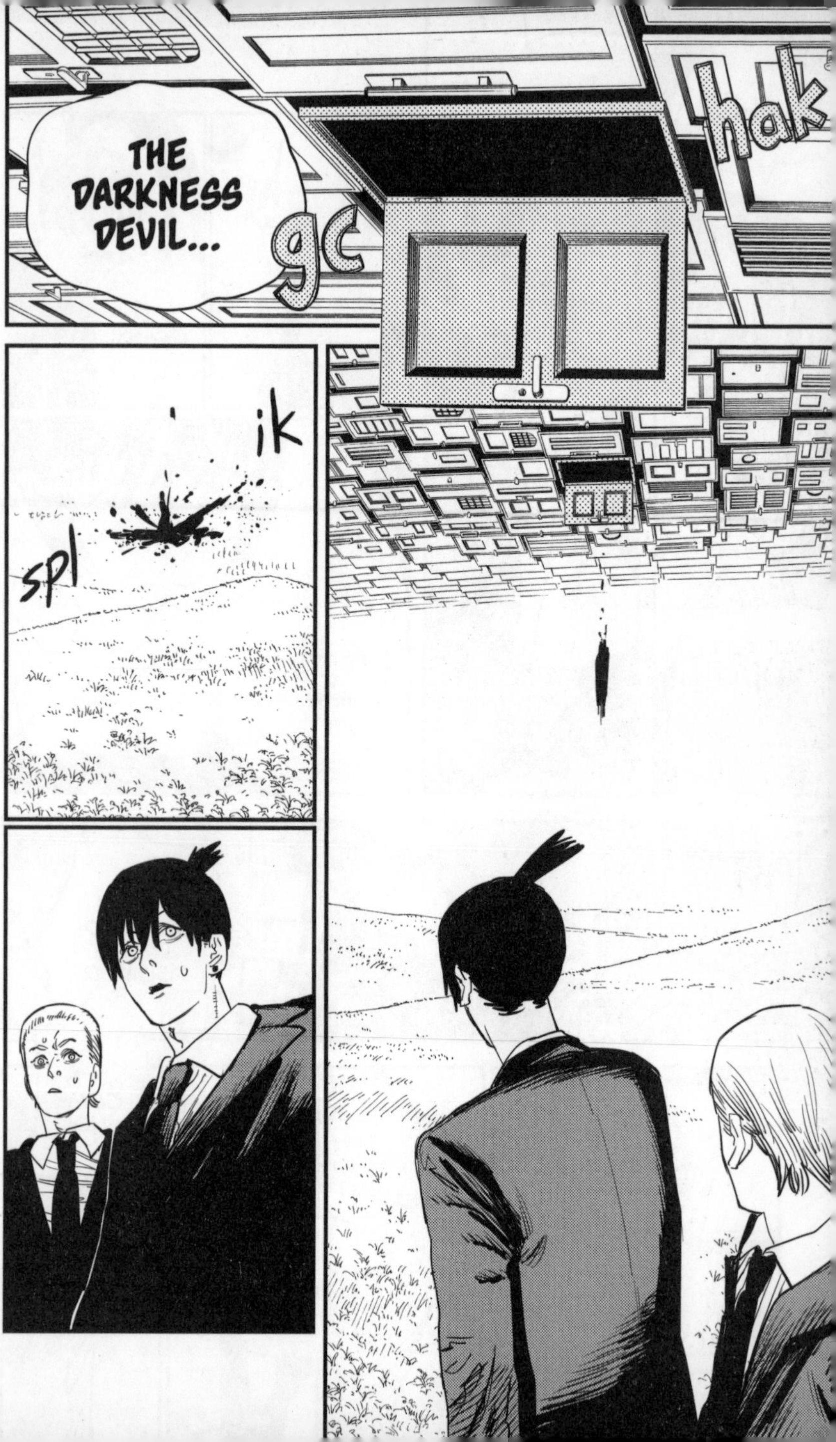
hak
THE DARKNESS DEVIL...
gc
ik
spl

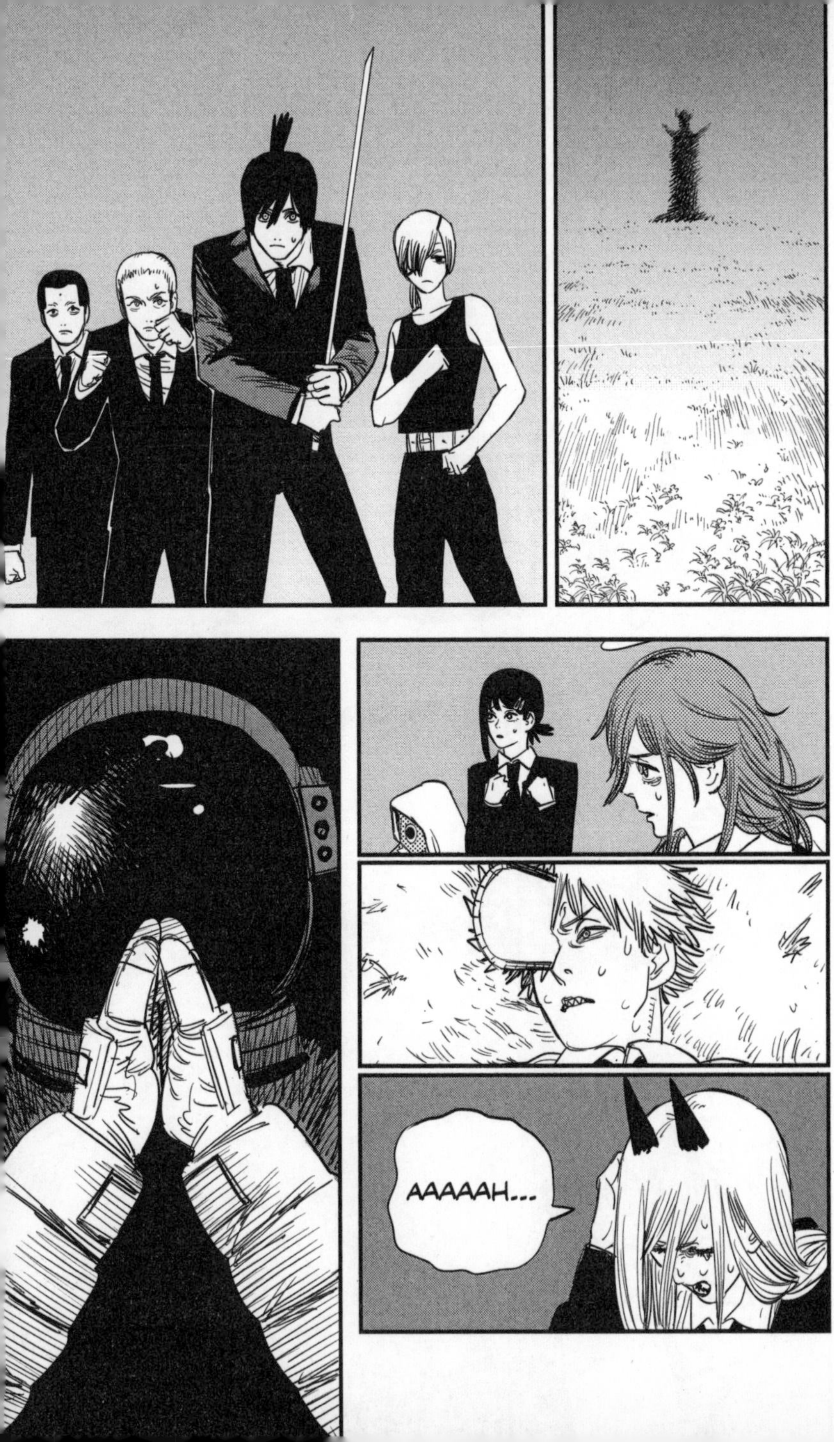
AAAAAH...

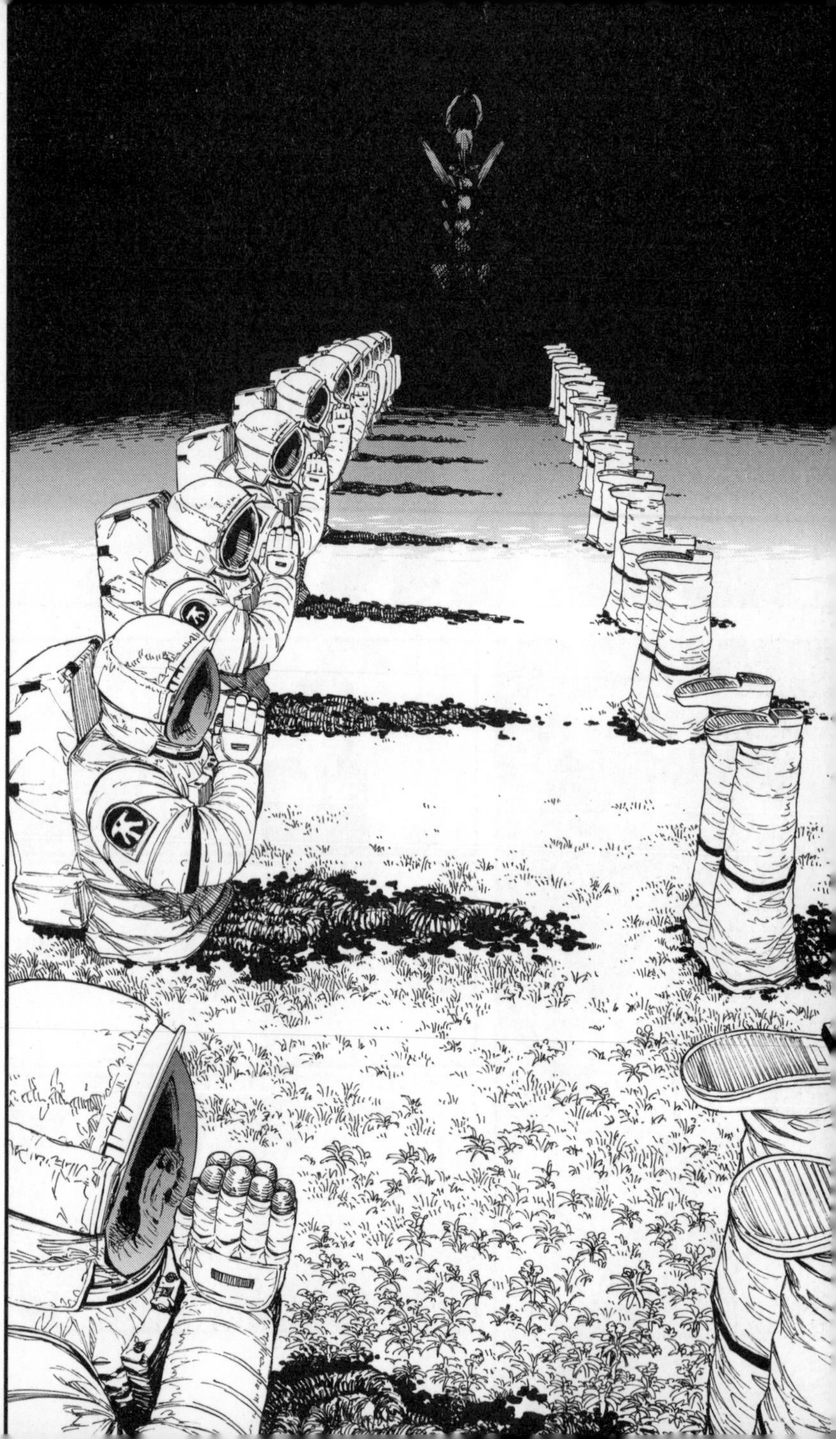

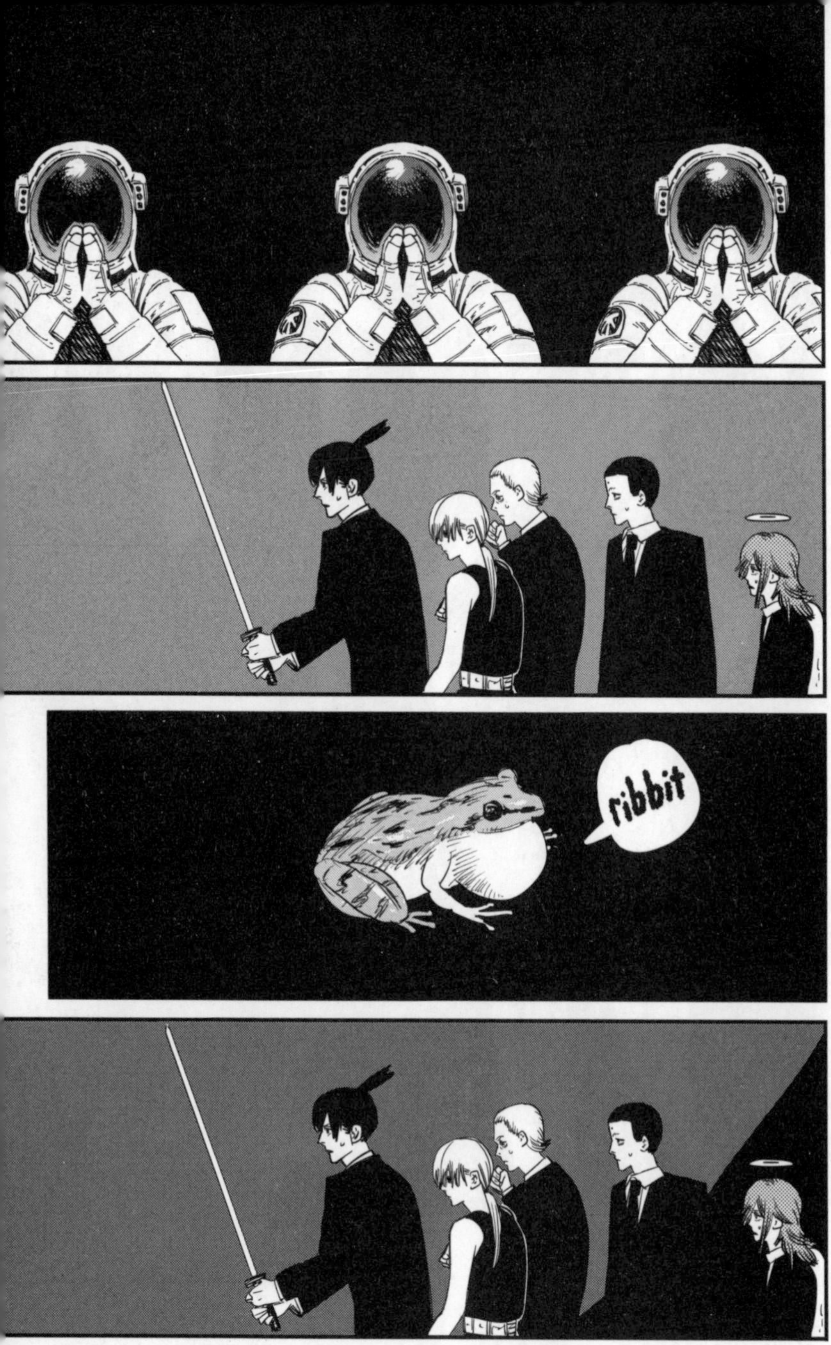
ribbit

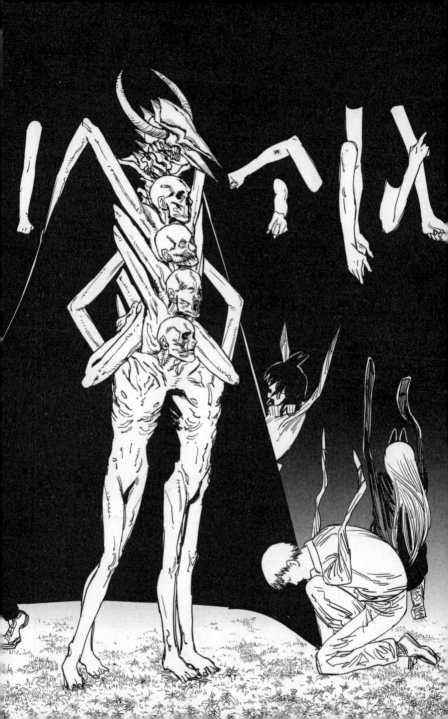

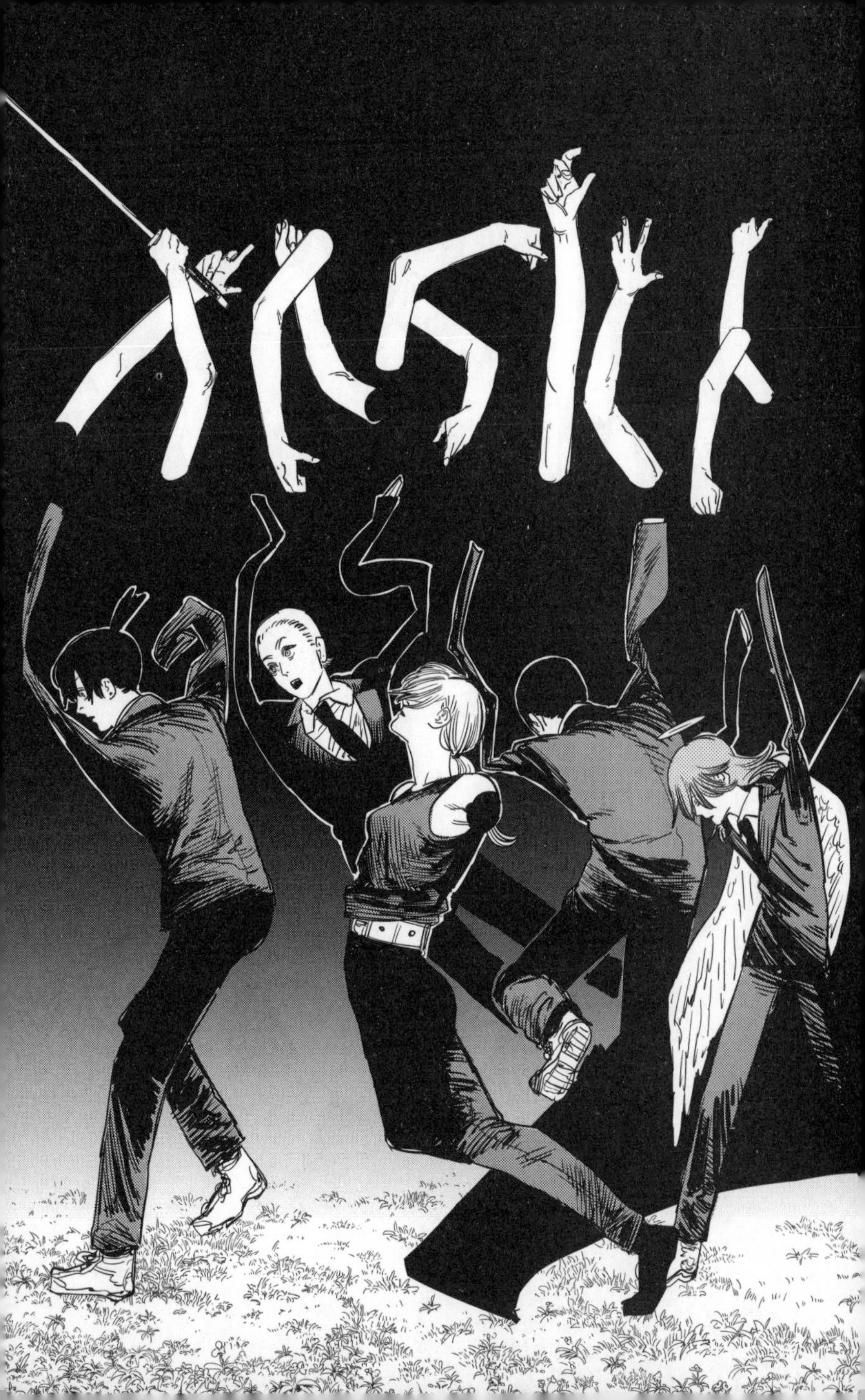

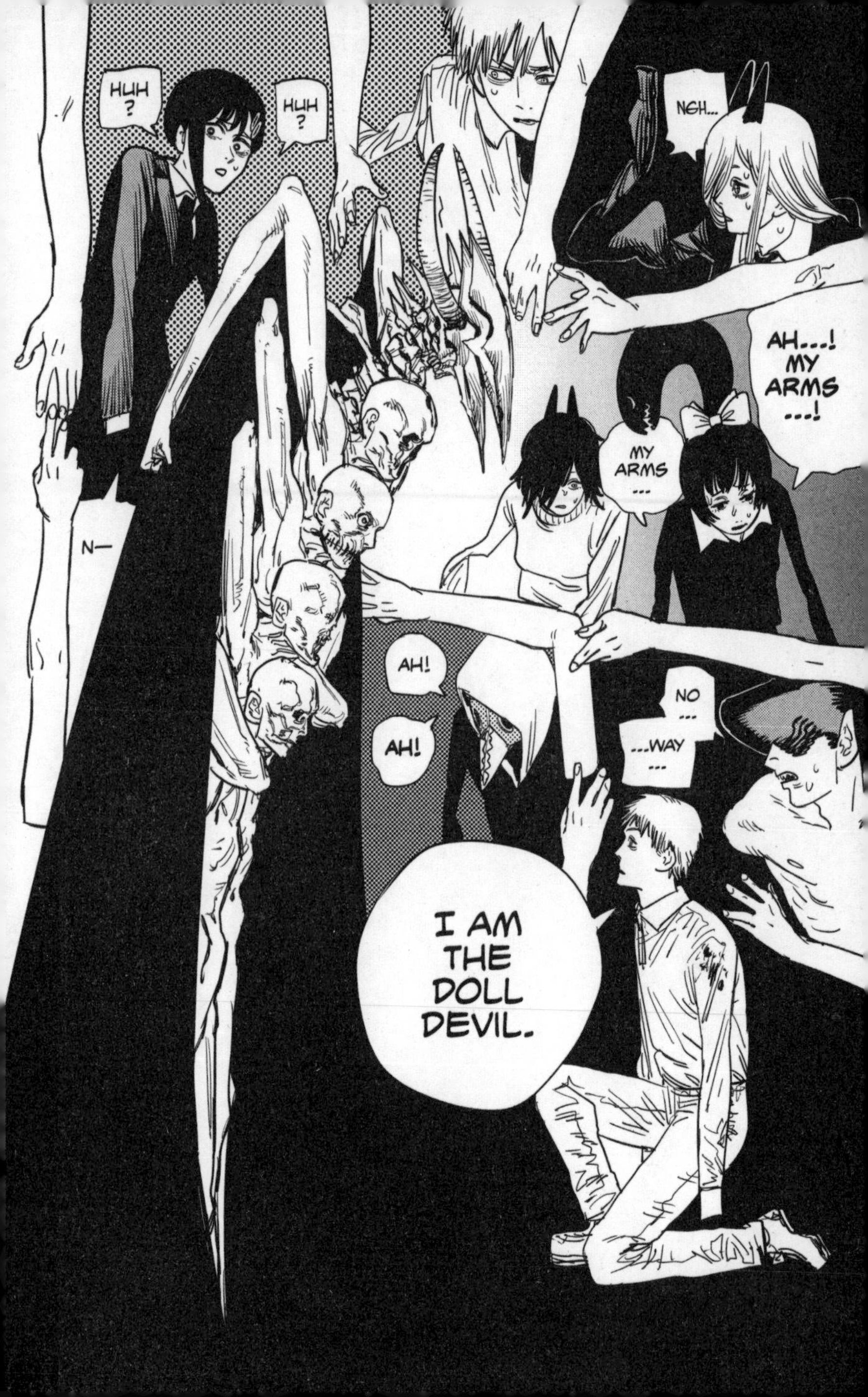
NGH...
HUH ?
HUH ?
N—
AH...! MY ARMS ...!
MY ARMS ...
NO ...
...WAY ...
AH!
AH!
I AM THE DOLL DEVIL.

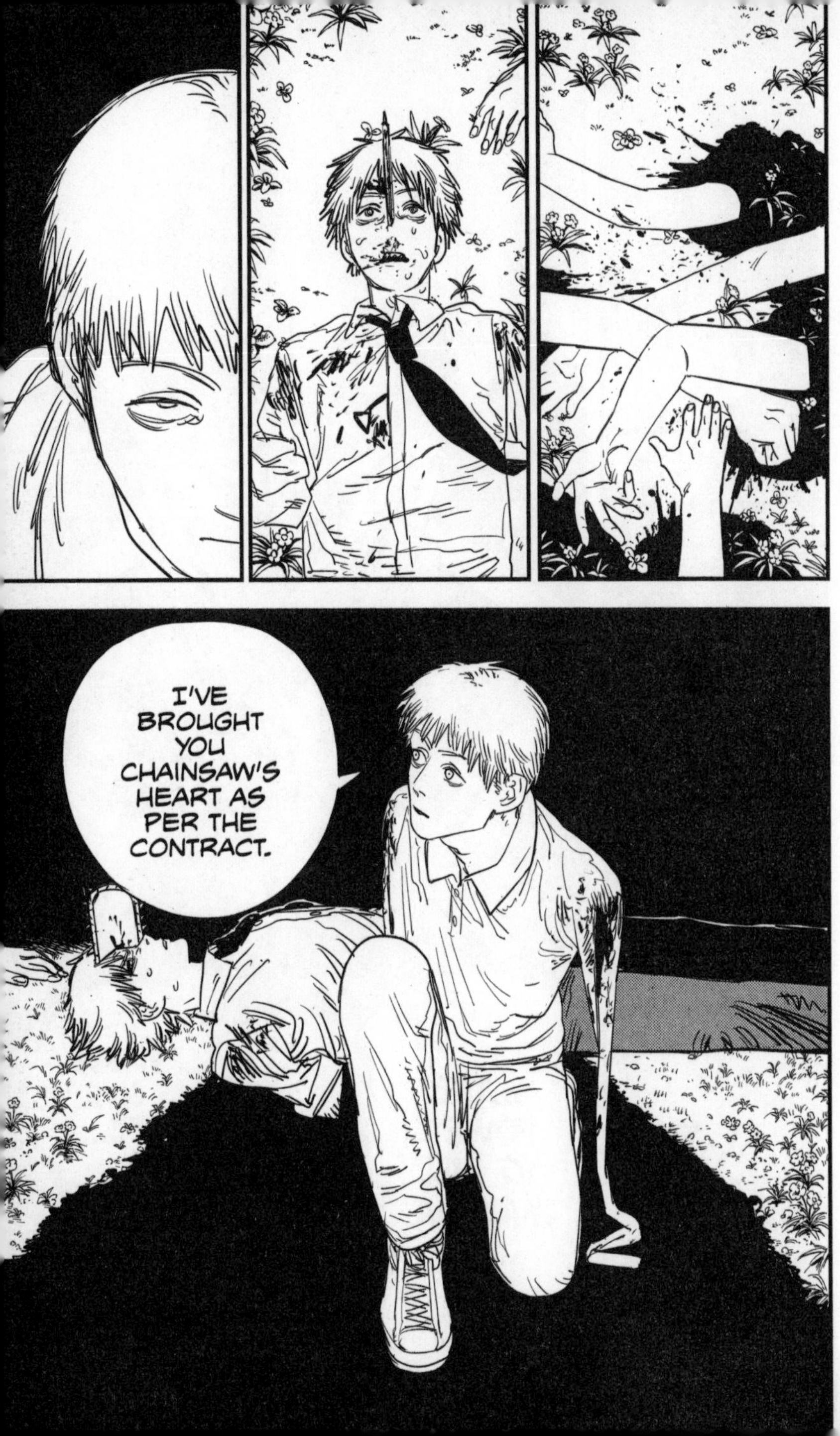
I'VE BROUGHT YOU CHAINSAW'S HEART AS PER THE CONTRACT.

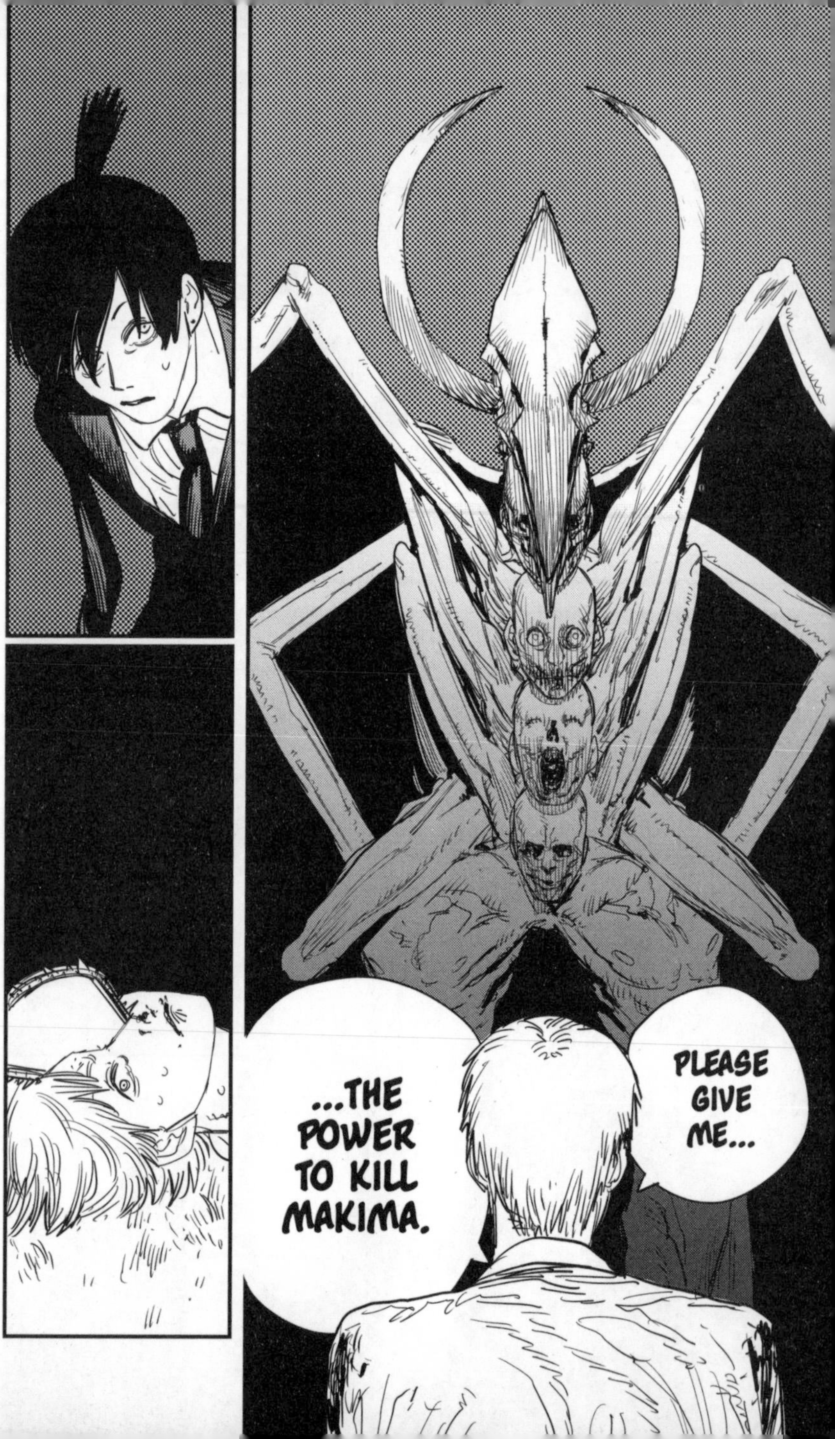
PLEASE GIVE ME...
...THE POWER TO KILL MAKIMA.

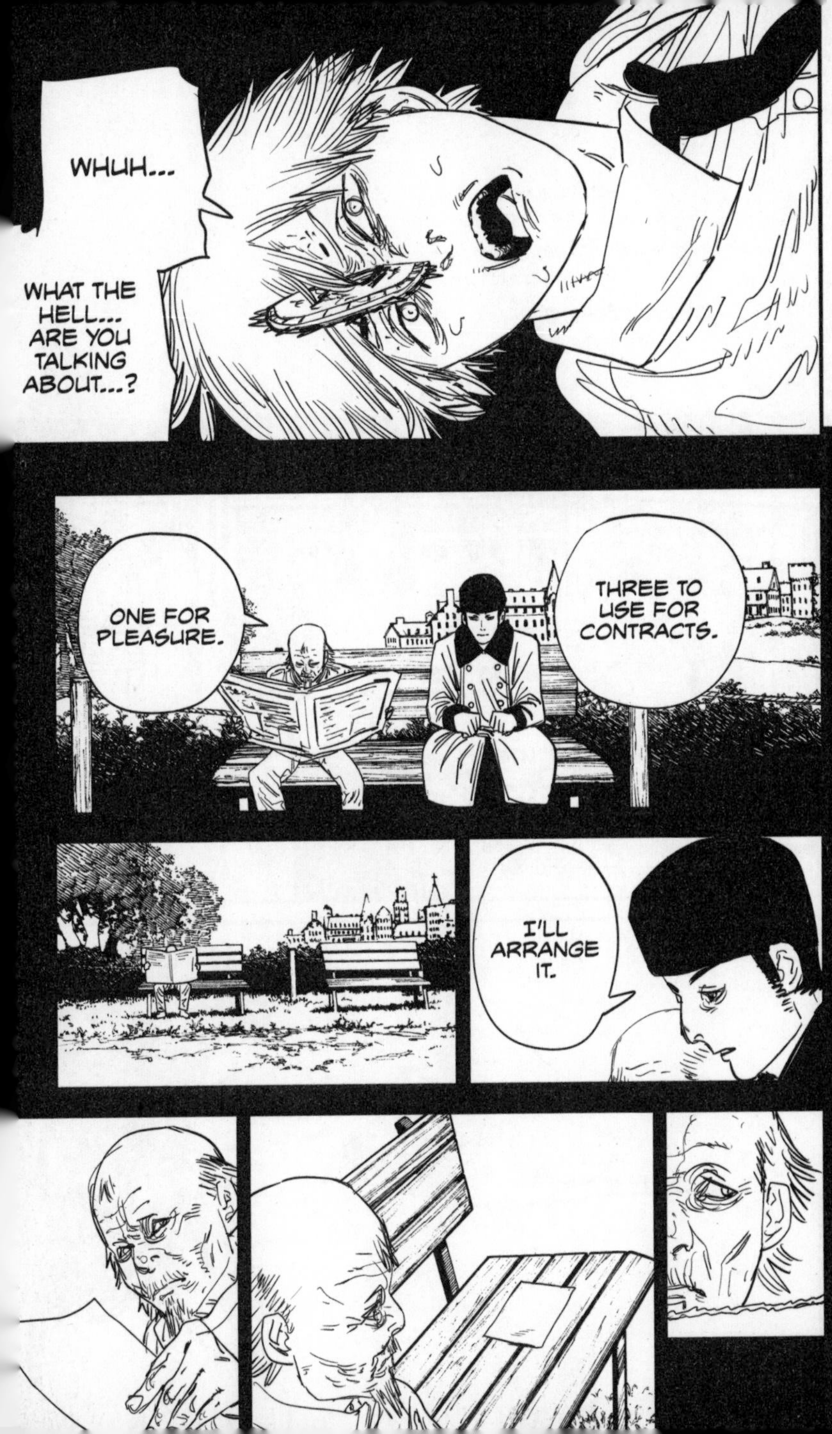
WHUH...
WHAT THE HELL... ARE YOU TALKING ABOUT...?
THREE TO USE FOR CONTRACTS.
ONE FOR PLEASURE.
I'LL ARRANGE IT.

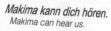

Makima kann dich hören.
Makima can hear us.

Der Tag des Untergangs ist nahe.
The day of reckoning is near.

Töte Makima.
Kill Makima.

A PIECE OF THE DARKNESS DEVIL'S FLESH...

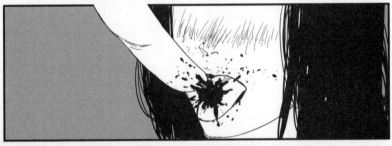

gulp

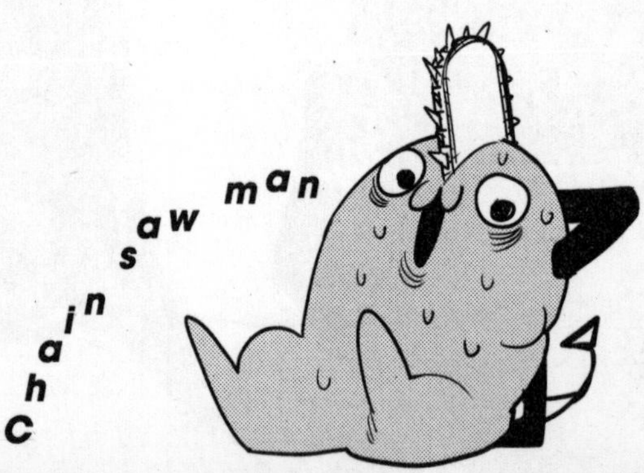
Chainsaw man

Chapter 65: The Darkness Devil

YOU'RE GONNA...

...KILL MAKIMA...?

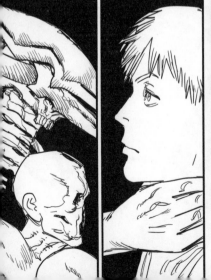

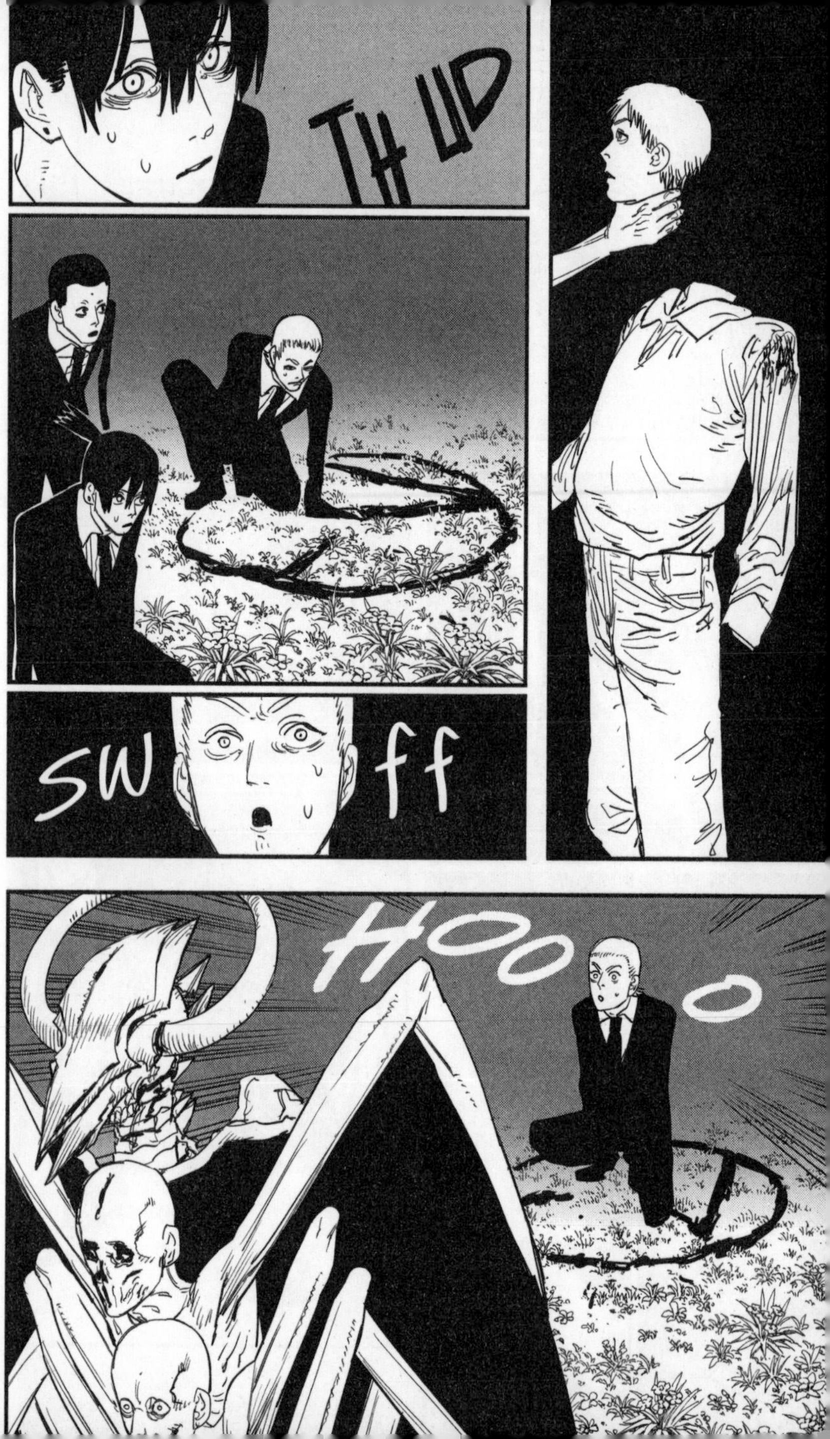
THUD
SWff
HOOOO

GRIP
GAH!
GHK!
AH!
THE STONE DEVIL...
KRAK

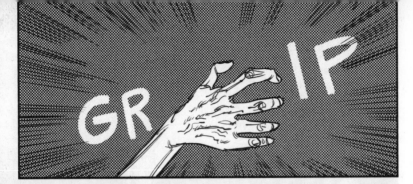

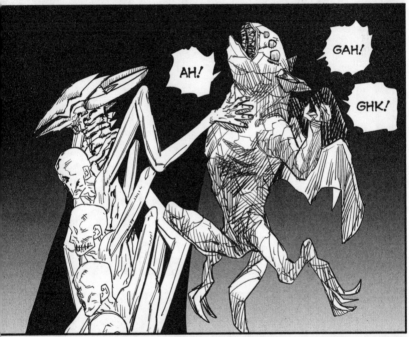

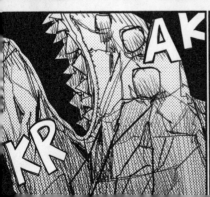

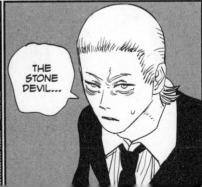

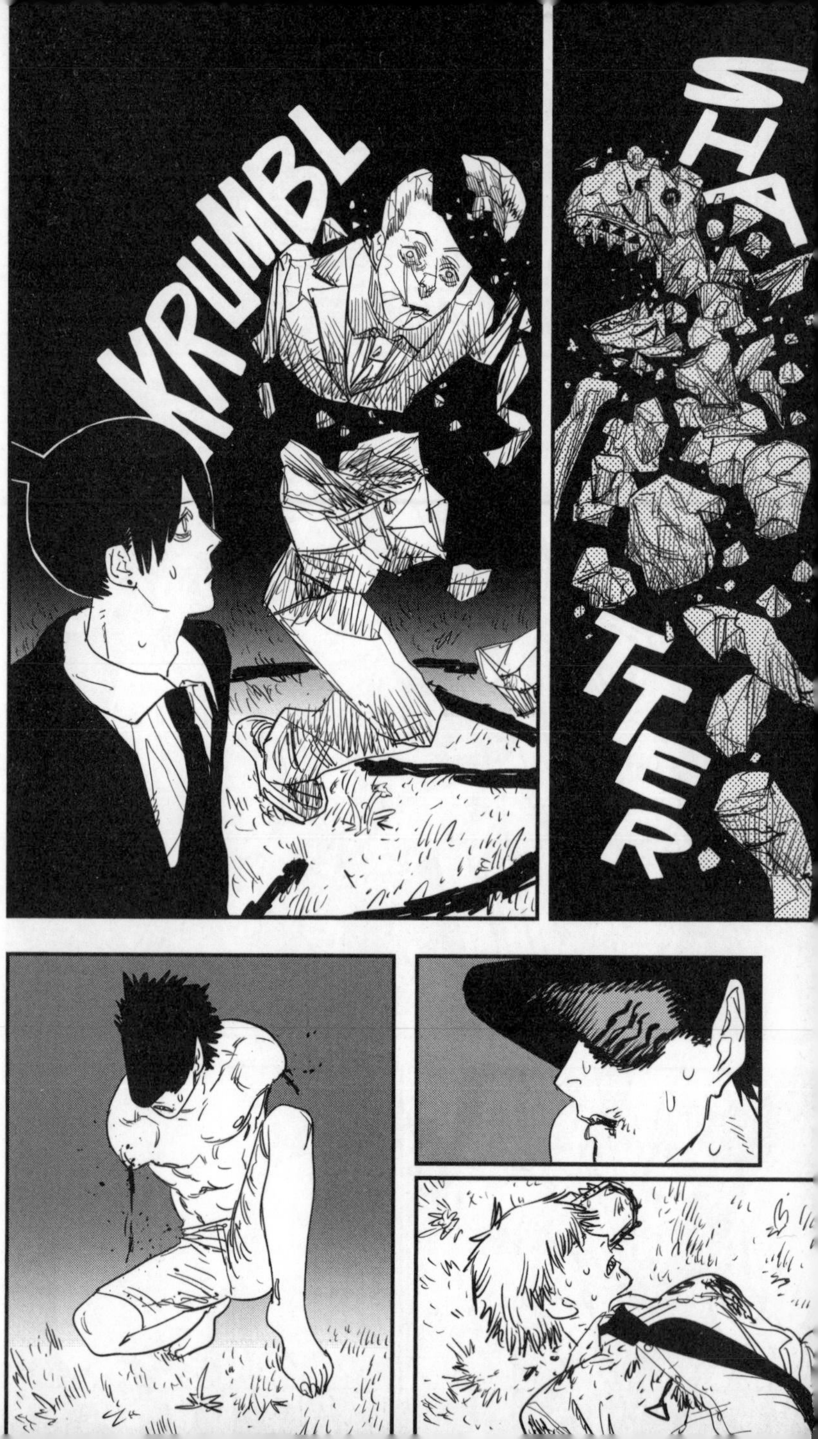
SHA
TTER
KRUMBL

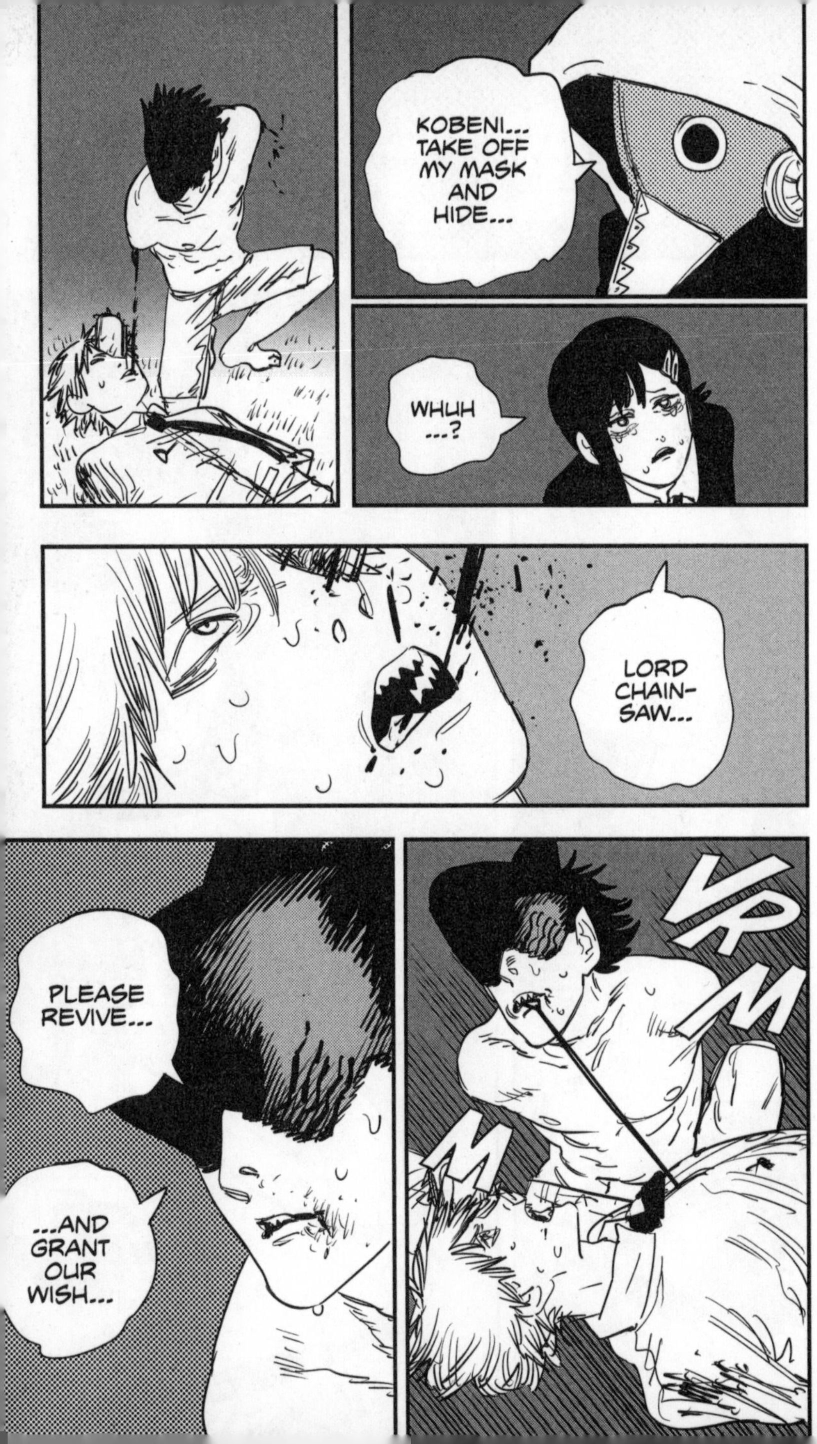
KOBENI... TAKE OFF MY MASK AND HIDE...
WHUH ...?
LORD CHAIN-SAW...
VRMM
PLEASE REVIVE...
...AND GRANT OUR WISH...

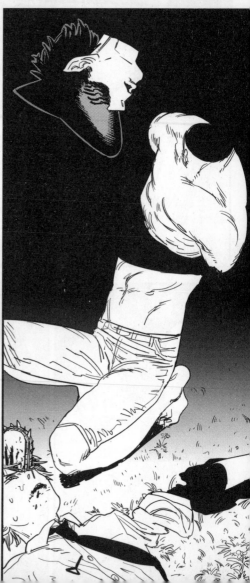

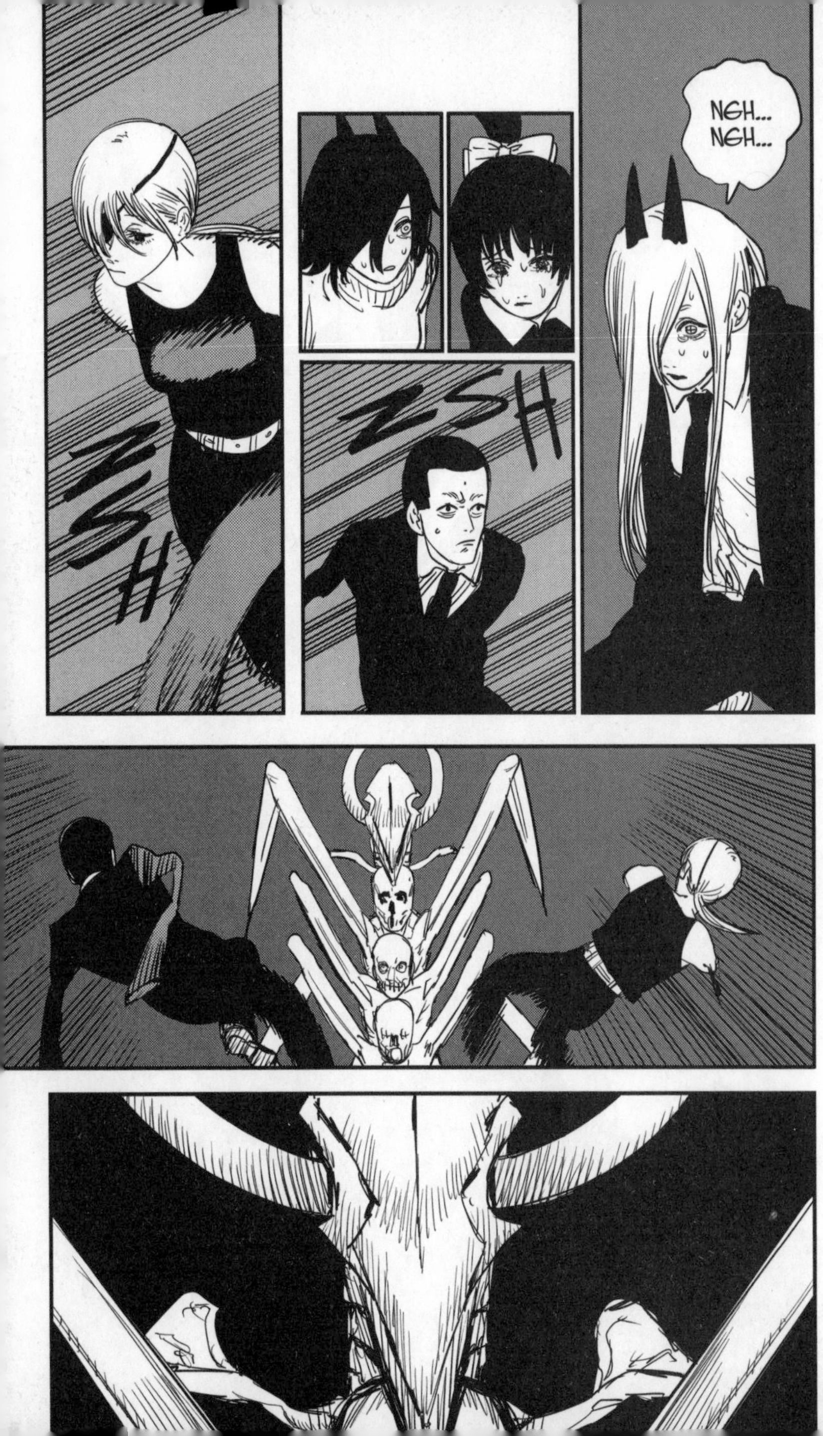
NGH... NGH...
ZSH
ZSH

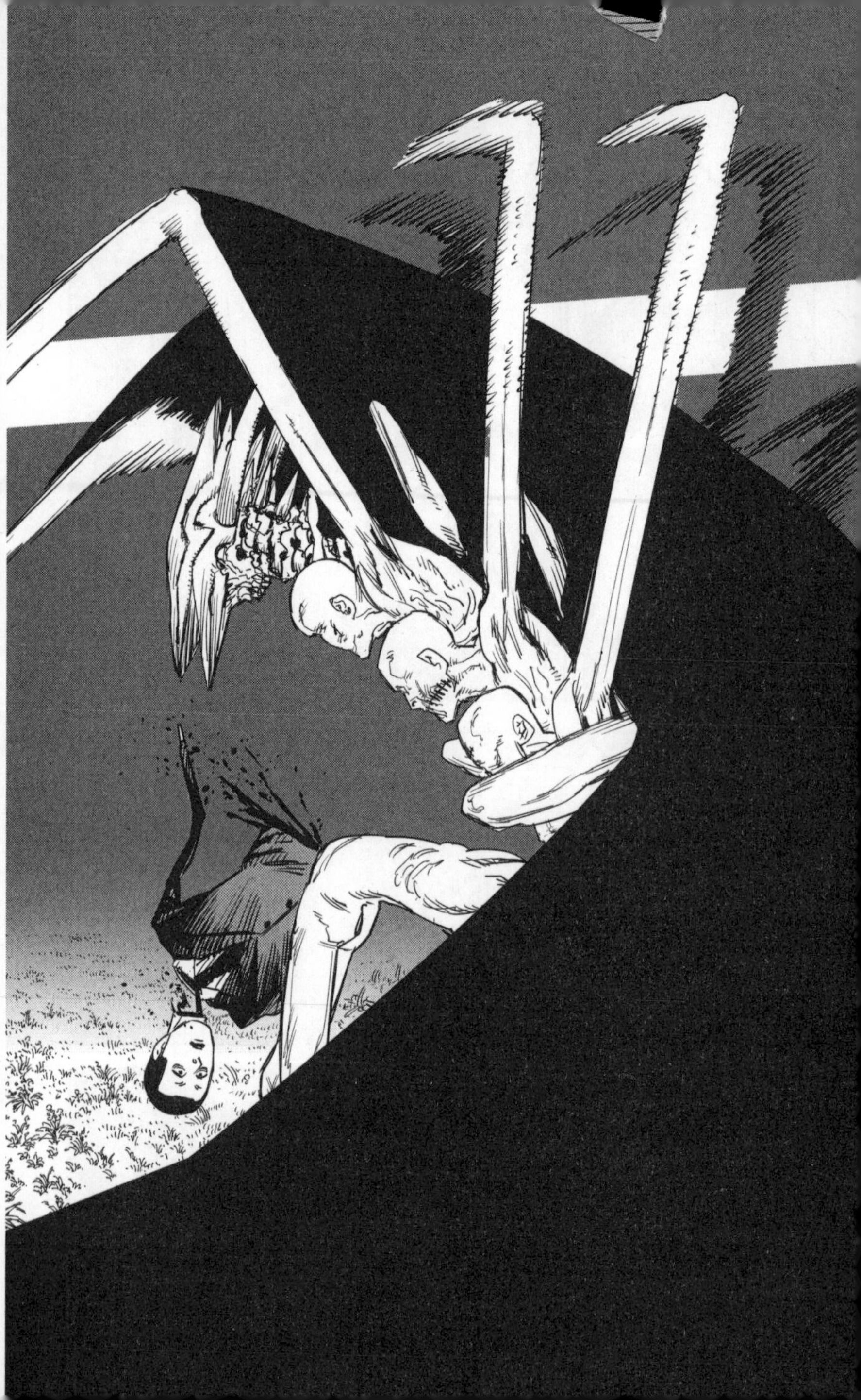

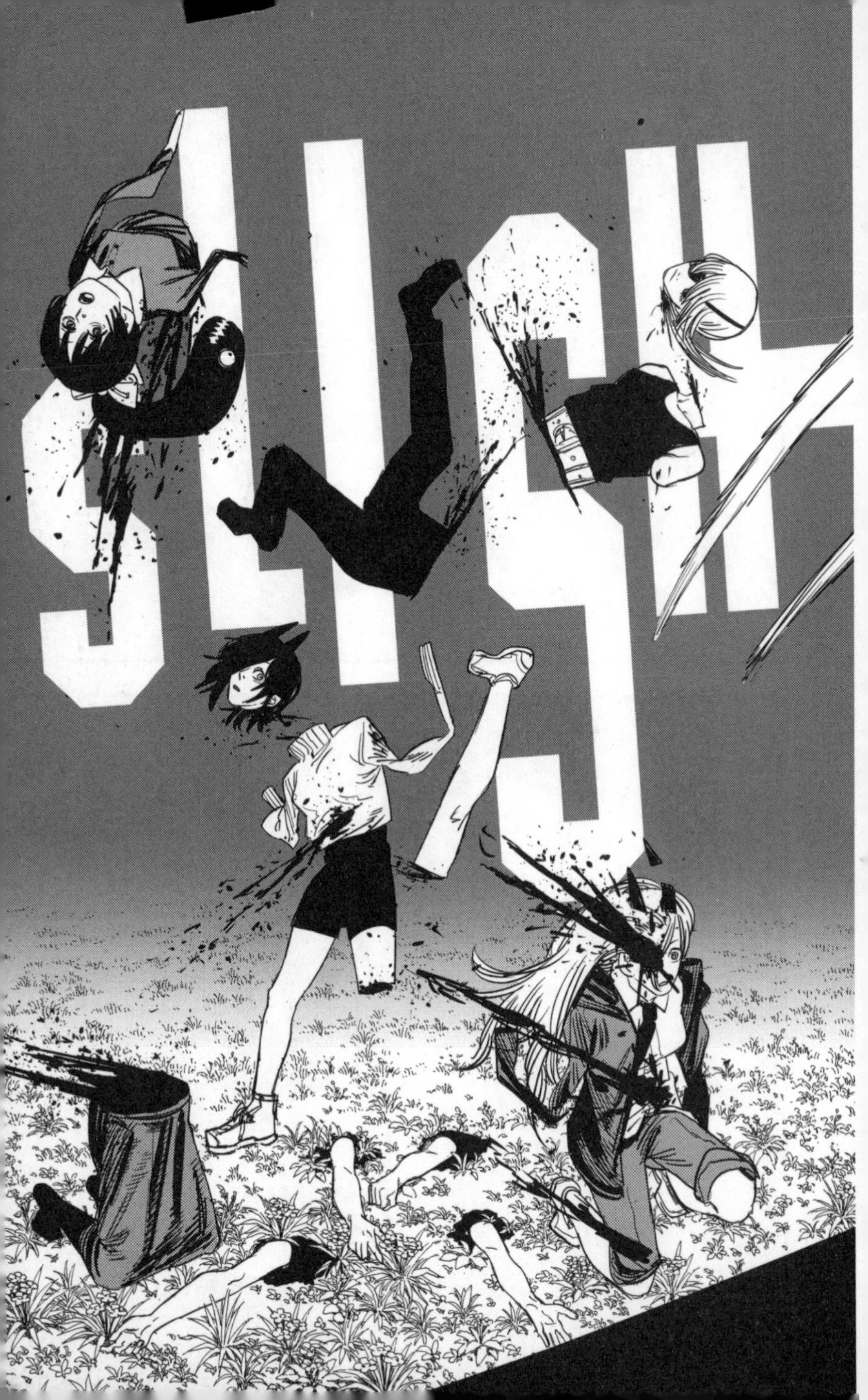
SLISH

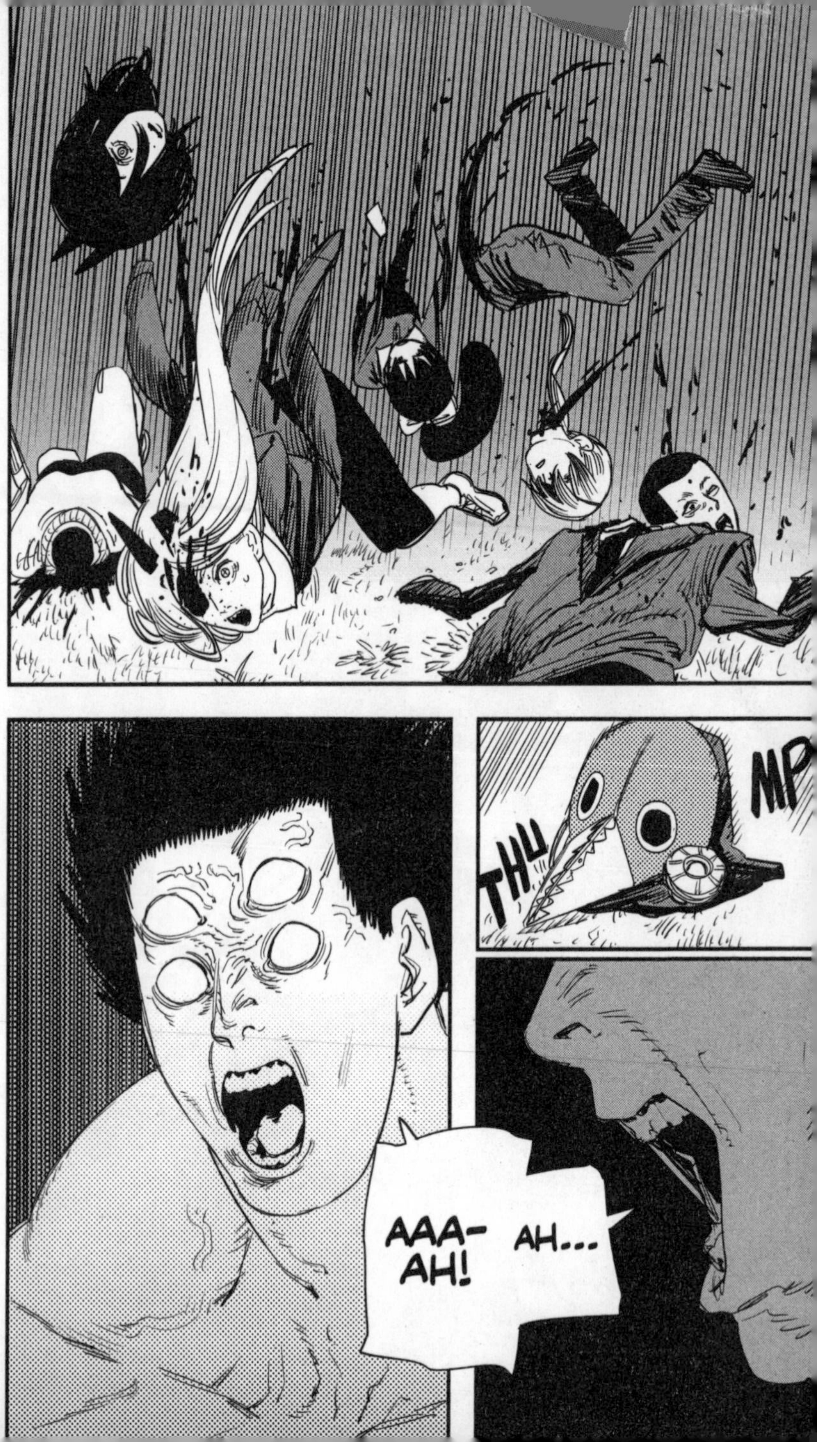
THUMP
AAA-AH! AH...

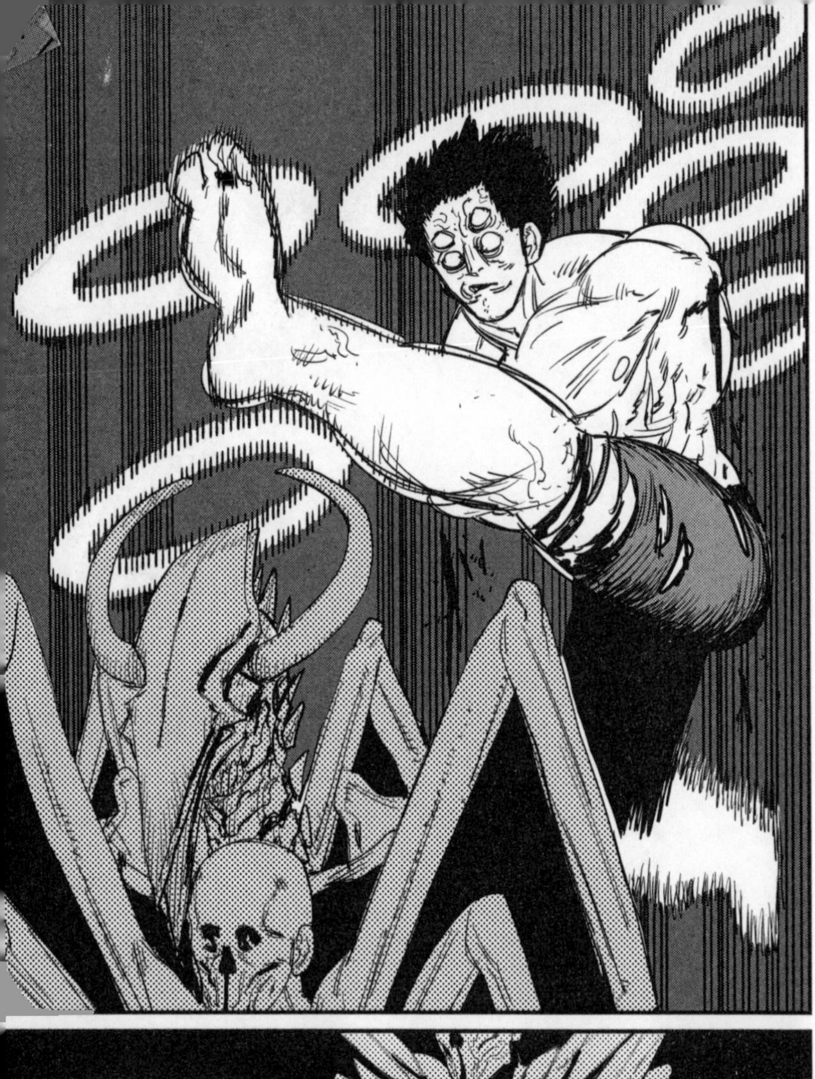
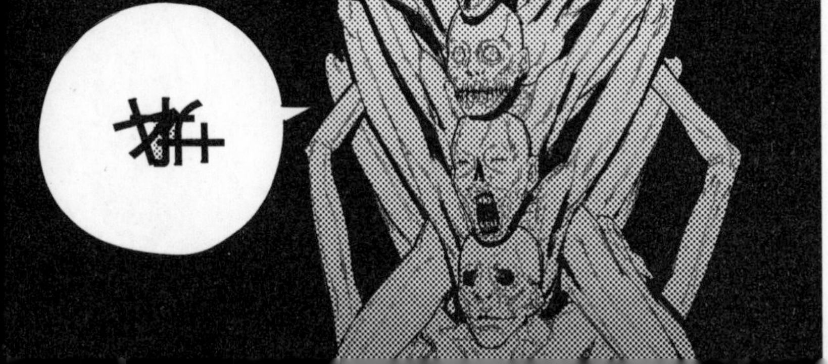

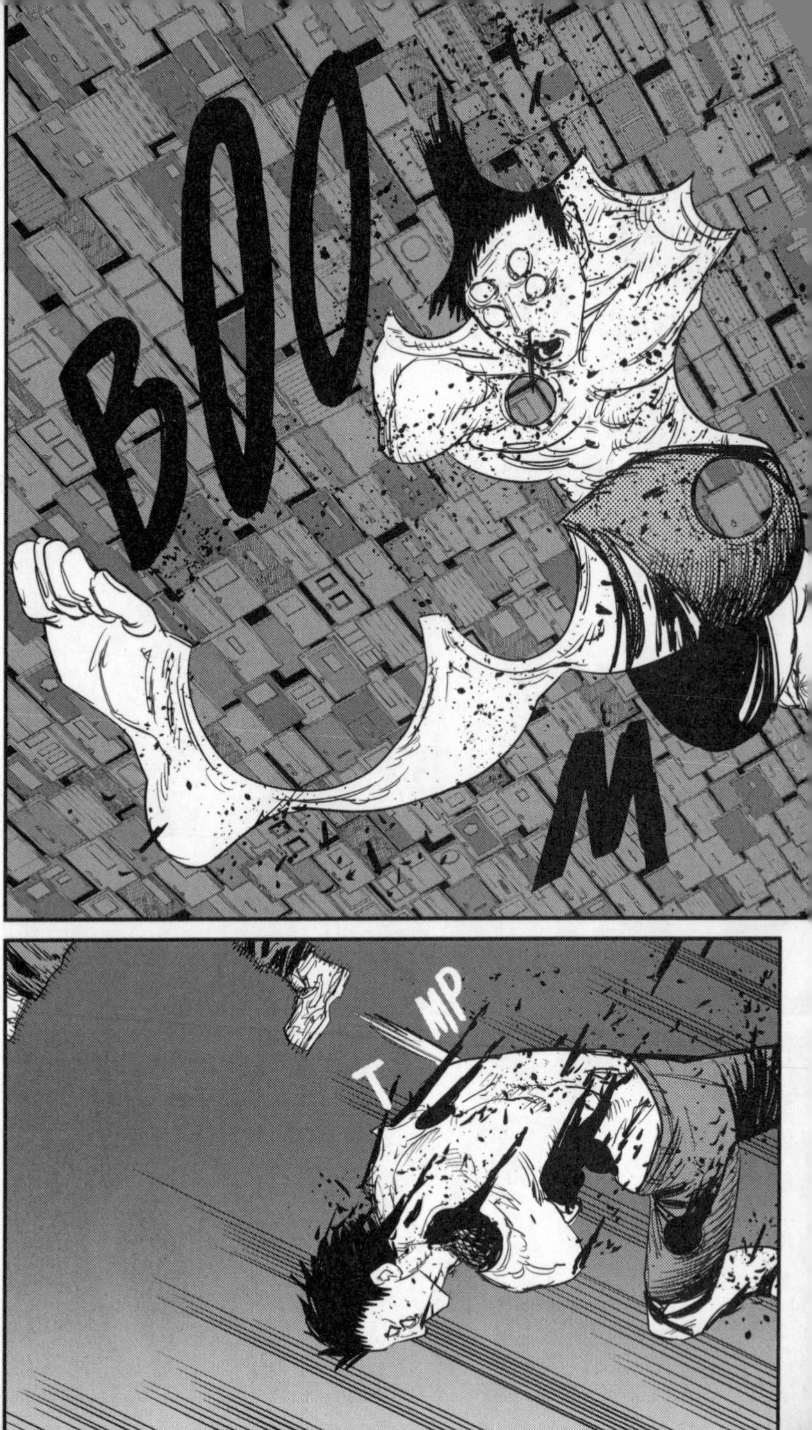
BOOM
T MP

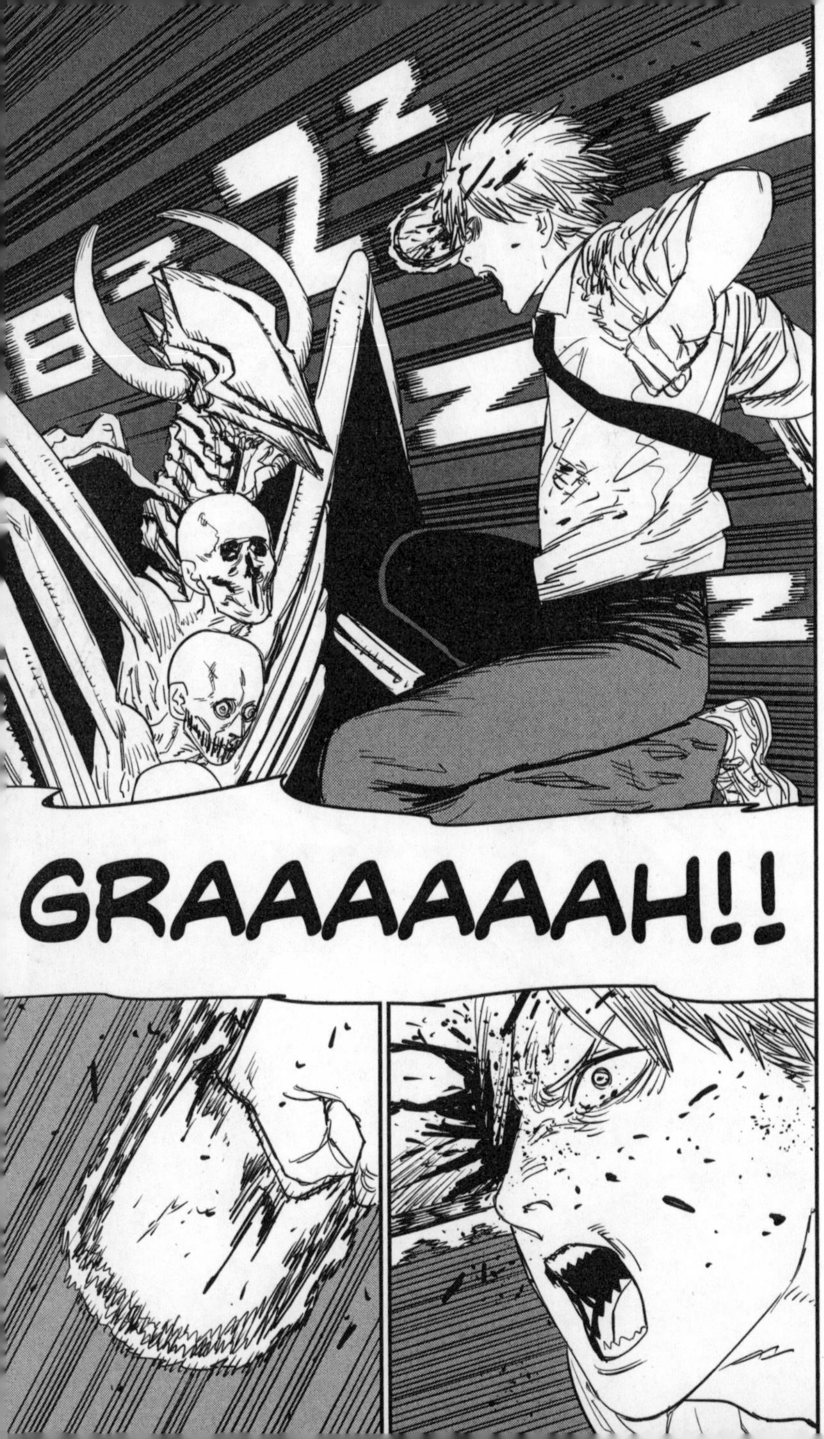
GRAAAAAAH!!

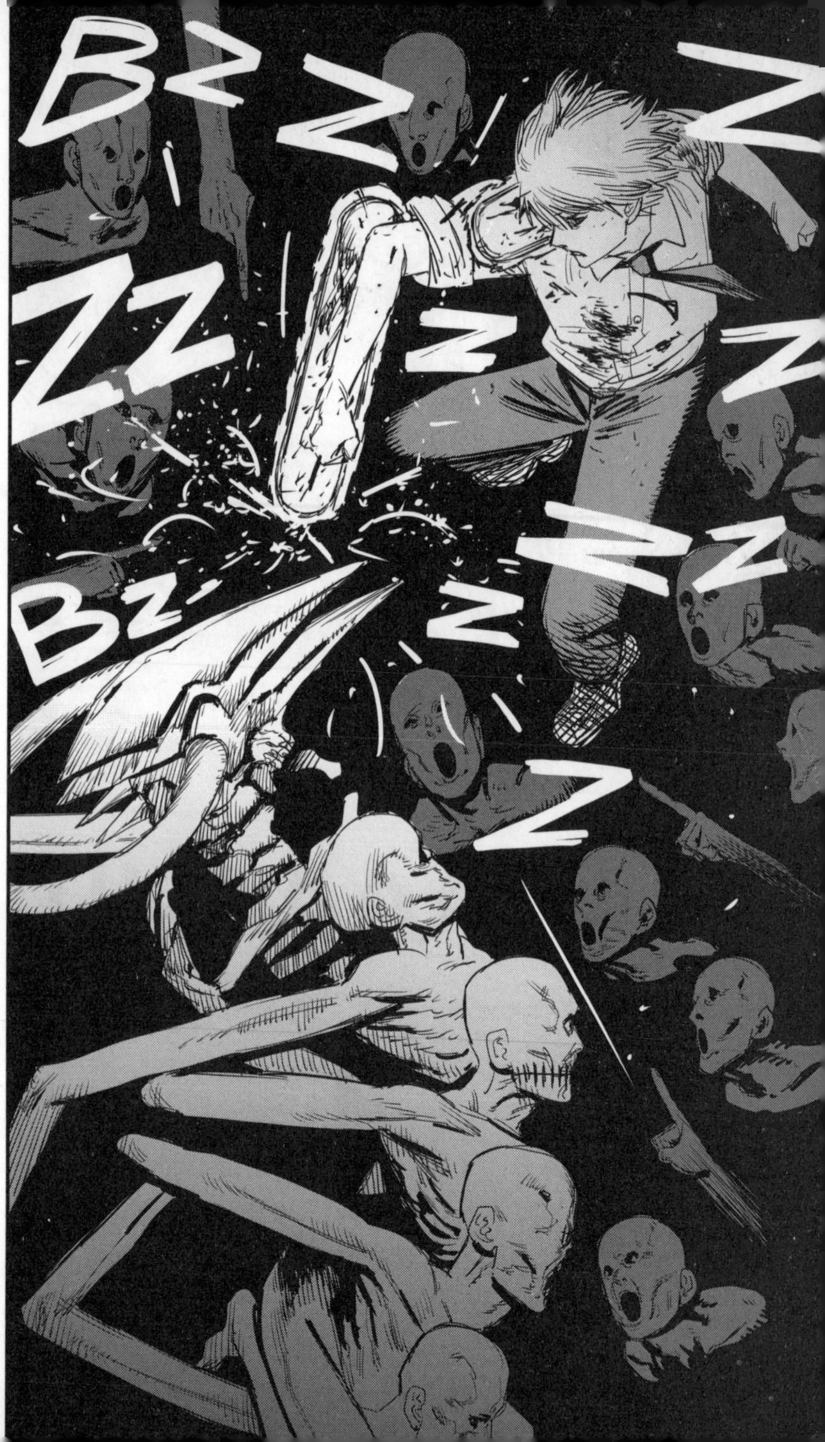
BZZZZZZ
BZZZZZ

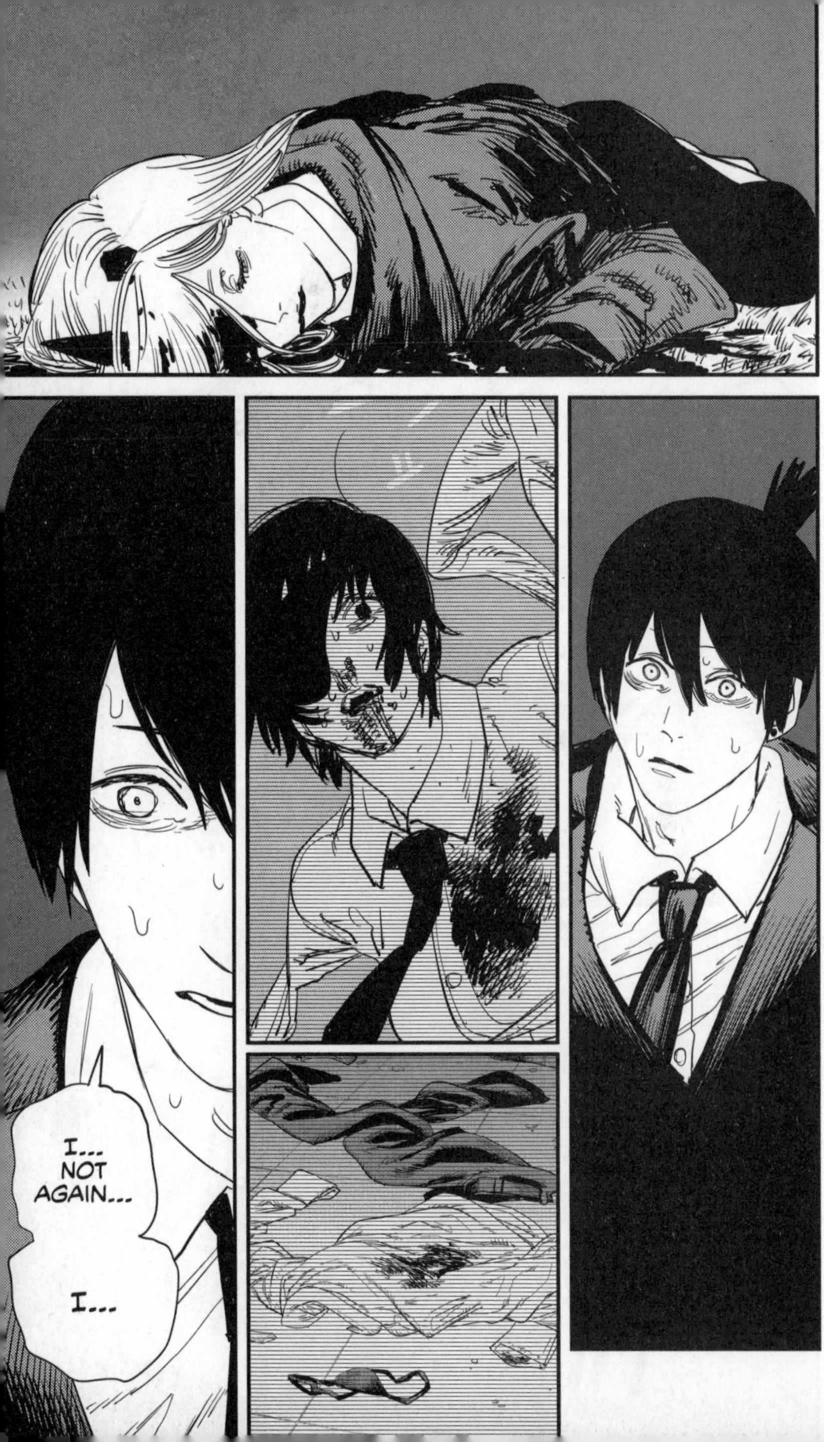
I... NOT AGAIN...
I...

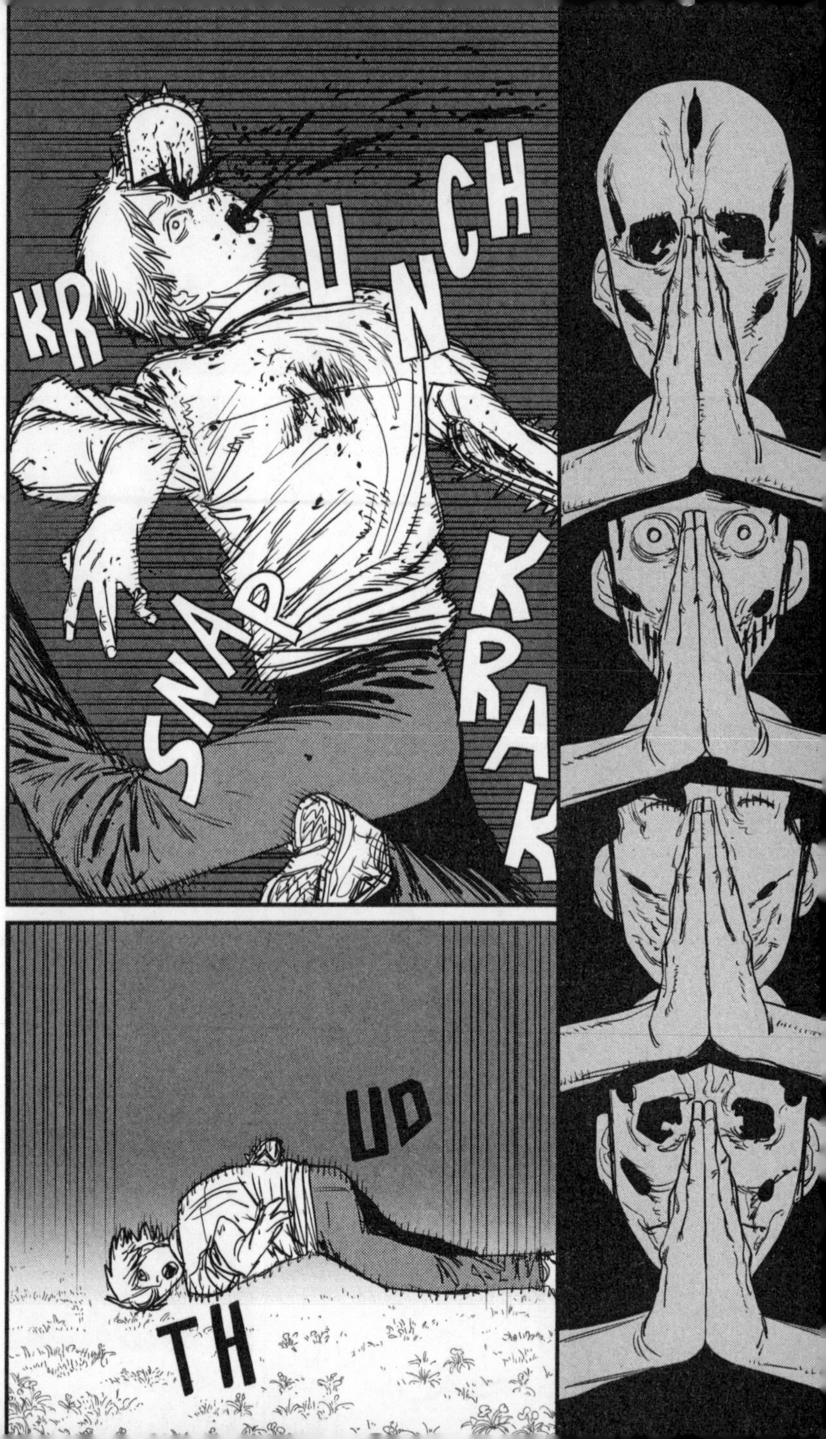
KRUNCH
KRAK
SNAP
THUD

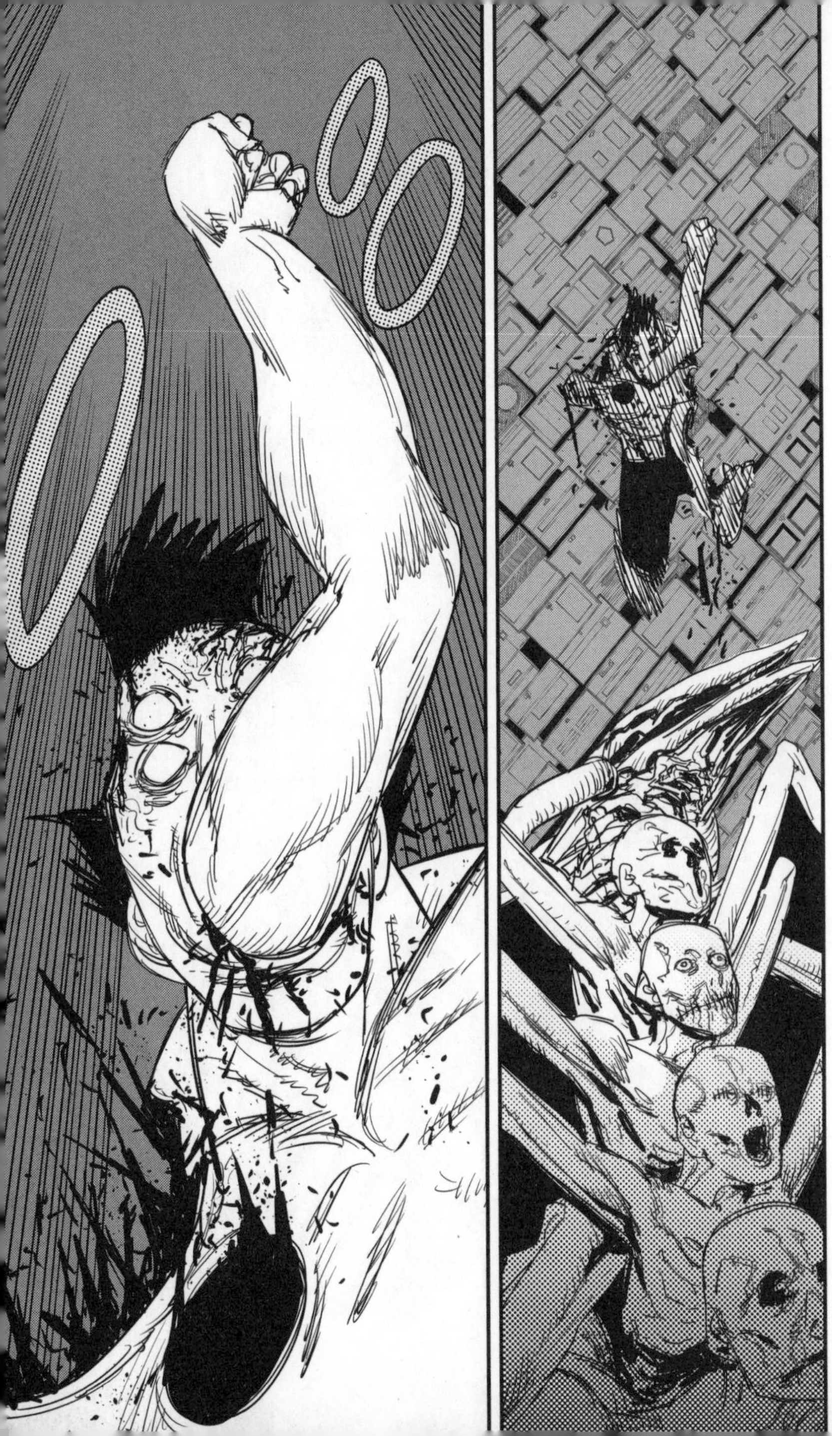

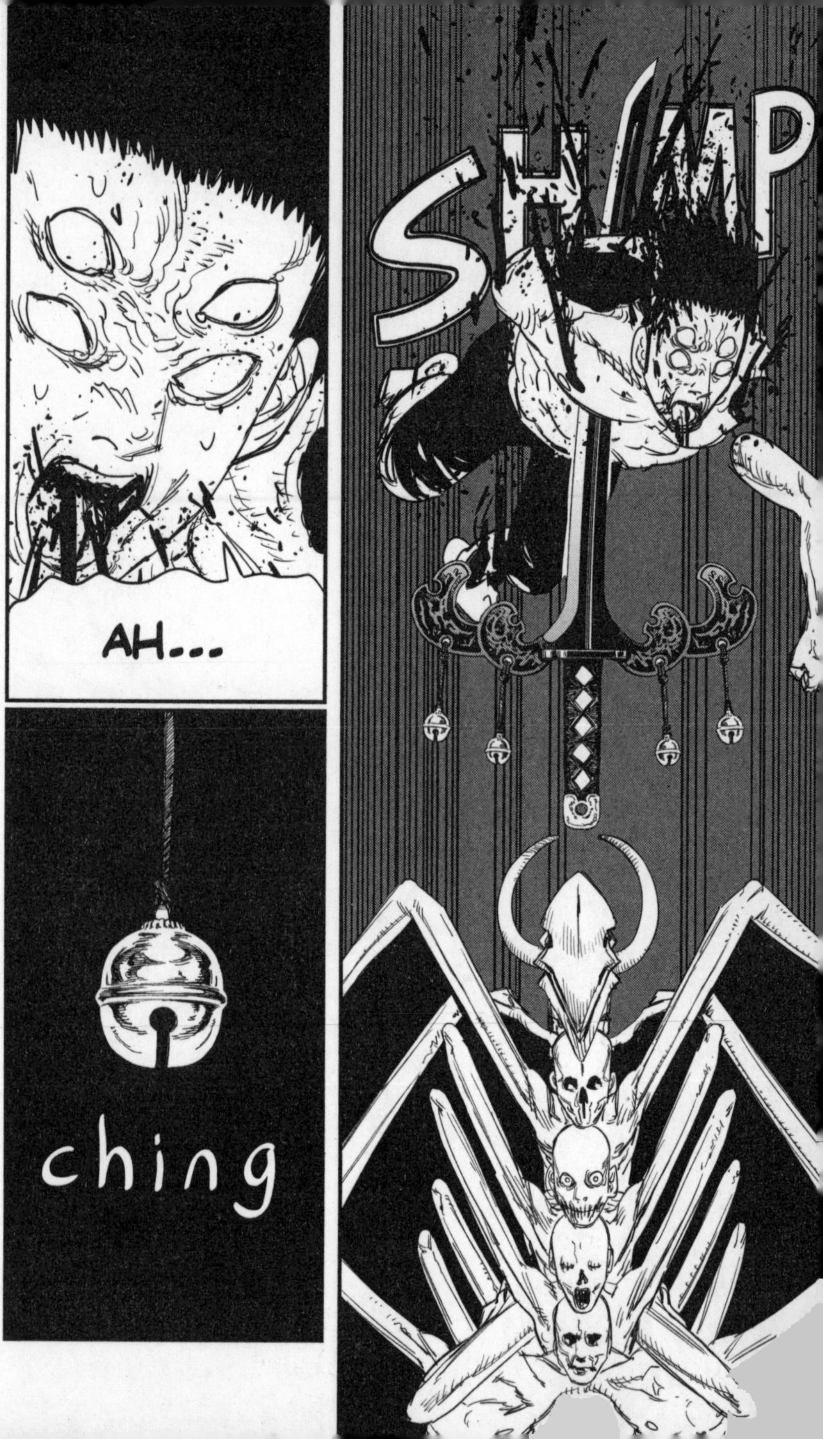
SHUMP
AH...
ching

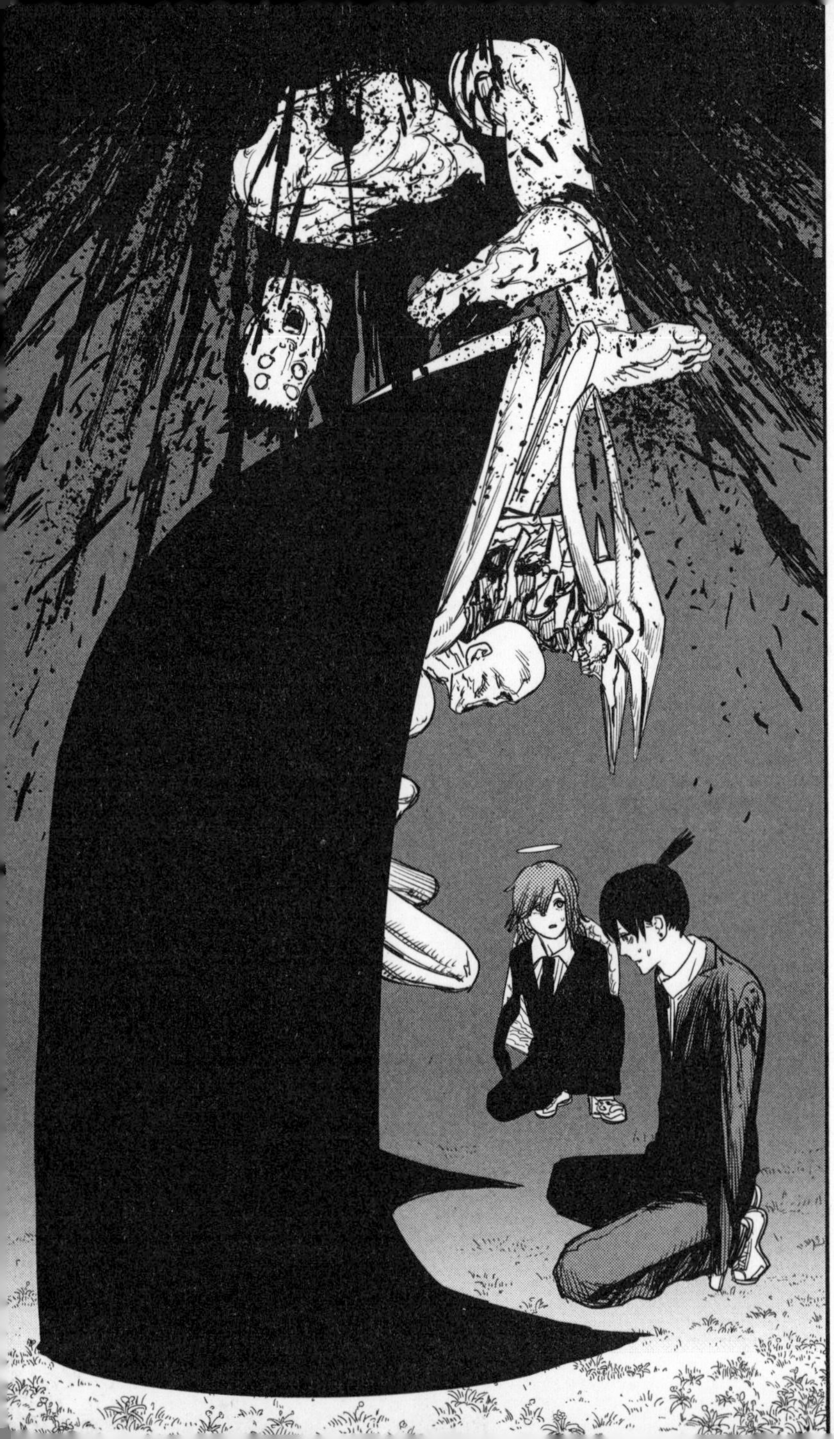

Chain saw man

Chapter 66: Woof!

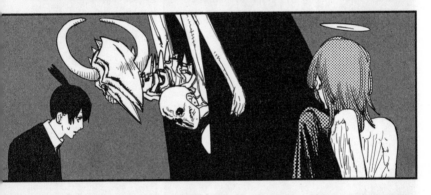

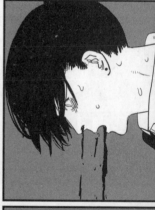

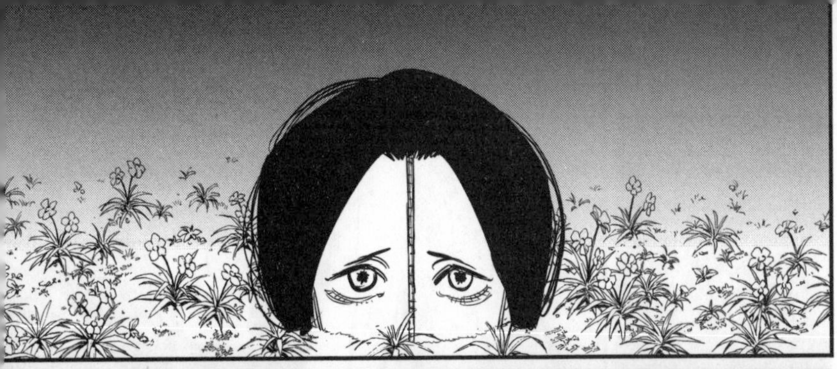
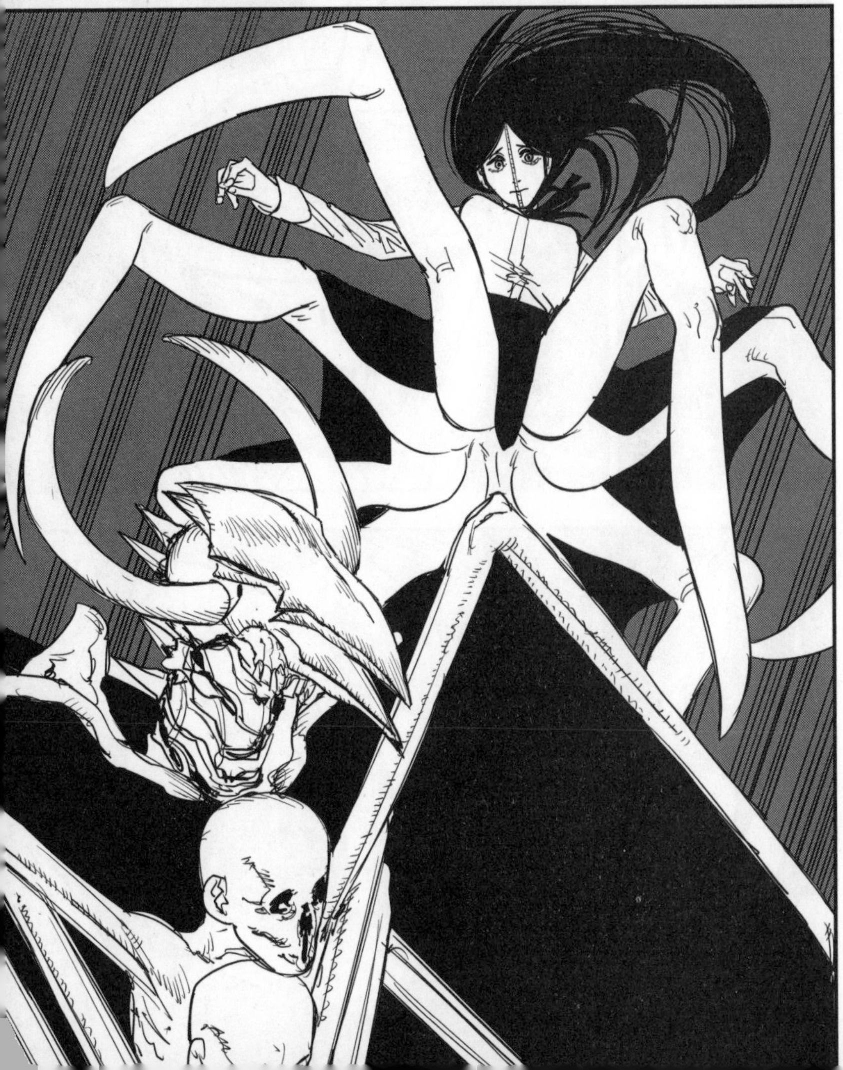

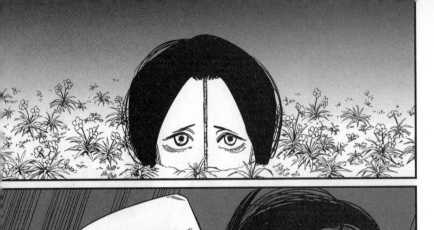

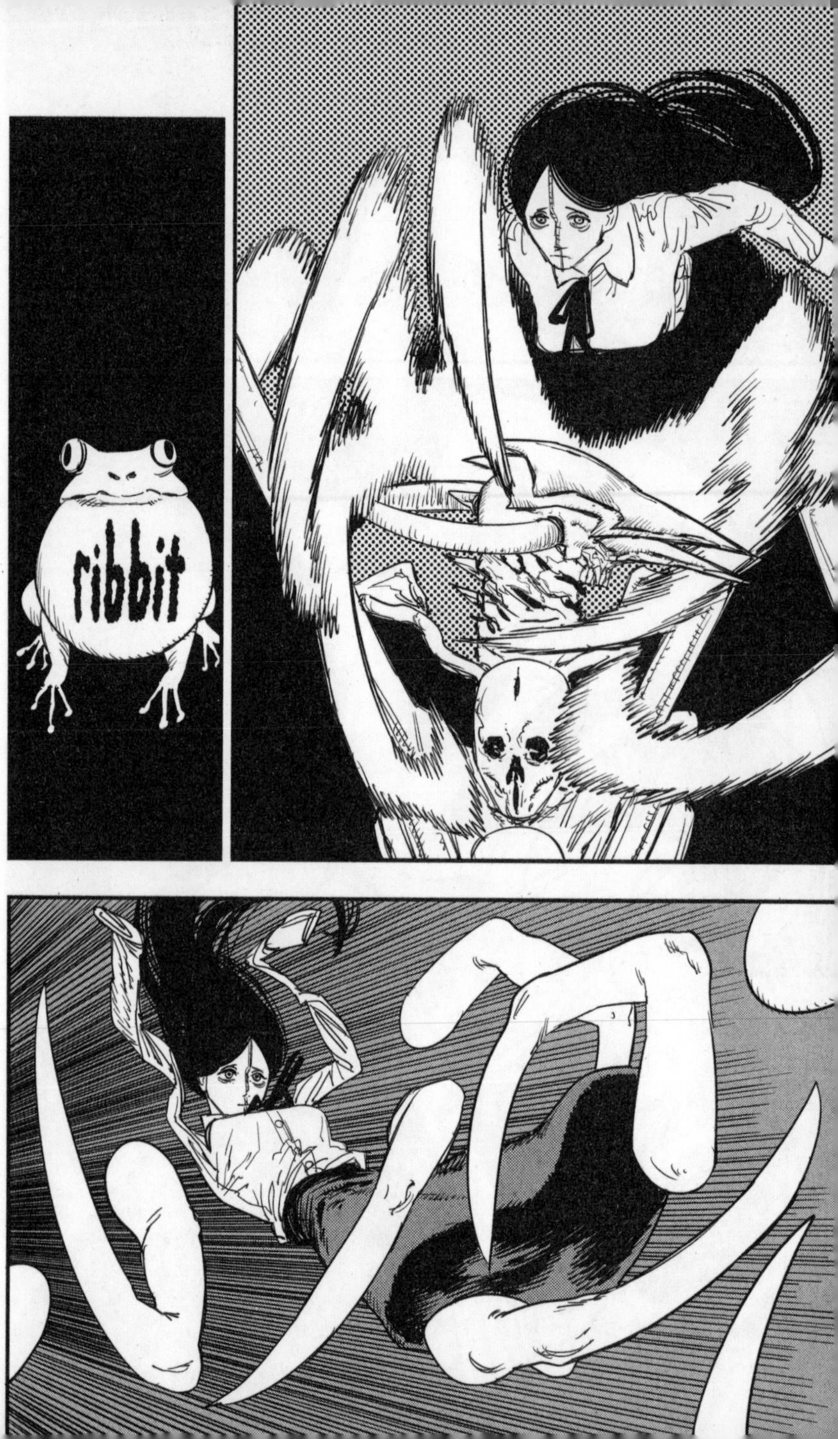
ribbit

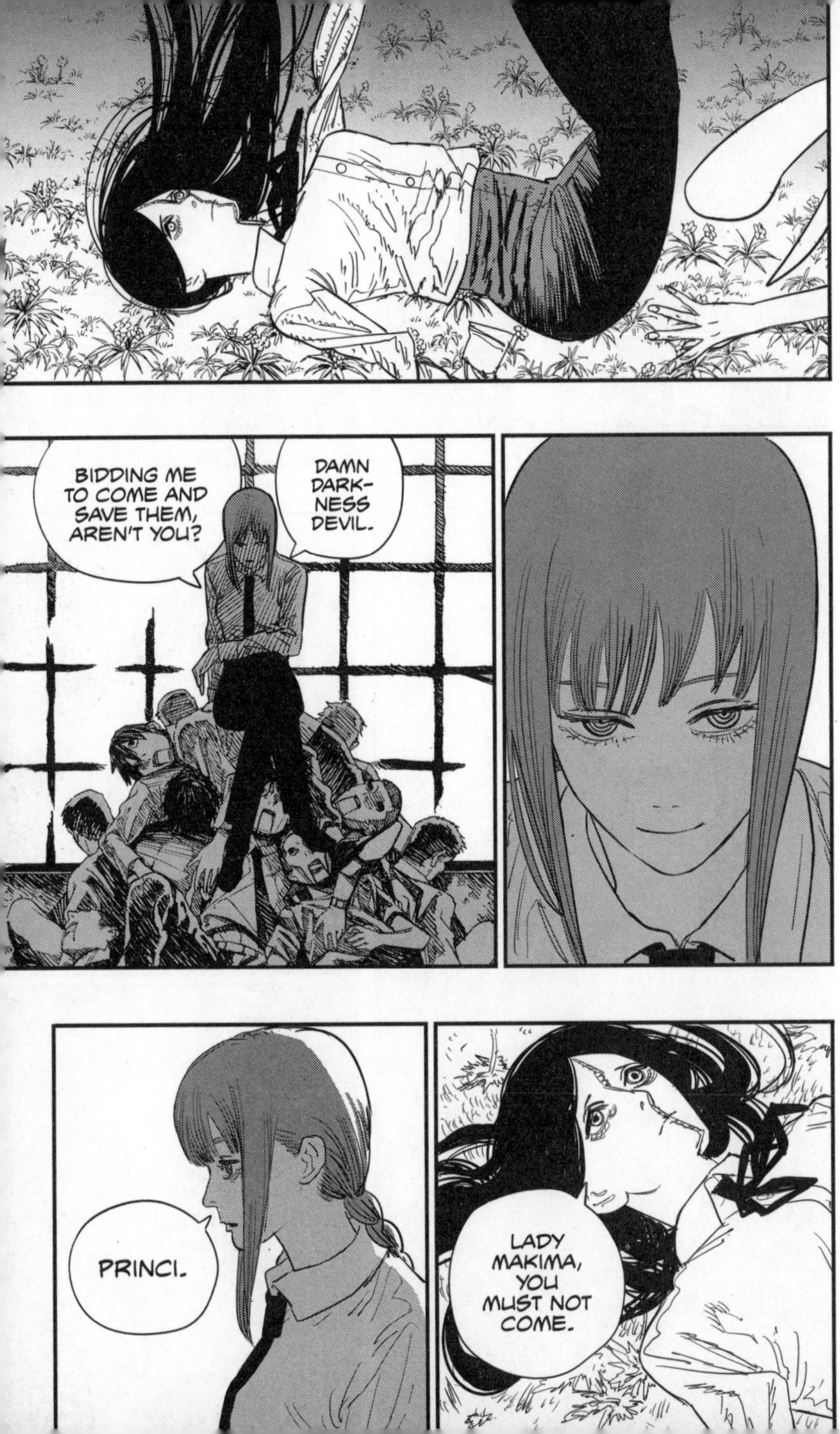
DAMN DARKNESS DEVIL.
BIDDING ME TO COME AND SAVE THEM, AREN'T YOU?
LADY MAKIMA, YOU MUST NOT COME.
PRINCI.

CALL ME.

AS YOU WISH.

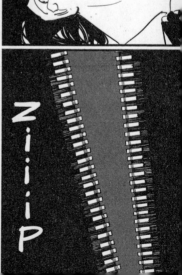

ZiiiiP

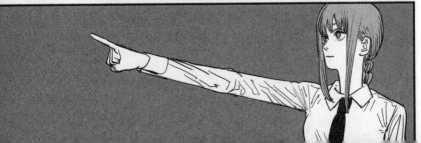

irk

sk

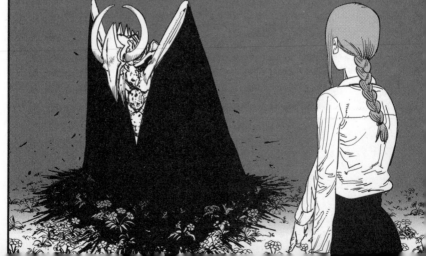

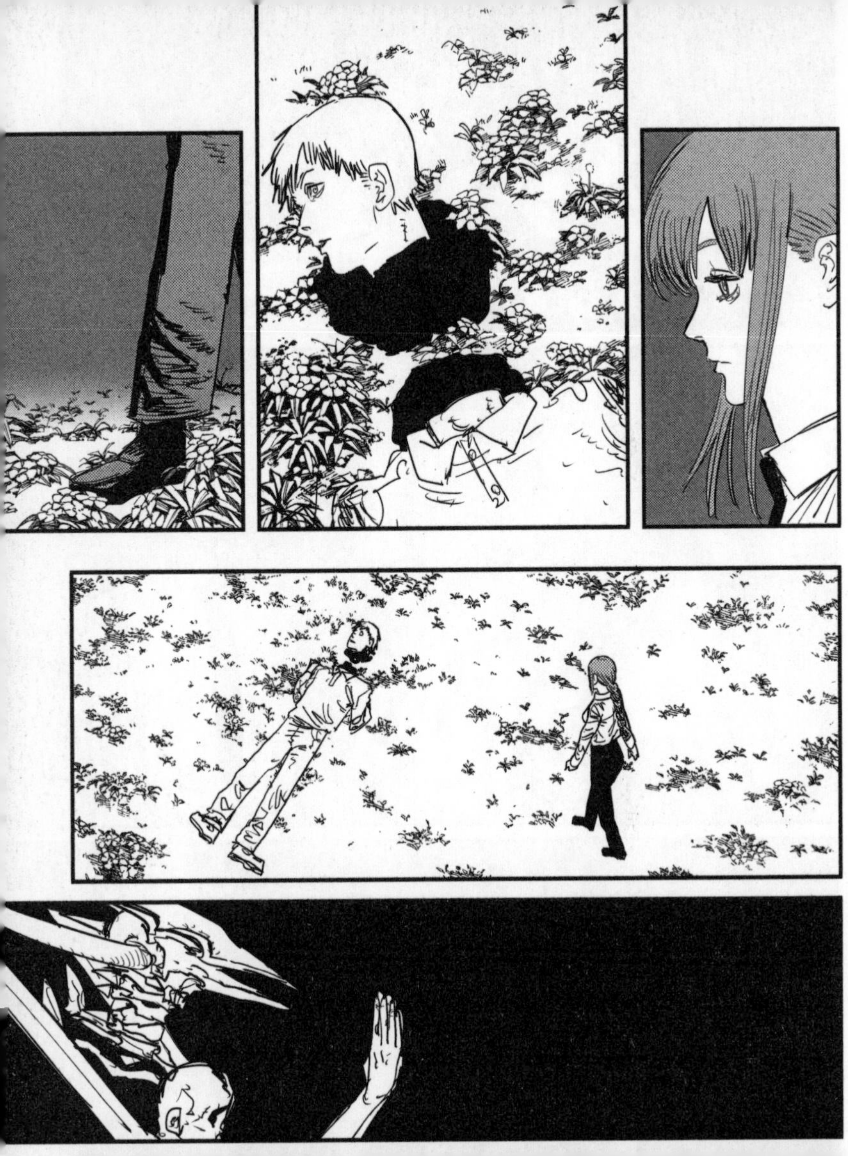

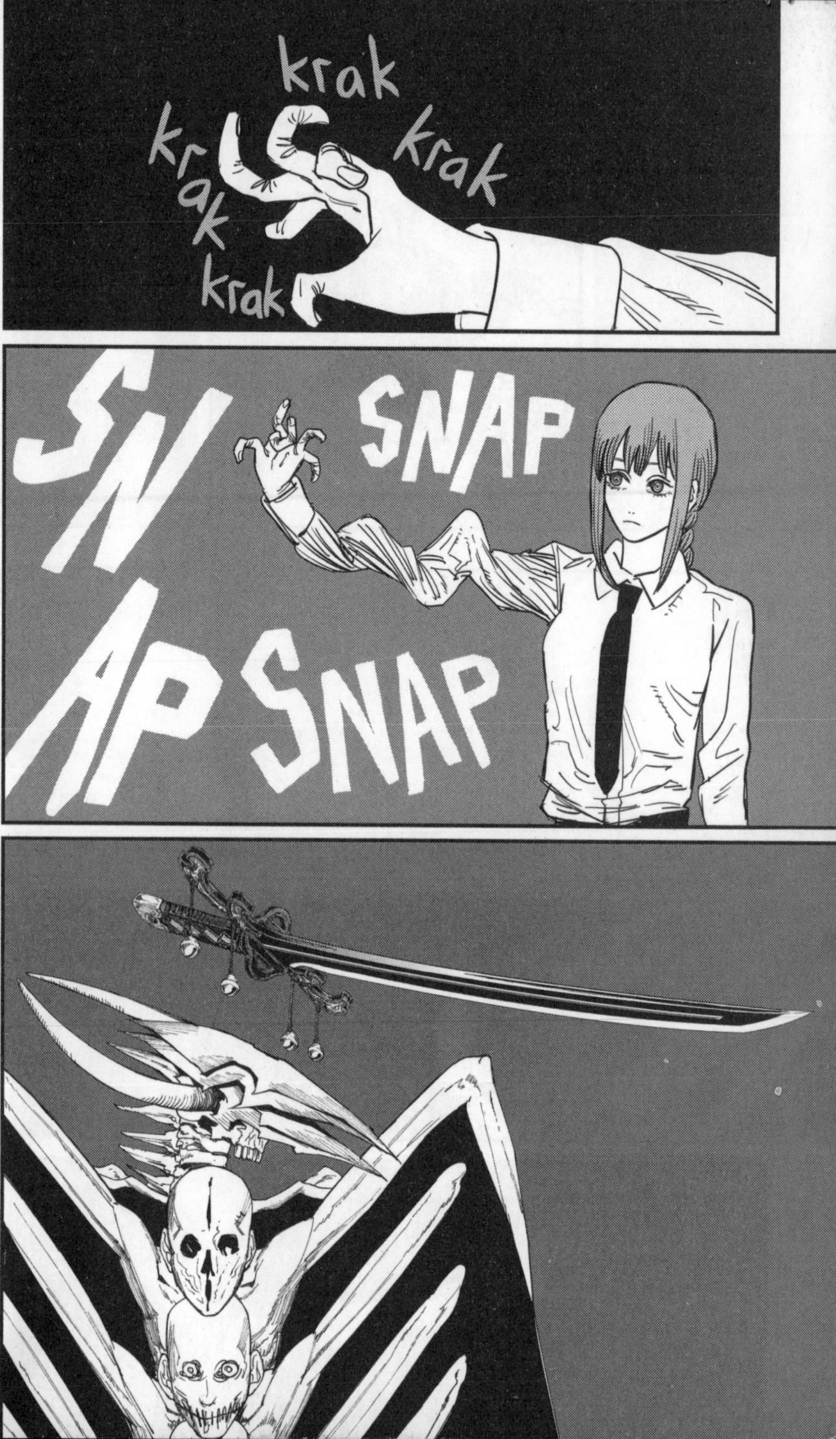
krak
krak
krak
krak
krak
SNAP
SNAP
SNAP

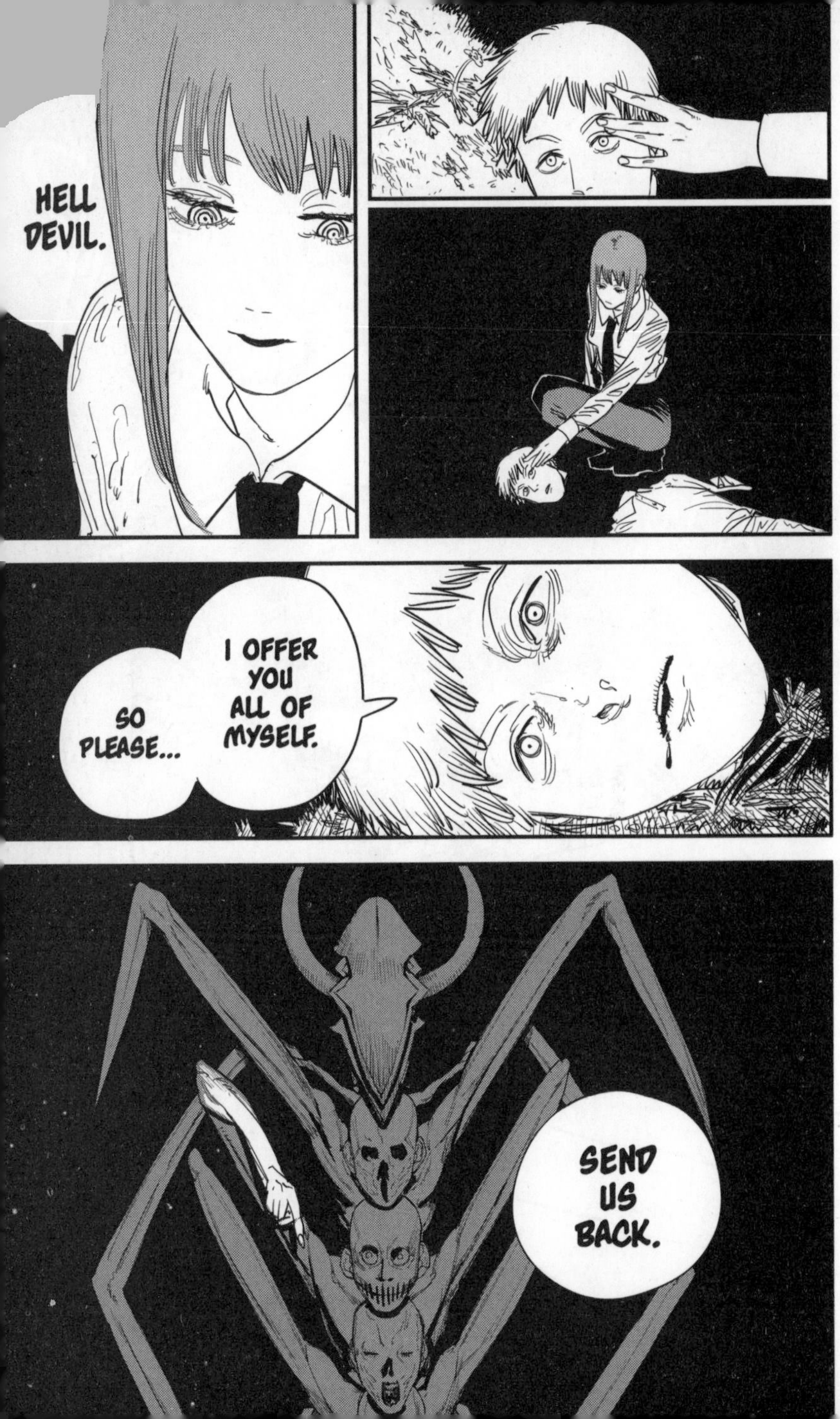
HELL DEVIL.
I OFFER YOU ALL OF MYSELF.
SO PLEASE...
SEND US BACK.

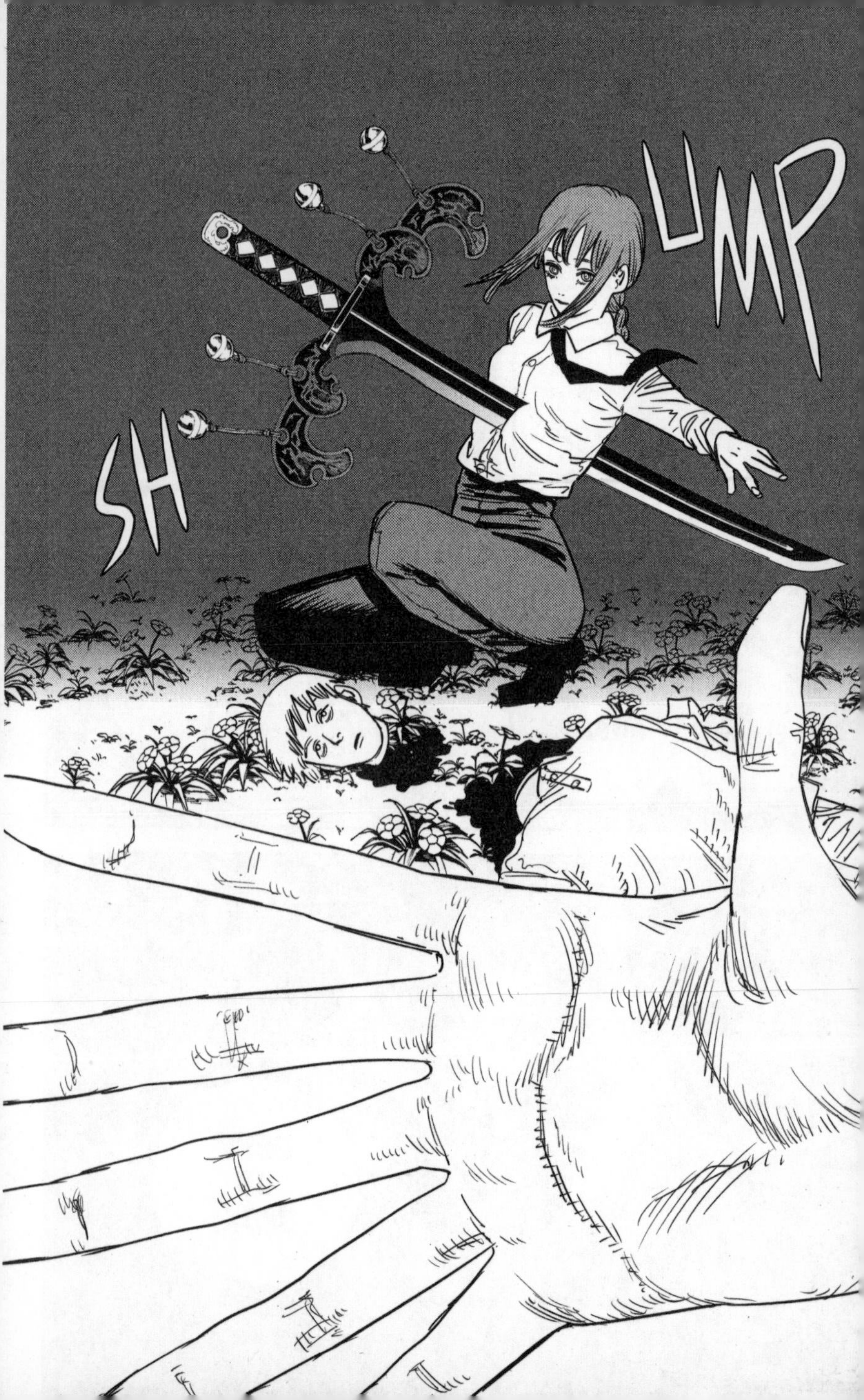
SH
UMP

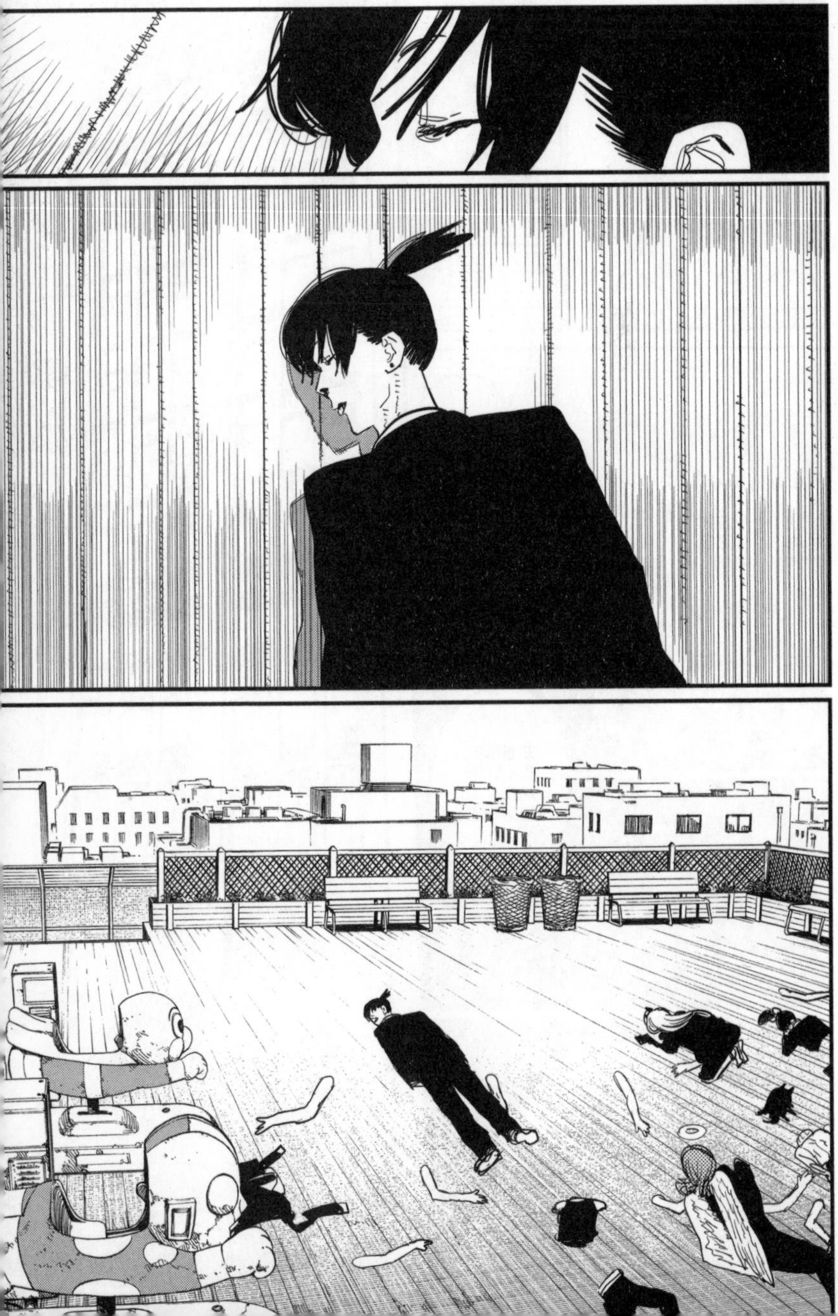

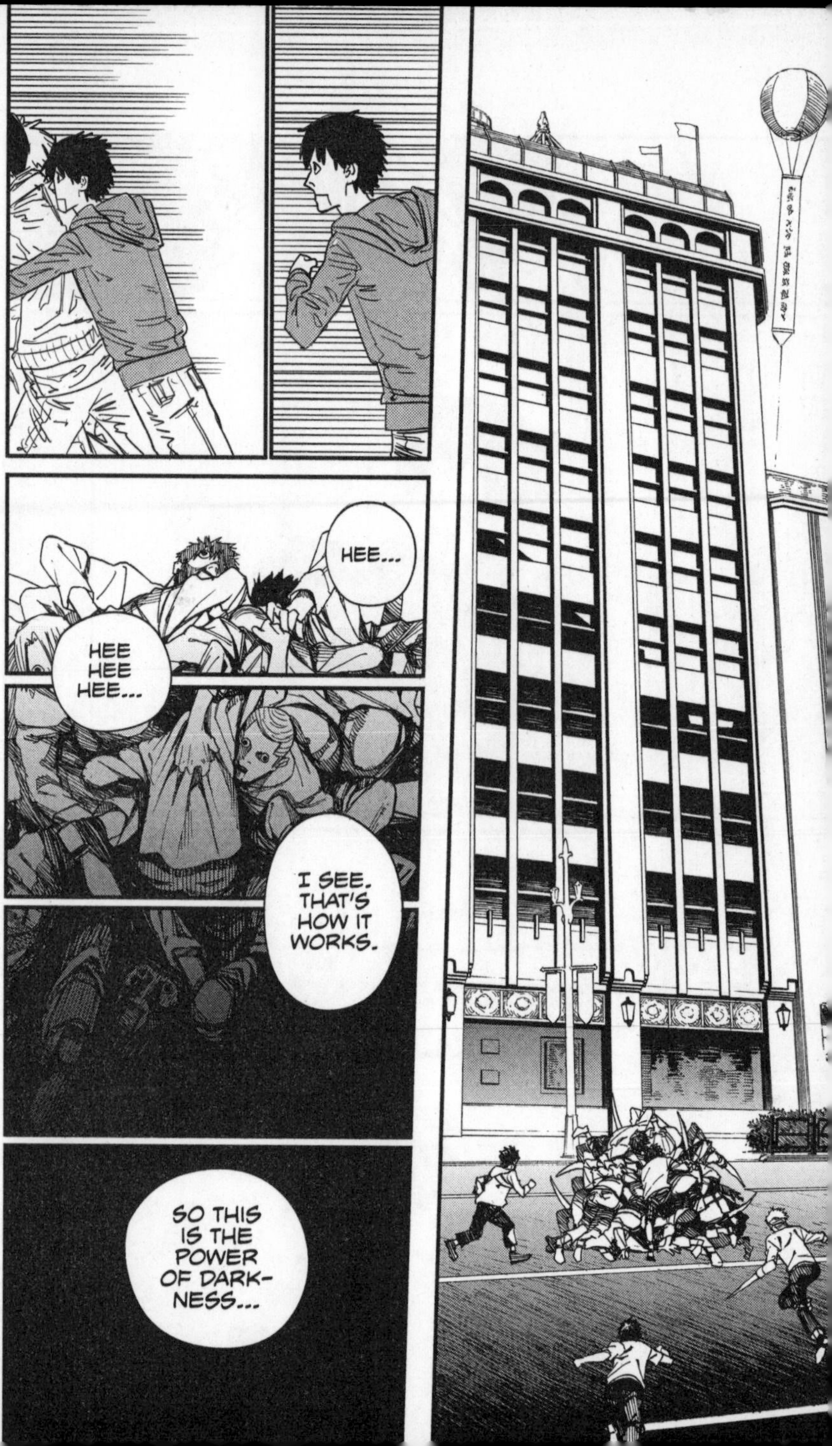
HEE...
HEE HEE HEE...
I SEE. THAT'S HOW IT WORKS.
SO THIS IS THE POWER OF DARK-NESS...

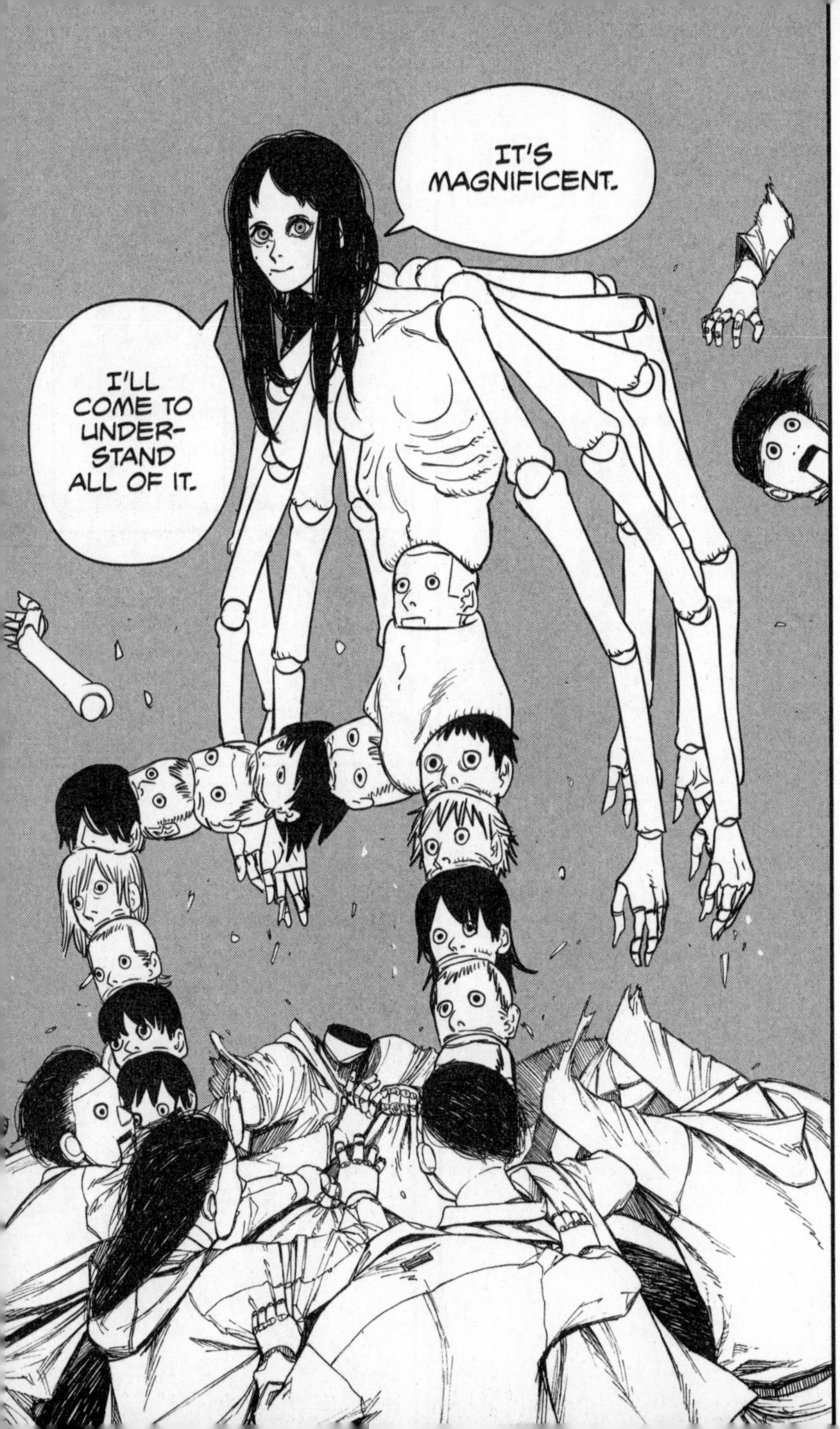
IT'S MAGNIFICENT.
I'LL COME TO UNDER-STAND ALL OF IT.

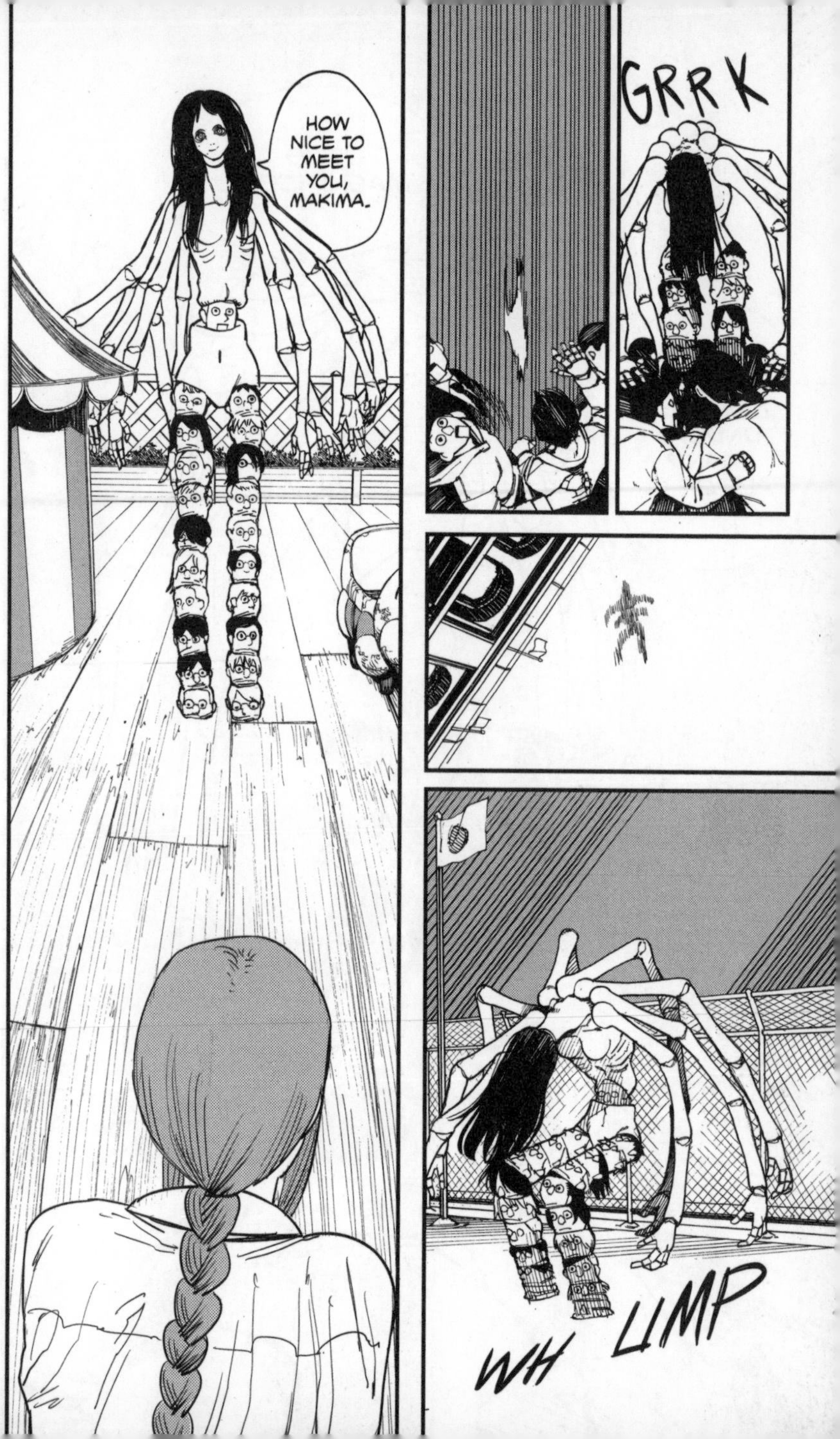
GRRK
WH UMP
HOW NICE TO MEET YOU, MAKIMA.

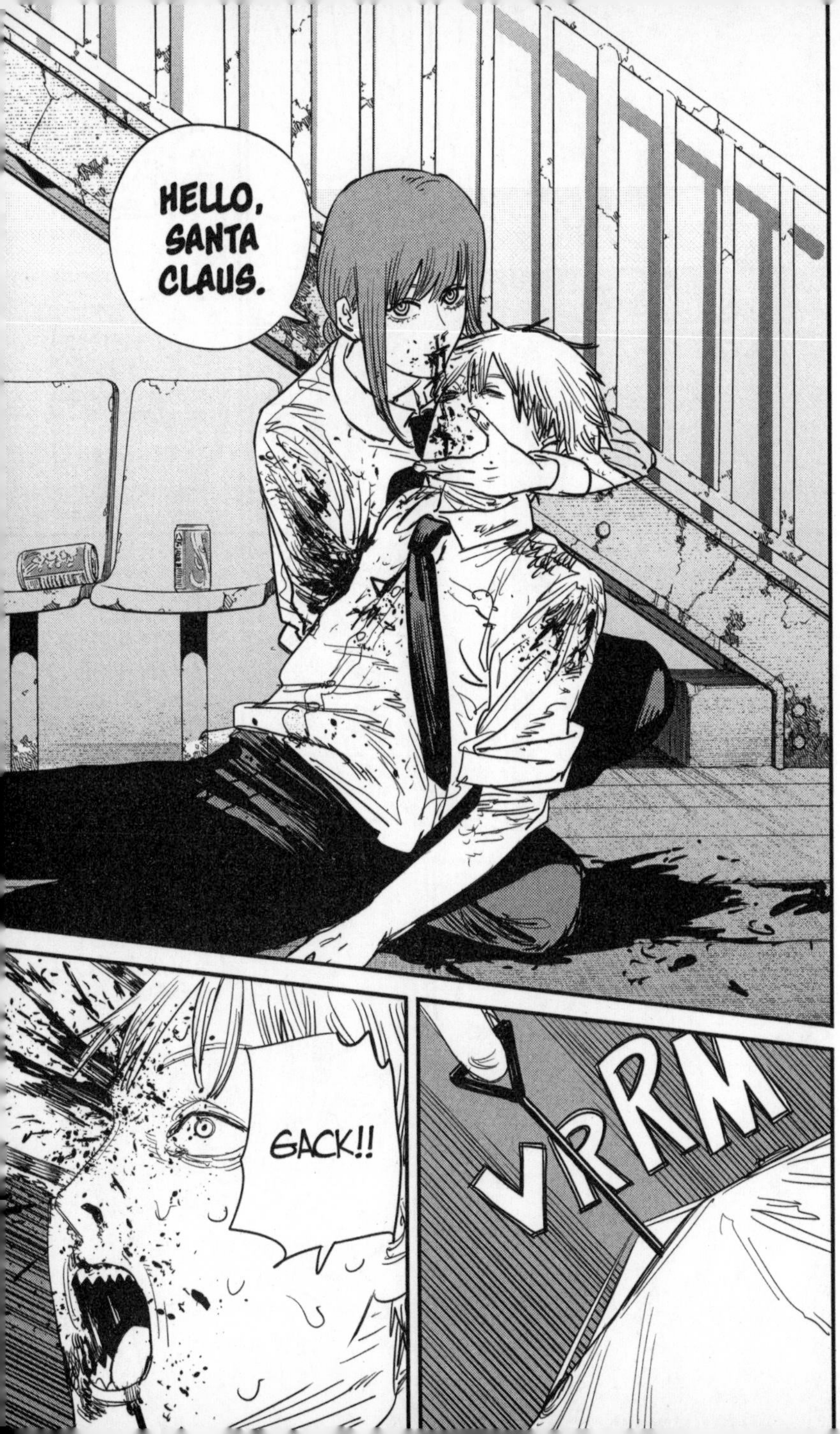
HELLO, SANTA CLAUS.
VRRM
GACK!!

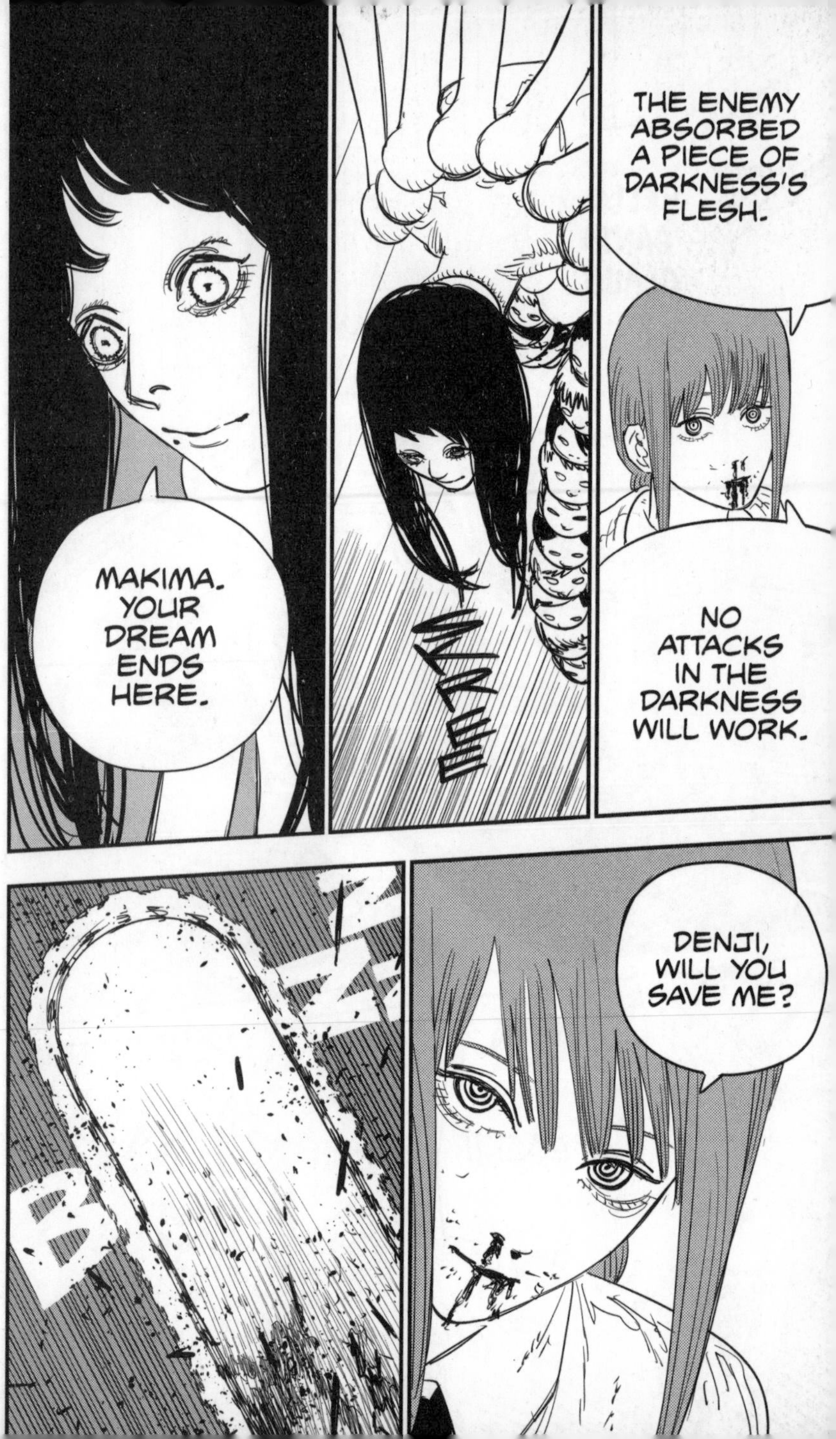
THE ENEMY ABSORBED A PIECE OF DARKNESS'S FLESH.
NO ATTACKS IN THE DARKNESS WILL WORK.
MAKIMA. YOUR DREAM ENDS HERE.
DENJI, WILL YOU SAVE ME?

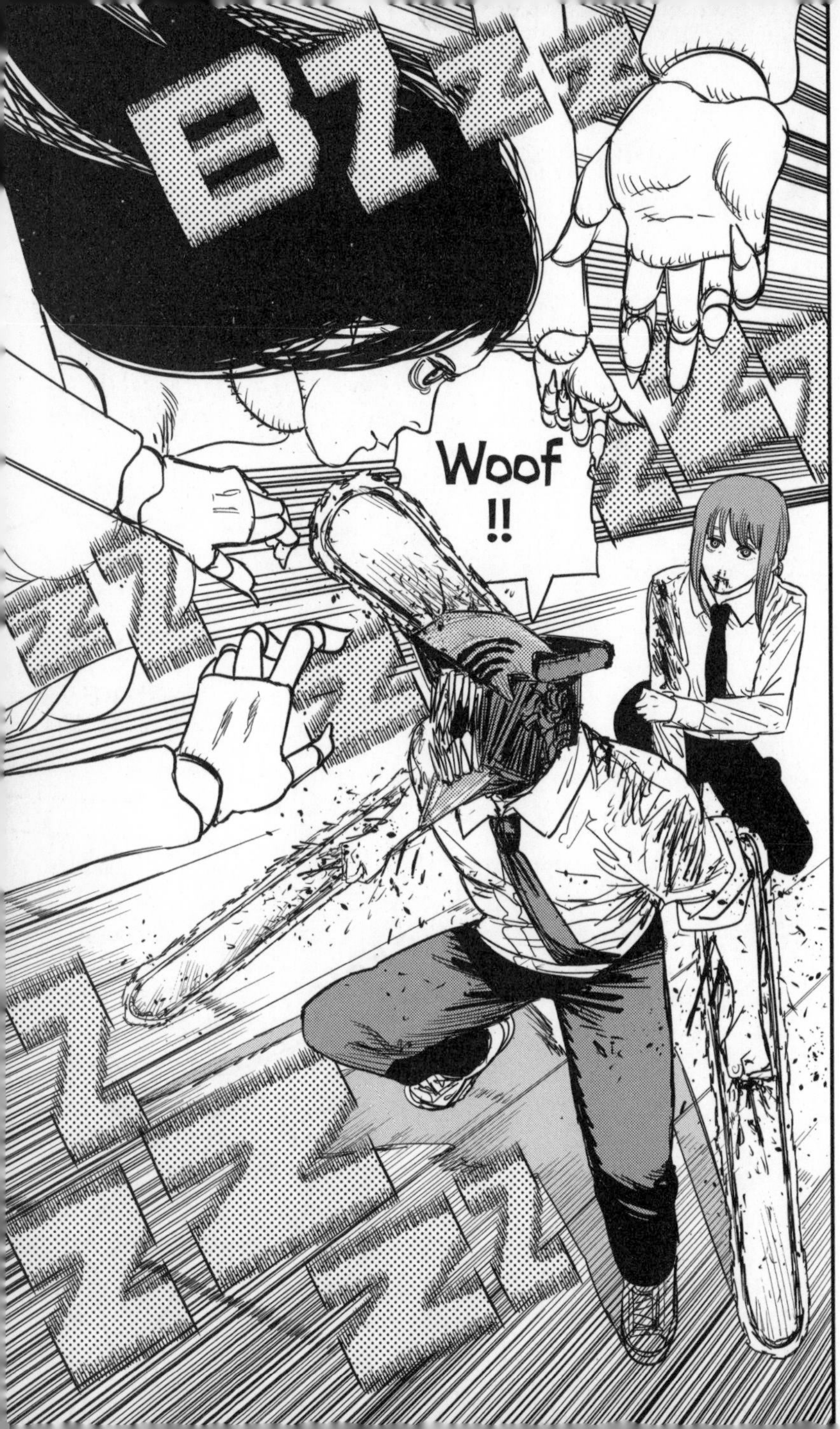

BZ
Woof !!

Chain
saw
man

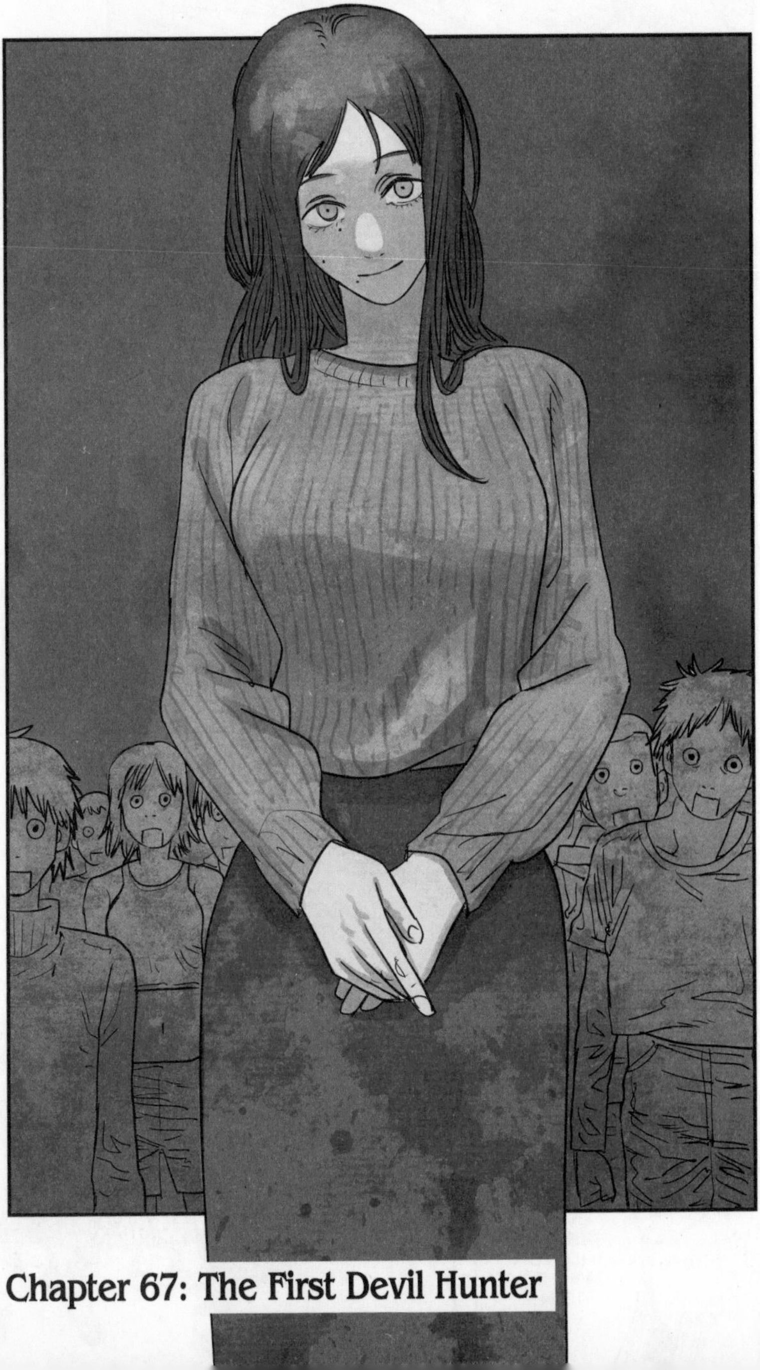

Chapter 67: The First Devil Hunter

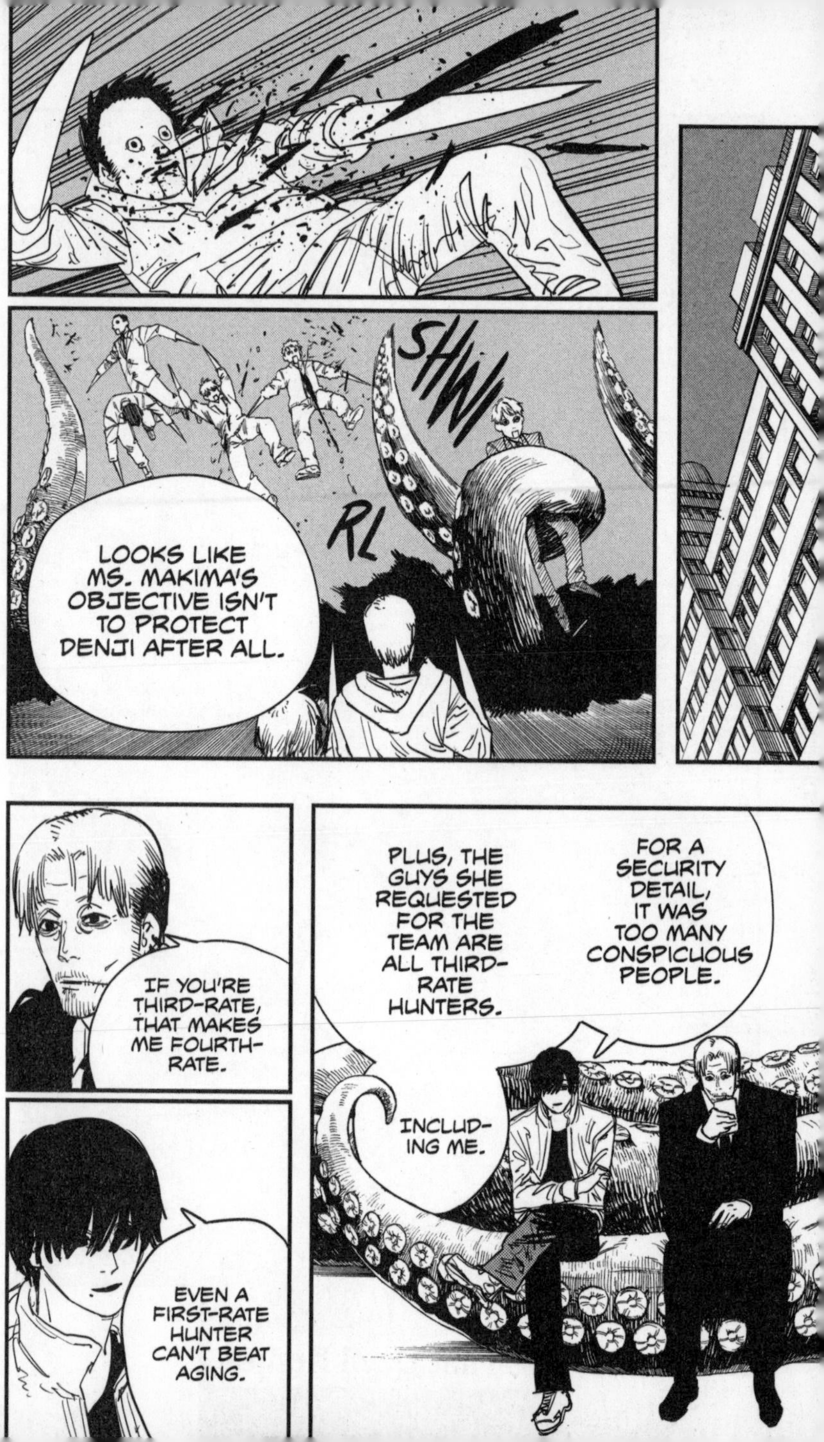
SHWI
RL
LOOKS LIKE MS. MAKIMA'S OBJECTIVE ISN'T TO PROTECT DENJI AFTER ALL.
FOR A SECURITY DETAIL, IT WAS TOO MANY CONSPICUOUS PEOPLE.
PLUS, THE GUYS SHE REQUESTED FOR THE TEAM ARE ALL THIRD-RATE HUNTERS.
INCLUDING ME.
IF YOU'RE THIRD-RATE, THAT MAKES ME FOURTH-RATE.
EVEN A FIRST-RATE HUNTER CAN'T BEAT AGING.

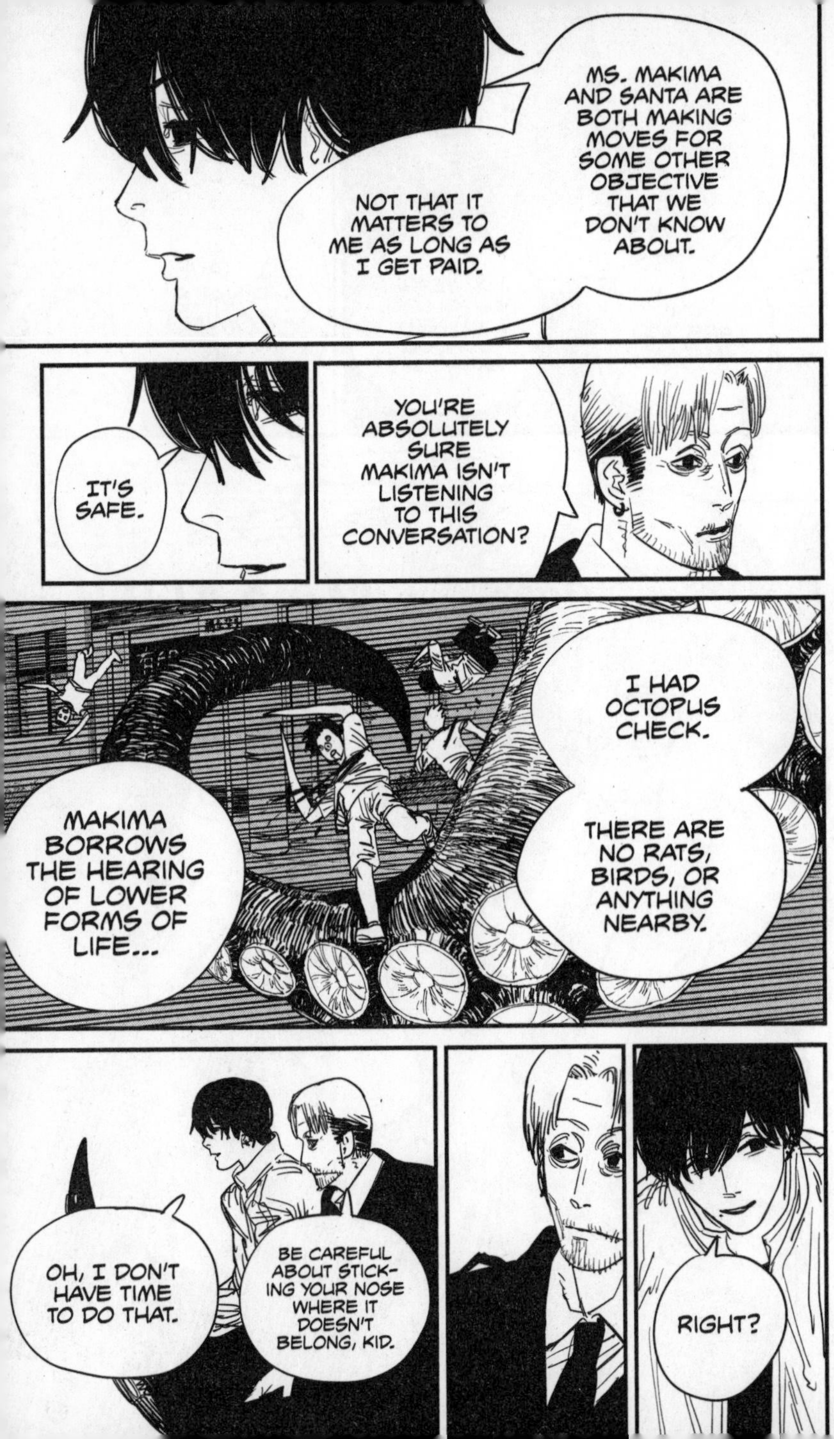
MS. MAKIMA AND SANTA ARE BOTH MAKING MOVES FOR SOME OTHER OBJECTIVE THAT WE DON'T KNOW ABOUT.
NOT THAT IT MATTERS TO ME AS LONG AS I GET PAID.
YOU'RE ABSOLUTELY SURE MAKIMA ISN'T LISTENING TO THIS CONVERSATION?
IT'S SAFE.
I HAD OCTOPUS CHECK.
THERE ARE NO RATS, BIRDS, OR ANYTHING NEARBY.
MAKIMA BORROWS THE HEARING OF LOWER FORMS OF LIFE...
RIGHT?
BE CAREFUL ABOUT STICK-ING YOUR NOSE WHERE IT DOESN'T BELONG, KID.
OH, I DON'T HAVE TIME TO DO THAT.

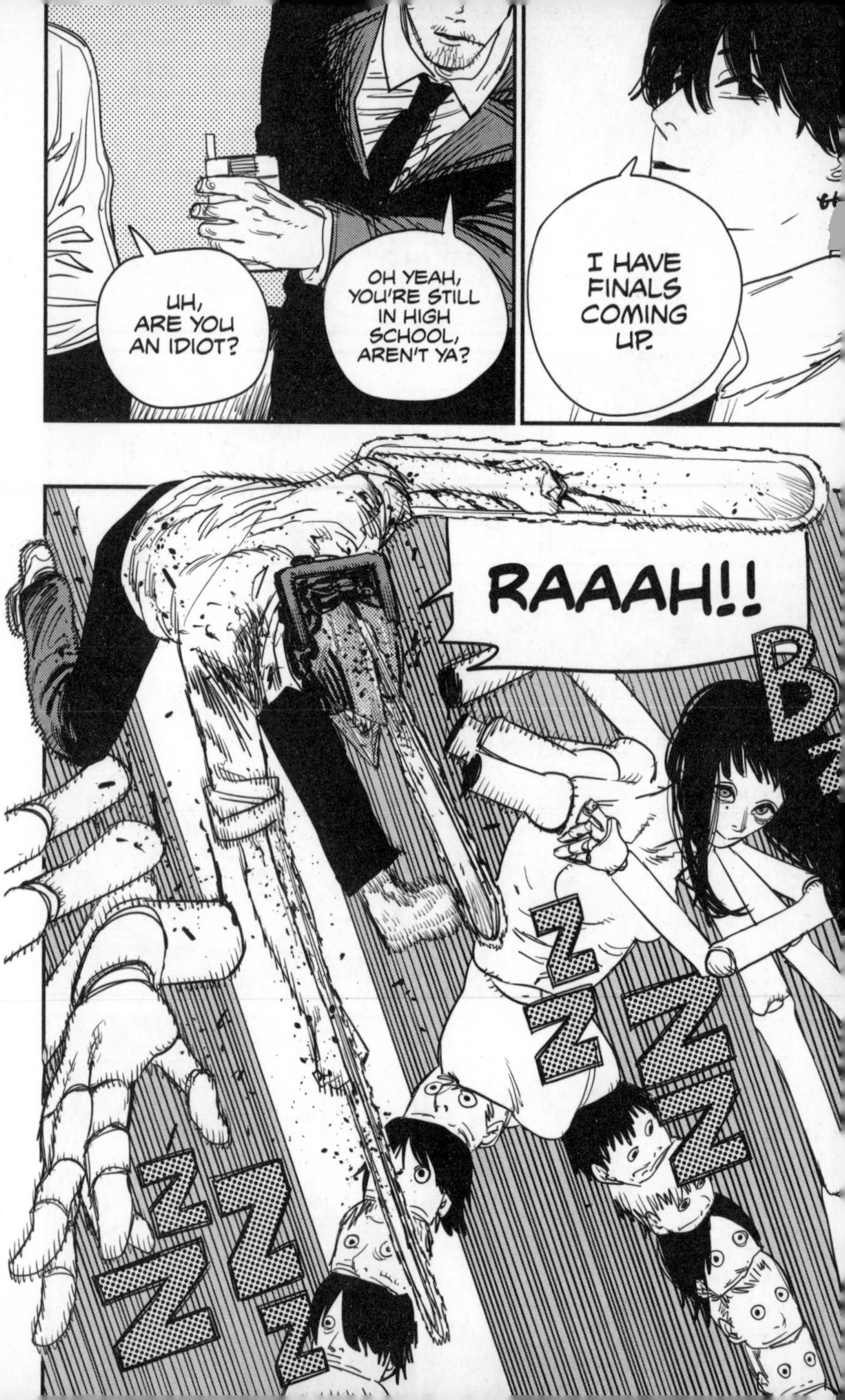
I HAVE FINALS COMING UP.
OH YEAH, YOU'RE STILL IN HIGH SCHOOL, AREN'T YA?
UH, ARE YOU AN IDIOT?
RAAAH!!

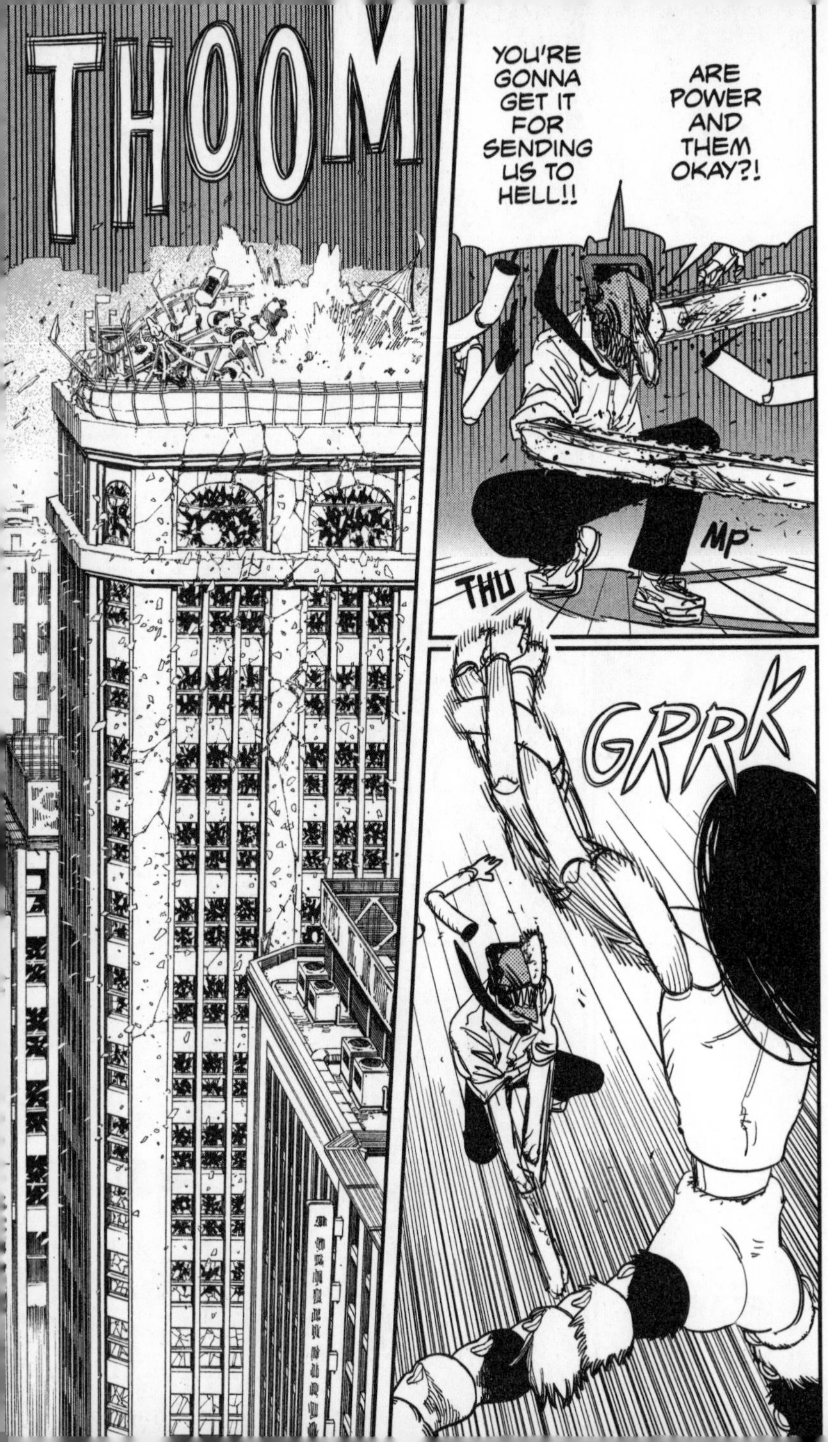
ARE POWER AND THEM OKAY?!
YOU'RE GONNA GET IT FOR SENDING US TO HELL!!
MP
THU
GRRK
THOOM

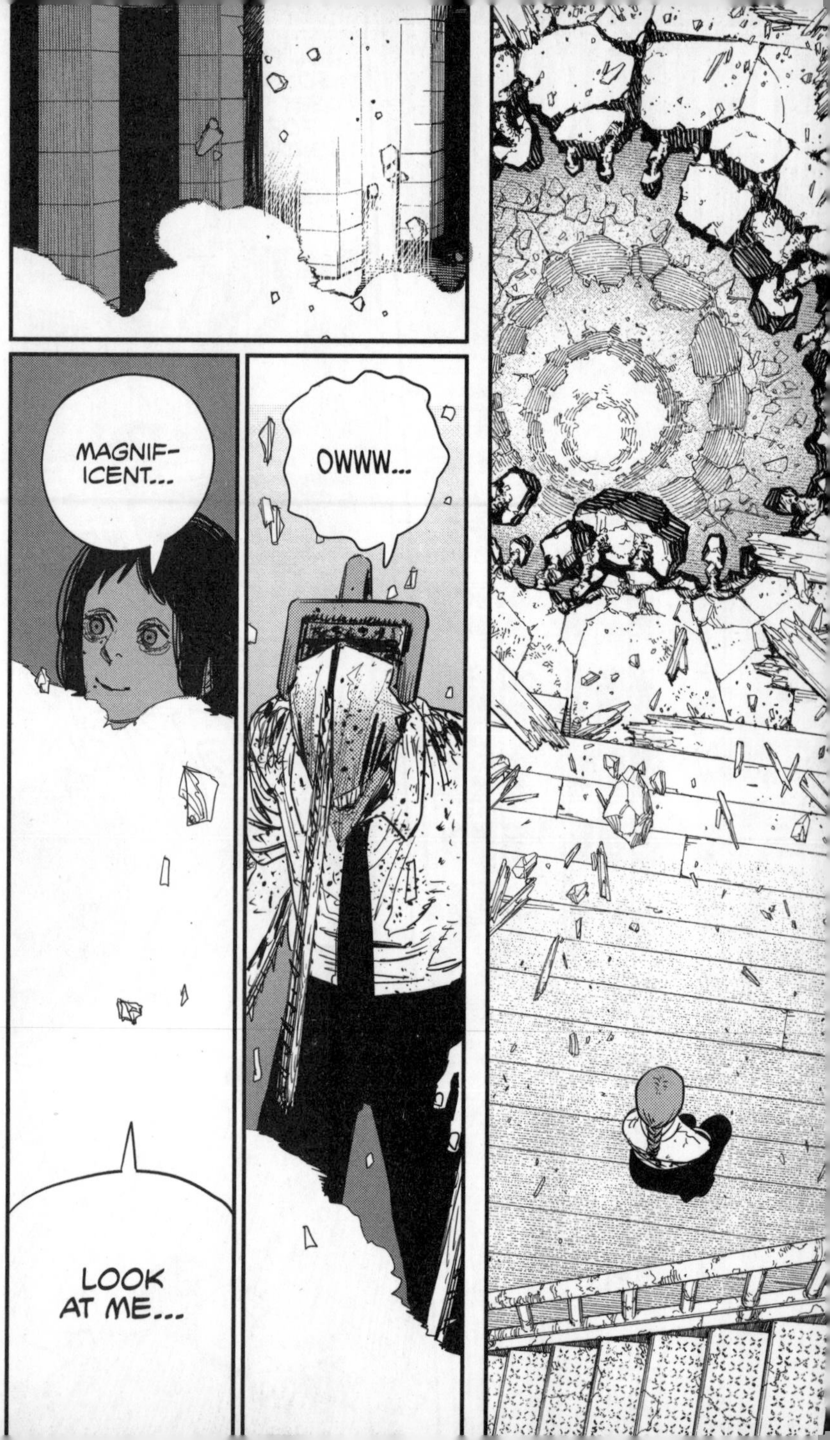
OWWW...
MAGNIF-ICENT...
LOOK AT ME...

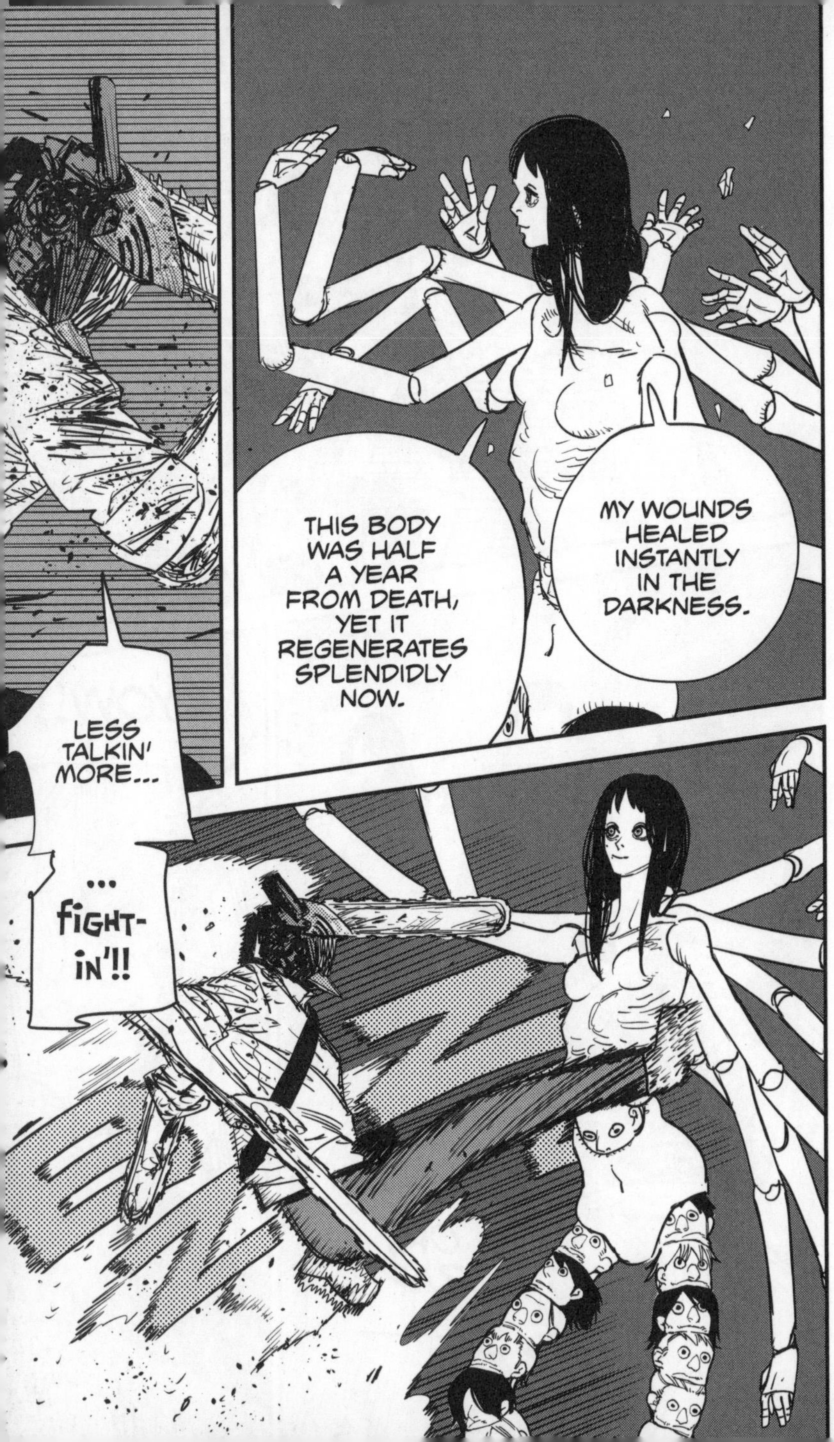
MY WOUNDS HEALED INSTANTLY IN THE DARKNESS.
THIS BODY WAS HALF A YEAR FROM DEATH, YET IT REGENERATES SPLENDIDLY NOW.
LESS TALKIN' MORE...
...FIGHT-IN'!!

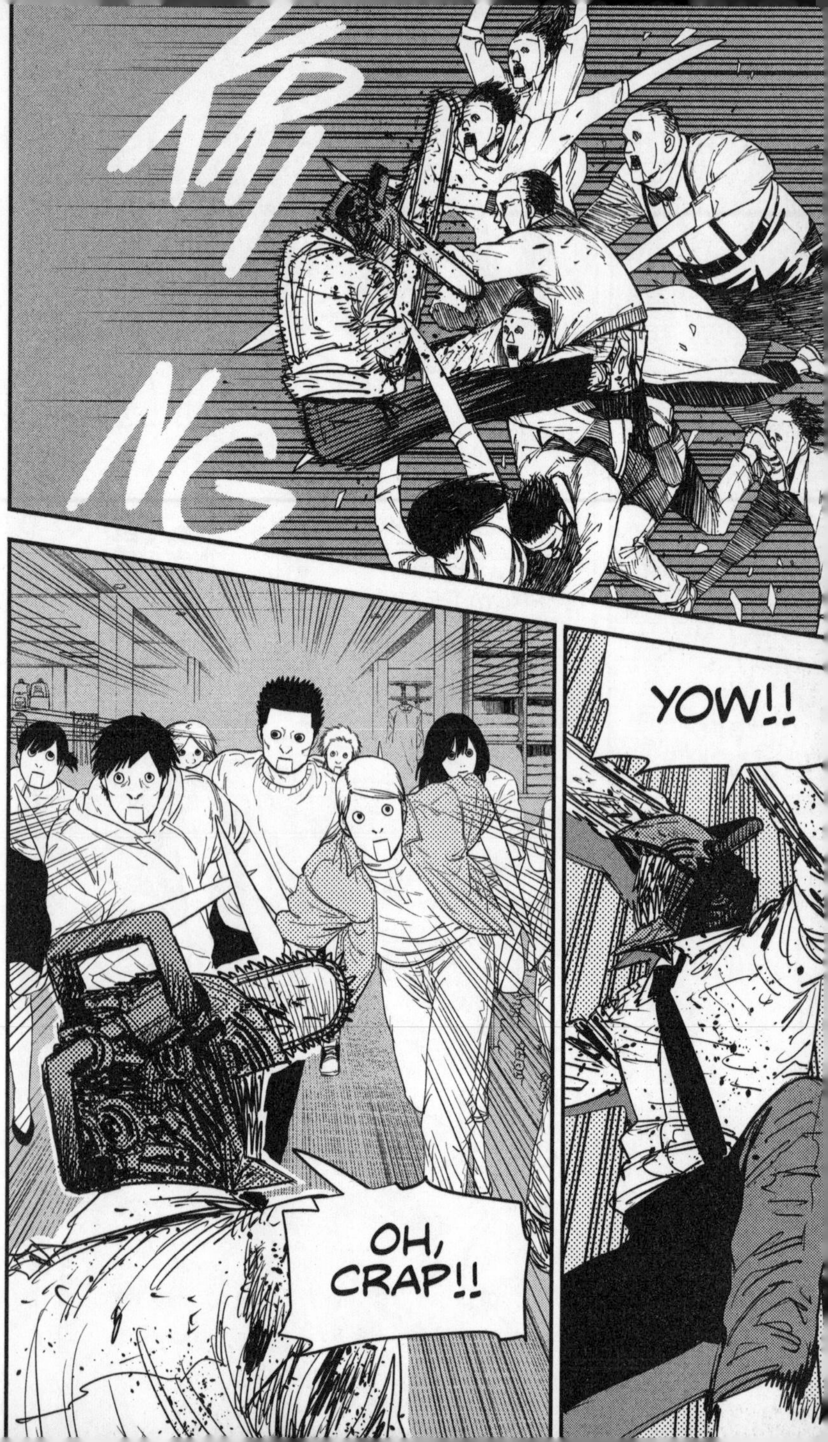
KRING
YOW!!
OH, CRAP!!

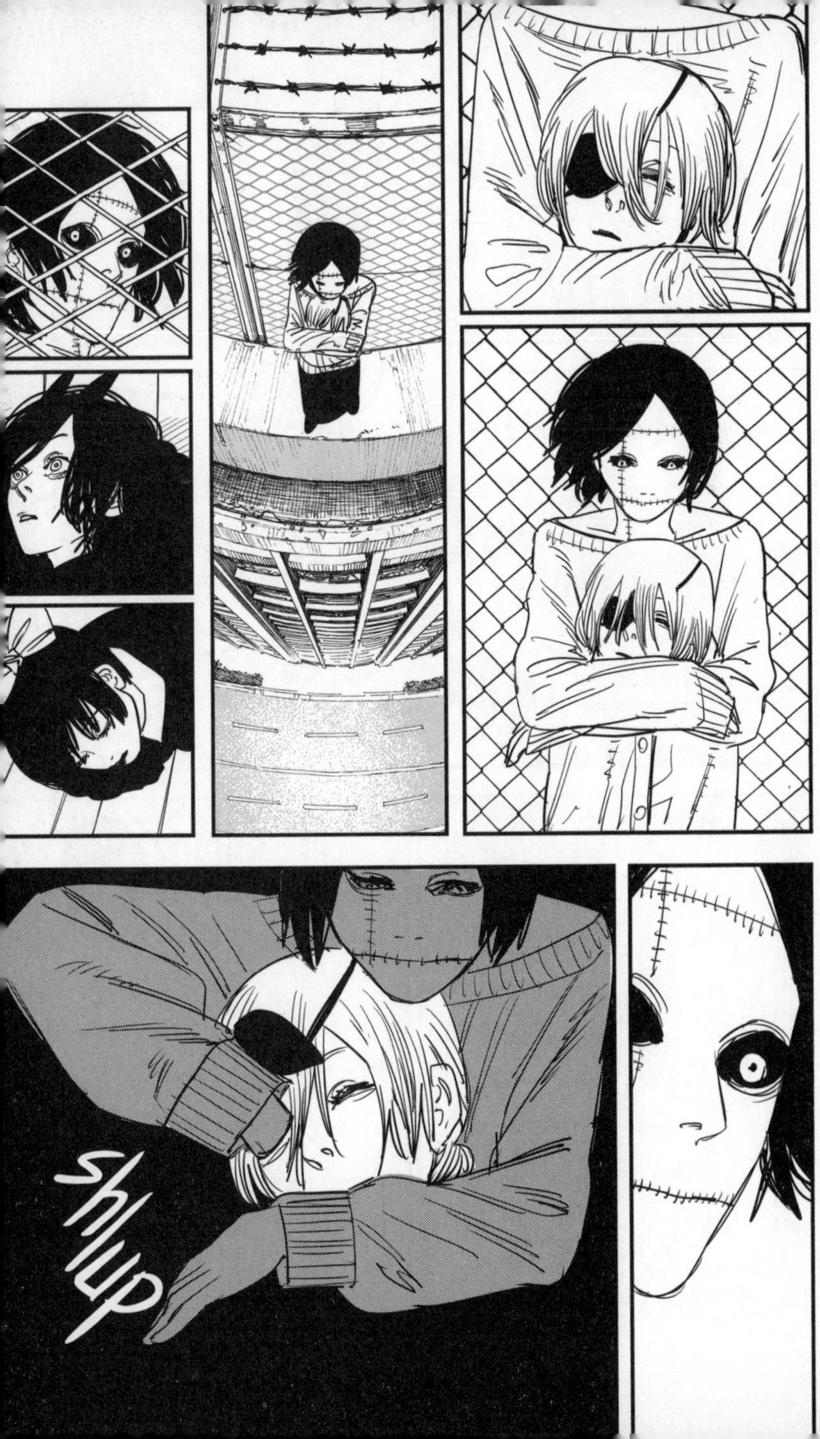
shlup

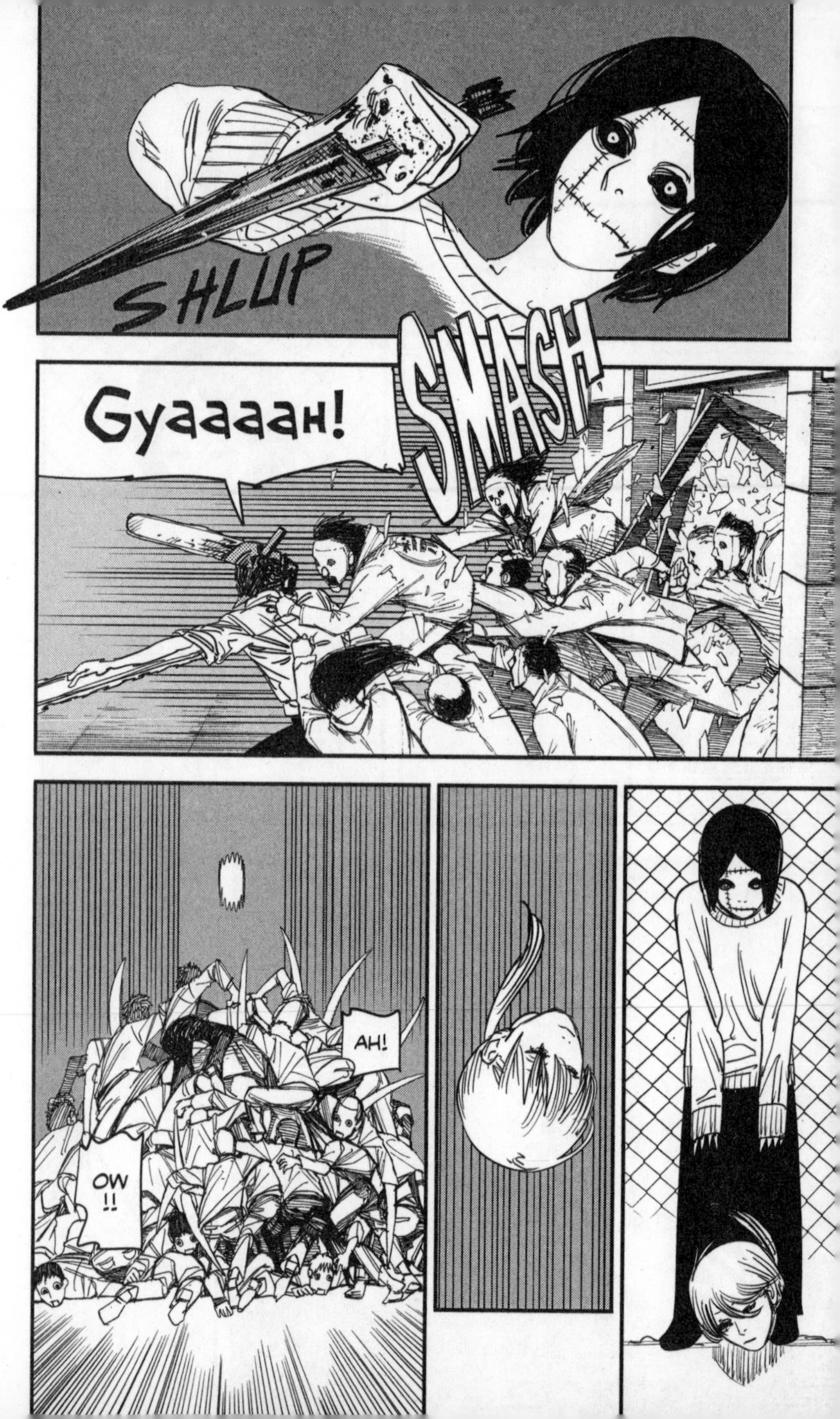
SHLUP
SMASH
Gyaaaaah!
AH!
OW !!

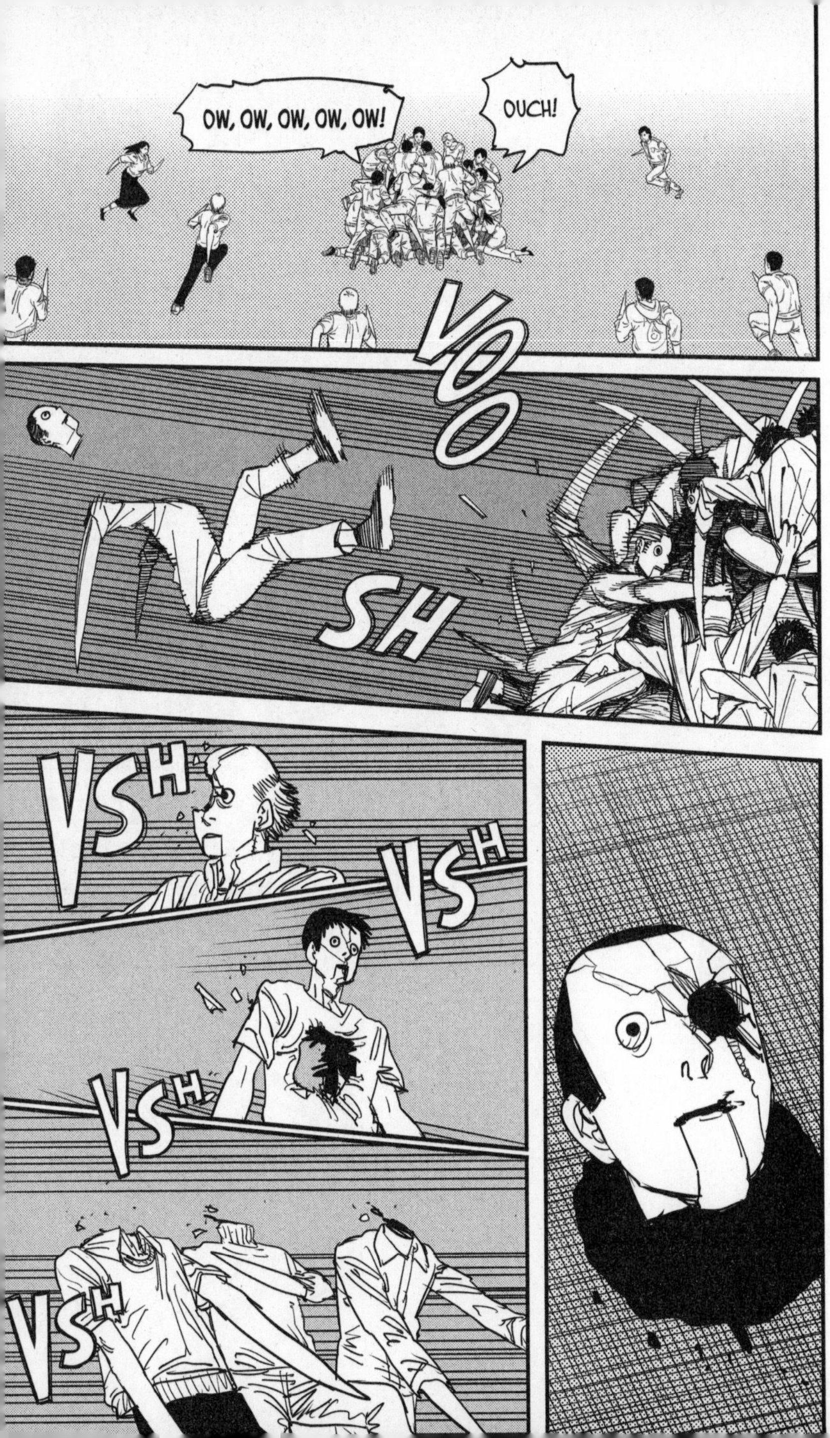
OUCH!
OW, OW, OW, OW, OW!
VOOSH
VSH
VSH
VSH
VSH

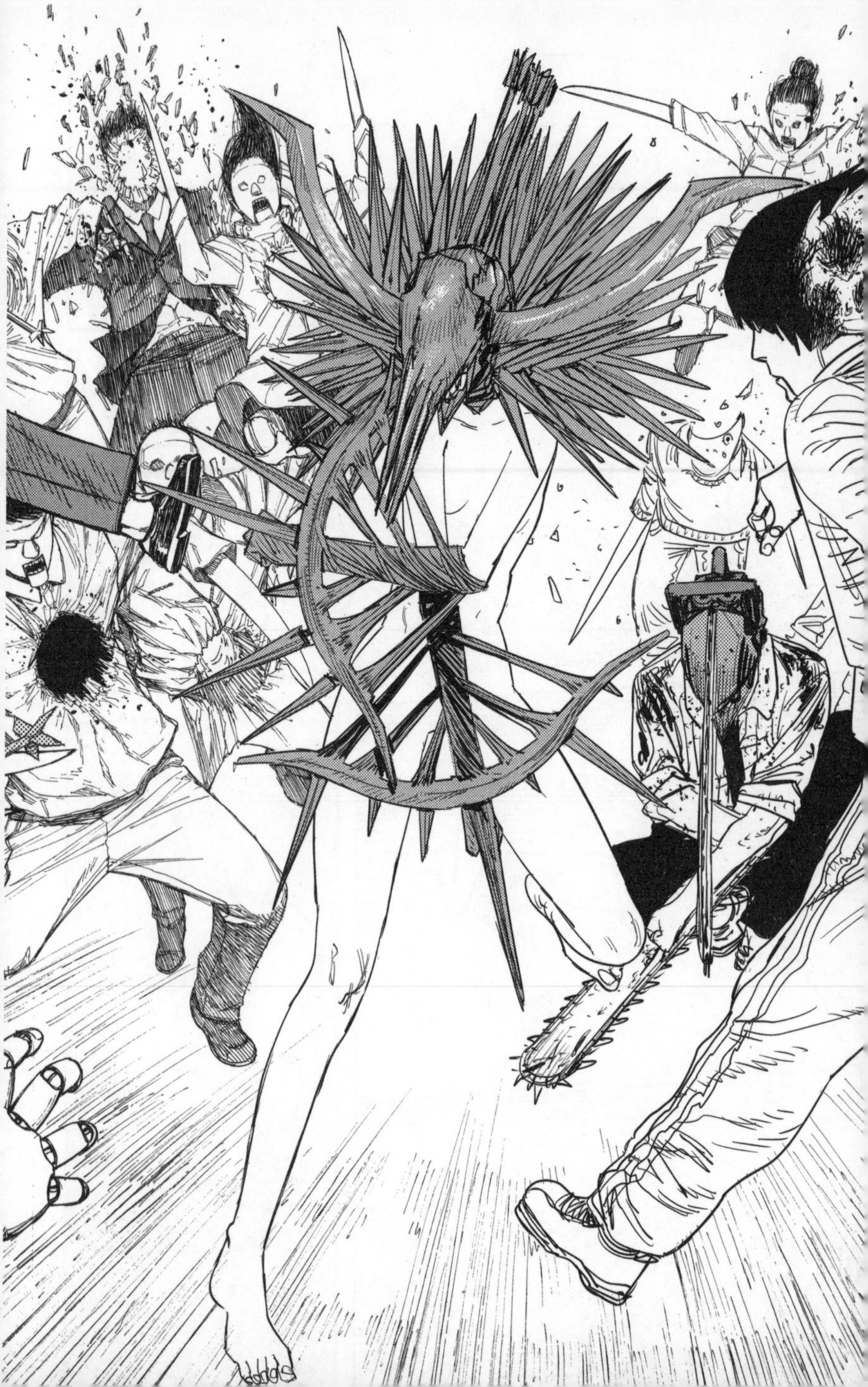

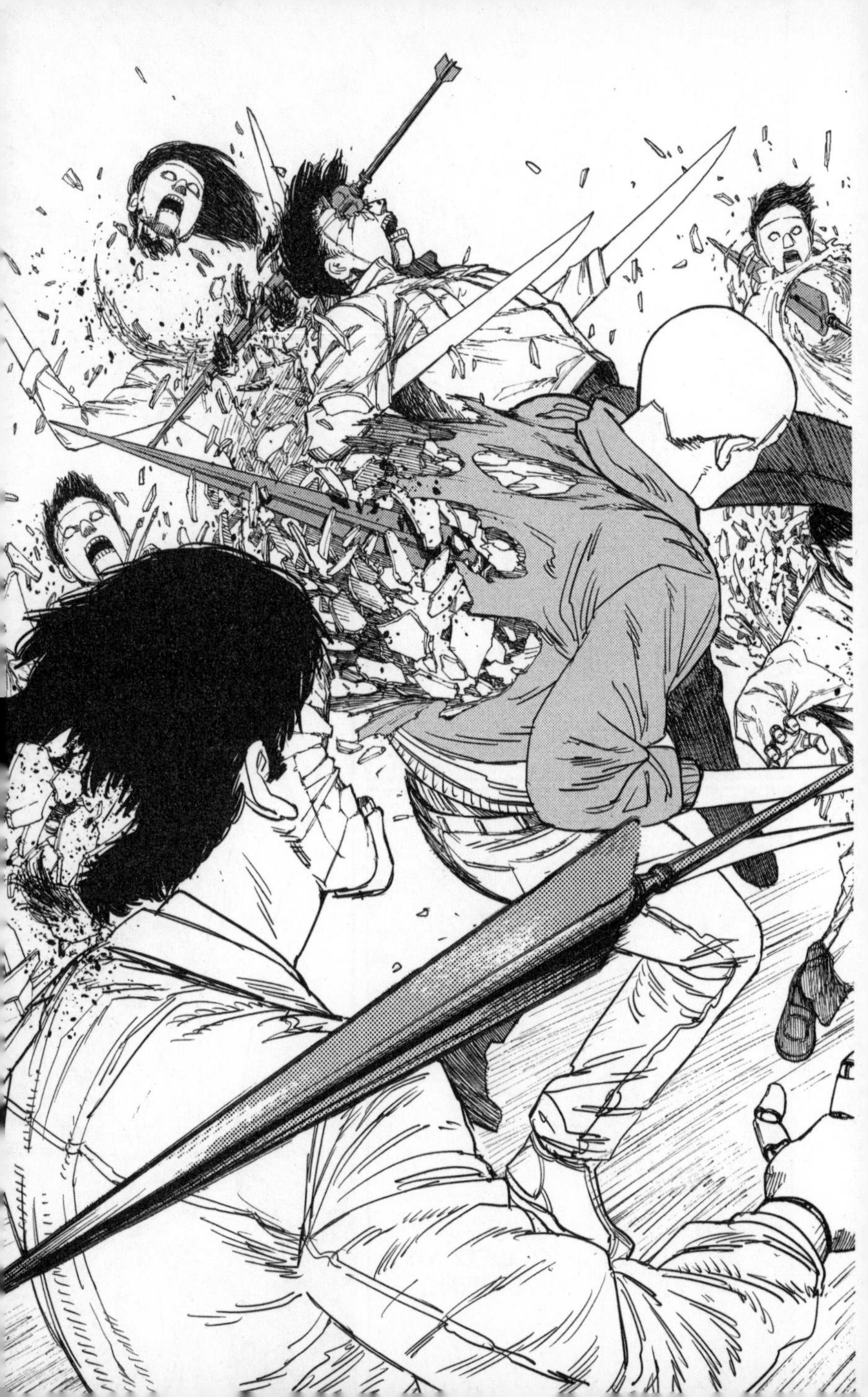

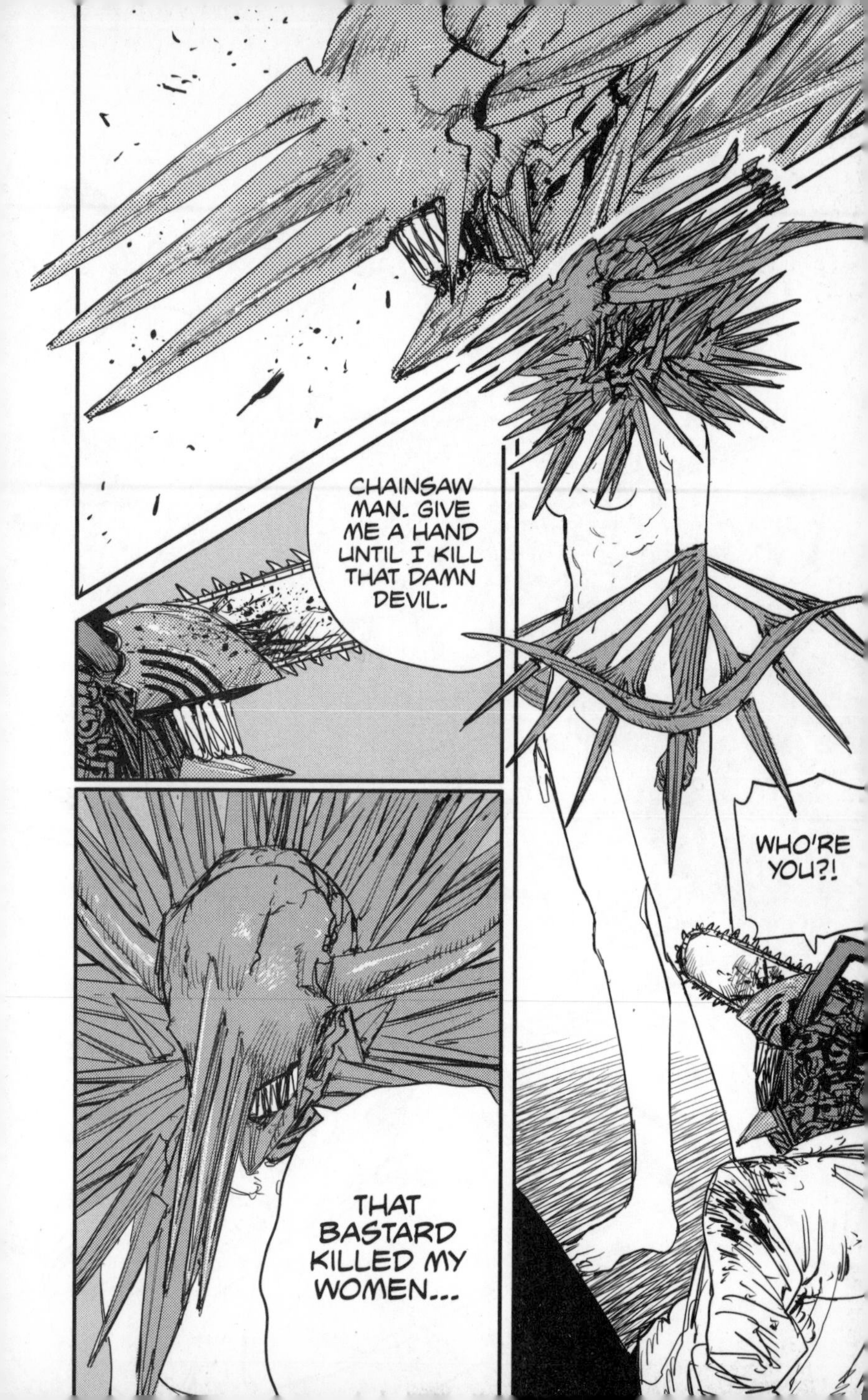
WHO'RE YOU?!
CHAINSAW MAN. GIVE ME A HAND UNTIL I KILL THAT DAMN DEVIL.
THAT BASTARD KILLED MY WOMEN...

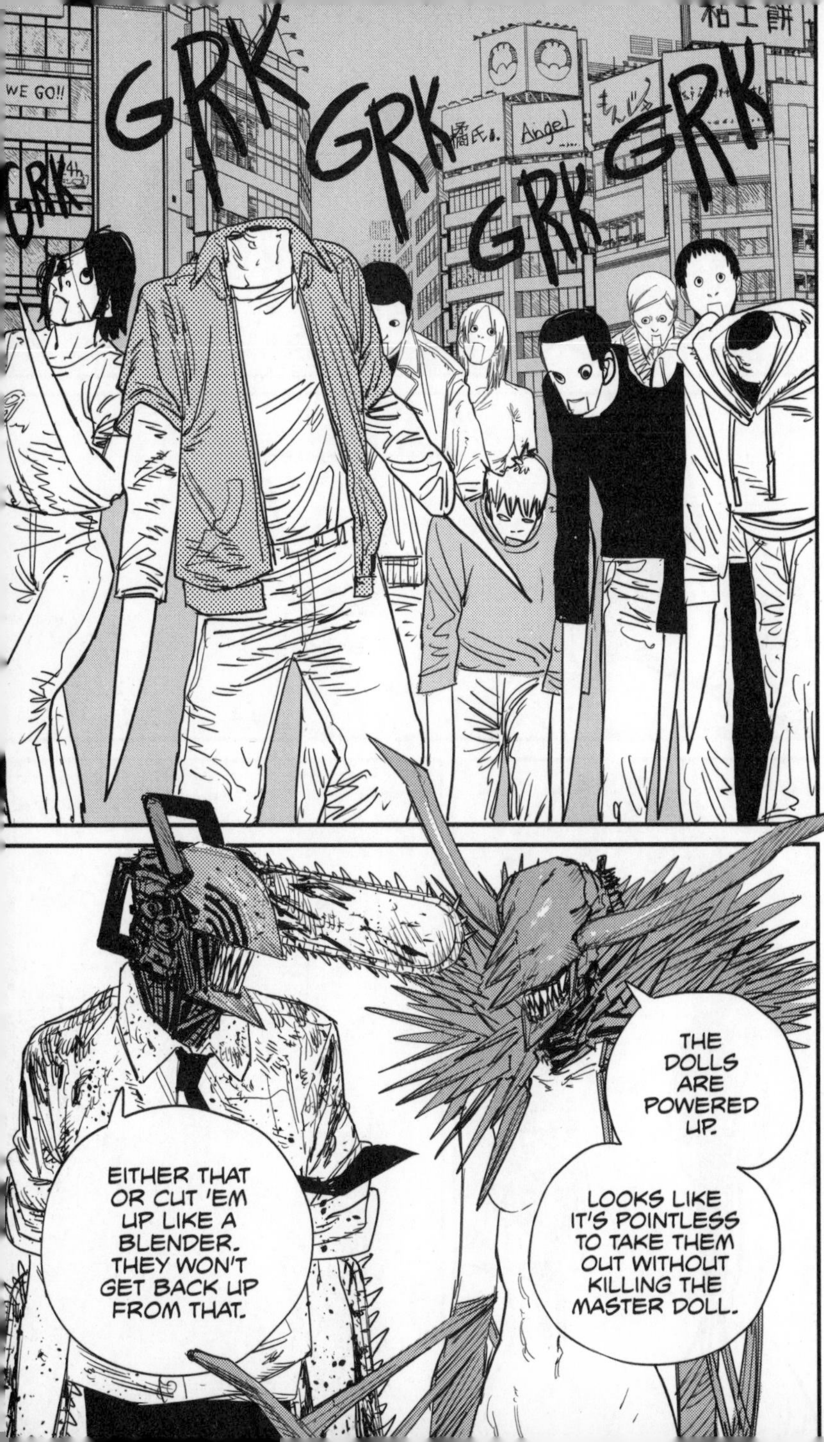
GRK
GRK
GRK
GRK
GRK
GRK
WE GO!!
Angel
THE DOLLS ARE POWERED UP.
LOOKS LIKE IT'S POINTLESS TO TAKE THEM OUT WITHOUT KILLING THE MASTER DOLL.
EITHER THAT OR CUT 'EM UP LIKE A BLENDER. THEY WON'T GET BACK UP FROM THAT.

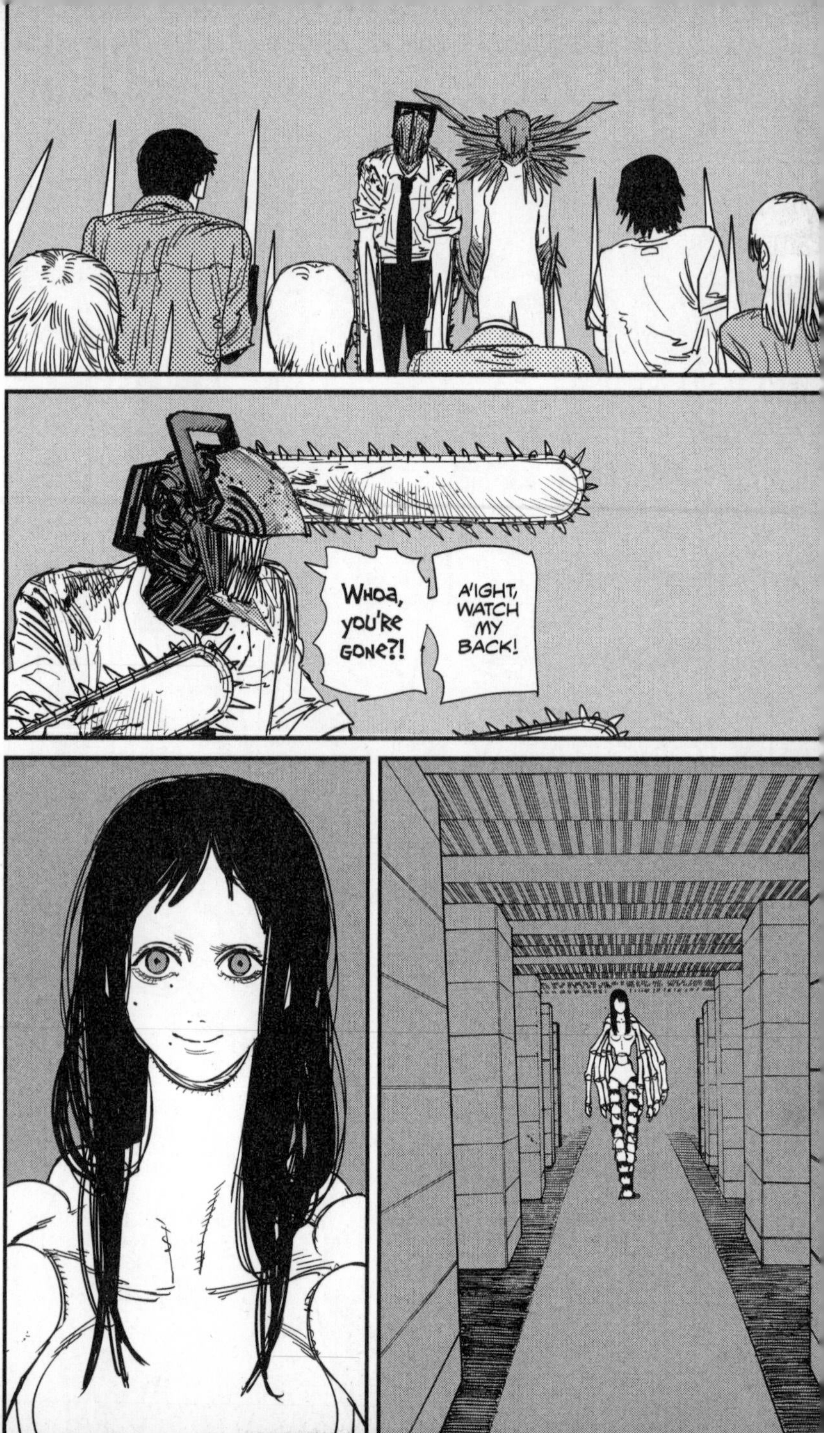
A'IGHT, WATCH MY BACK!
Whoa, you're gone?!

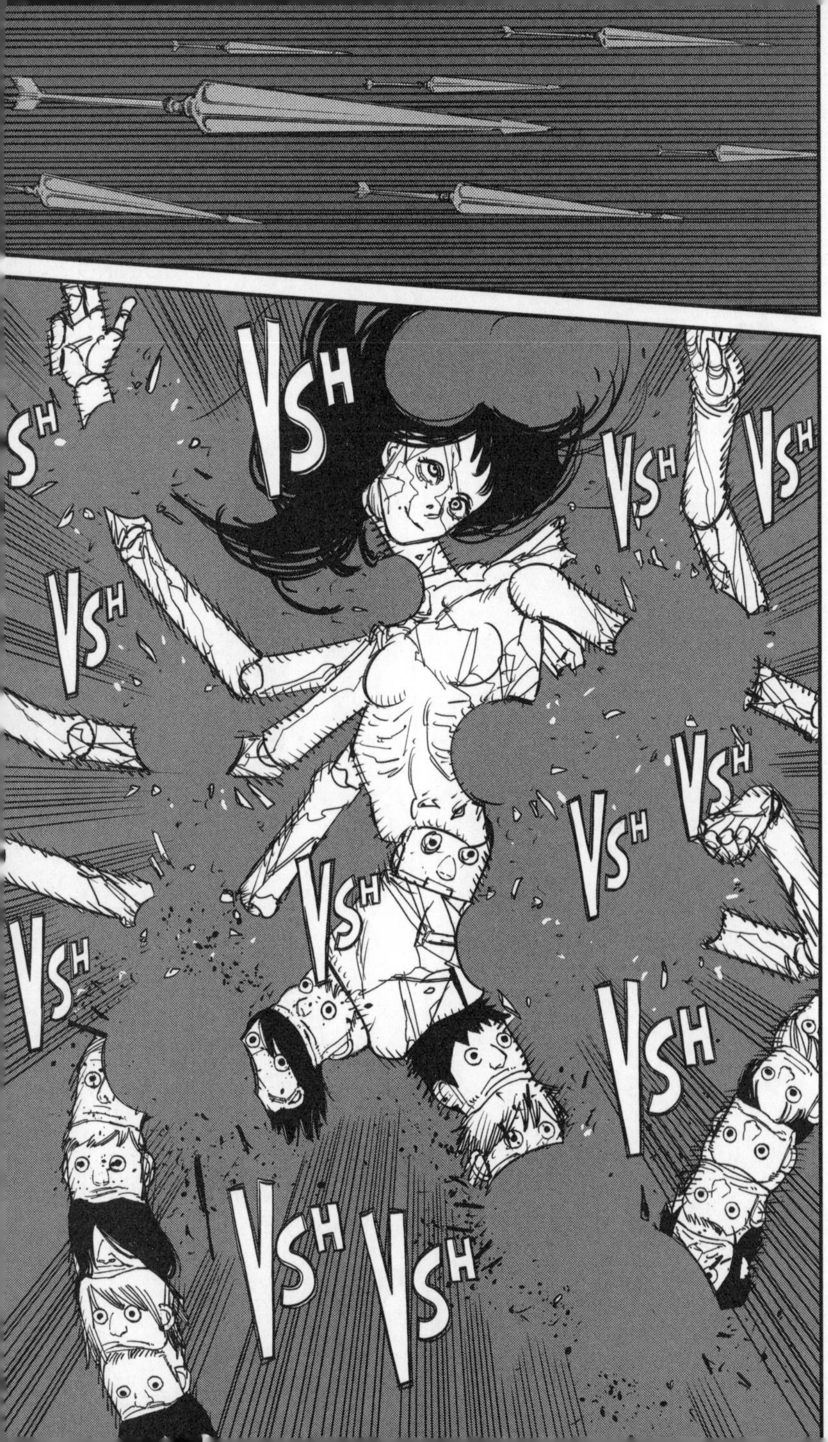
VSH
VSH
VSH
SH
VSH
VSH
VSH
VSH
VSH
VSH
VSH
VSH

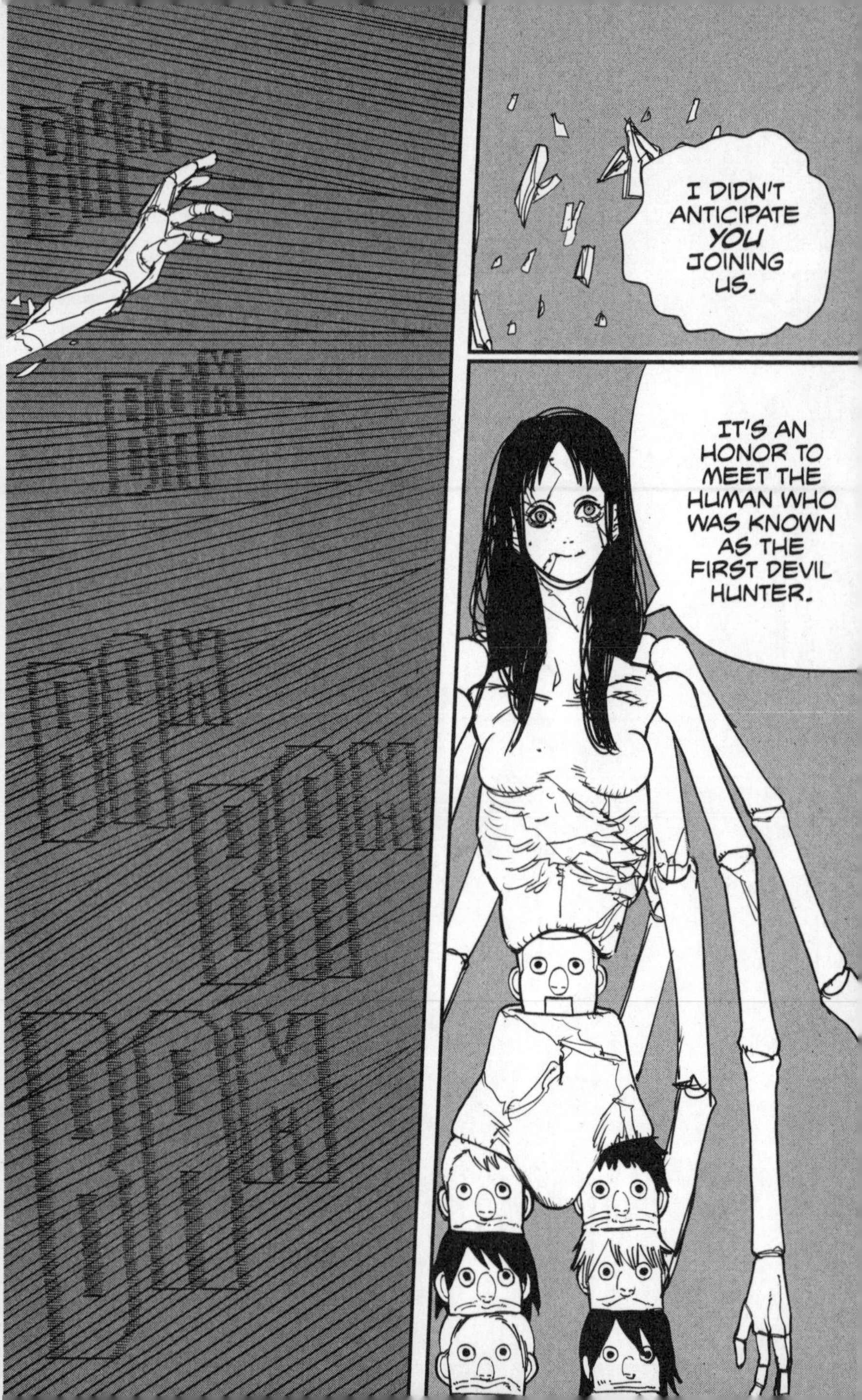
I DIDN'T ANTICIPATE *YOU* JOINING US.
IT'S AN HONOR TO MEET THE HUMAN WHO WAS KNOWN AS THE FIRST DEVIL HUNTER.

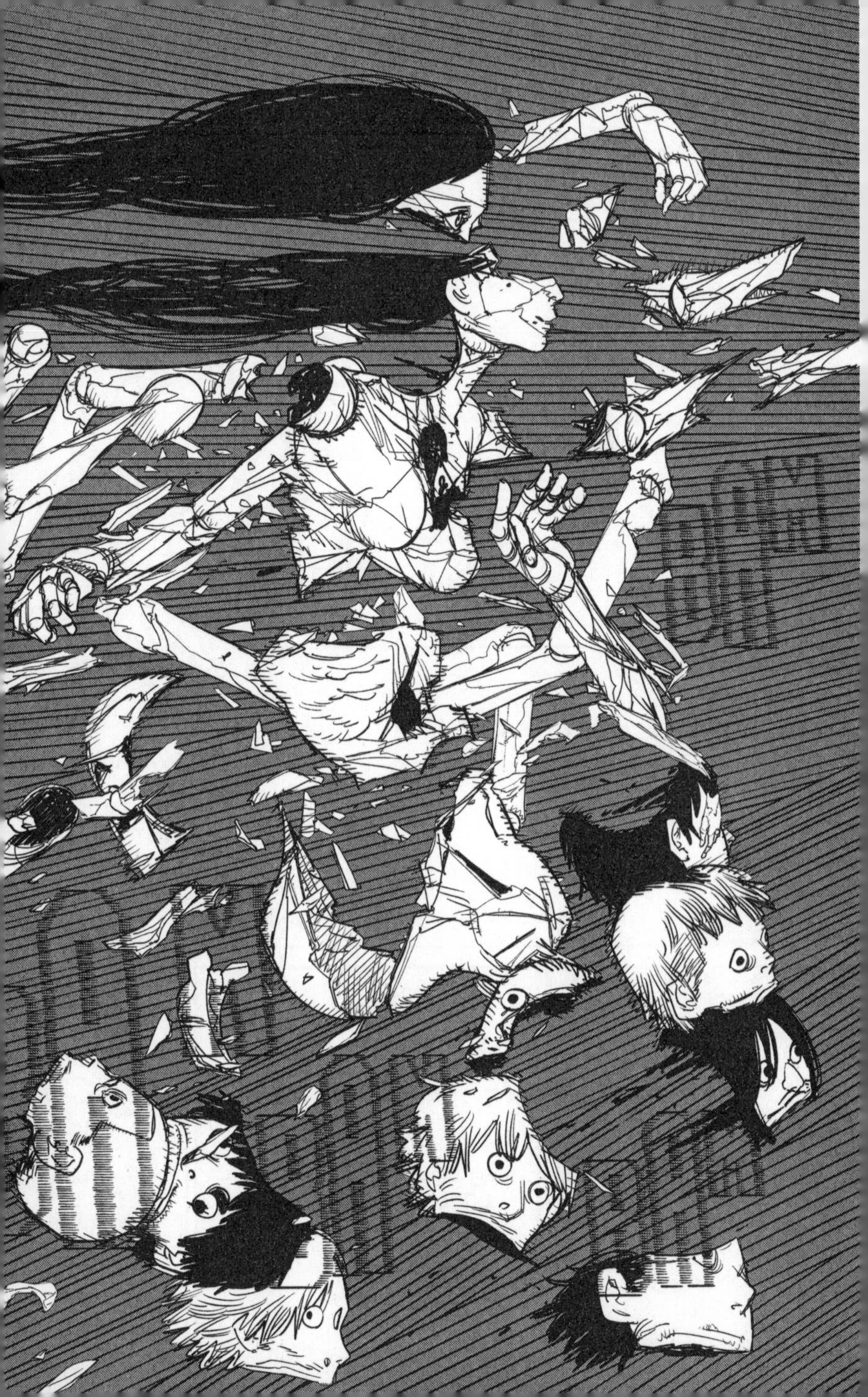

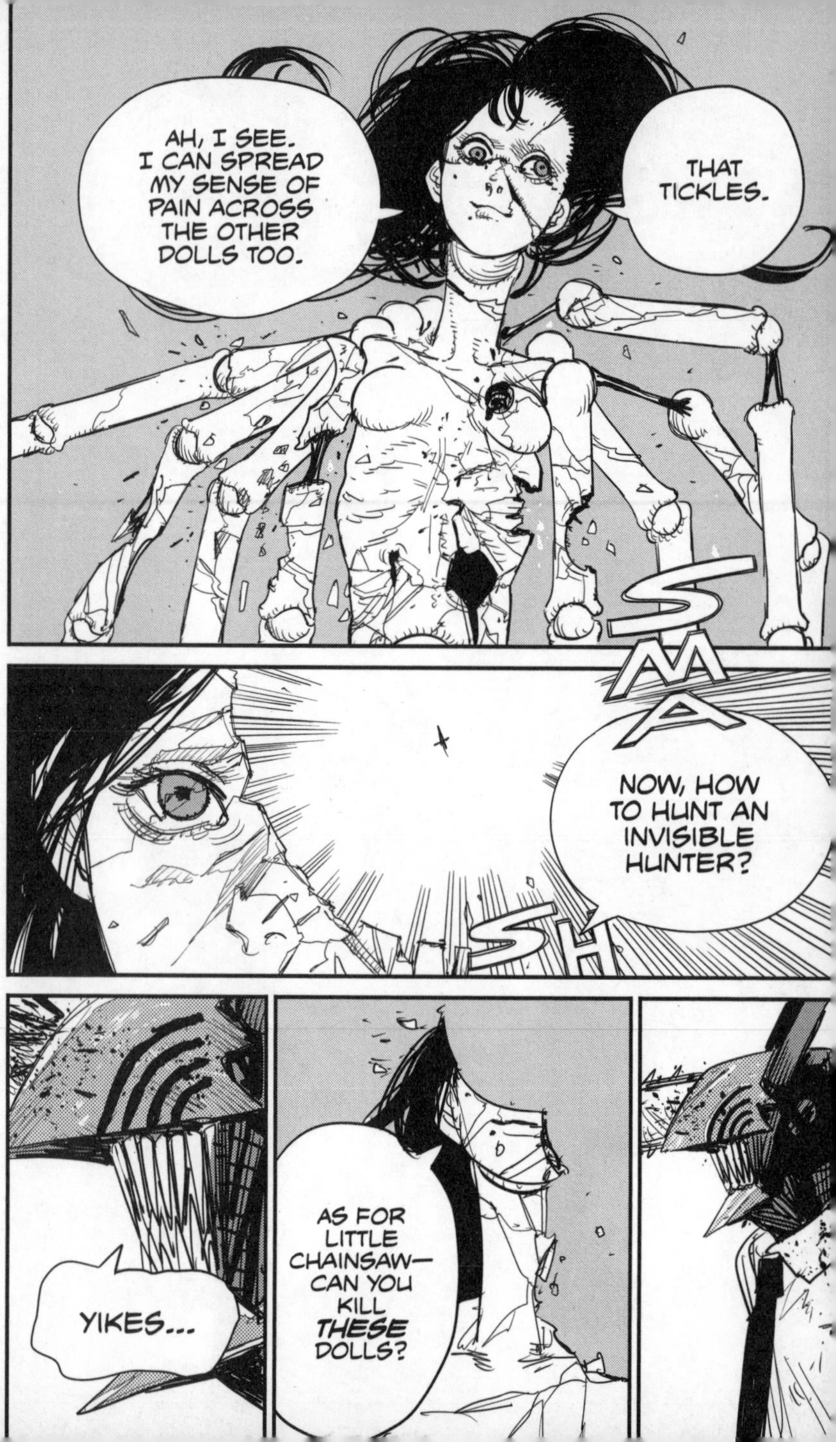
THAT TICKLES.
AH, I SEE. I CAN SPREAD MY SENSE OF PAIN ACROSS THE OTHER DOLLS TOO.
SMASH
NOW, HOW TO HUNT AN INVISIBLE HUNTER?
AS FOR LITTLE CHAINSAW— CAN YOU KILL *THESE* DOLLS?
YIKES...

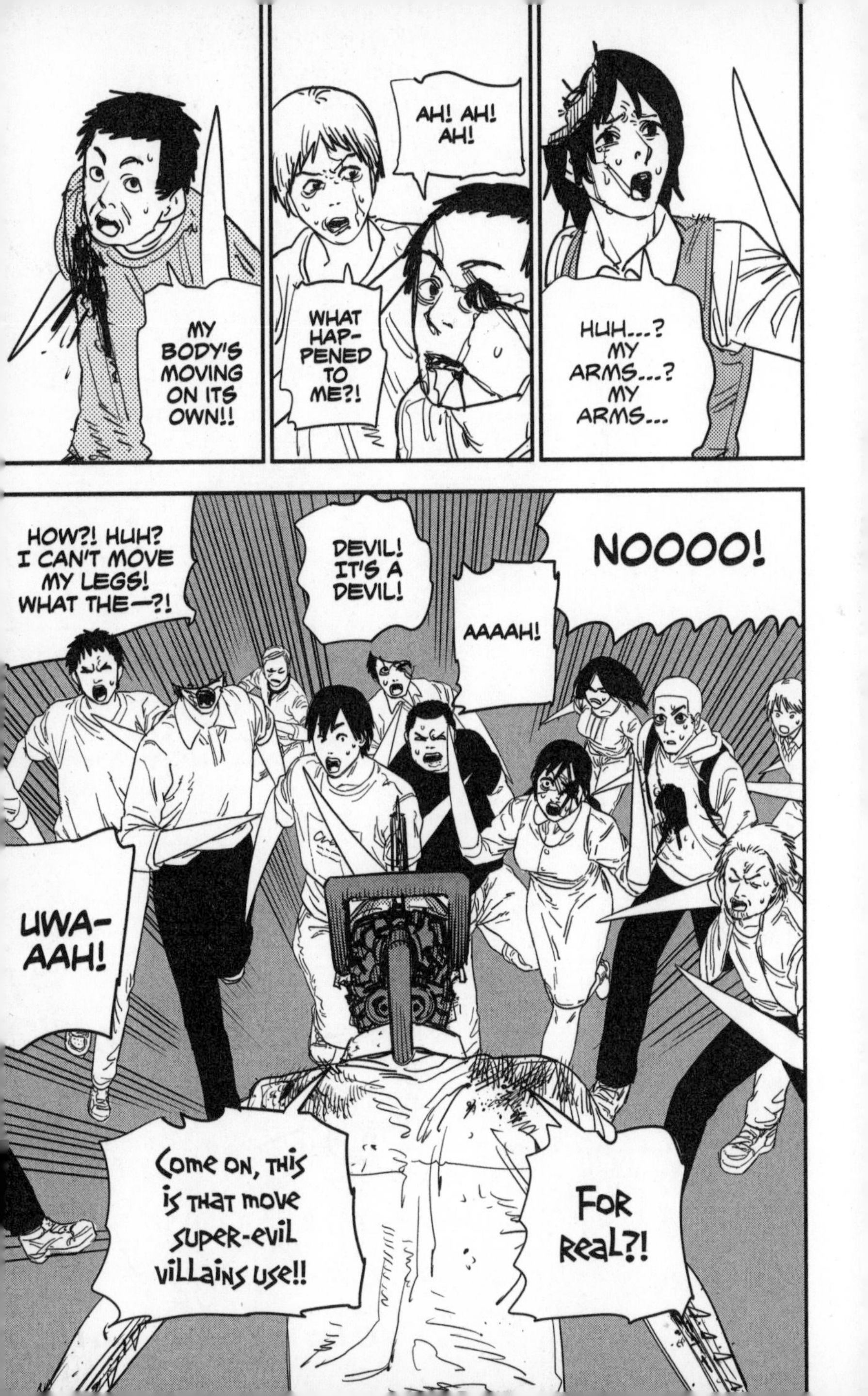
HUH...? MY ARMS...? MY ARMS...
AH! AH! AH!
WHAT HAP-PENED TO ME?!
MY BODY'S MOVING ON ITS OWN!!
NOOOO!
DEVIL! IT'S A DEVIL!
AAAAH!
HOW?! HUH? I CAN'T MOVE MY LEGS! WHAT THE—?!
UWA-AAH!
FOR real?!
Come on, this is that move super-evil villains use!!

Chain saw man

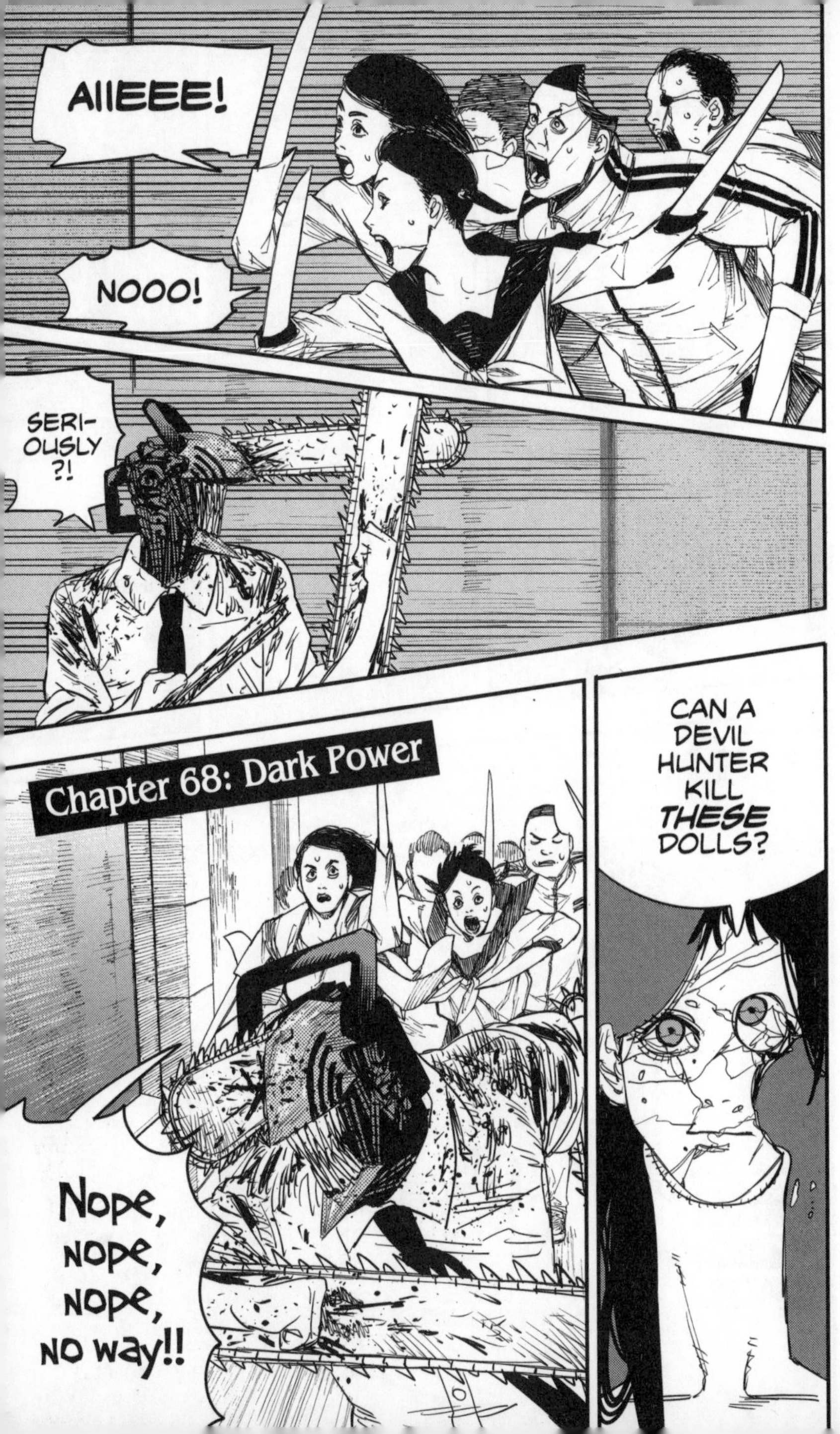
AIIEEE!
NOOO!
SERI-OUSLY ?!
CAN A DEVIL HUNTER KILL *THESE* DOLLS?
Chapter 68: Dark Power
Nope, nope, nope, no way!!

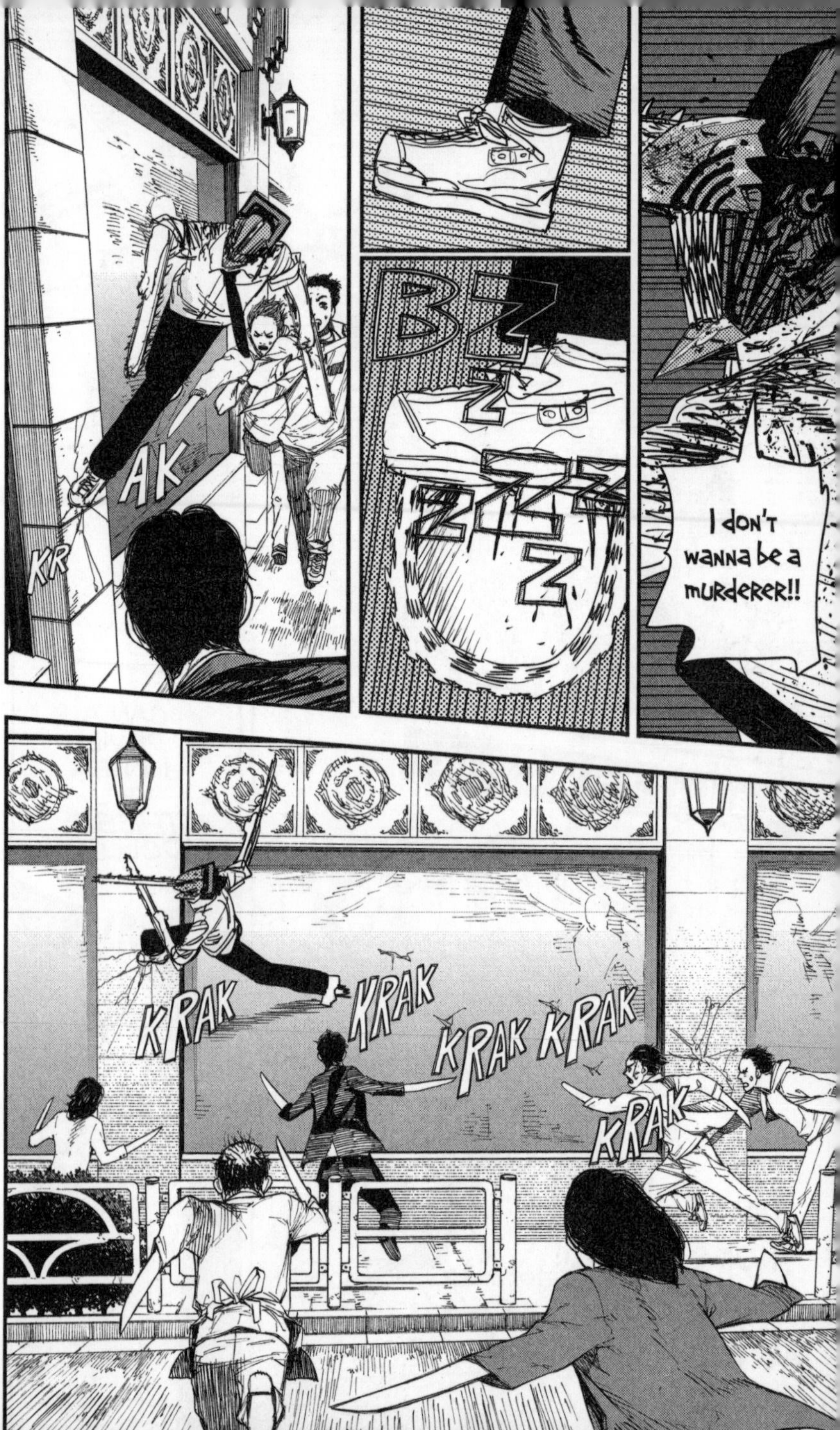
I don't wanna be a murderer!!
BZZZ
ZZZZ
KR
AK
KRAK
KRAK KRAK
KRAK
KRAK

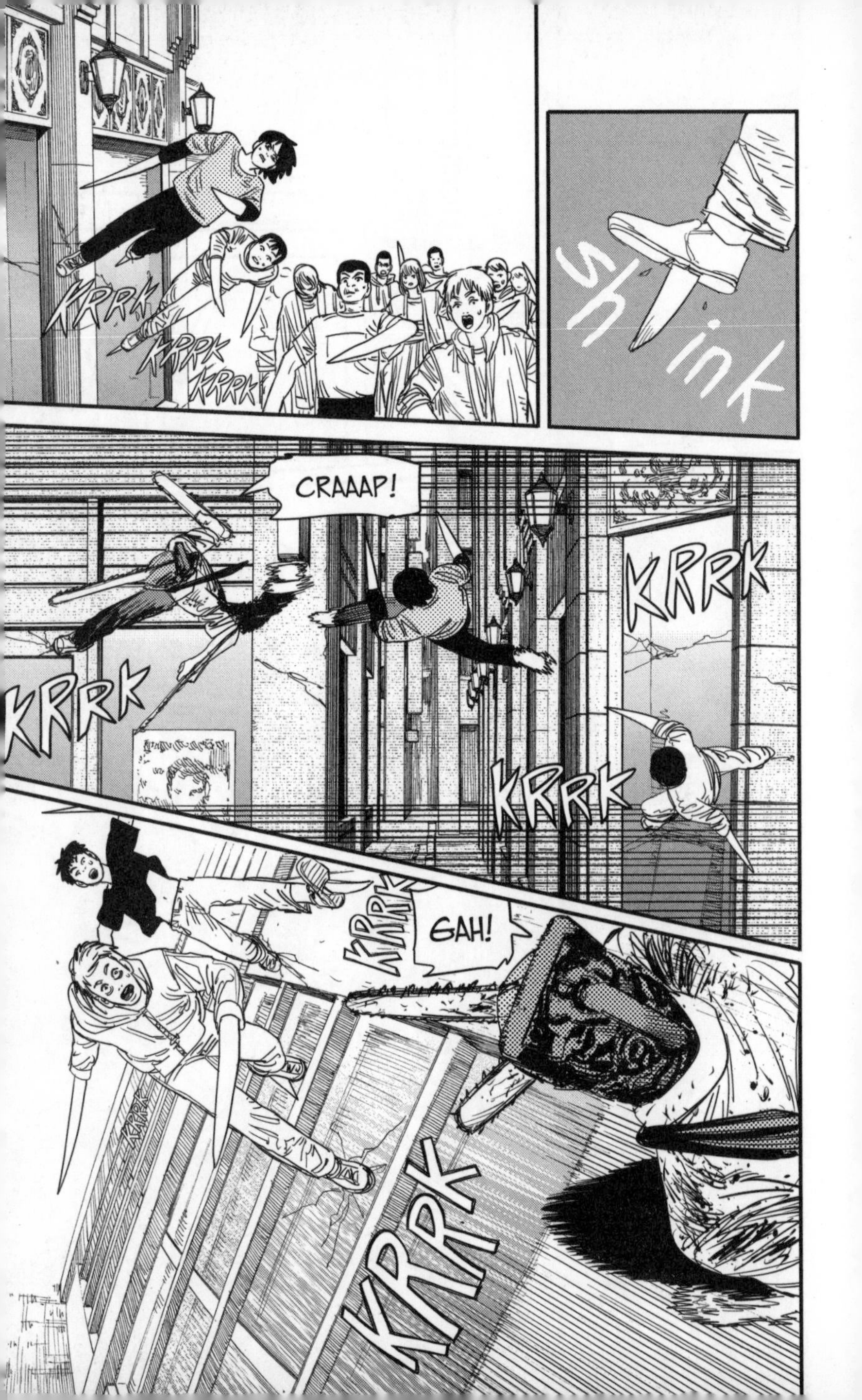
shink
KRRK
KRRK
KRRK
CRAAAP!
KRRK
KRRK
KRRK
GAH!
KRRK
KRRK

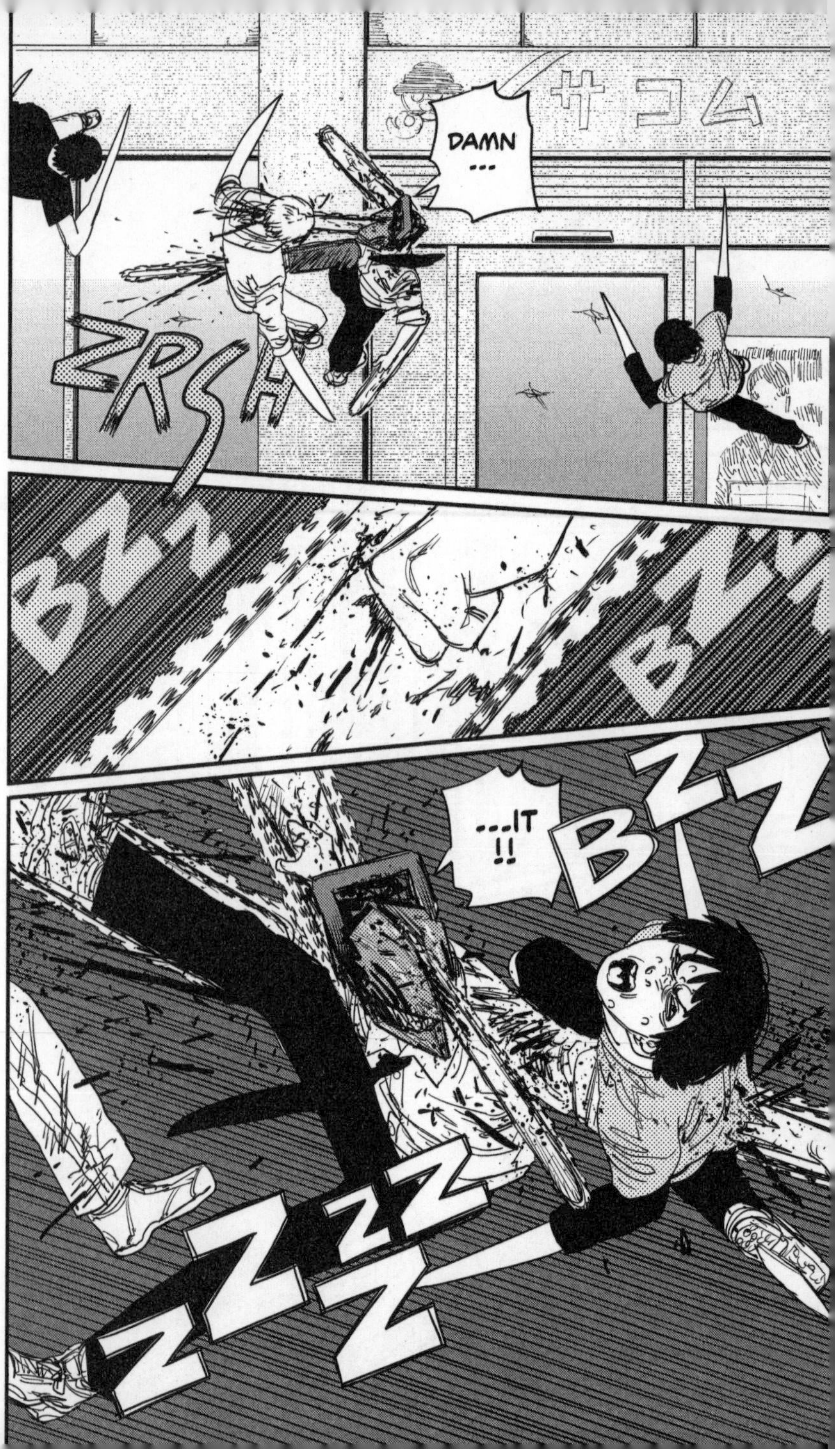
サコム
DAMN ---
ZRSH
BZZ
BZZ
BZZ
---IT !!
ZZZZ

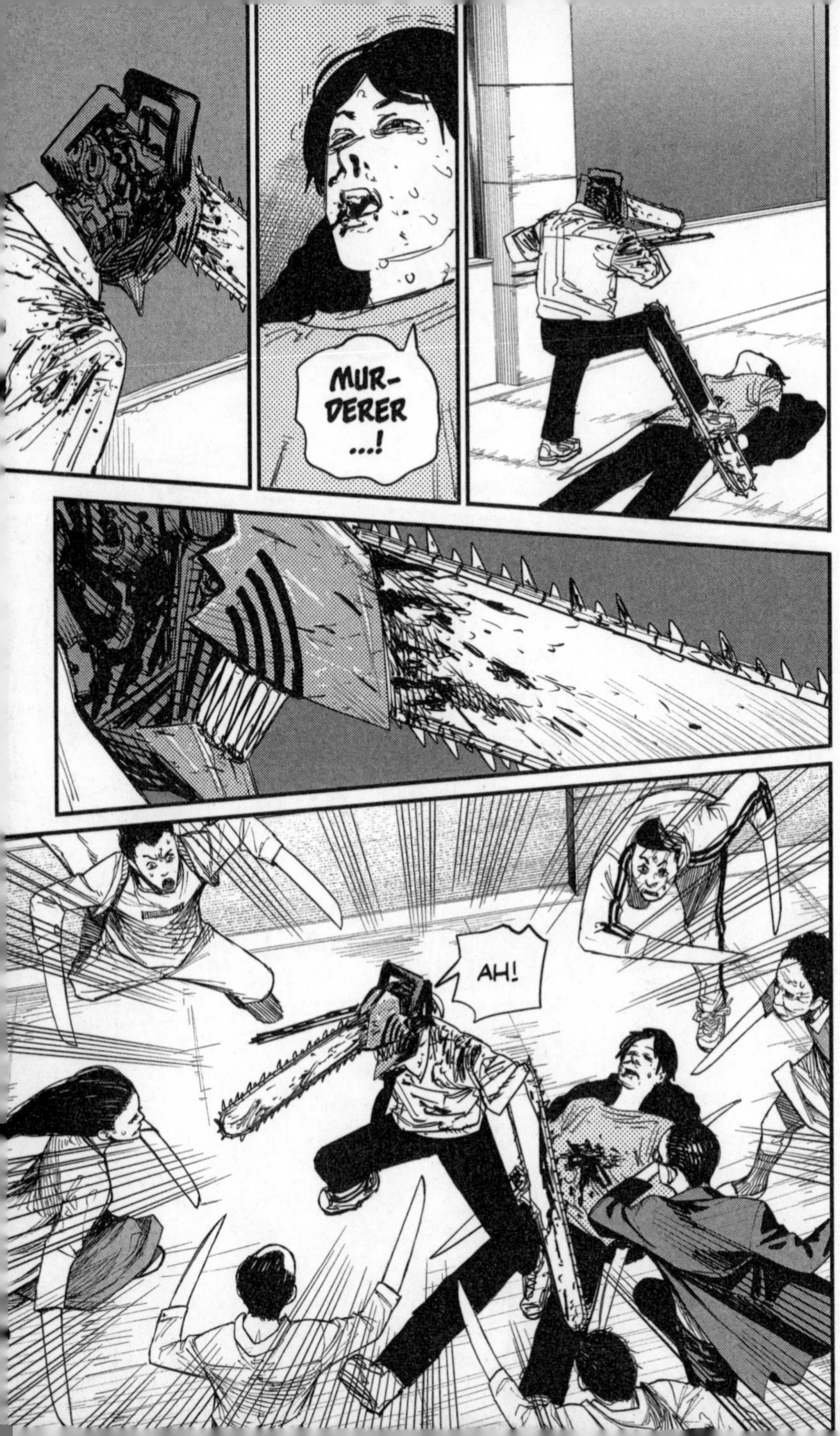
MUR-DERER ...!
AH!

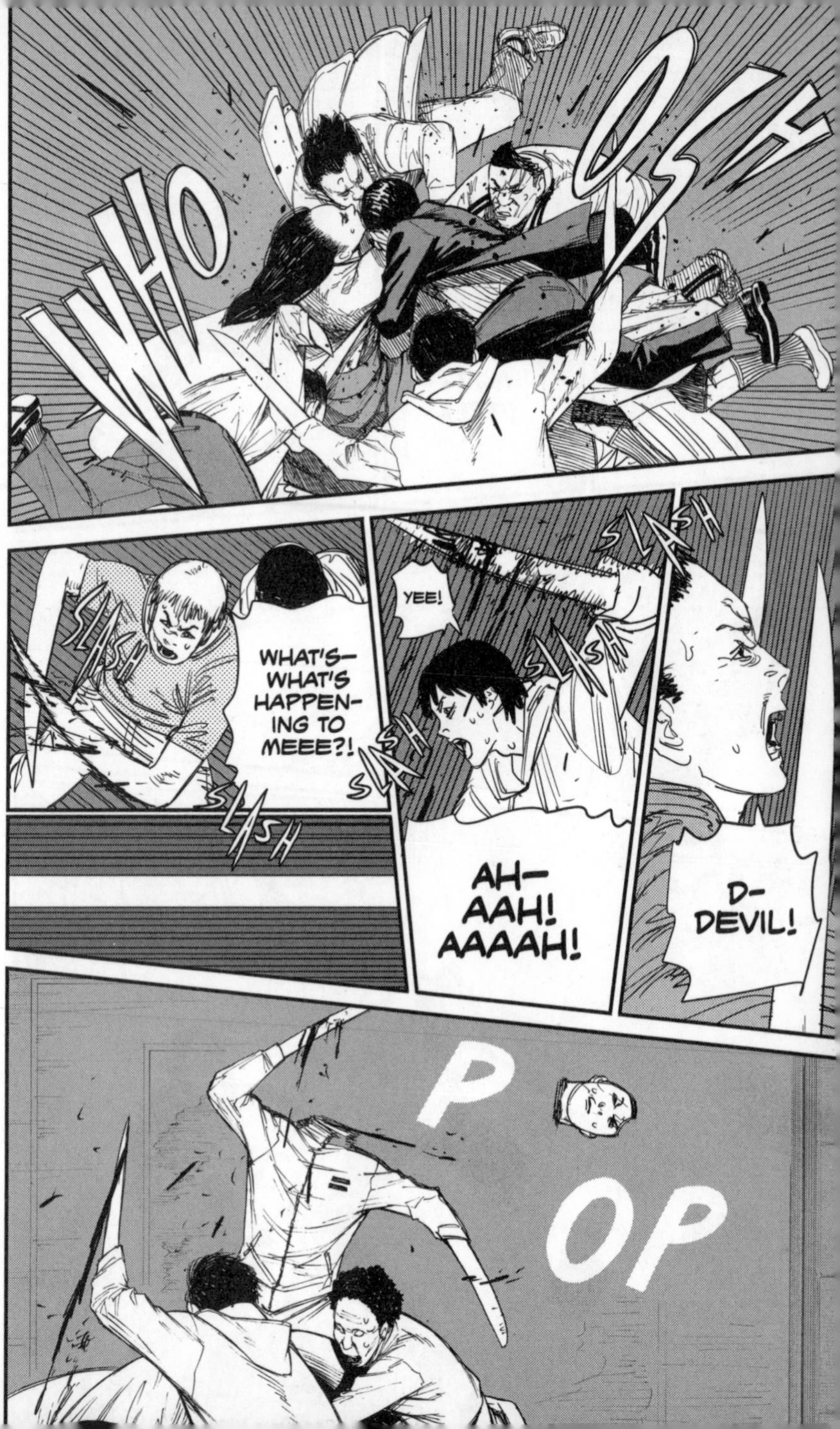
WHOOSH
D-DEVIL!
SLASH
YEE!
SLASH
SLASH
AH-AAH! AAAAH!
SLASH
WHAT'S—WHAT'S HAPPENING TO MEEE?!
SLASH
POP

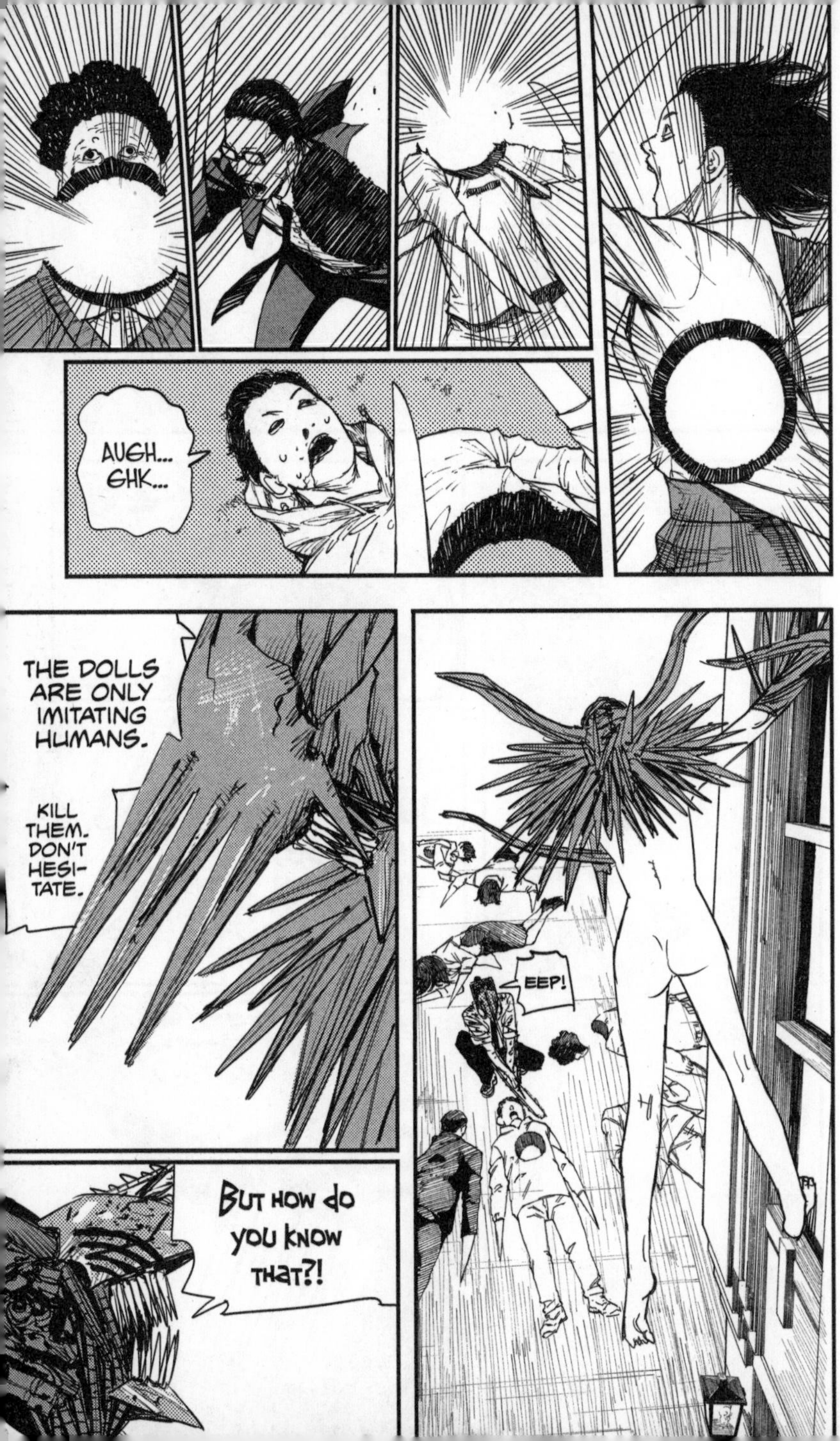
AUGH... GHK...
THE DOLLS ARE ONLY IMITATING HUMANS.
KILL THEM. DON'T HESITATE.
EEP!
BUT HOW DO YOU KNOW THAT?!

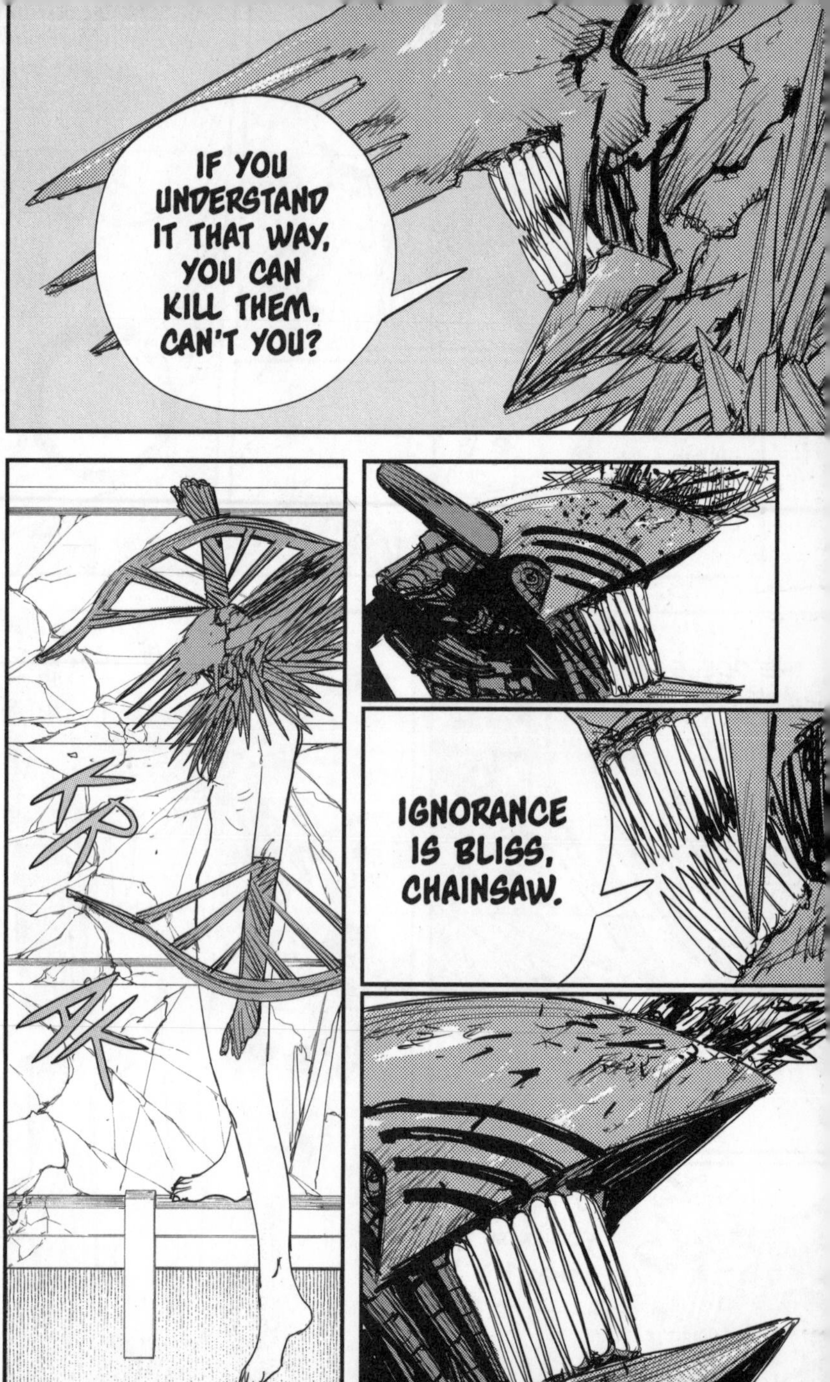
IF YOU UNDERSTAND IT THAT WAY, YOU CAN KILL THEM, CAN'T YOU?
IGNORANCE IS BLISS, CHAINSAW.
KRAK

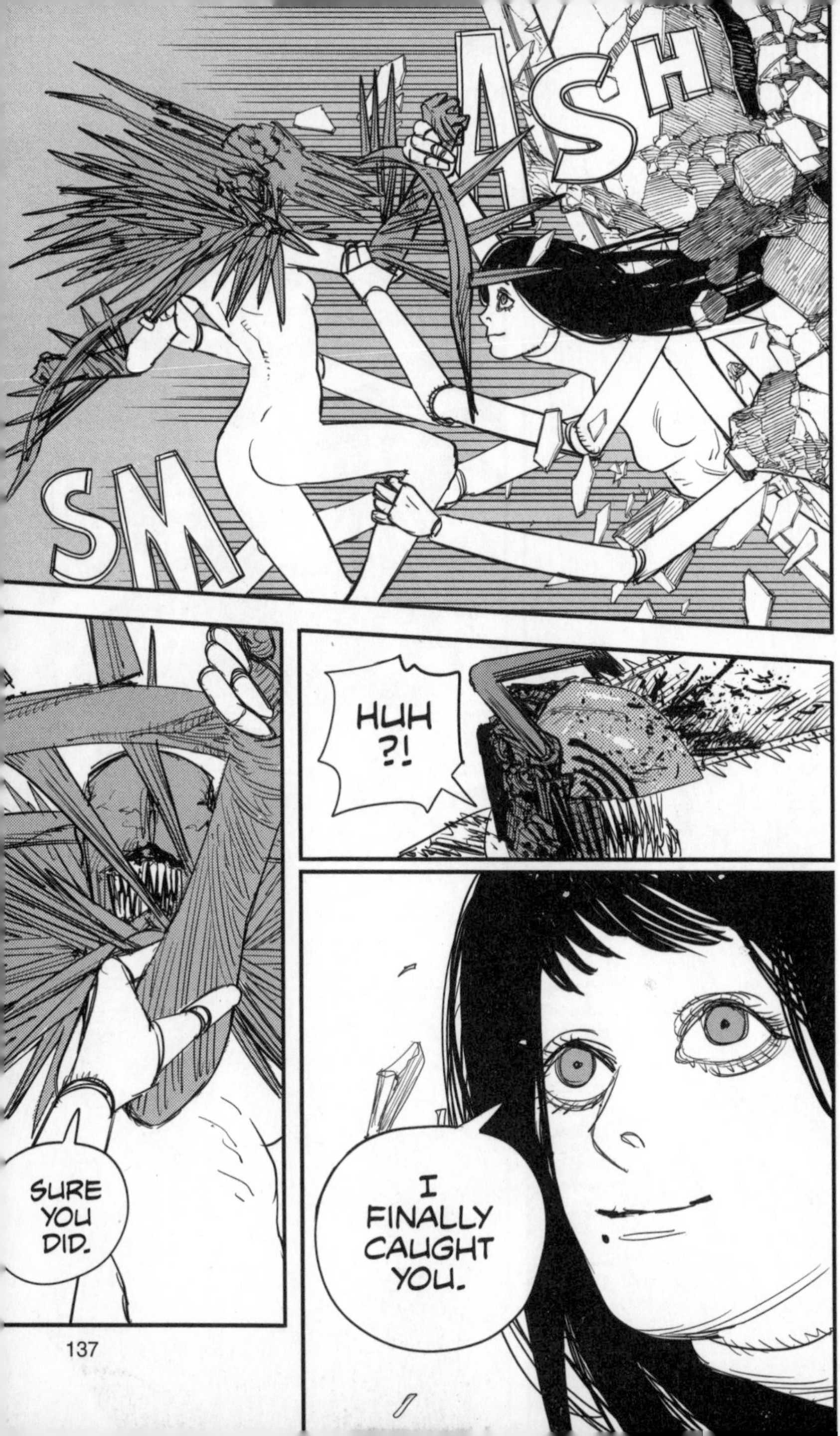
SMASH
HUH ?!
I FINALLY CAUGHT YOU.
SURE YOU DID.

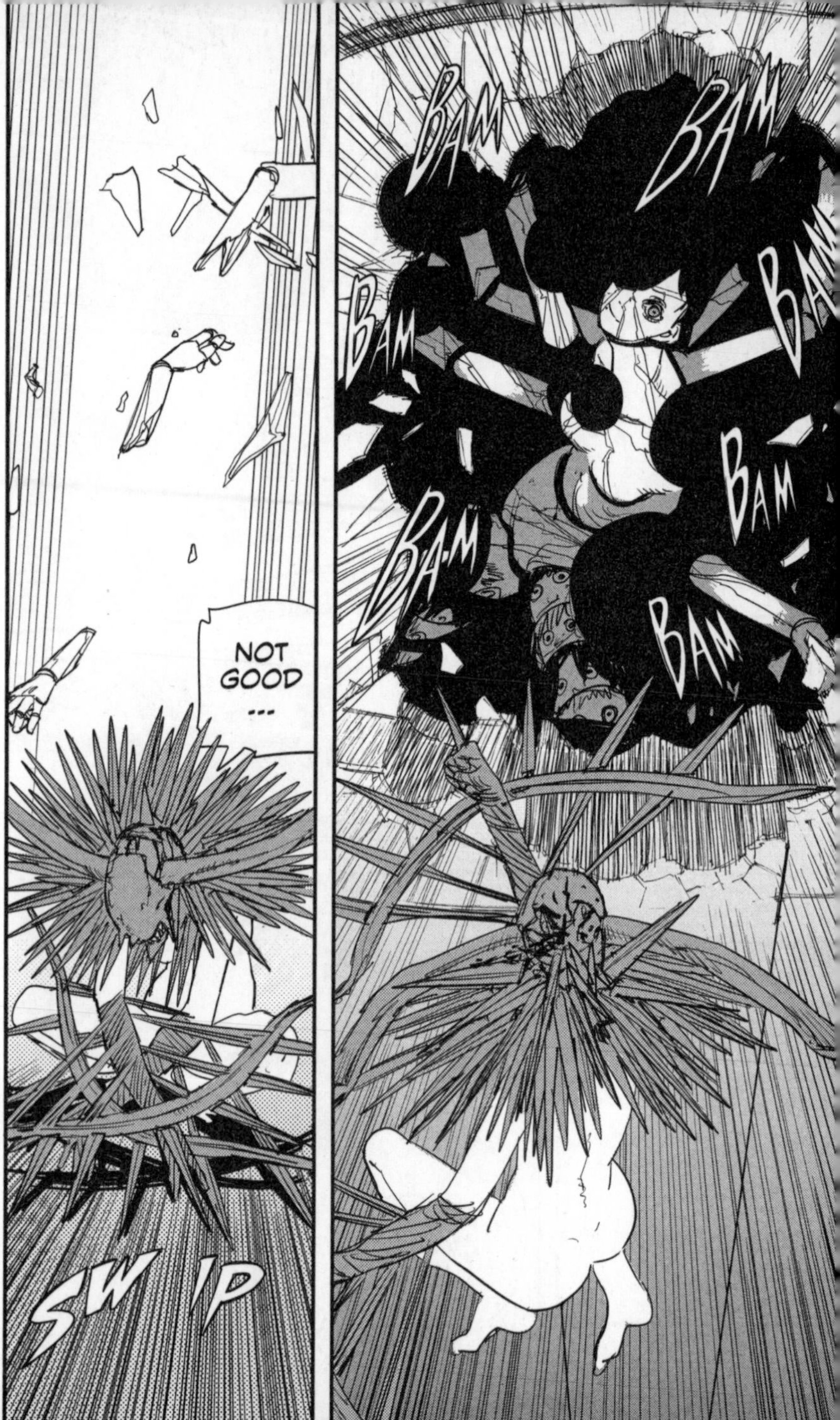
BAM
BAM
BAM
BAM
BAM
BAM
BAM
NOT GOOD ...
SWIP

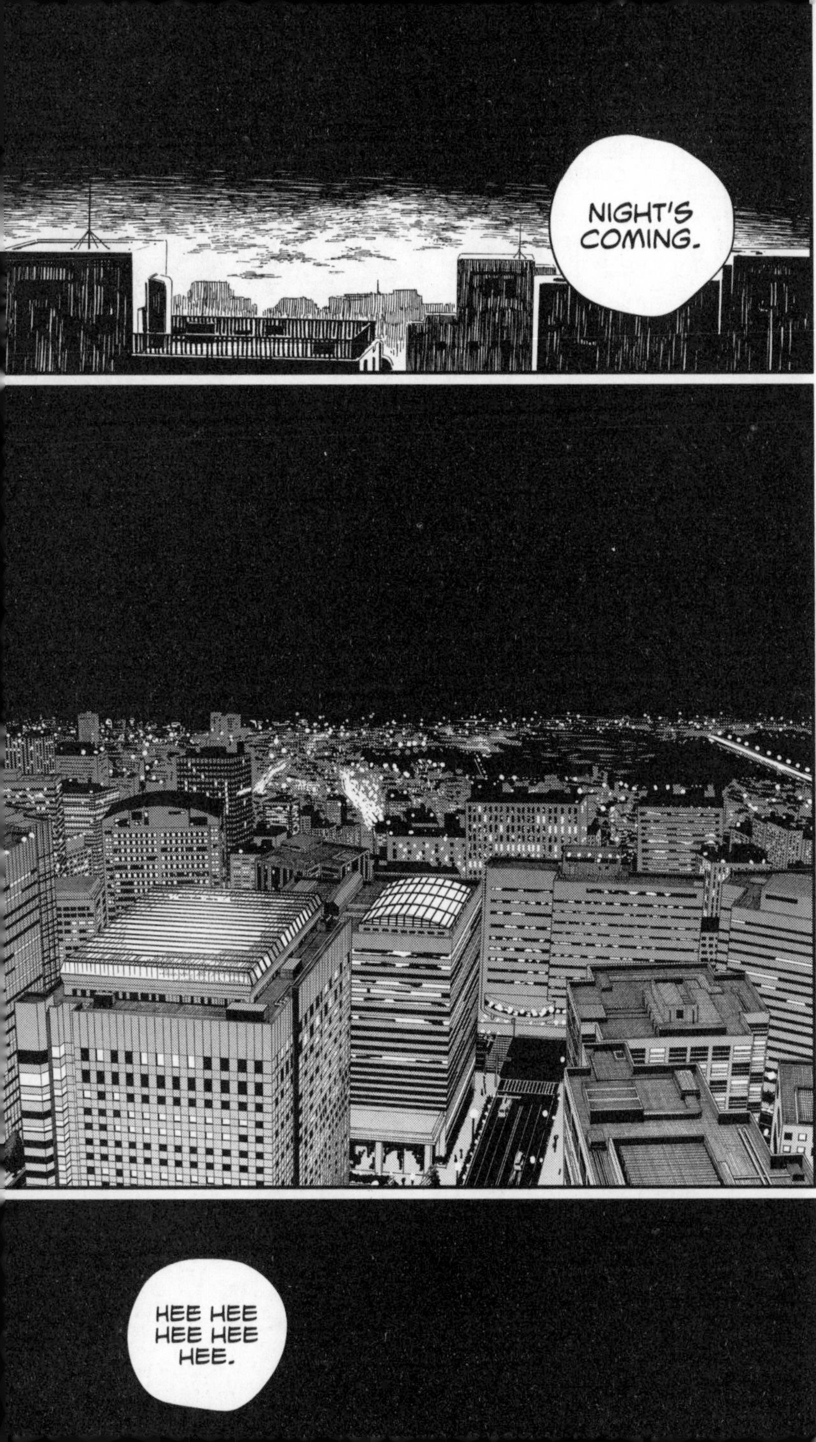
NIGHT'S COMING.
HEE HEE HEE HEE HEE.

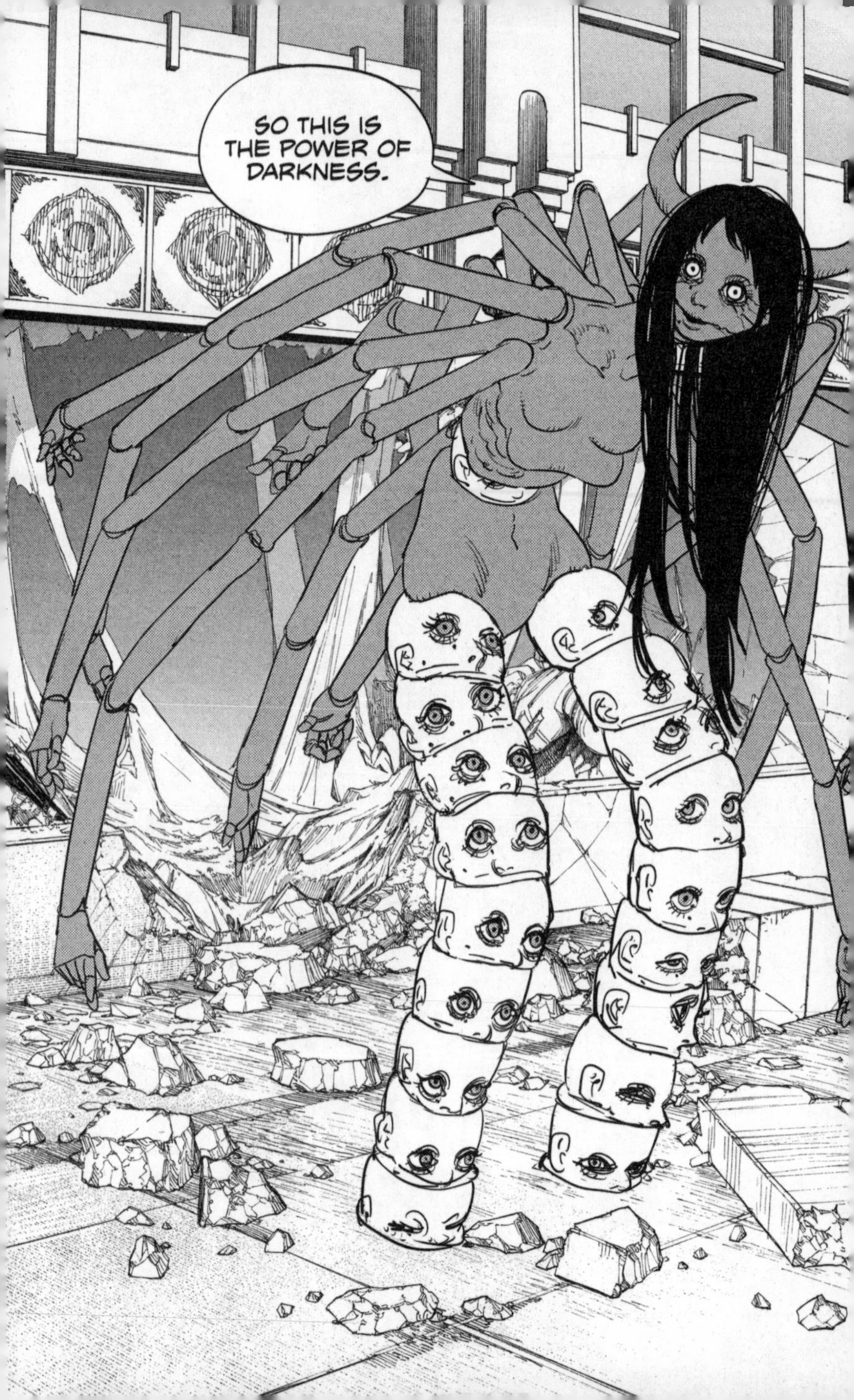
SO THIS IS THE POWER OF DARKNESS.

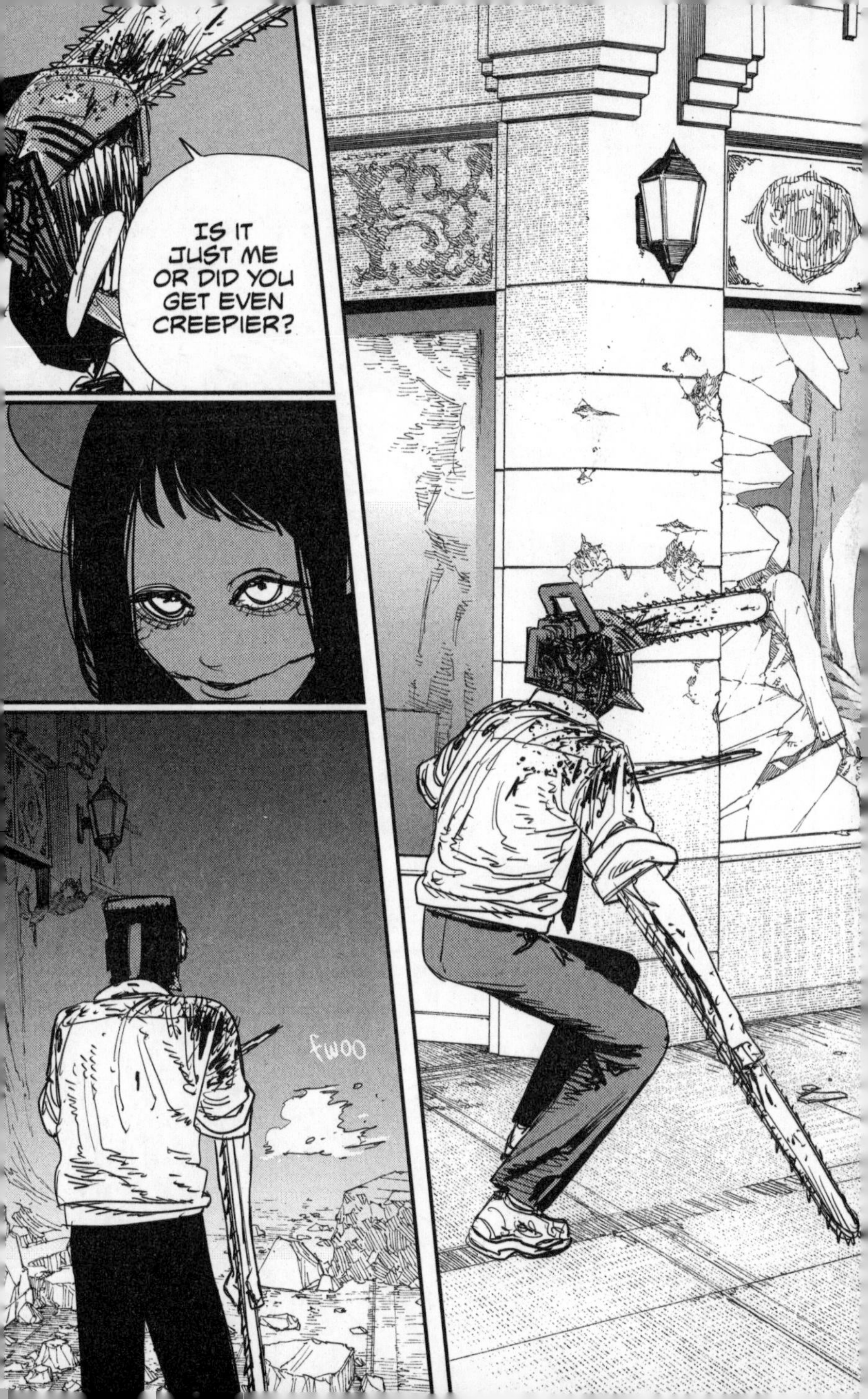
IS IT JUST ME OR DID YOU GET EVEN CREEPIER?
fwoo

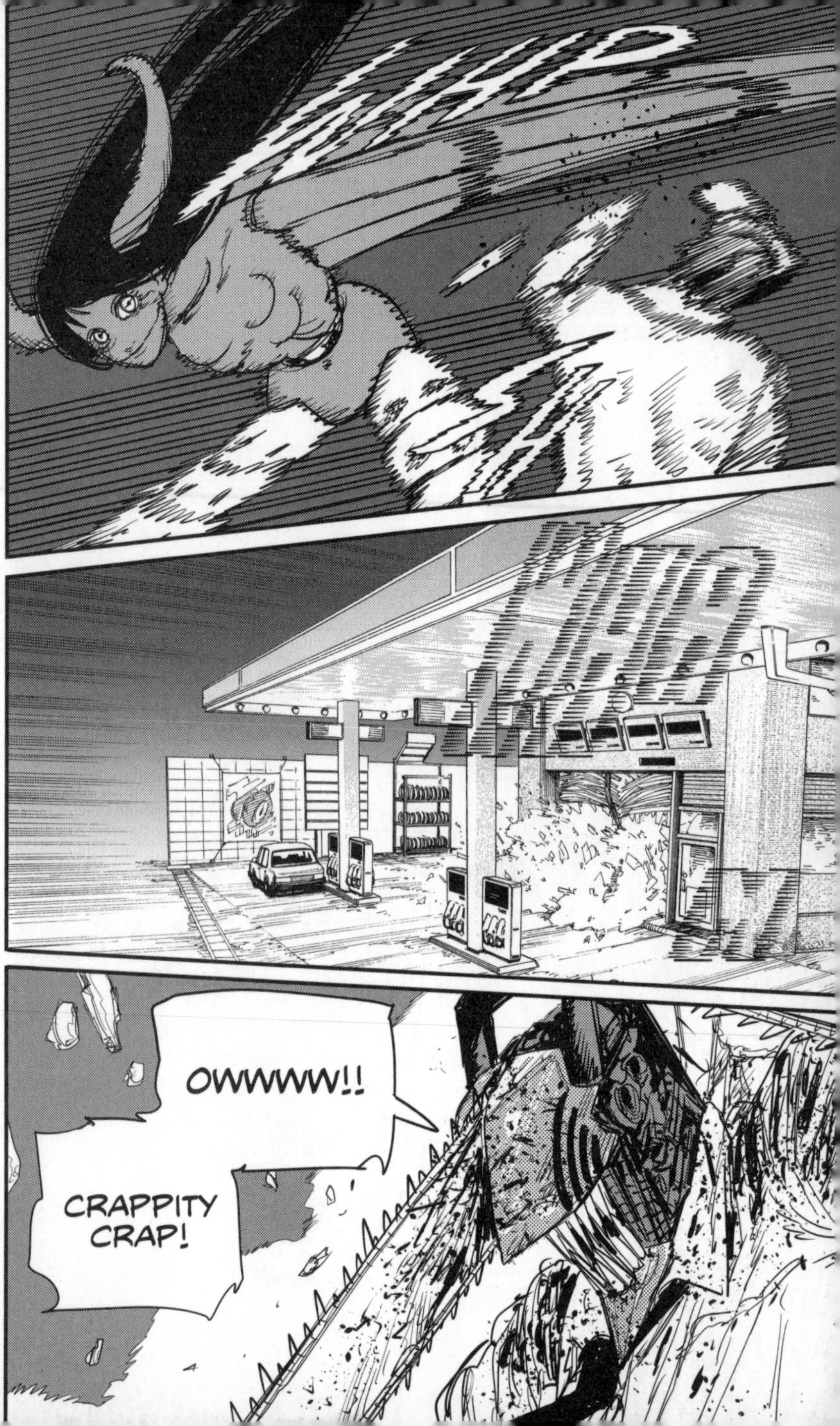
OWWWW!!
CRAPPITY CRAP!

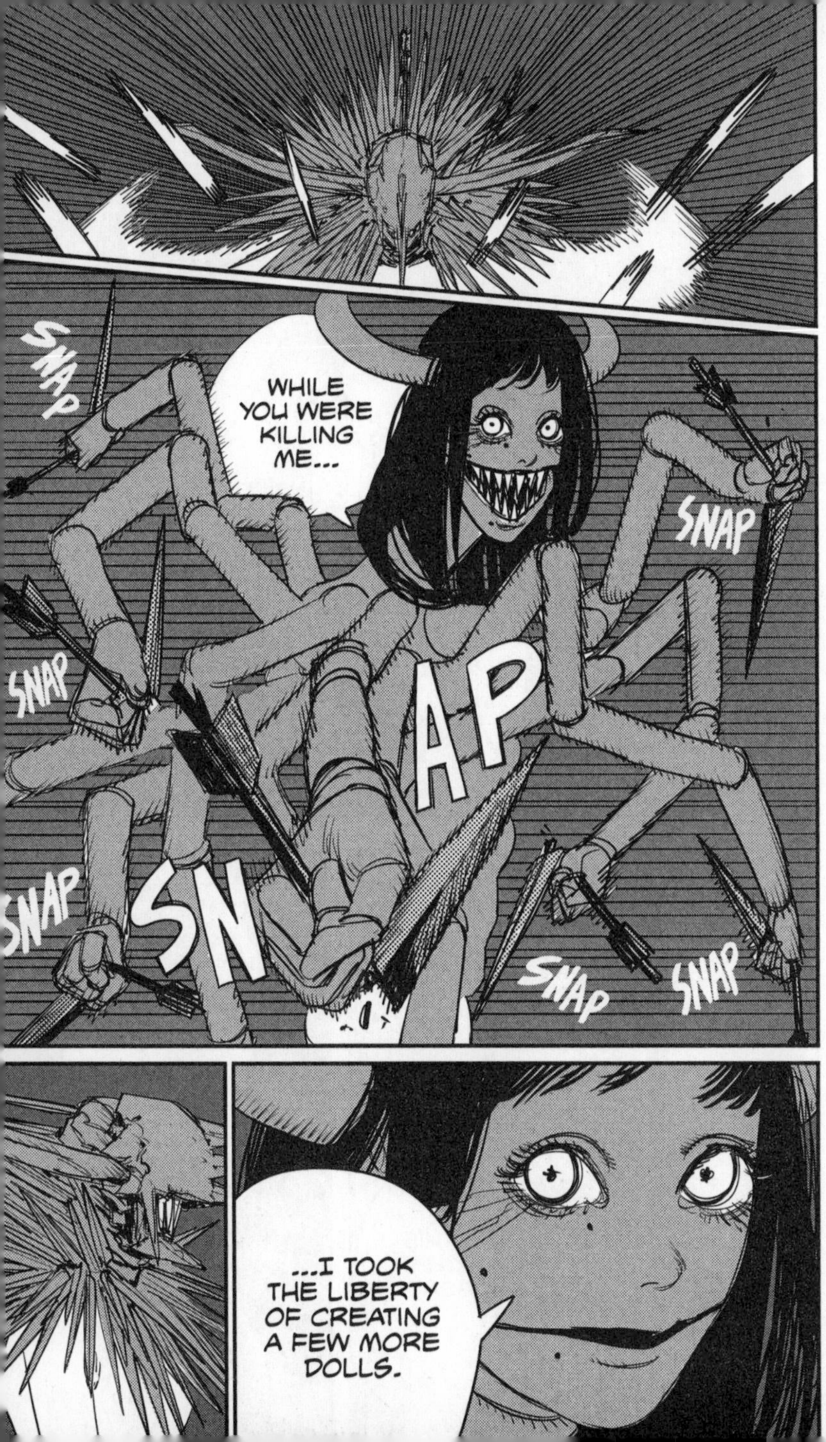
WHILE YOU WERE KILLING ME...
SNAP
SNAP
SNAP
SNAP
SNAP
SNAP
SNAP
...I TOOK THE LIBERTY OF CREATING A FEW MORE DOLLS.

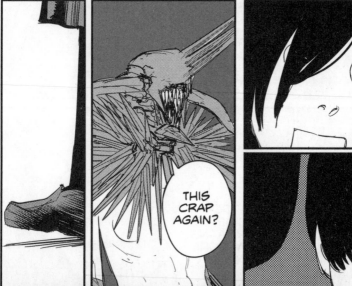

THIS
CRAP
AGAIN?

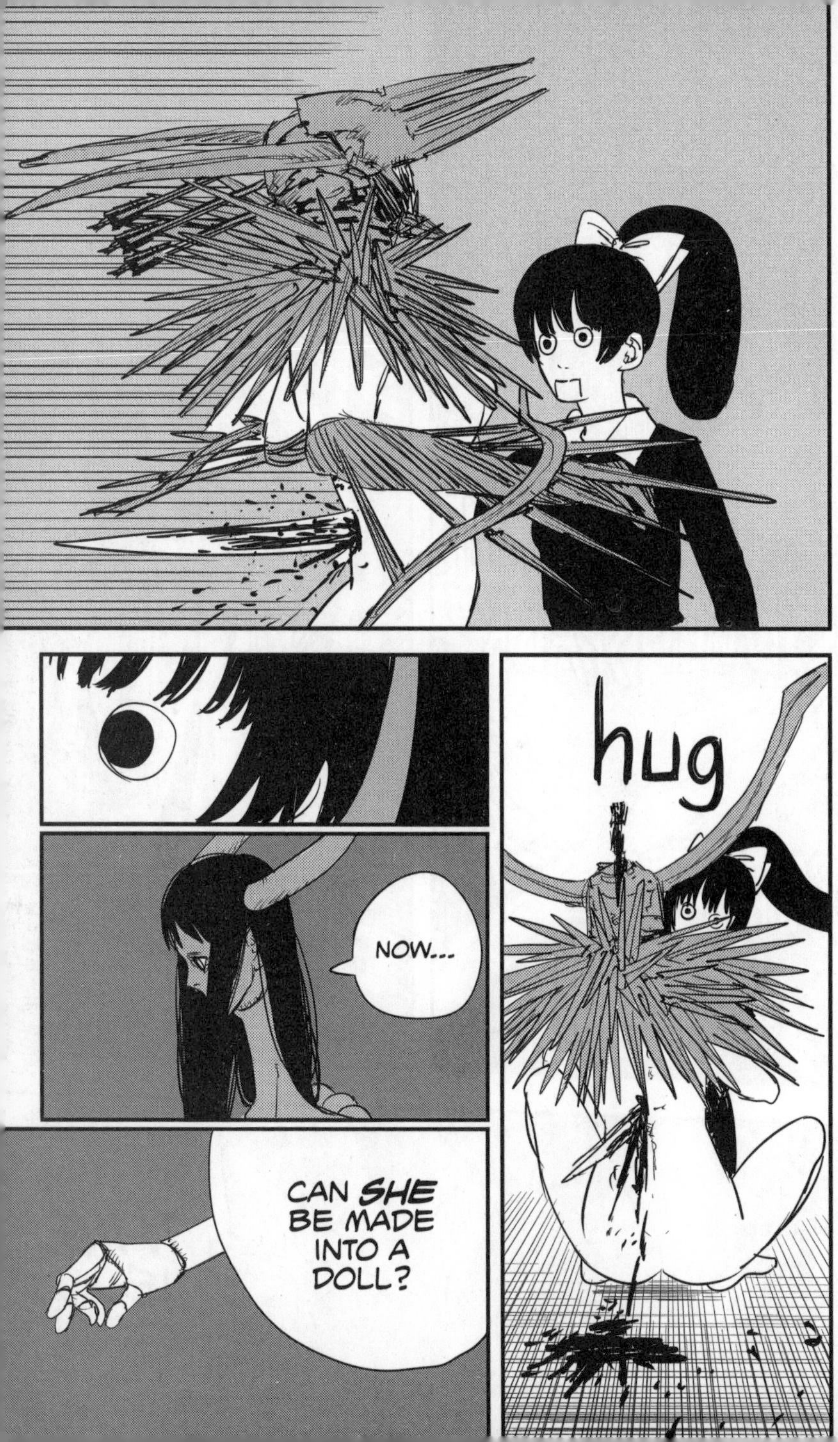
hug
NOW...
CAN *SHE* BE MADE INTO A DOLL?

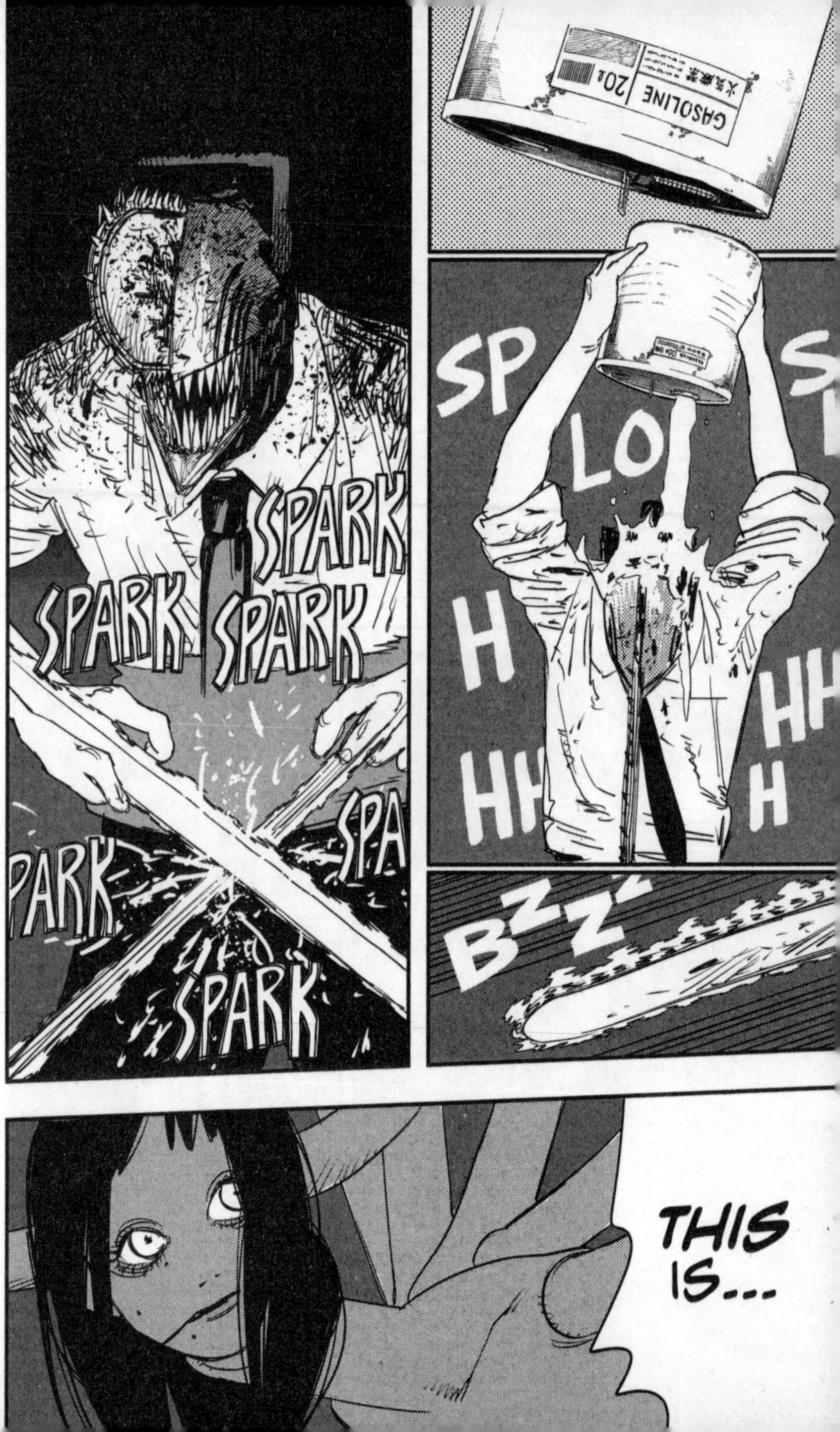
GASOLINE 20ℓ
SP LO S H HH HH H
BZZZ
SPARK
SPARK
SPARK
SPA
PARK
SPARK
THIS IS...

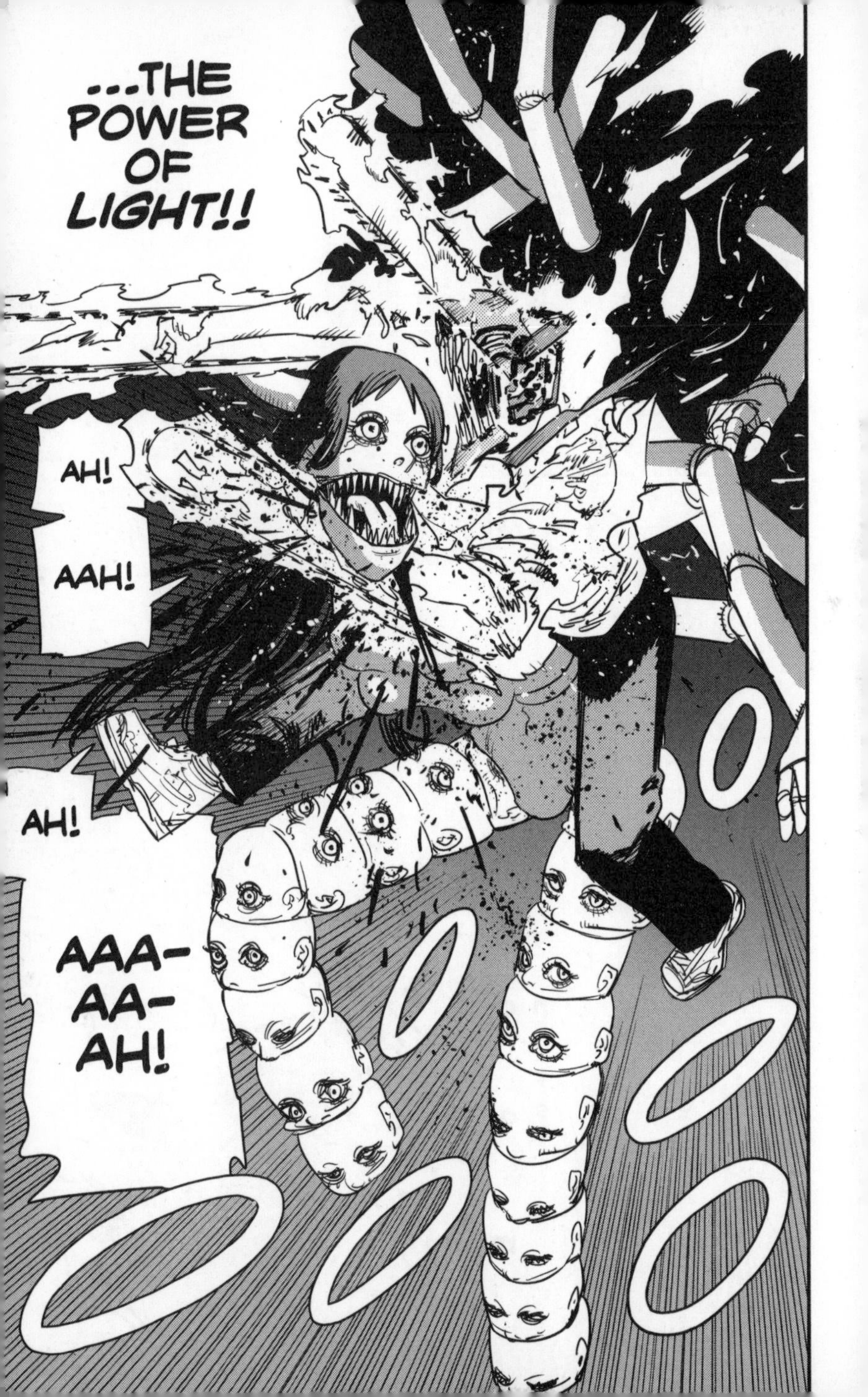
...THE POWER OF LIGHT!!
AH!
AAH!
AH!
AAA-AA-AH!

C
h a i n

s a w

m a n

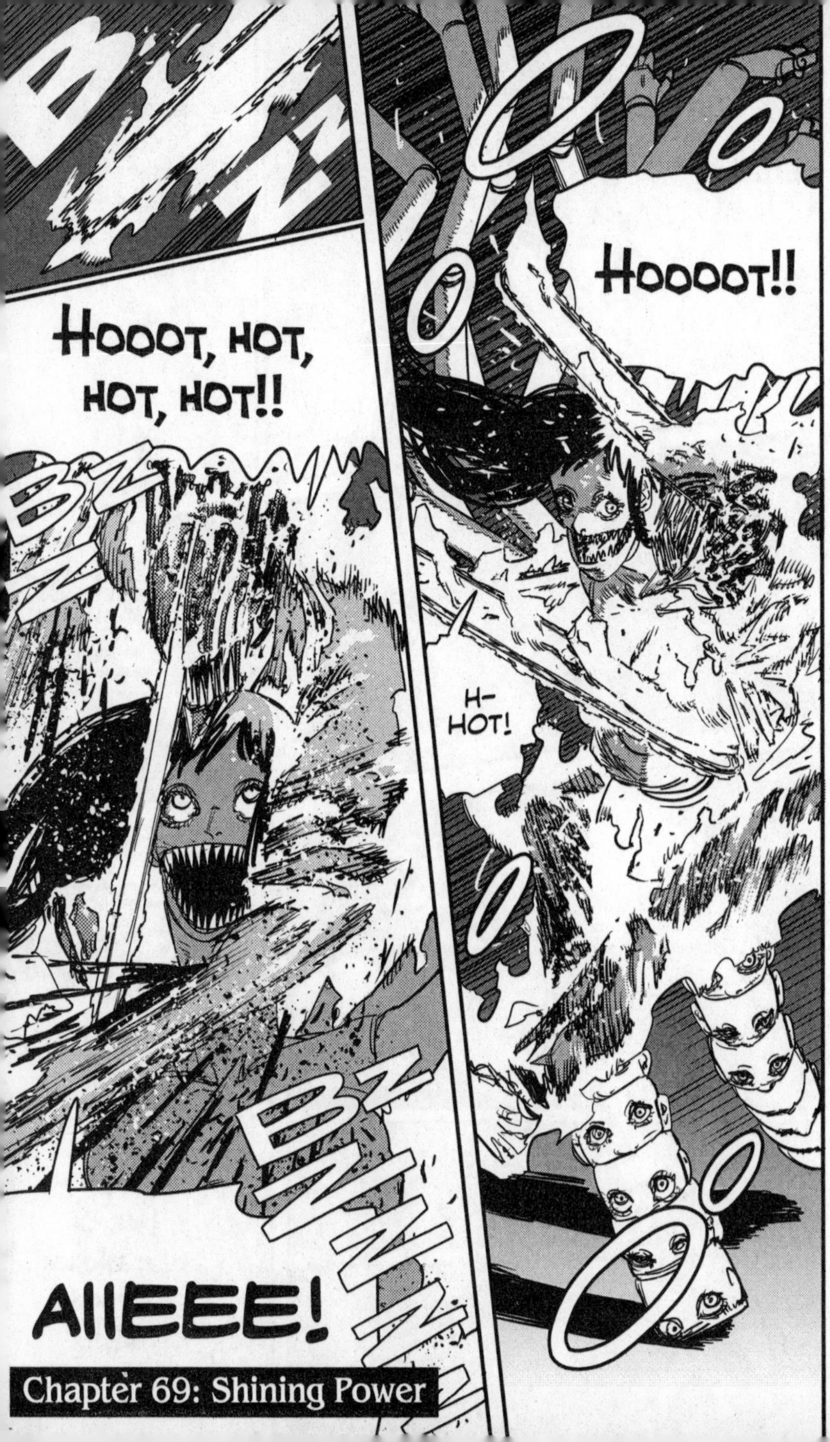
HOOOOT!!
H-
HOT!
HOOOT, HOT,
HOT, HOT!!
AIIEEE!

Chapter 69: Shining Power

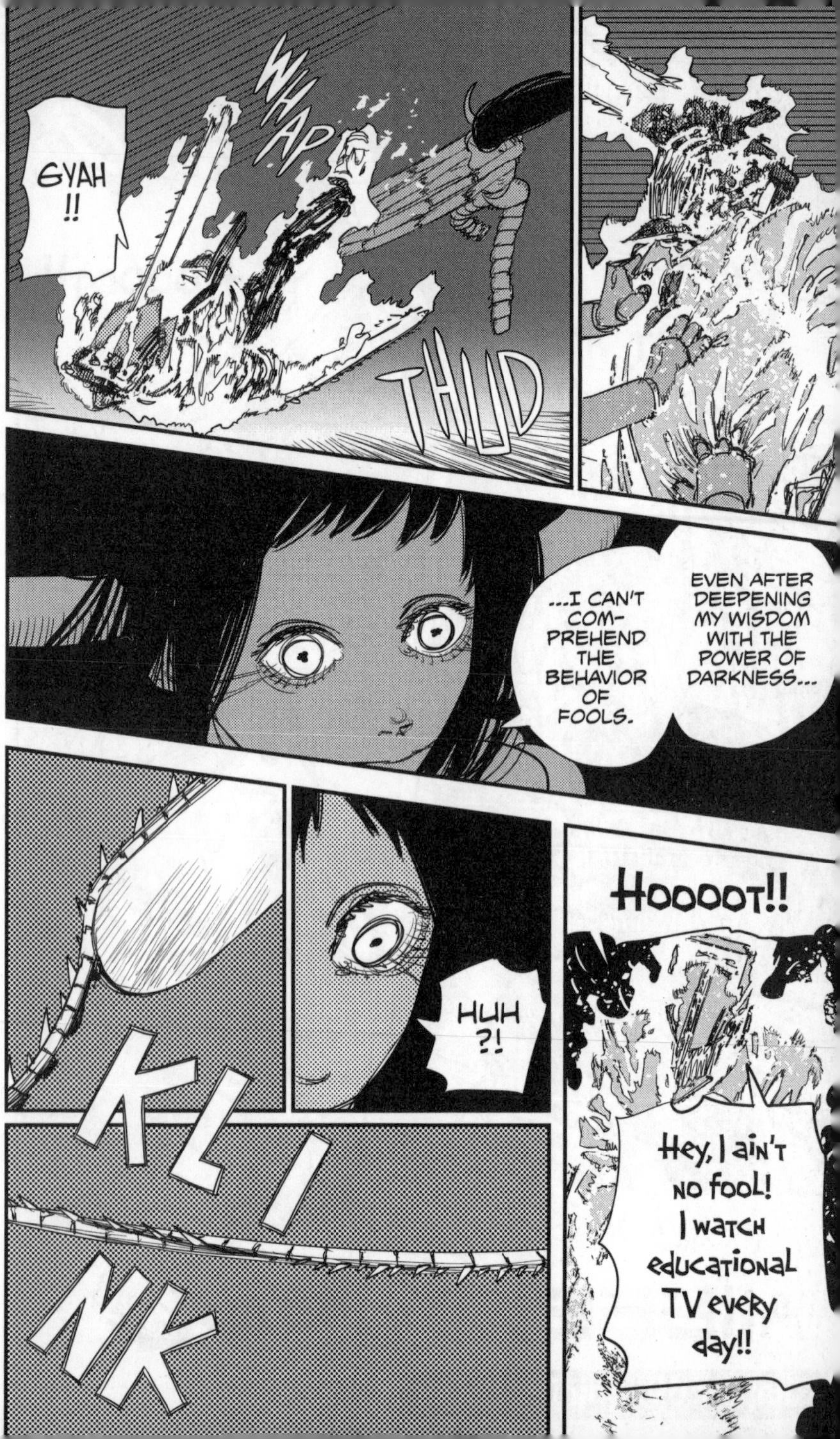
WHAP
GYAH!!
THUD
EVEN AFTER DEEPENING MY WISDOM WITH THE POWER OF DARKNESS...
...I CAN'T COM-PREHEND THE BEHAVIOR OF FOOLS.
HOOOOT!!
Hey, I ain't no fool! I watch educational TV every day!!
HUH?!
KLINK

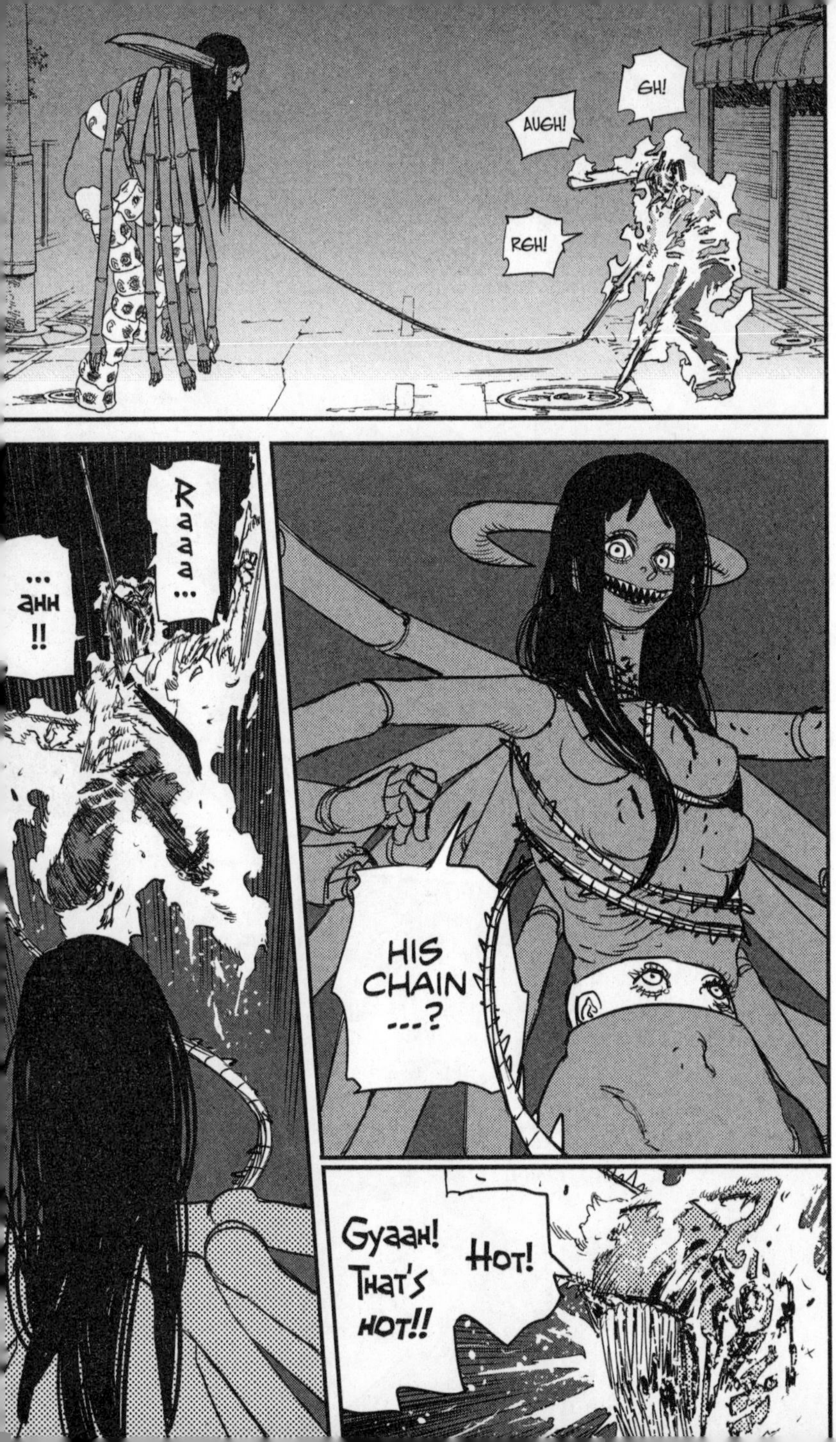
GH!
AUGH!
RGH!
HIS CHAIN ---?
HOT!
Gyaah! That's hot!!
Raaa...
...ahh!!

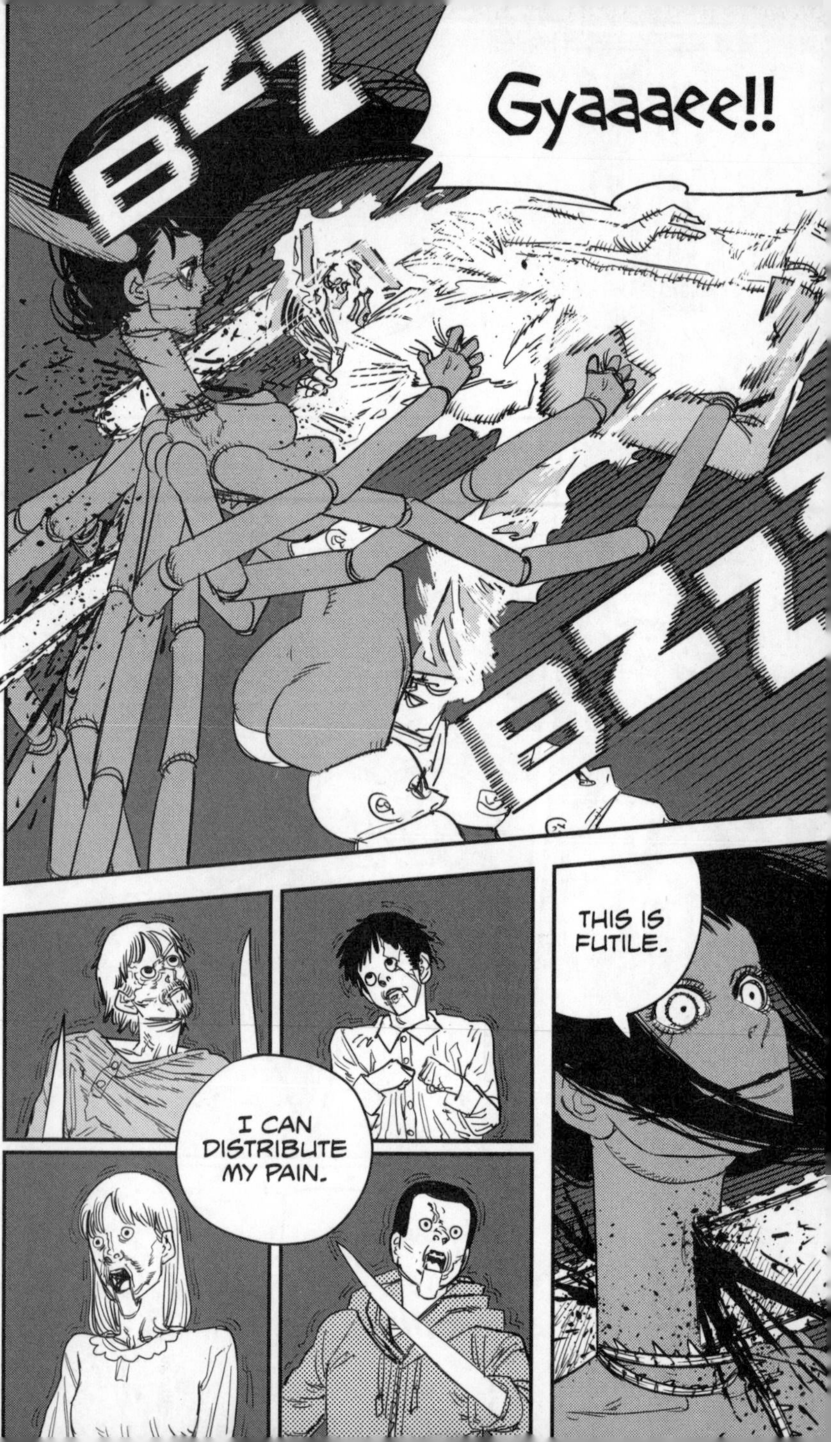
Gyaaaee!!
BZZ
BZZ
THIS IS FUTILE.
I CAN DISTRIBUTE MY PAIN.

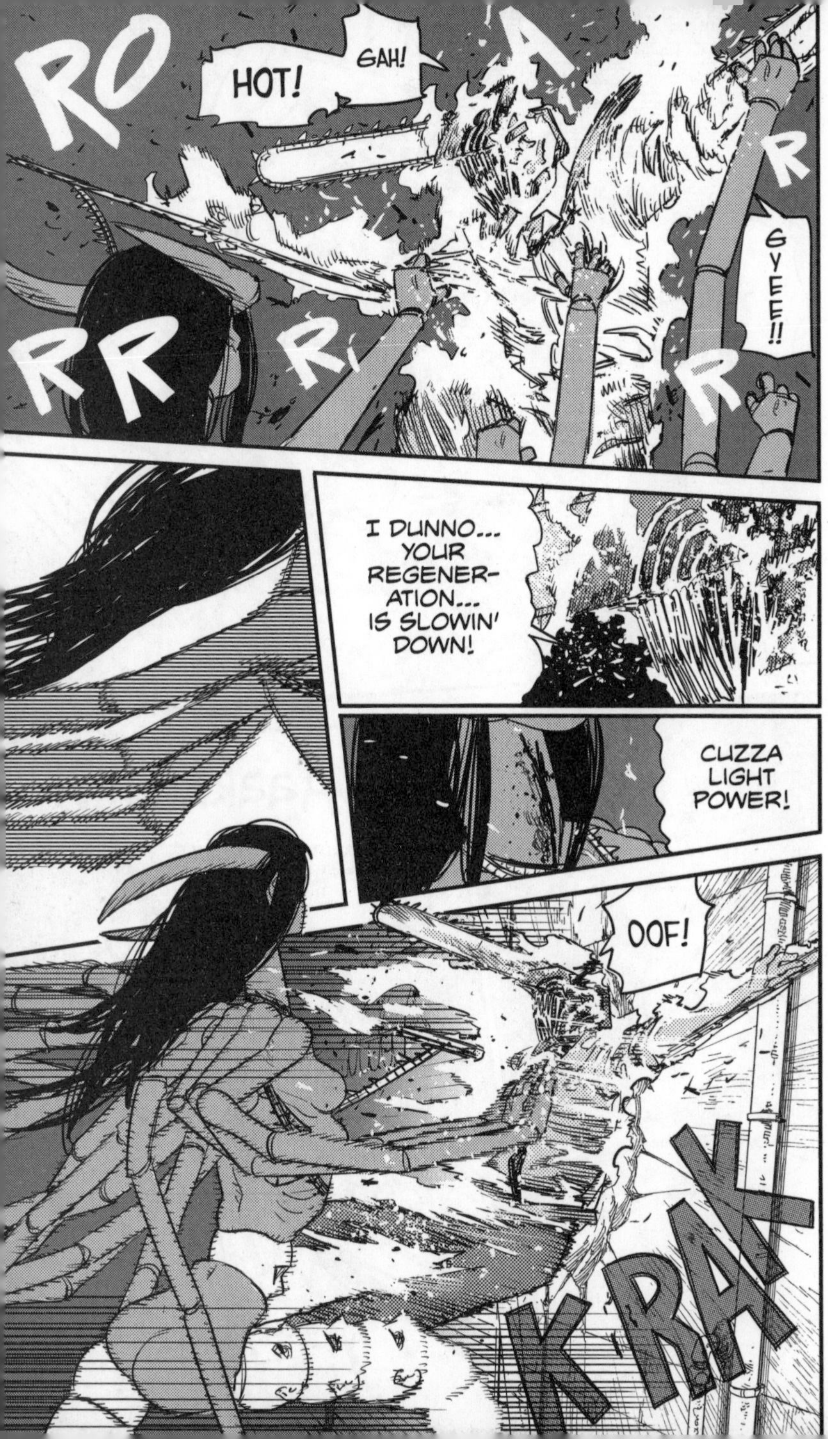
GAH!
HOT!
GYEEE!!
RO
A
R
RR
R
R
I DUNNO... YOUR REGENER-ATION... IS SLOWIN' DOWN!
CUZZA LIGHT POWER!
OOF!
KRAK

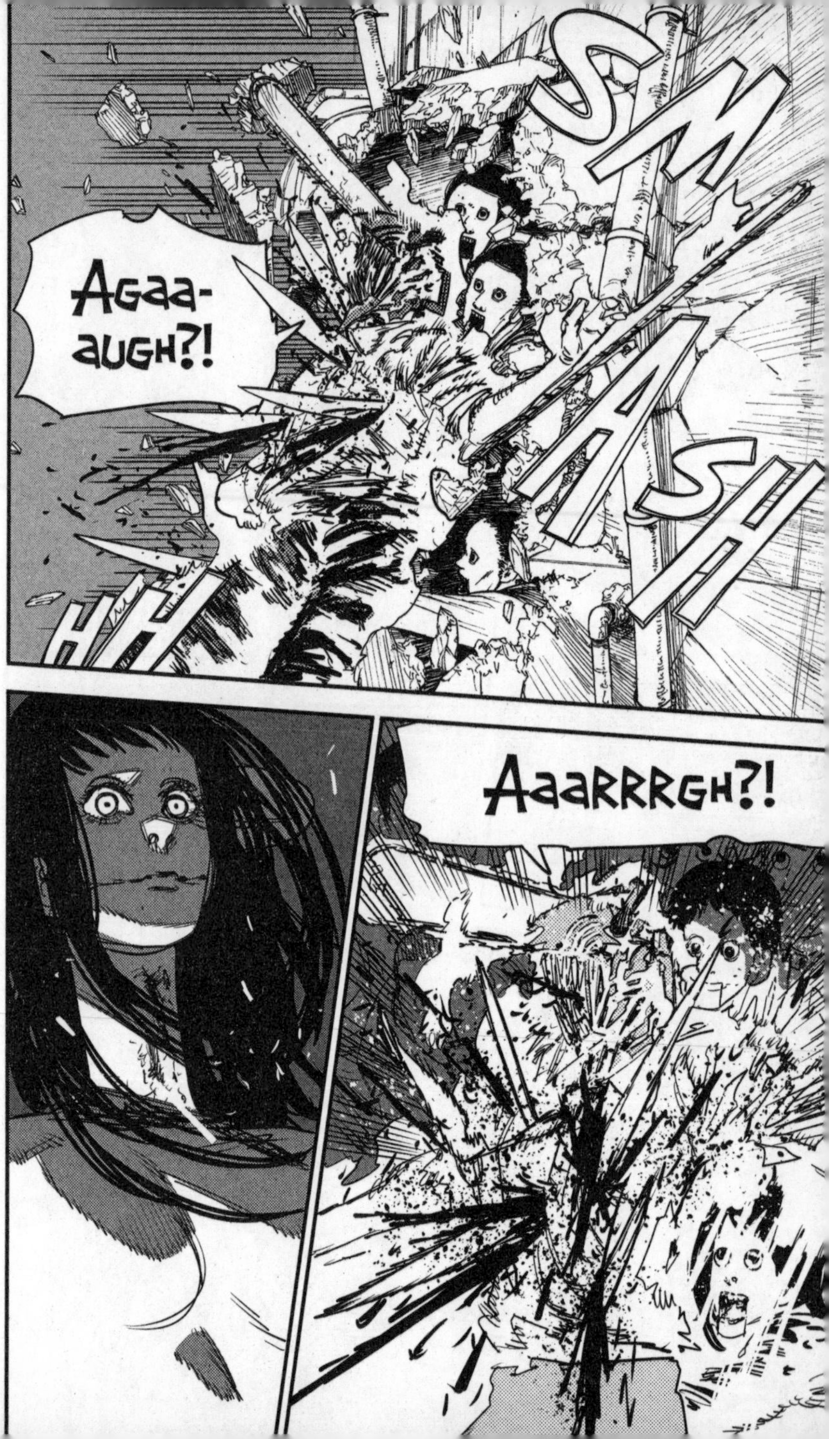
SMASHH
Agaaa-augh?!
Aaarrrgh?!

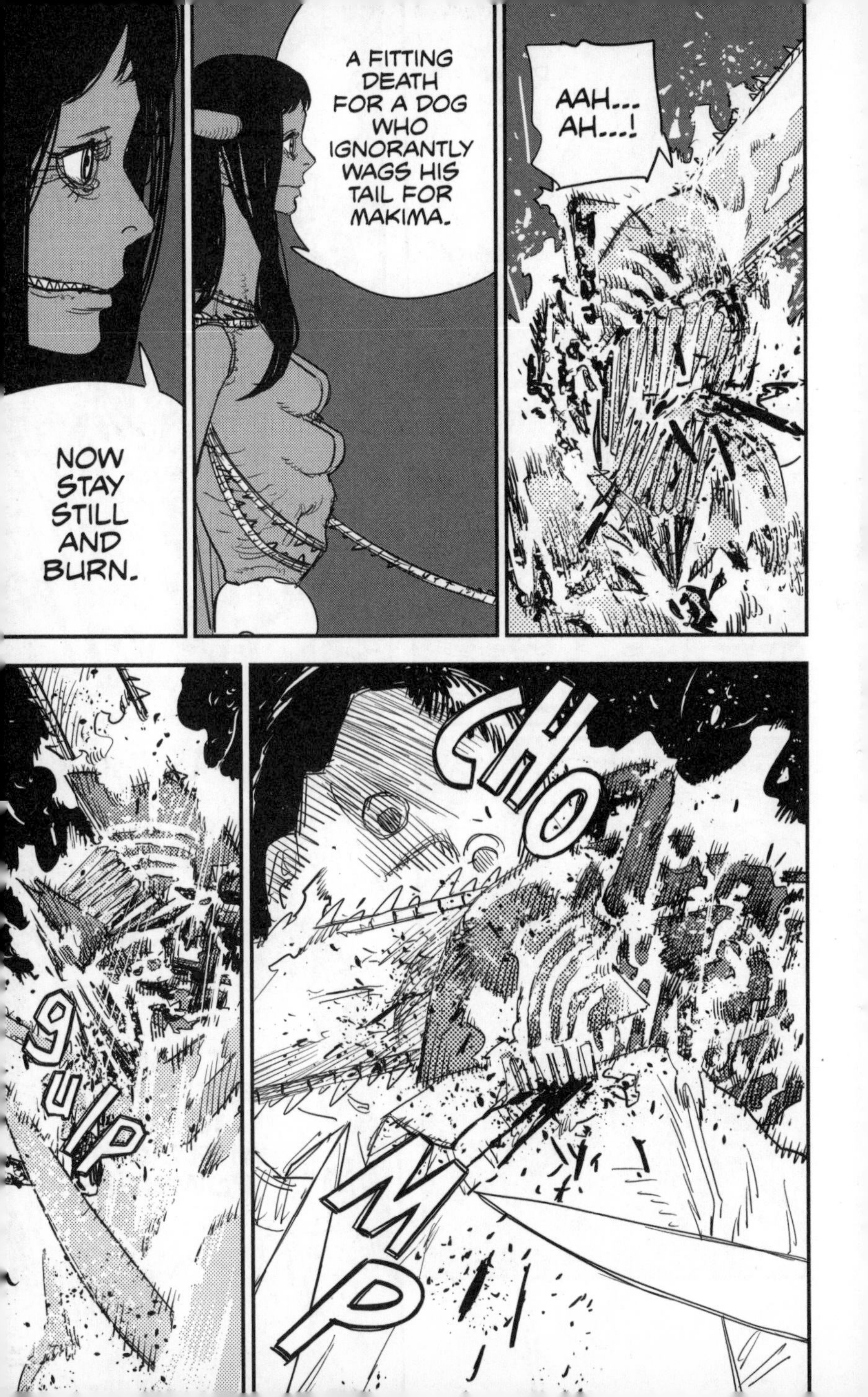
AAH...
AH...!
A FITTING DEATH FOR A DOG WHO IGNORANTLY WAGS HIS TAIL FOR MAKIMA.
NOW STAY STILL AND BURN.
CHOMP
gulp

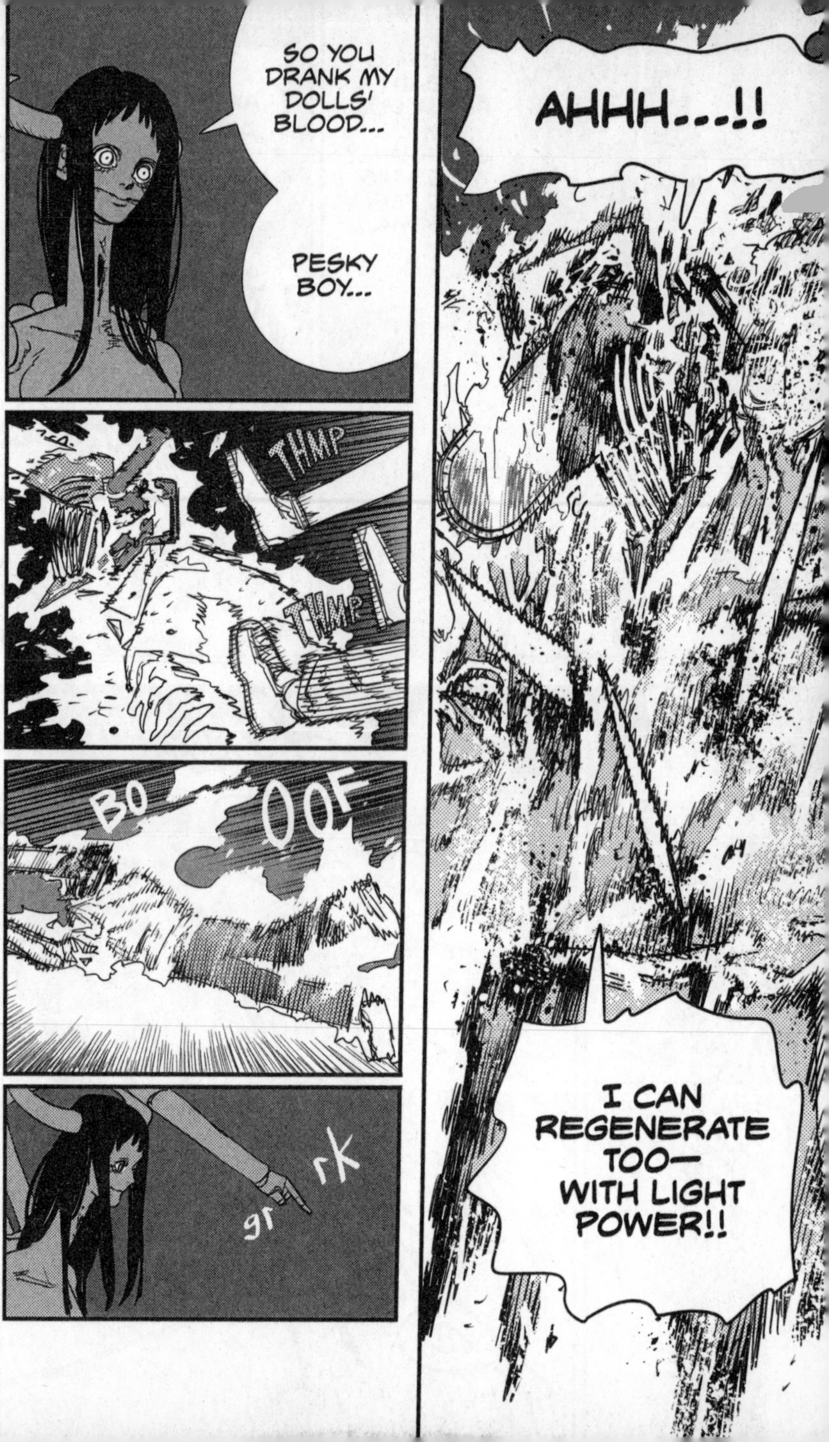
AHHH...!!
I CAN REGENERATE TOO—WITH LIGHT POWER!!
SO YOU DRANK MY DOLLS' BLOOD...
PESKY BOY...
THMP
THMP
BO
OOF
rk
gr

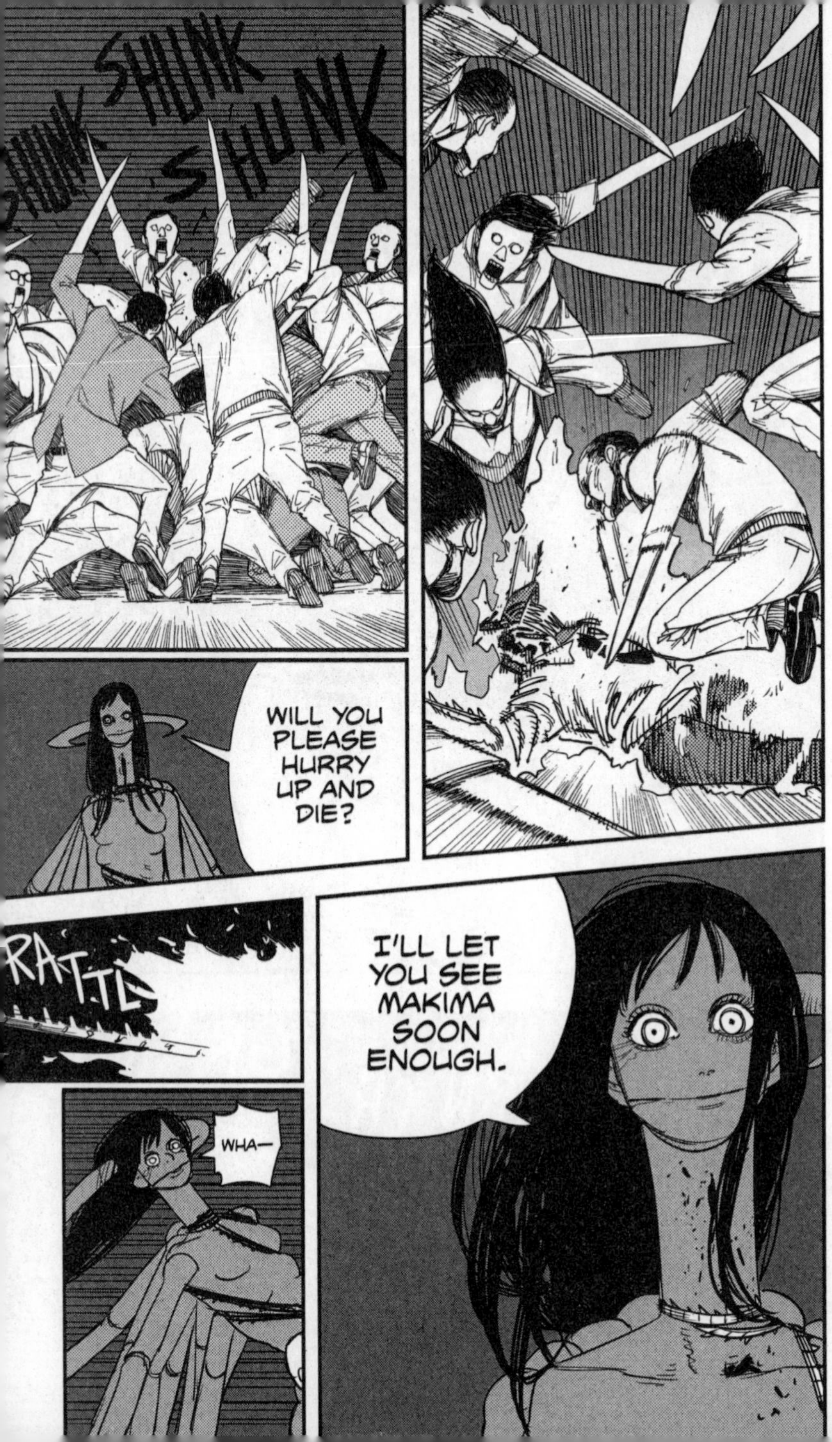
SHUNK
SHUNK
SHUNK
WILL YOU PLEASE HURRY UP AND DIE?
I'LL LET YOU SEE MAKIMA SOON ENOUGH.
RATTL
WHA—

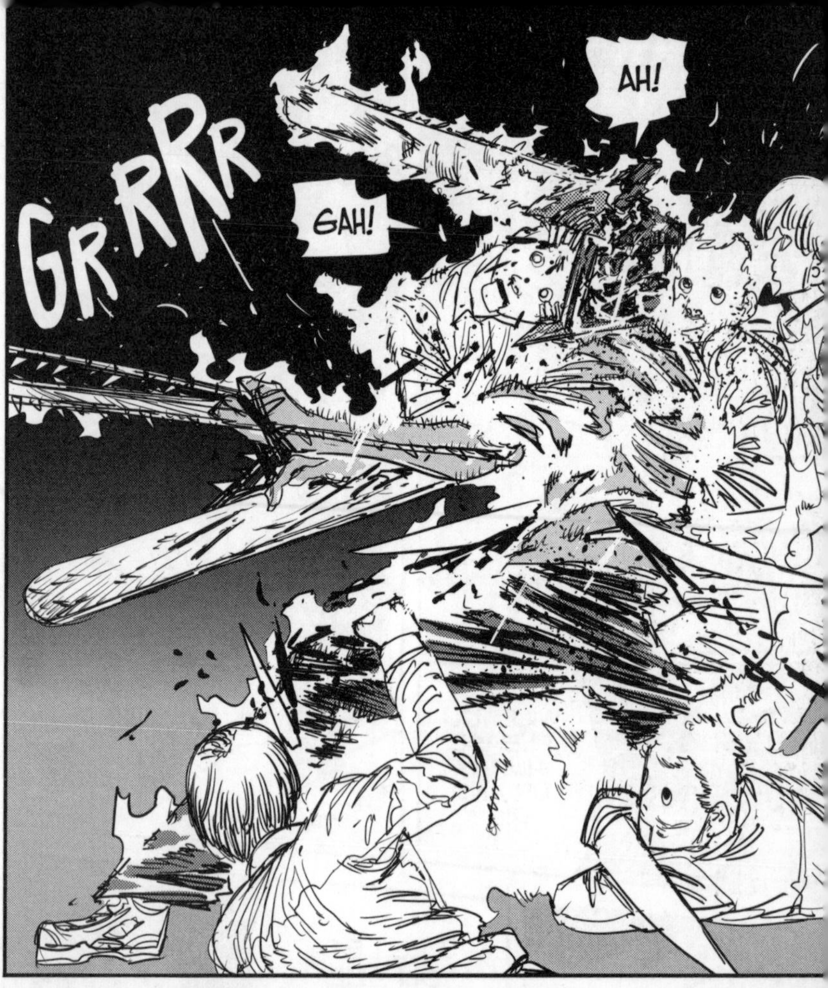
AH!
GAH!
GRRRR

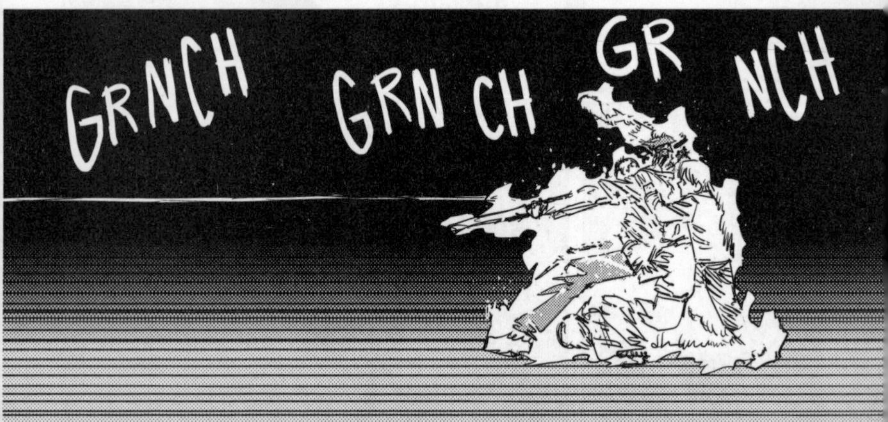
GRNCH
GRN CH
GR NCH

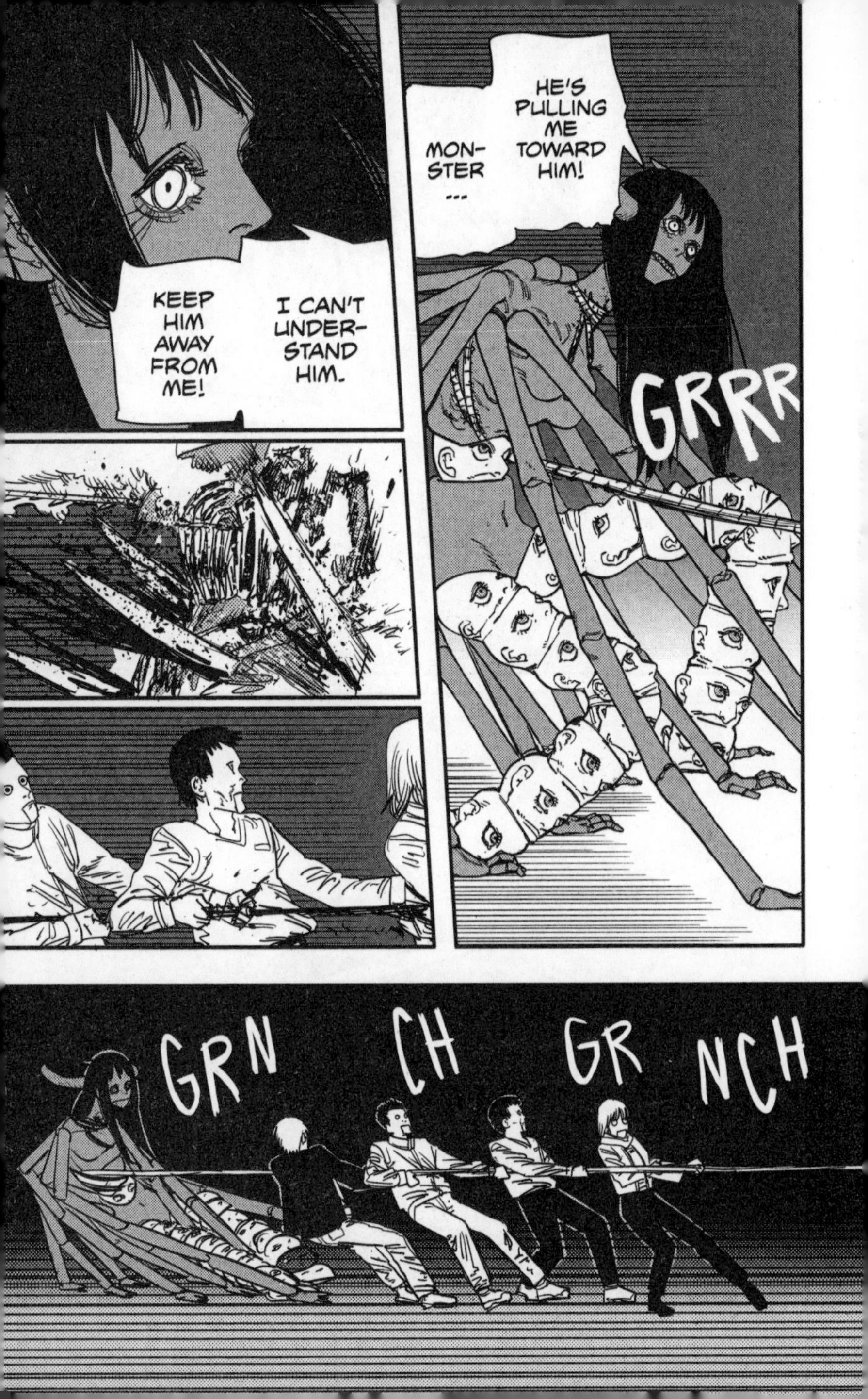
HE'S PULLING ME TOWARD HIM!
MON-STER...
GRRR
I CAN'T UNDER-STAND HIM.
KEEP HIM AWAY FROM ME!
GRN CH GR NCH

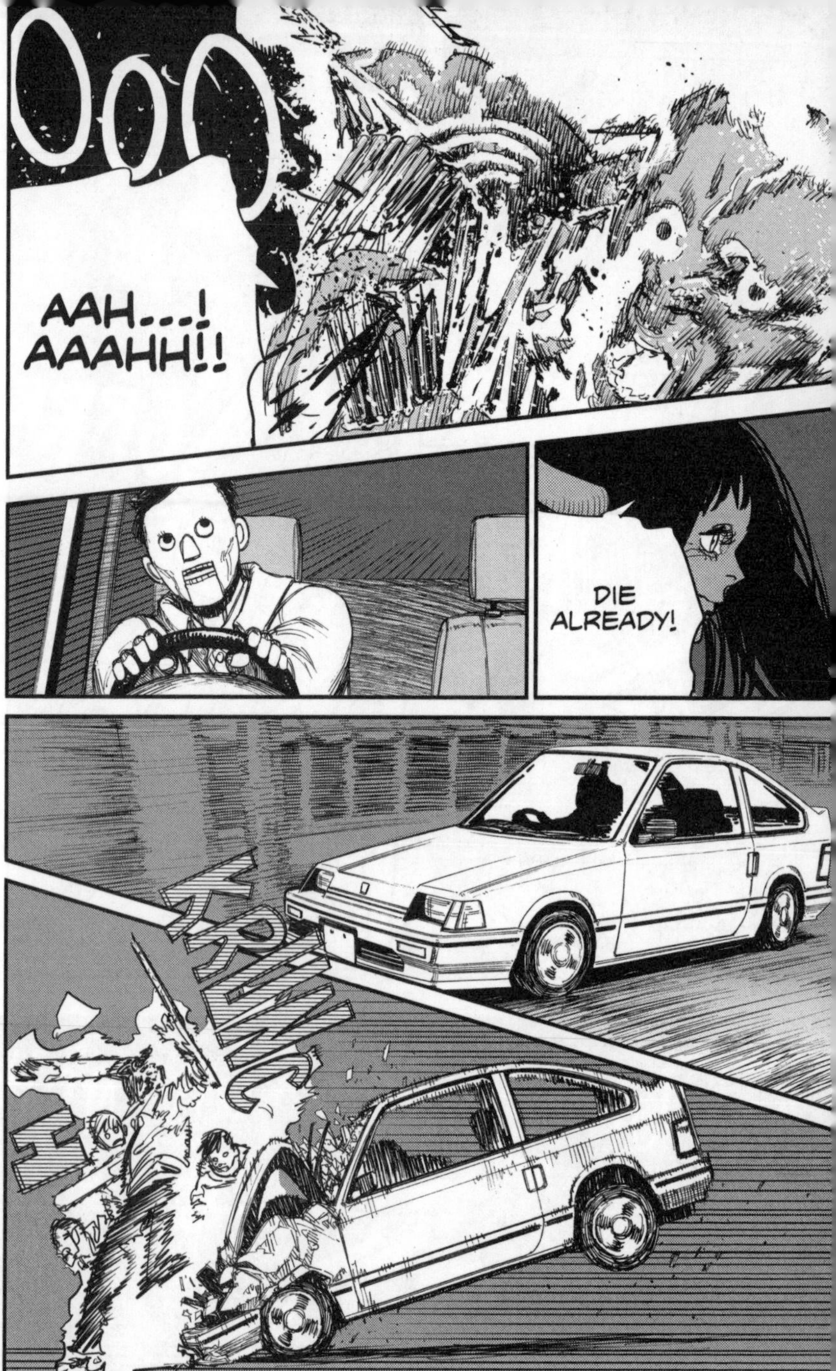
AAH...!
AAAHH!!
DIE ALREADY!
KRUNCH

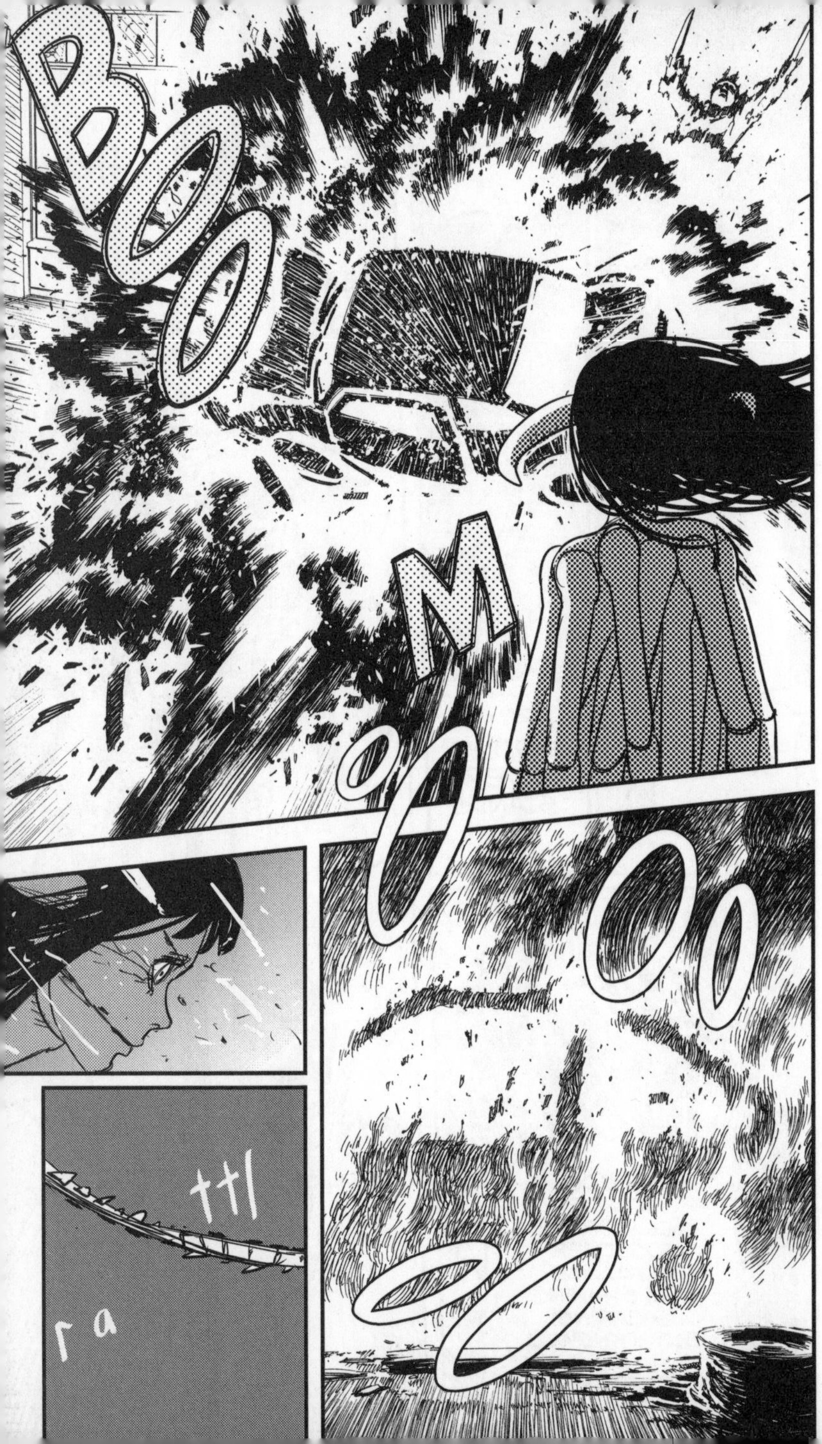
BOOOM

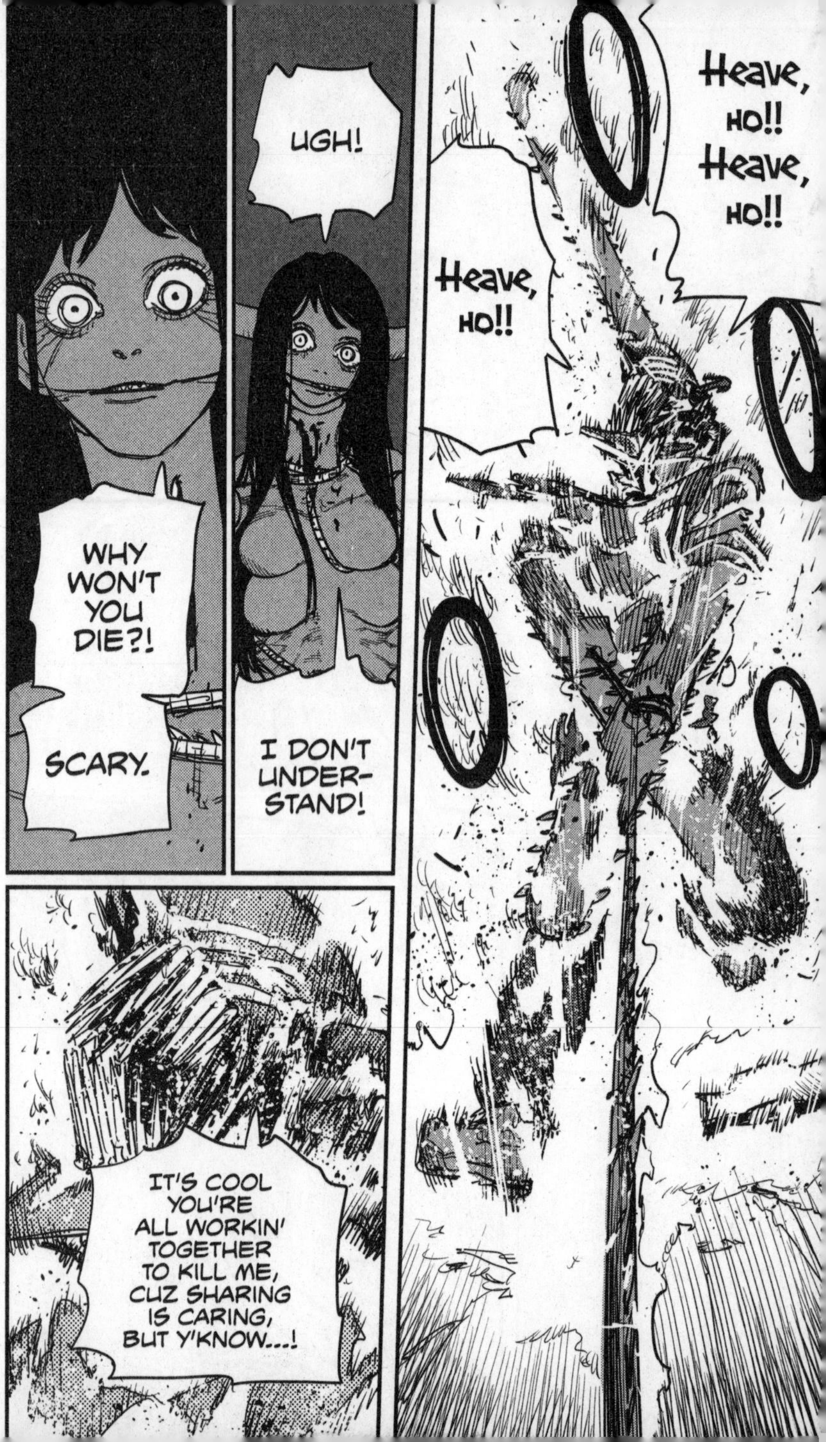
Heave, HO!! Heave, HO!!
Heave, HO!!
UGH!
I DON'T UNDERSTAND!
WHY WON'T YOU DIE?!
SCARY.
IT'S COOL YOU'RE ALL WORKIN' TOGETHER TO KILL ME, CUZ SHARING IS CARING, BUT Y'KNOW...!

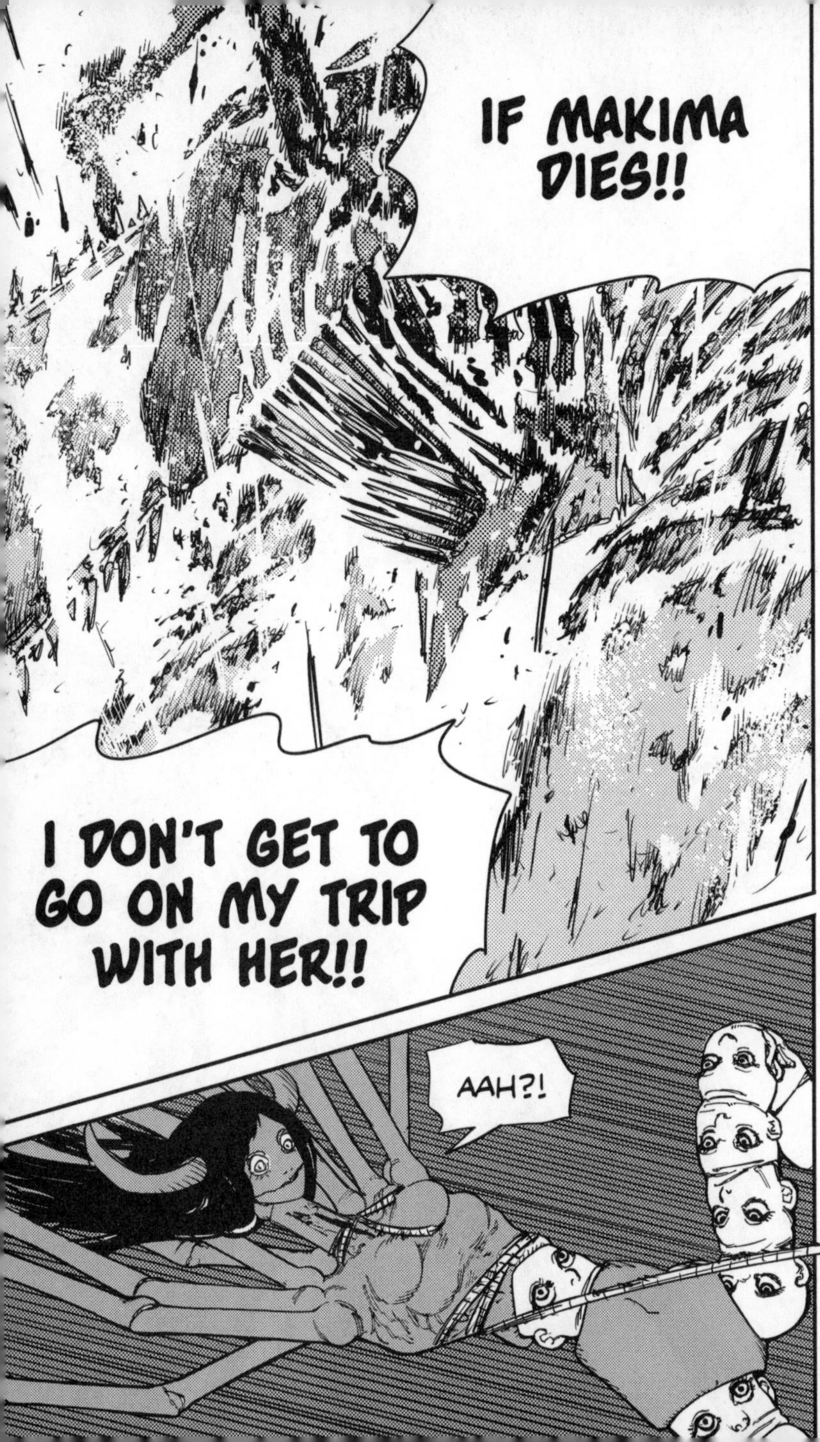
IF MAKIMA DIES!!
I DON'T GET TO GO ON MY TRIP WITH HER!!
AAH?!

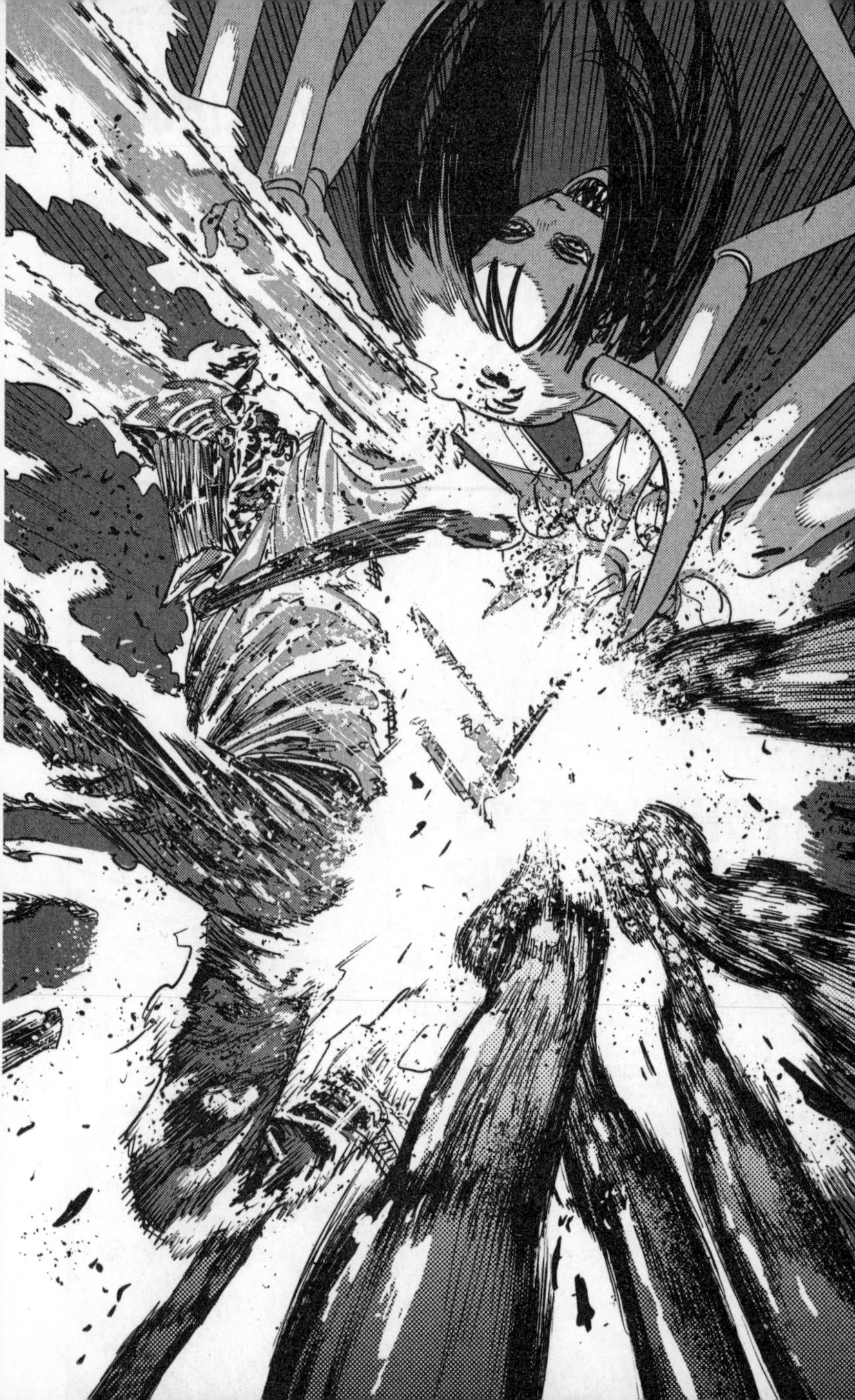

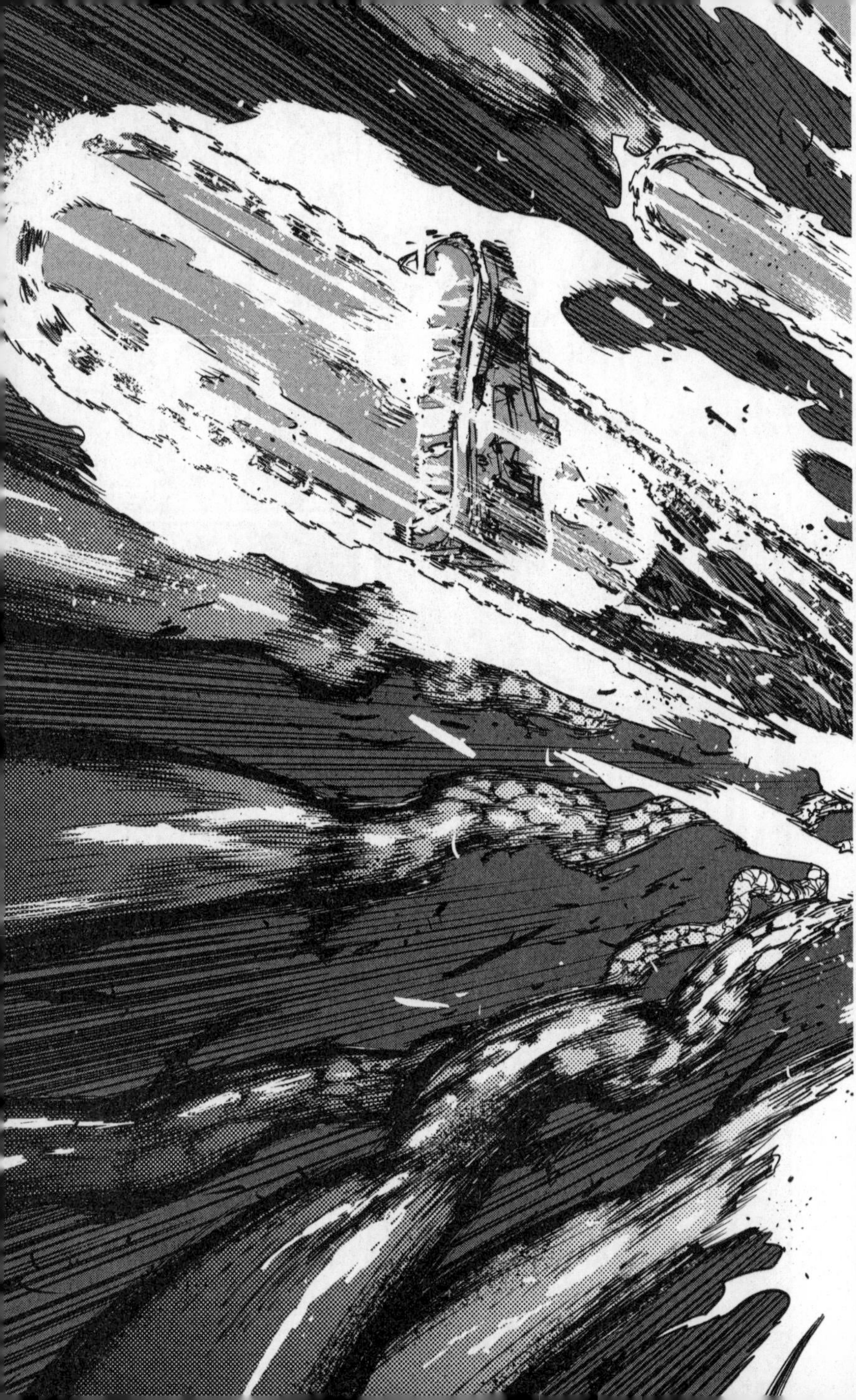

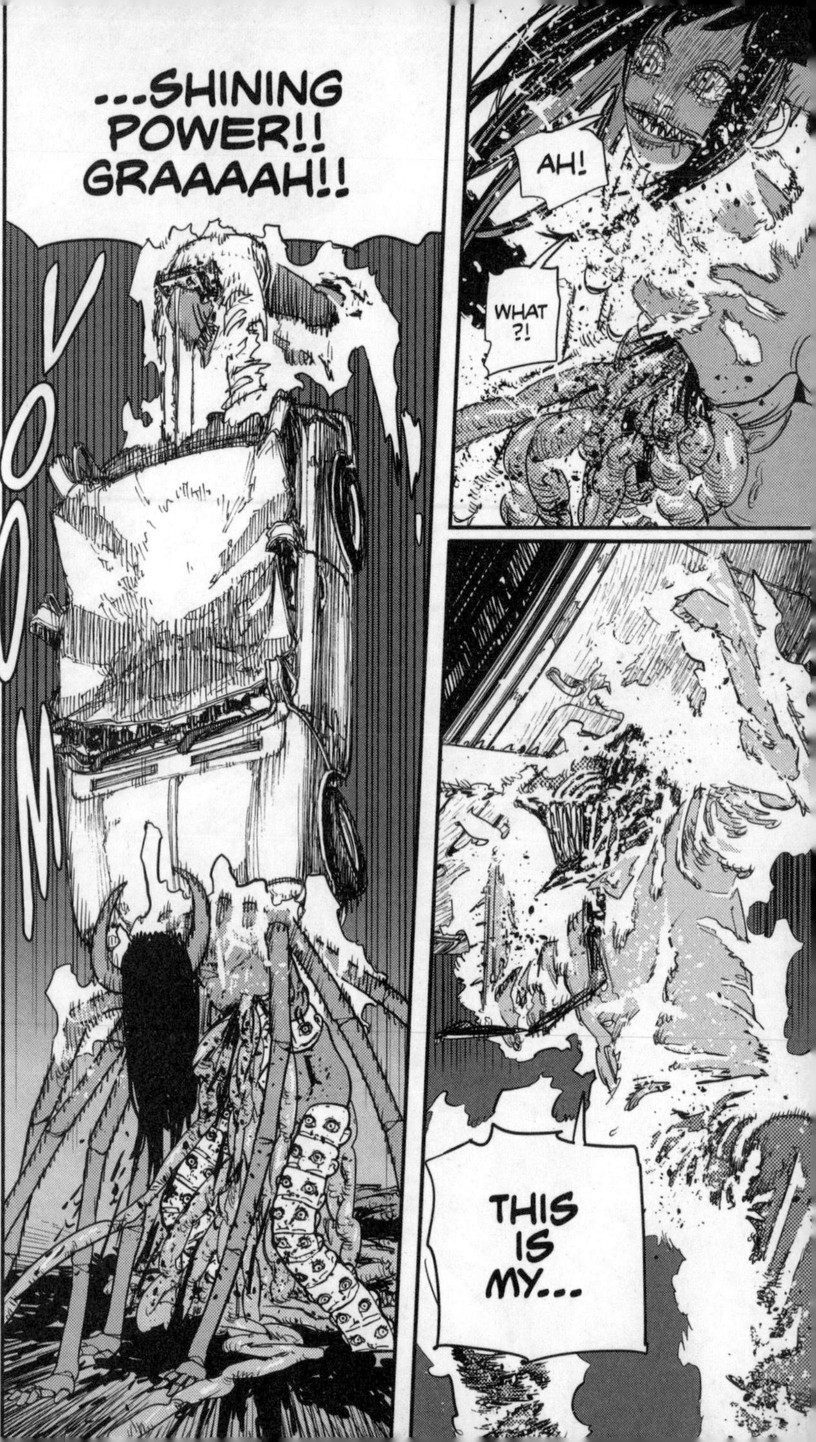
AH!
WHAT?!
THIS IS MY...
...SHINING POWER!! GRAAAAH!!
VOOM

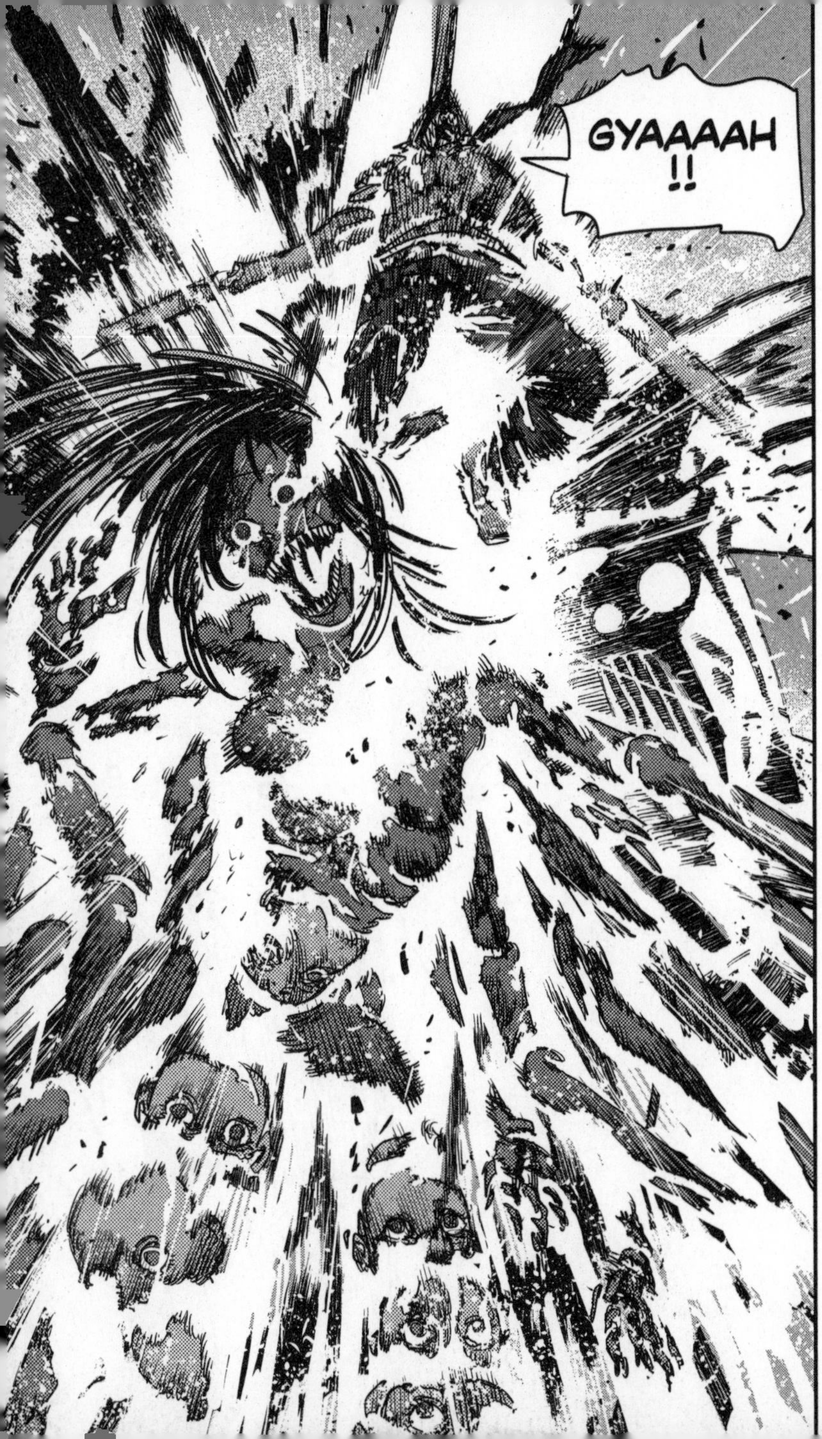
GYAAAAH !!

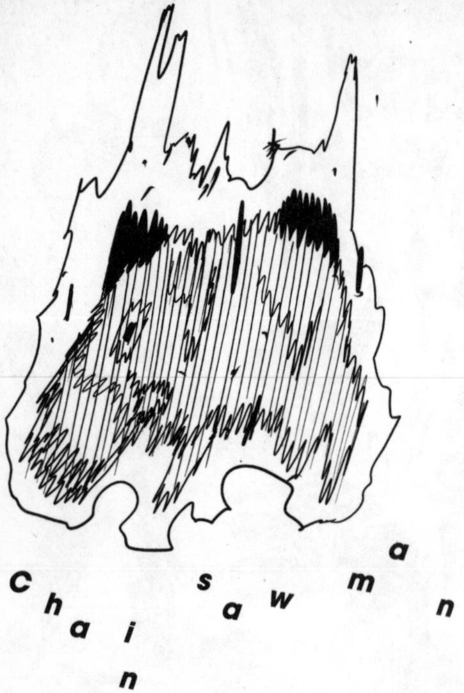
Chainsaw man

SPLATTER

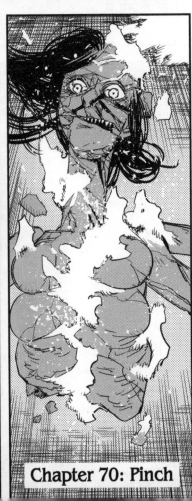

Chapter 70: Pinch

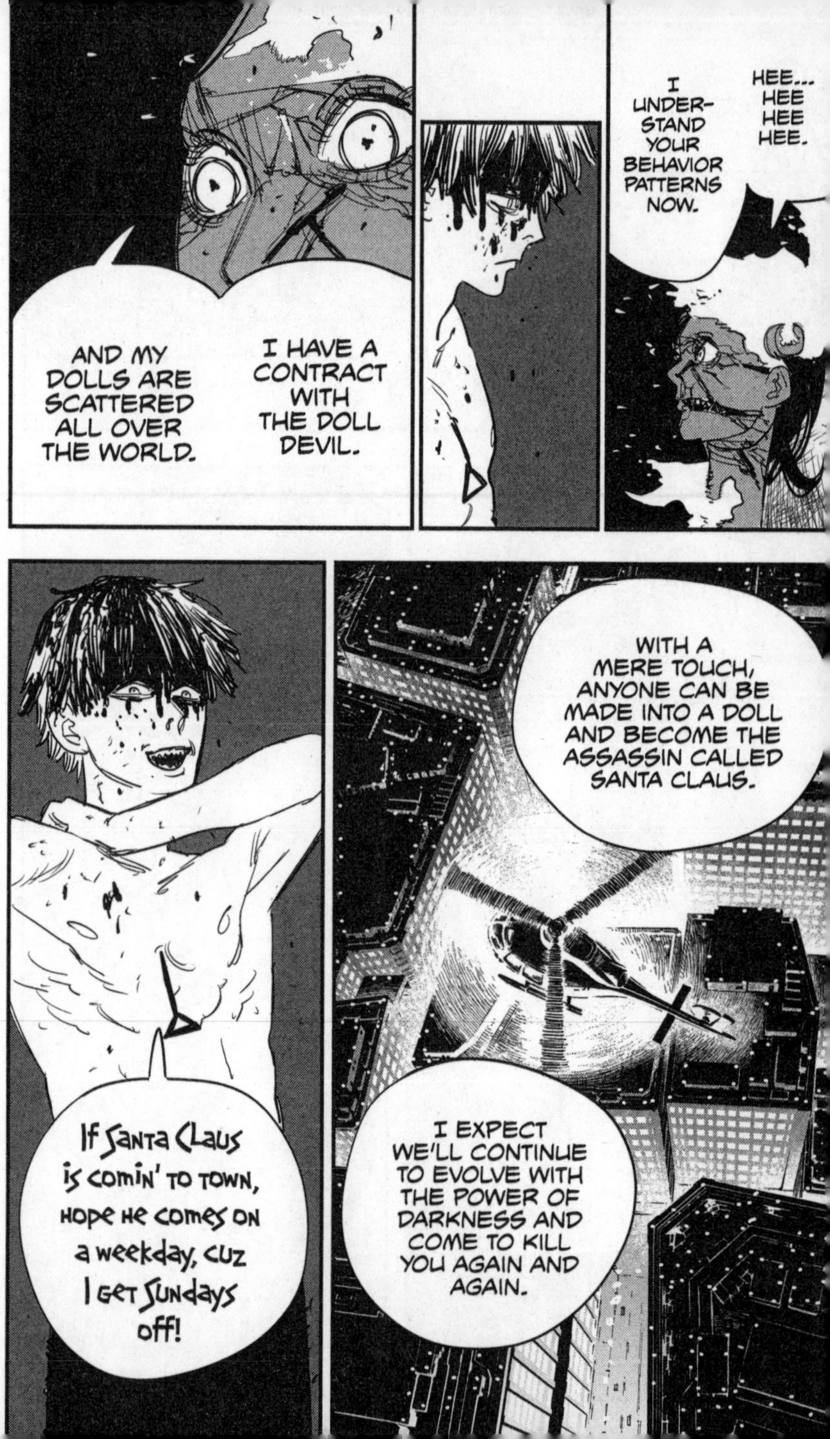
HEE... HEE HEE HEE.
I UNDERSTAND YOUR BEHAVIOR PATTERNS NOW.
I HAVE A CONTRACT WITH THE DOLL DEVIL.
AND MY DOLLS ARE SCATTERED ALL OVER THE WORLD.
WITH A MERE TOUCH, ANYONE CAN BE MADE INTO A DOLL AND BECOME THE ASSASSIN CALLED SANTA CLAUS.
I EXPECT WE'LL CONTINUE TO EVOLVE WITH THE POWER OF DARKNESS AND COME TO KILL YOU AGAIN AND AGAIN.
If Santa Claus is comin' to town, hope he comes on a weekday, cuz I get Sundays off!

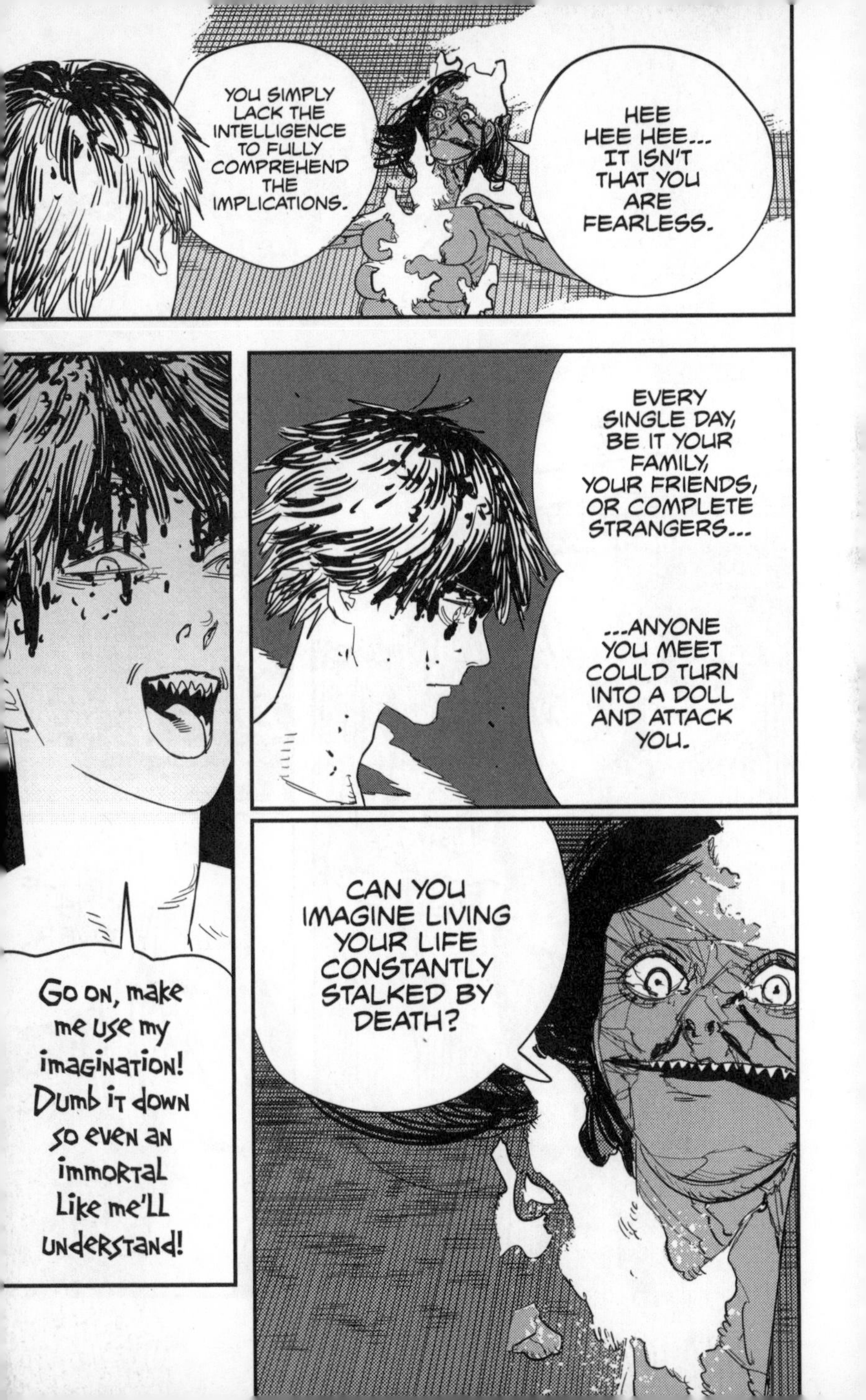
HEE HEE HEE... IT ISN'T THAT YOU ARE FEARLESS.
YOU SIMPLY LACK THE INTELLIGENCE TO FULLY COMPREHEND THE IMPLICATIONS.
EVERY SINGLE DAY, BE IT YOUR FAMILY, YOUR FRIENDS, OR COMPLETE STRANGERS...
...ANYONE YOU MEET COULD TURN INTO A DOLL AND ATTACK YOU.
CAN YOU IMAGINE LIVING YOUR LIFE CONSTANTLY STALKED BY DEATH?
Go on, make me use my imagination! Dumb it down so even an immortal like me'll understand!

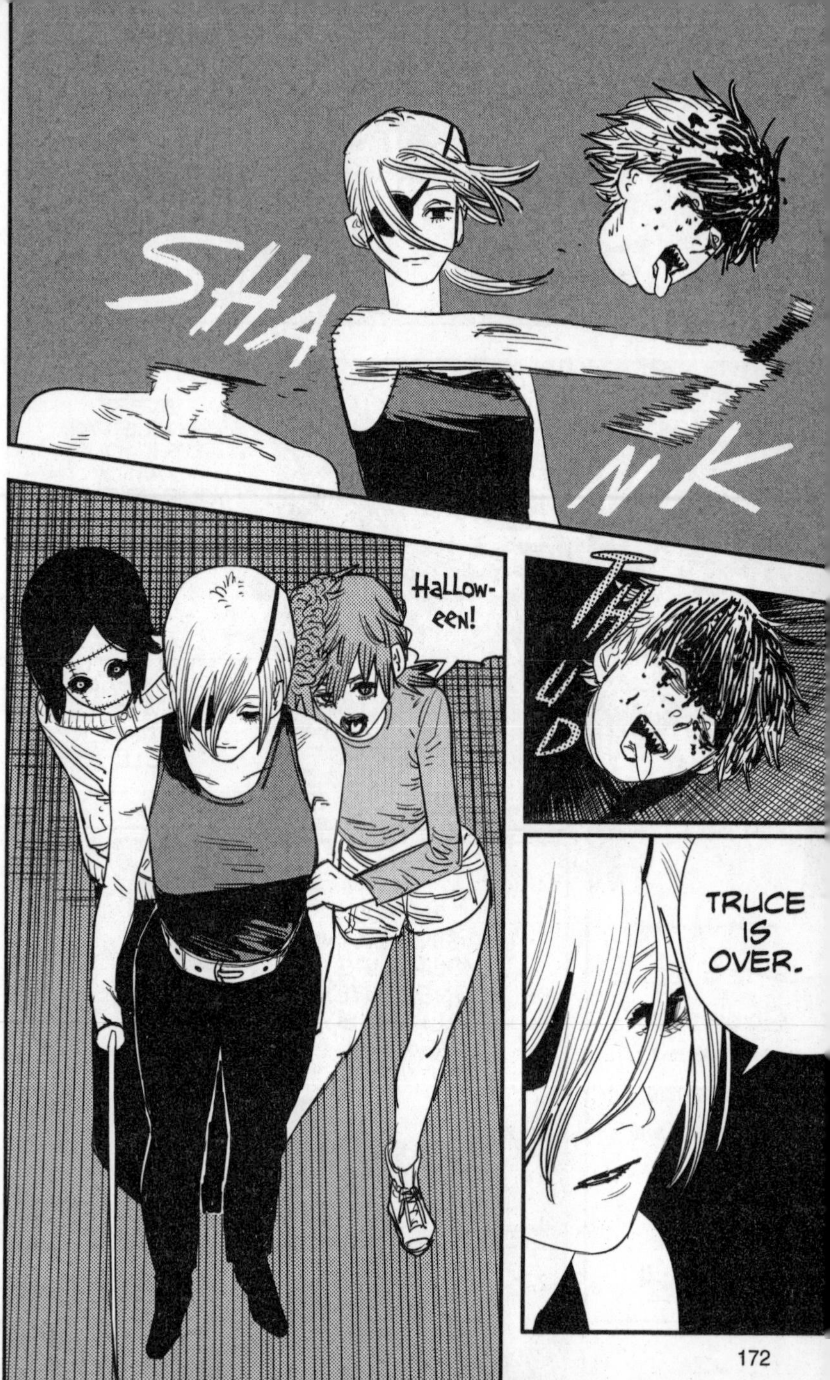
SHANK
THUD
TRUCE IS OVER.
Hallow-een!

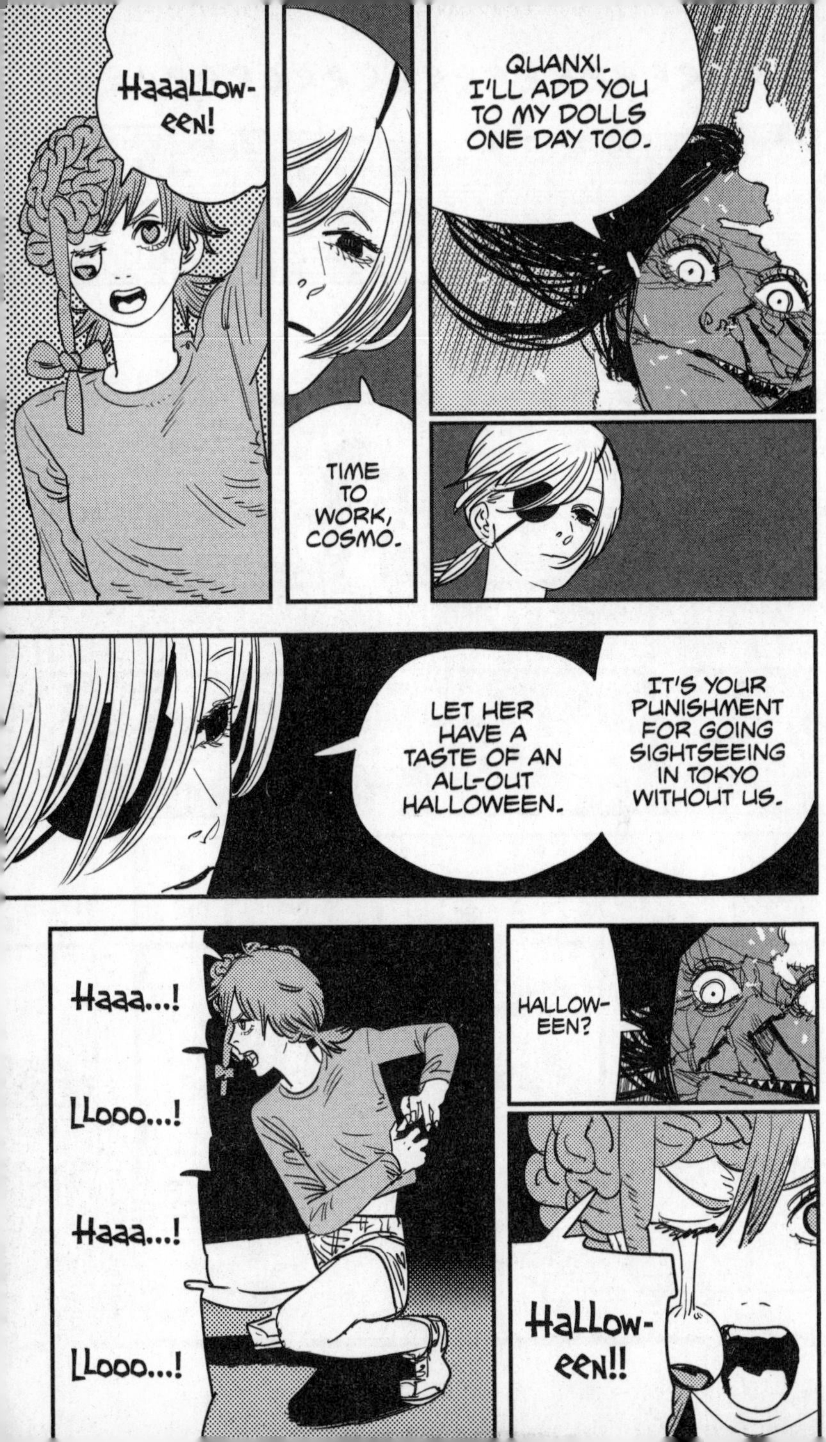
QUANXI. I'LL ADD YOU TO MY DOLLS ONE DAY TOO.
TIME TO WORK, COSMO.
Haaallow-een!
IT'S YOUR PUNISHMENT FOR GOING SIGHTSEEING IN TOKYO WITHOUT US.
LET HER HAVE A TASTE OF AN ALL-OUT HALLOWEEN.
HALLOW-EEN?
Hallow-een!!
Haaa...!
Llooo...!
Haaa...!
Llooo...!

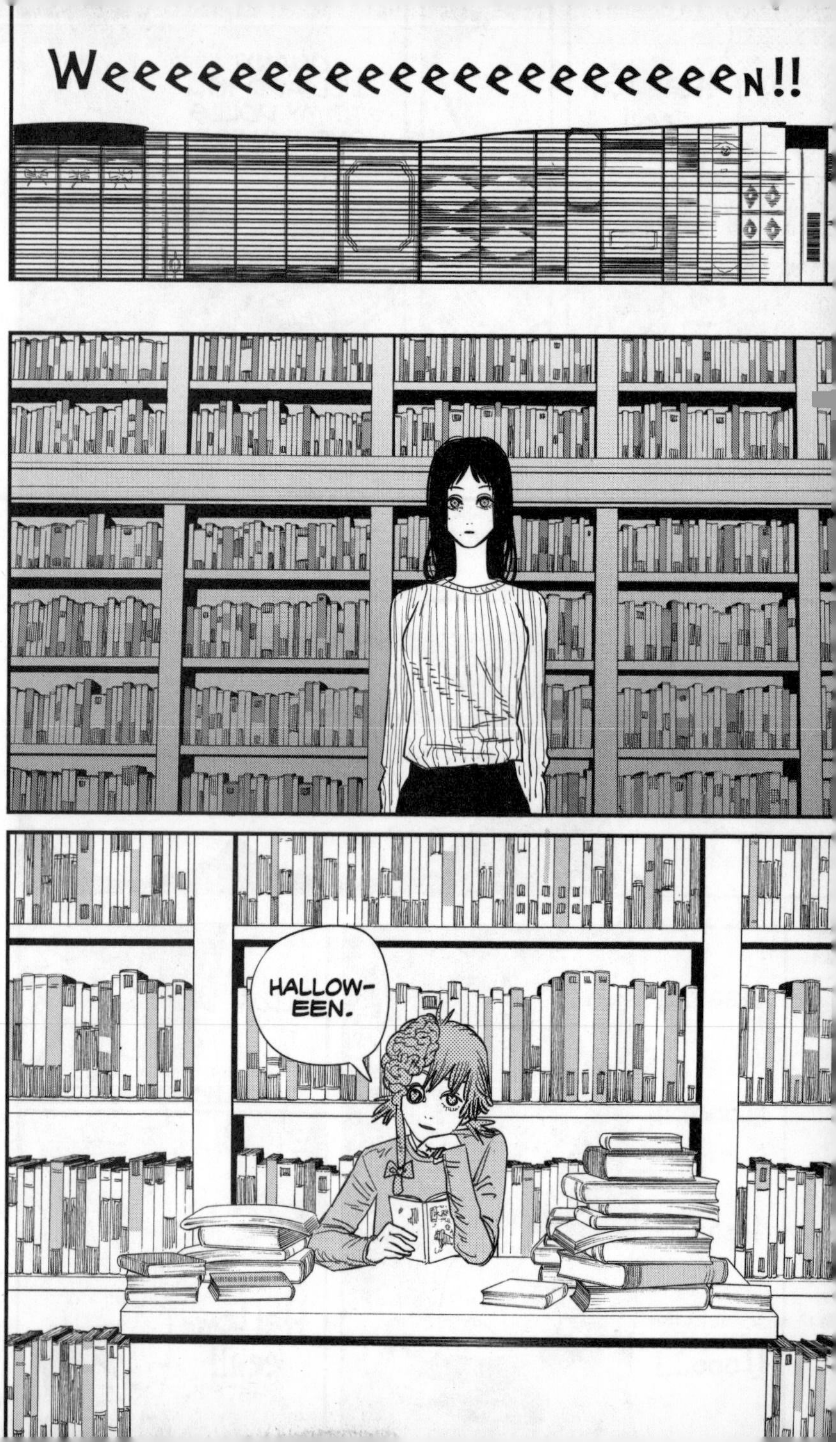
WEEEEEEEEEEEEEEEEEEEEEEEEN!!
HALLOW-EEN.

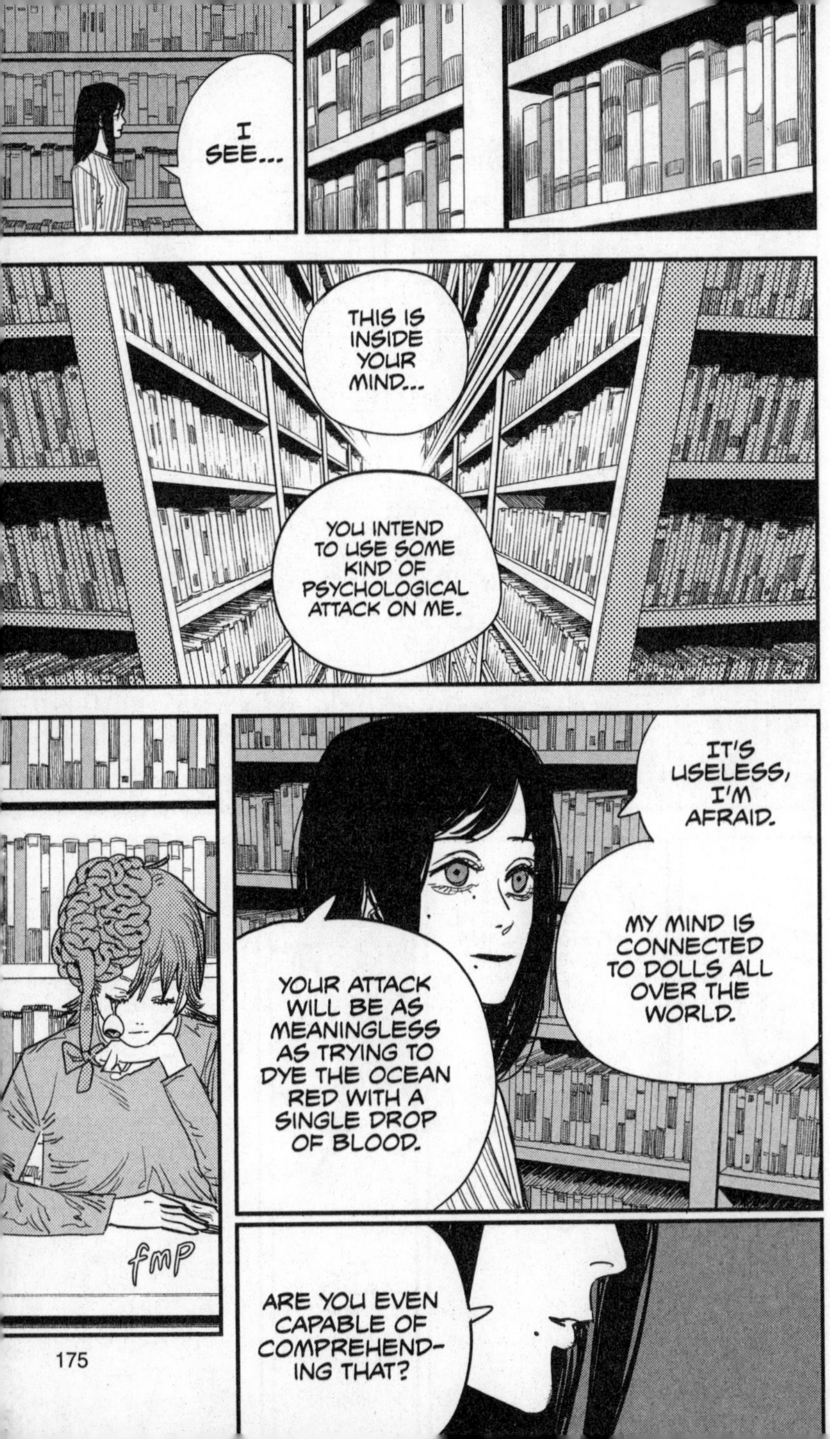
I SEE...
THIS IS INSIDE YOUR MIND...
YOU INTEND TO USE SOME KIND OF PSYCHOLOGICAL ATTACK ON ME.
IT'S USELESS, I'M AFRAID.
MY MIND IS CONNECTED TO DOLLS ALL OVER THE WORLD.
YOUR ATTACK WILL BE AS MEANINGLESS AS TRYING TO DYE THE OCEAN RED WITH A SINGLE DROP OF BLOOD.
ARE YOU EVEN CAPABLE OF COMPREHENDING THAT?
fmp

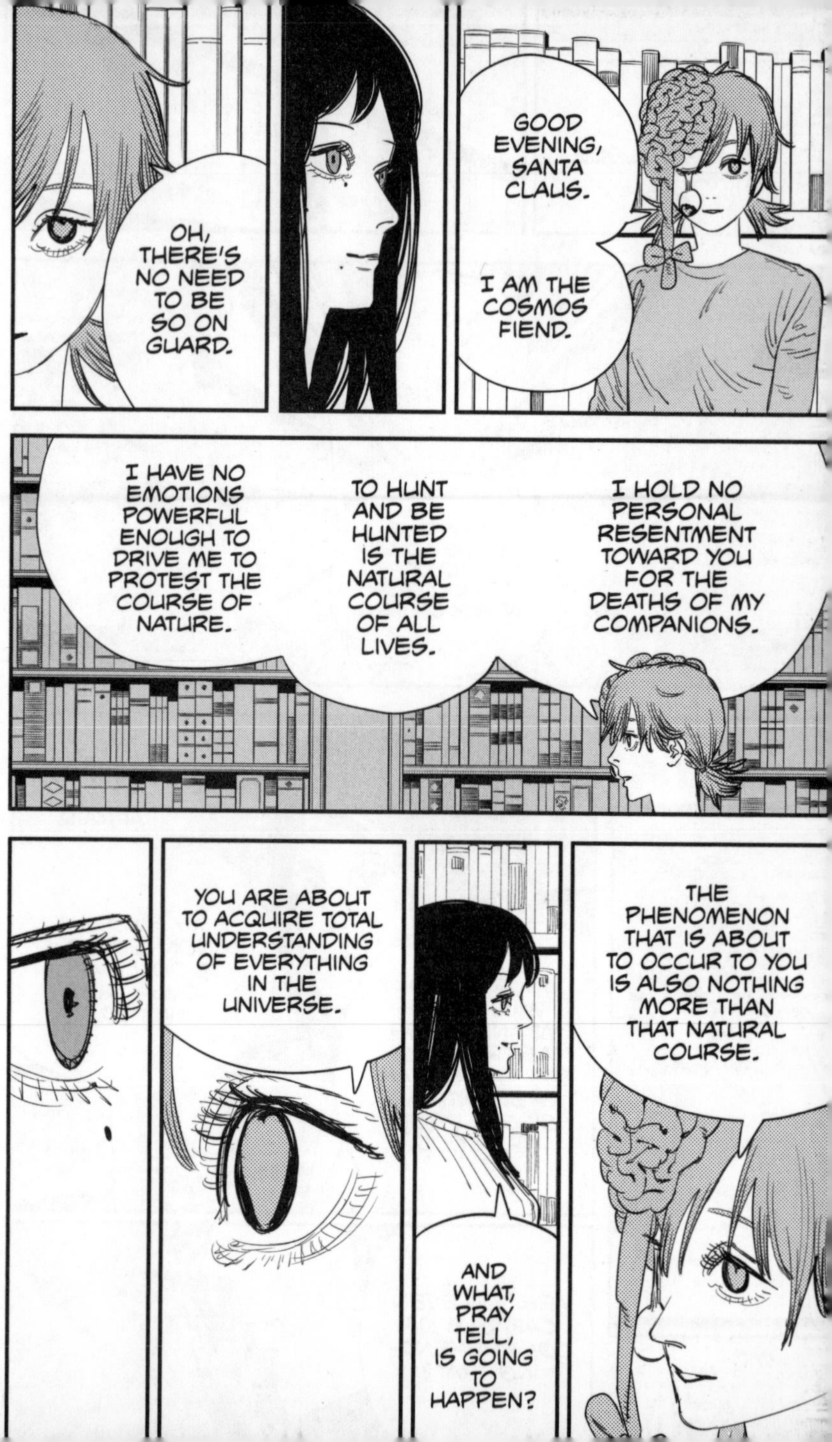
GOOD EVENING, SANTA CLAUS.
I AM THE COSMOS FIEND.
OH, THERE'S NO NEED TO BE SO ON GUARD.
I HOLD NO PERSONAL RESENTMENT TOWARD YOU FOR THE DEATHS OF MY COMPANIONS.
TO HUNT AND BE HUNTED IS THE NATURAL COURSE OF ALL LIVES.
I HAVE NO EMOTIONS POWERFUL ENOUGH TO DRIVE ME TO PROTEST THE COURSE OF NATURE.
THE PHENOMENON THAT IS ABOUT TO OCCUR TO YOU IS ALSO NOTHING MORE THAN THAT NATURAL COURSE.
AND WHAT, PRAY TELL, IS GOING TO HAPPEN?
YOU ARE ABOUT TO ACQUIRE TOTAL UNDERSTANDING OF EVERYTHING IN THE UNIVERSE.

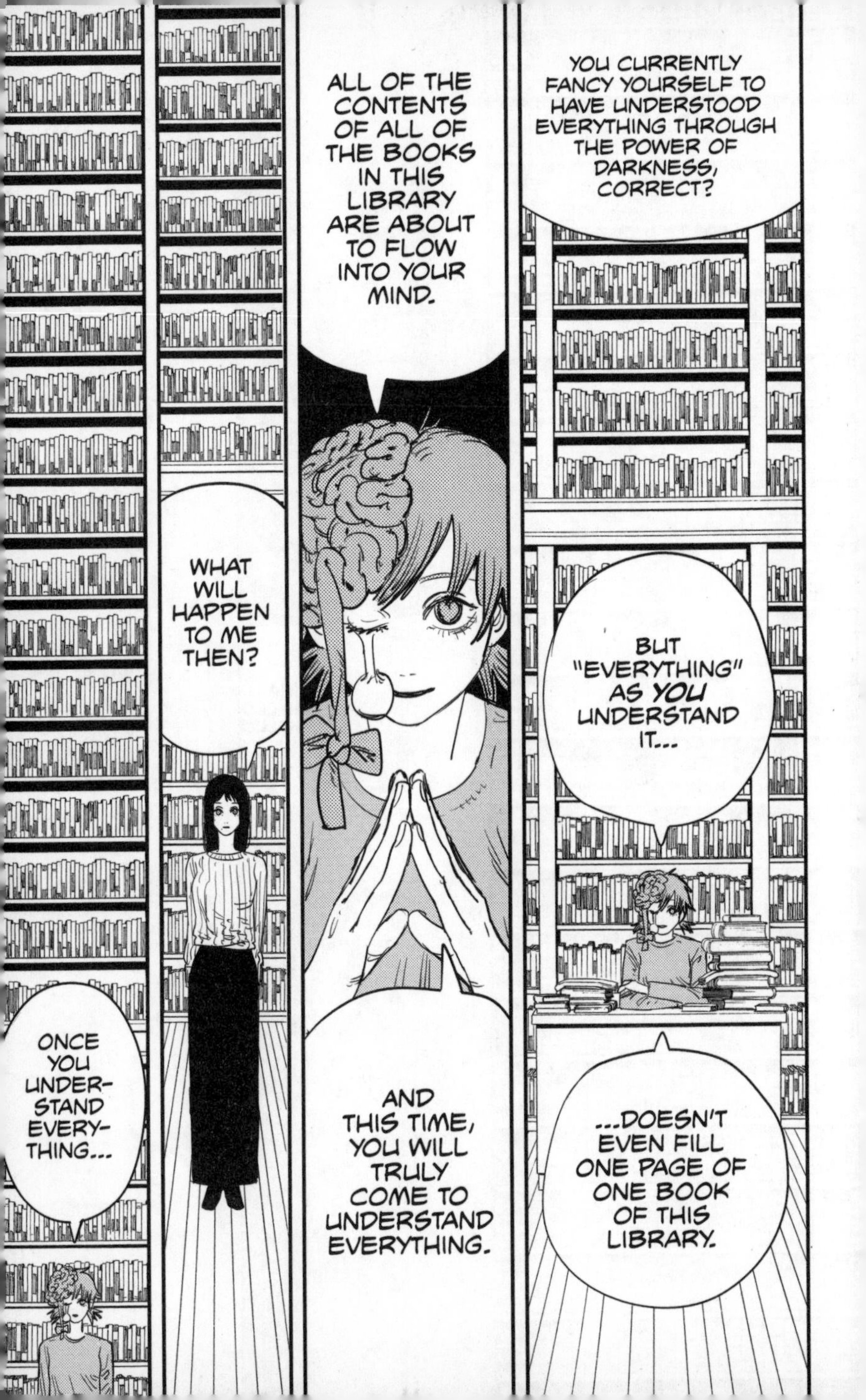
YOU CURRENTLY FANCY YOURSELF TO HAVE UNDERSTOOD EVERYTHING THROUGH THE POWER OF DARKNESS, CORRECT?
BUT "EVERYTHING" AS *YOU* UNDERSTAND IT...
...DOESN'T EVEN FILL ONE PAGE OF ONE BOOK OF THIS LIBRARY.
ALL OF THE CONTENTS OF ALL OF THE BOOKS IN THIS LIBRARY ARE ABOUT TO FLOW INTO YOUR MIND.
AND THIS TIME, YOU WILL TRULY COME TO UNDERSTAND EVERYTHING.
WHAT WILL HAPPEN TO ME THEN?
ONCE YOU UNDER-STAND EVERY-THING...

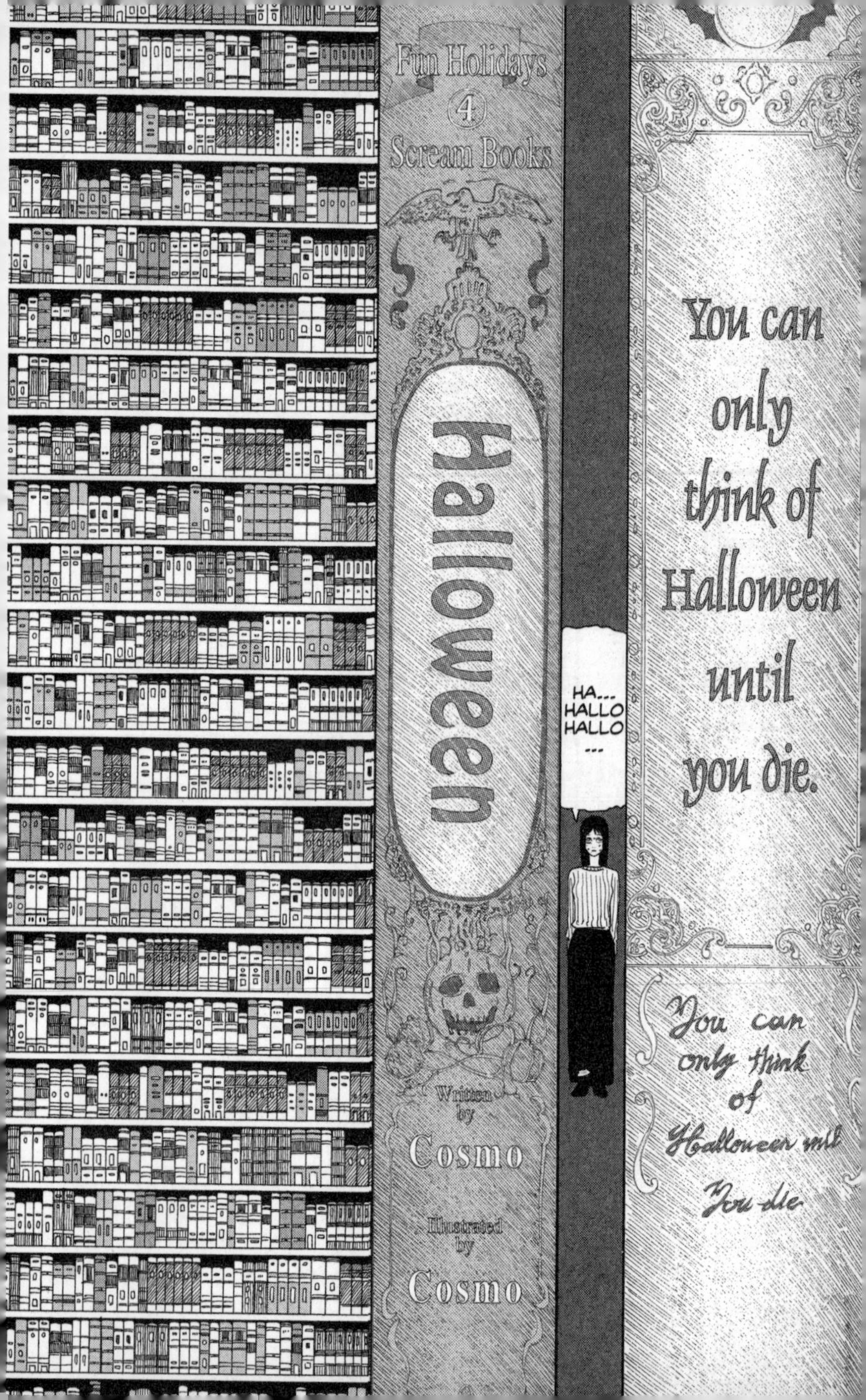
You can only think of Halloween until you die.
You can
only think
of
Halloween util
You die
HA... HALLO HALLO ...
Fun Holidays
4
Scream Books
Halloween
Written by
Cosmo
Illustrated by
Cosmo

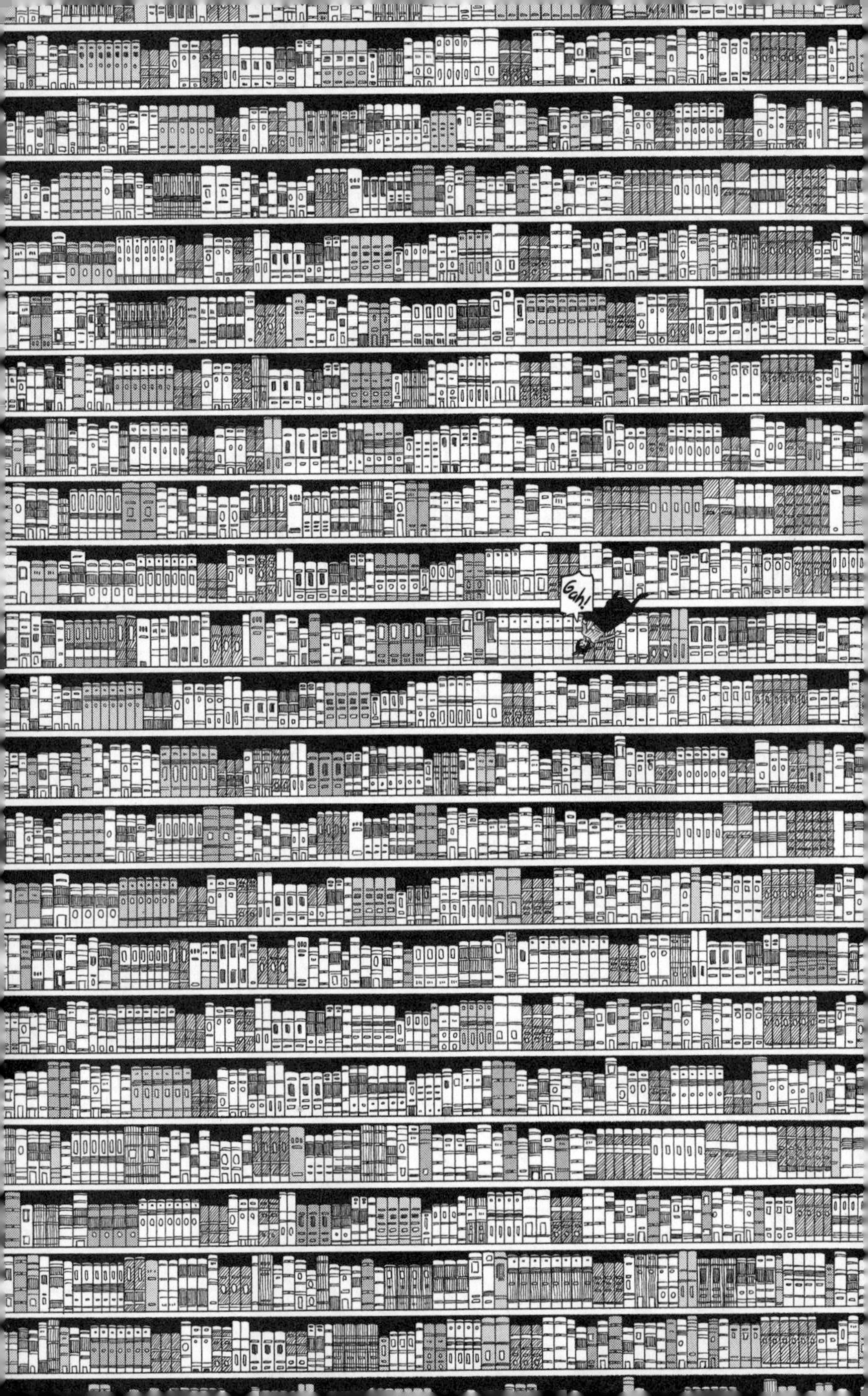
Gah!

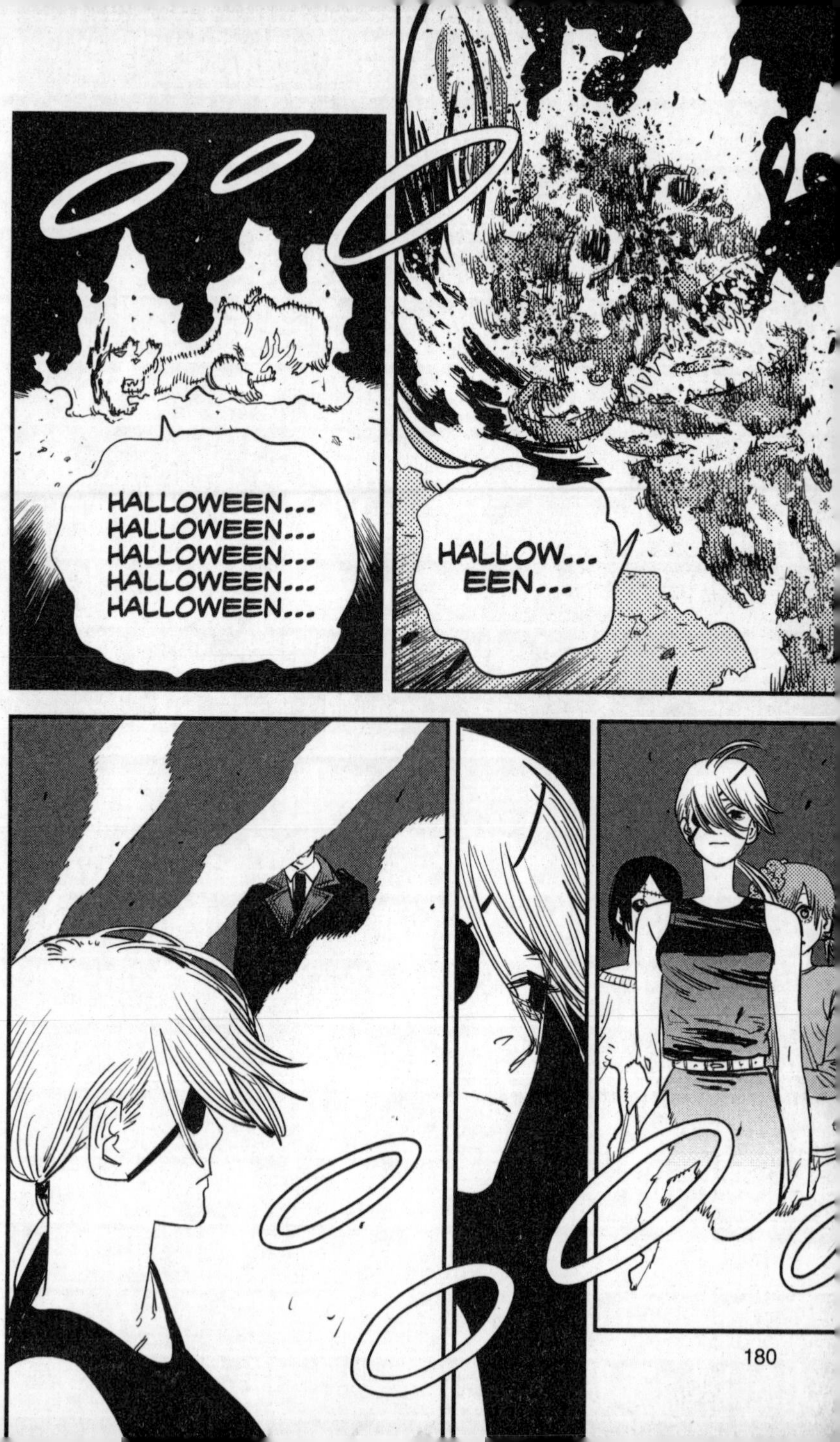
HALLOW... EEN...
HALLOWEEN... HALLOWEEN... HALLOWEEN... HALLOWEEN... HALLOWEEN...

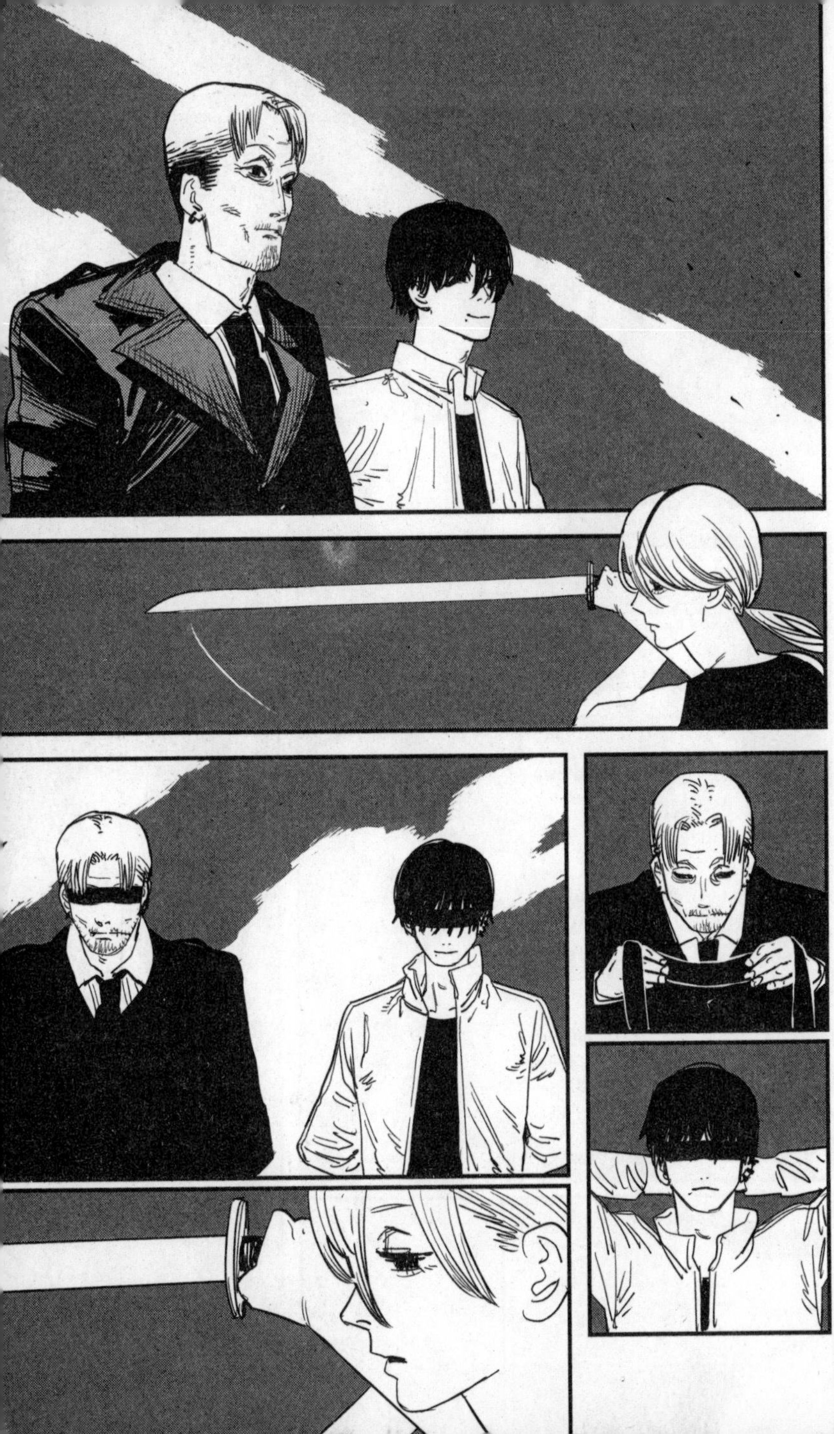

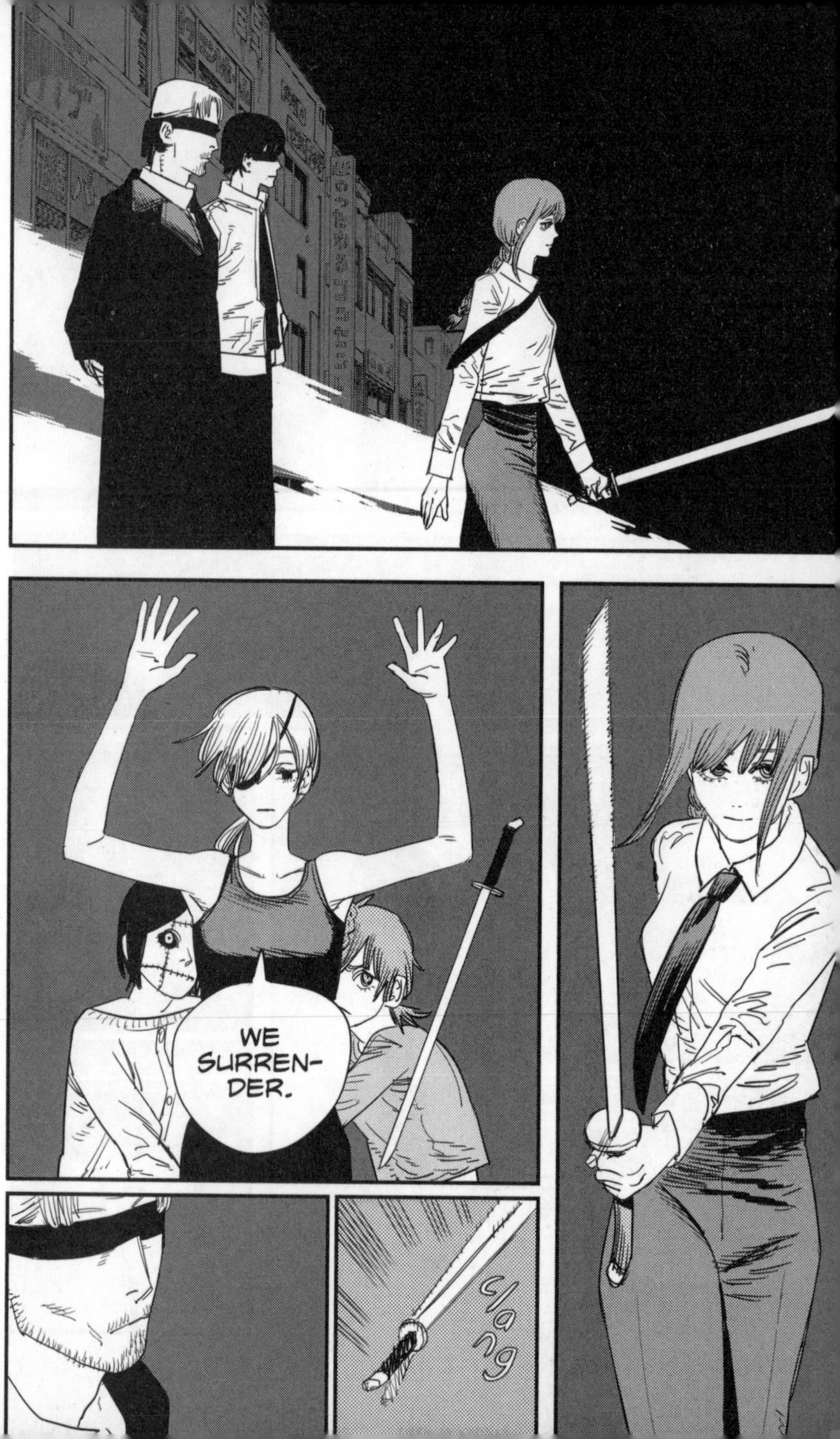
WE SURREN-DER.
clang

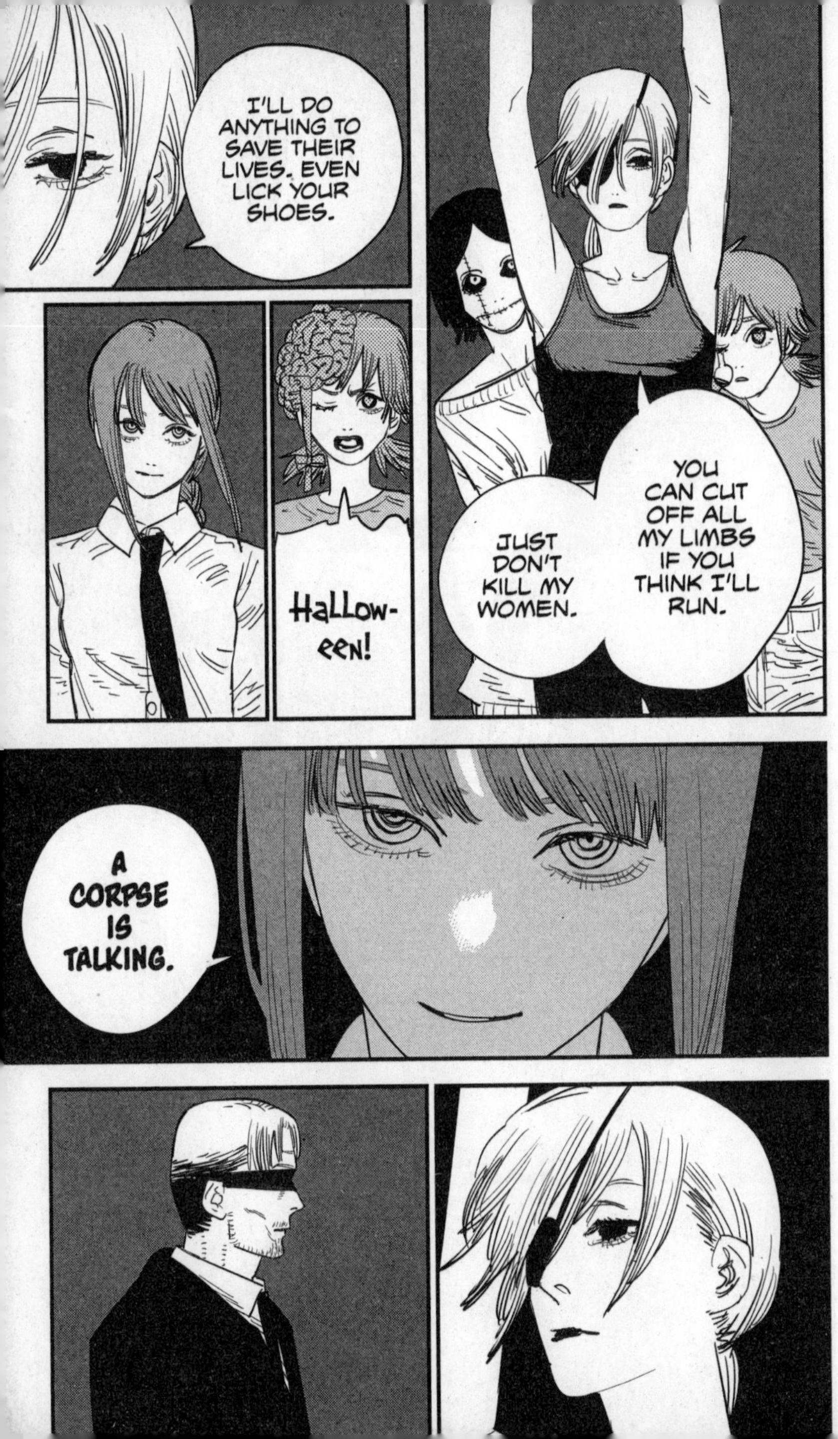
YOU CAN CUT OFF ALL MY LIMBS IF YOU THINK I'LL RUN.
JUST DON'T KILL MY WOMEN.
I'LL DO ANYTHING TO SAVE THEIR LIVES. EVEN LICK YOUR SHOES.
Hallow-een!
A CORPSE IS TALKING.

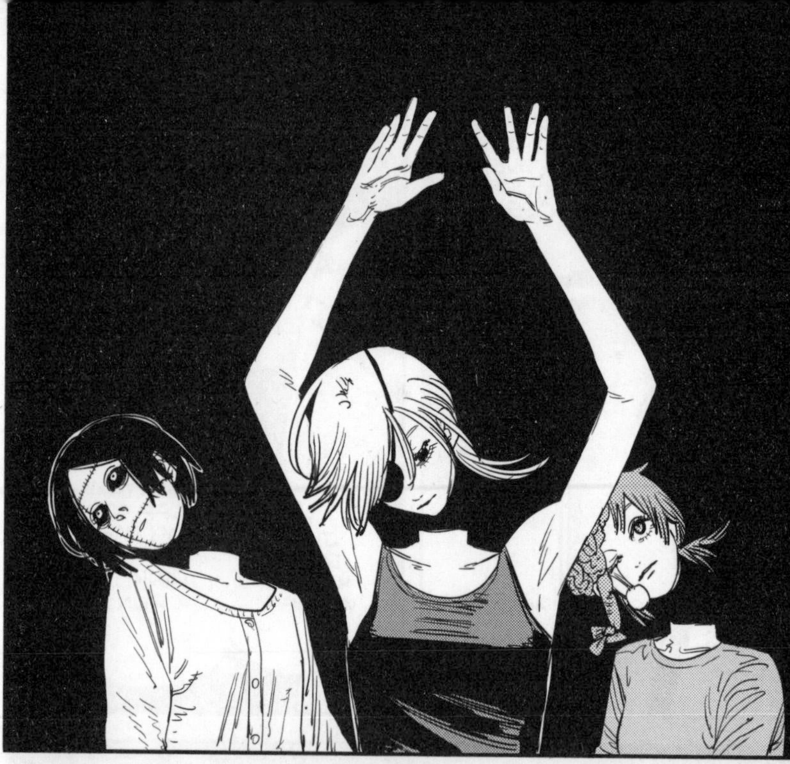

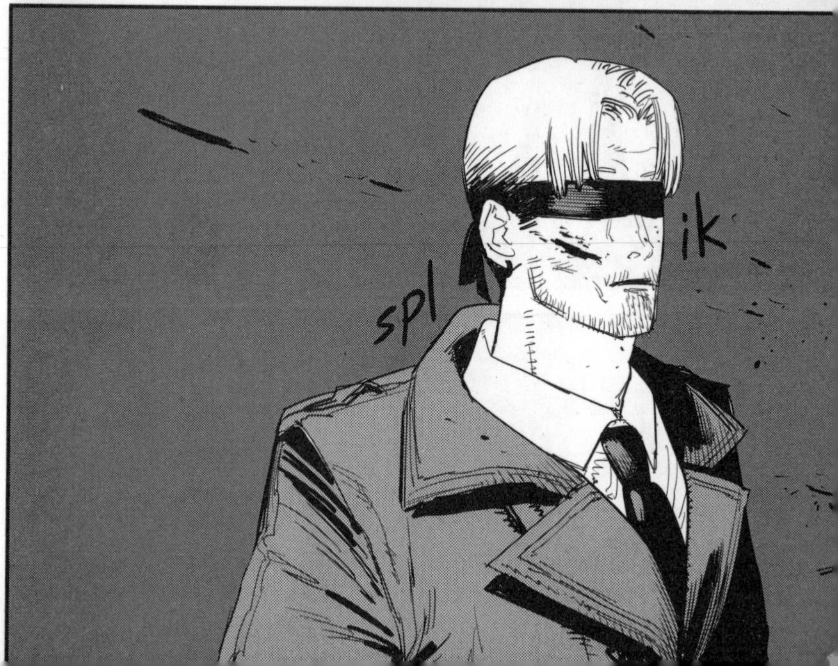
spl
ik

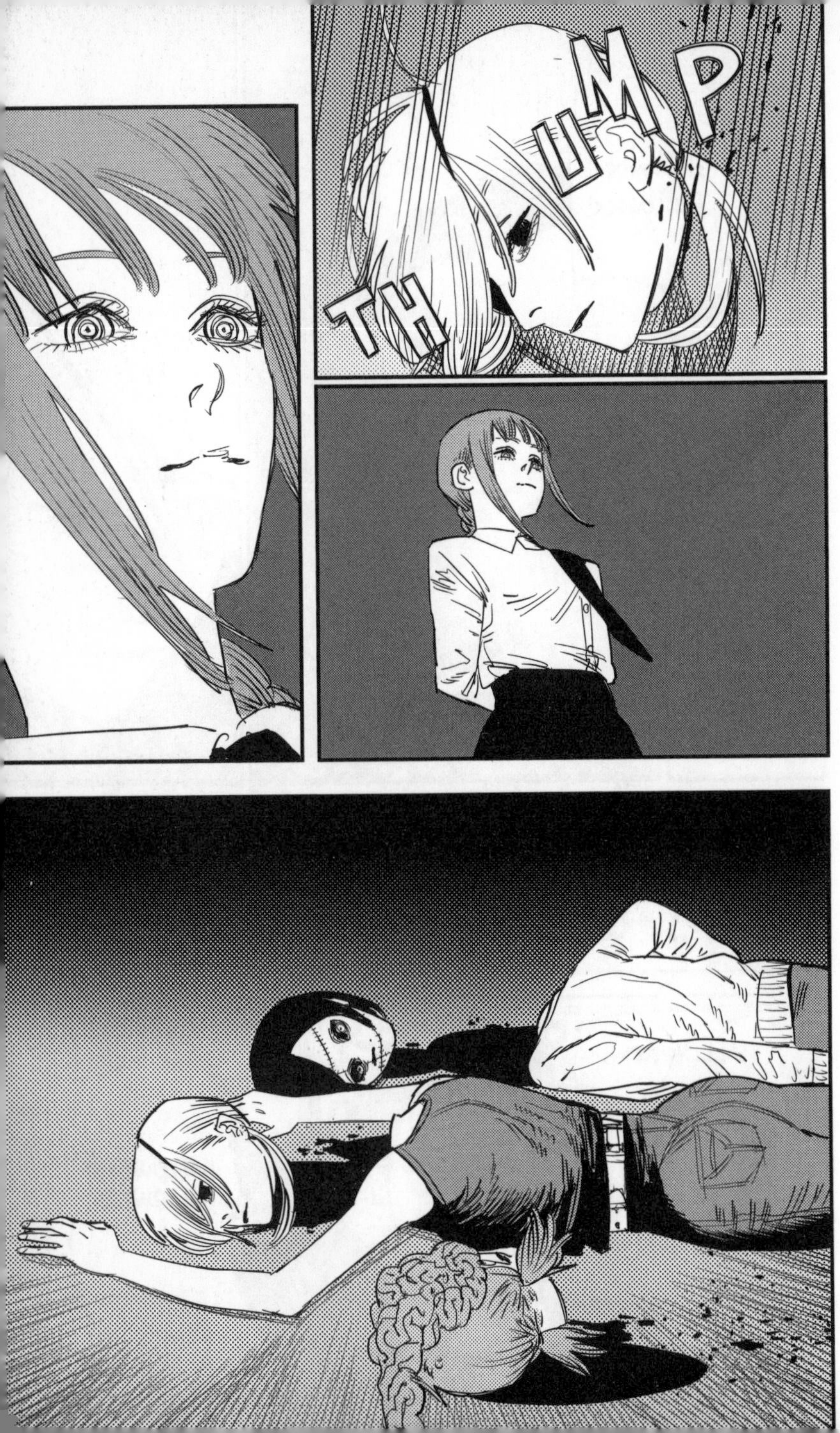
THUMP

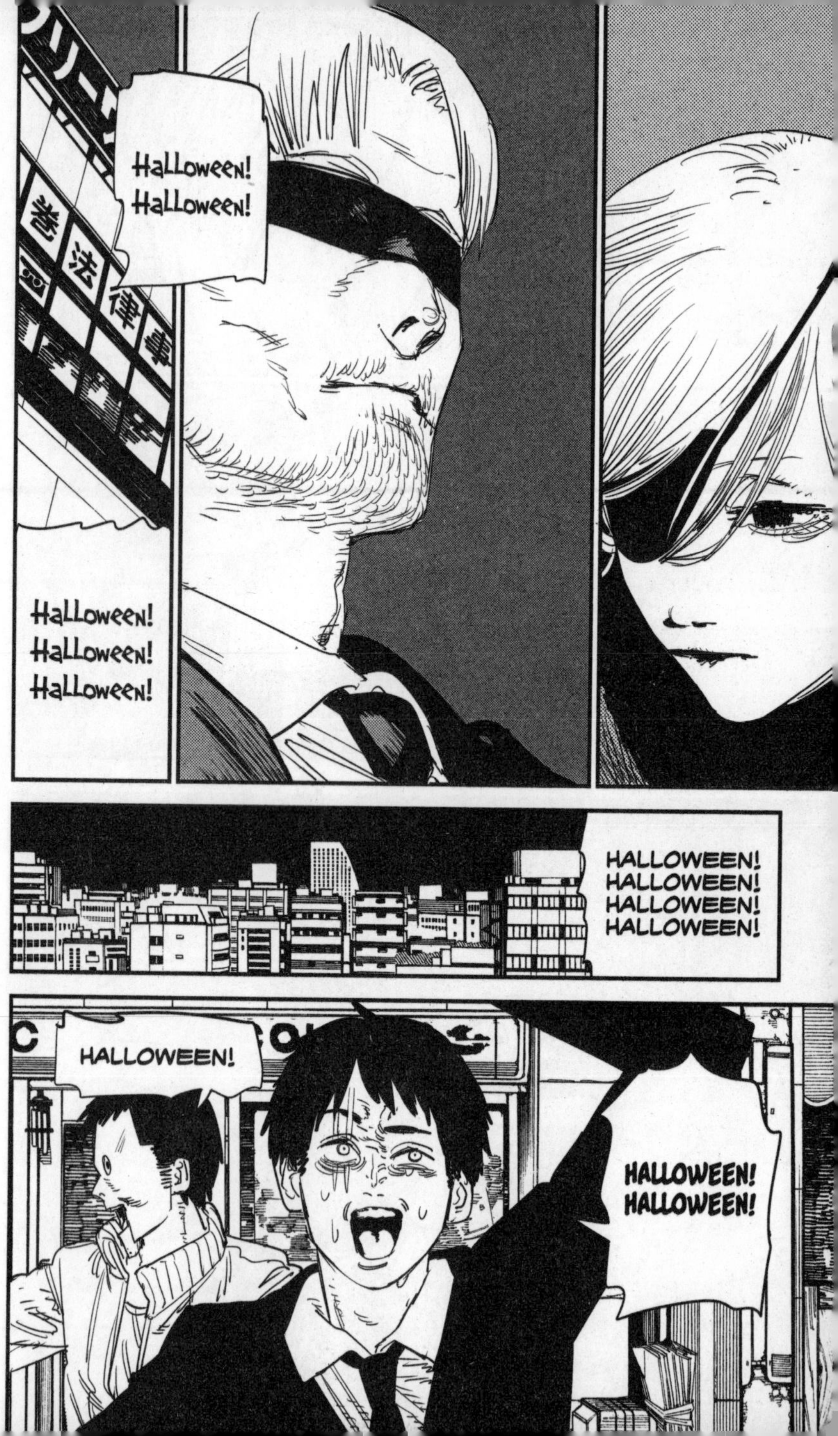
Halloween!
Halloween!
Halloween!
Halloween!
Halloween!
HALLOWEEN!
HALLOWEEN!
HALLOWEEN!
HALLOWEEN!
HALLOWEEN!
HALLOWEEN!
HALLOWEEN!

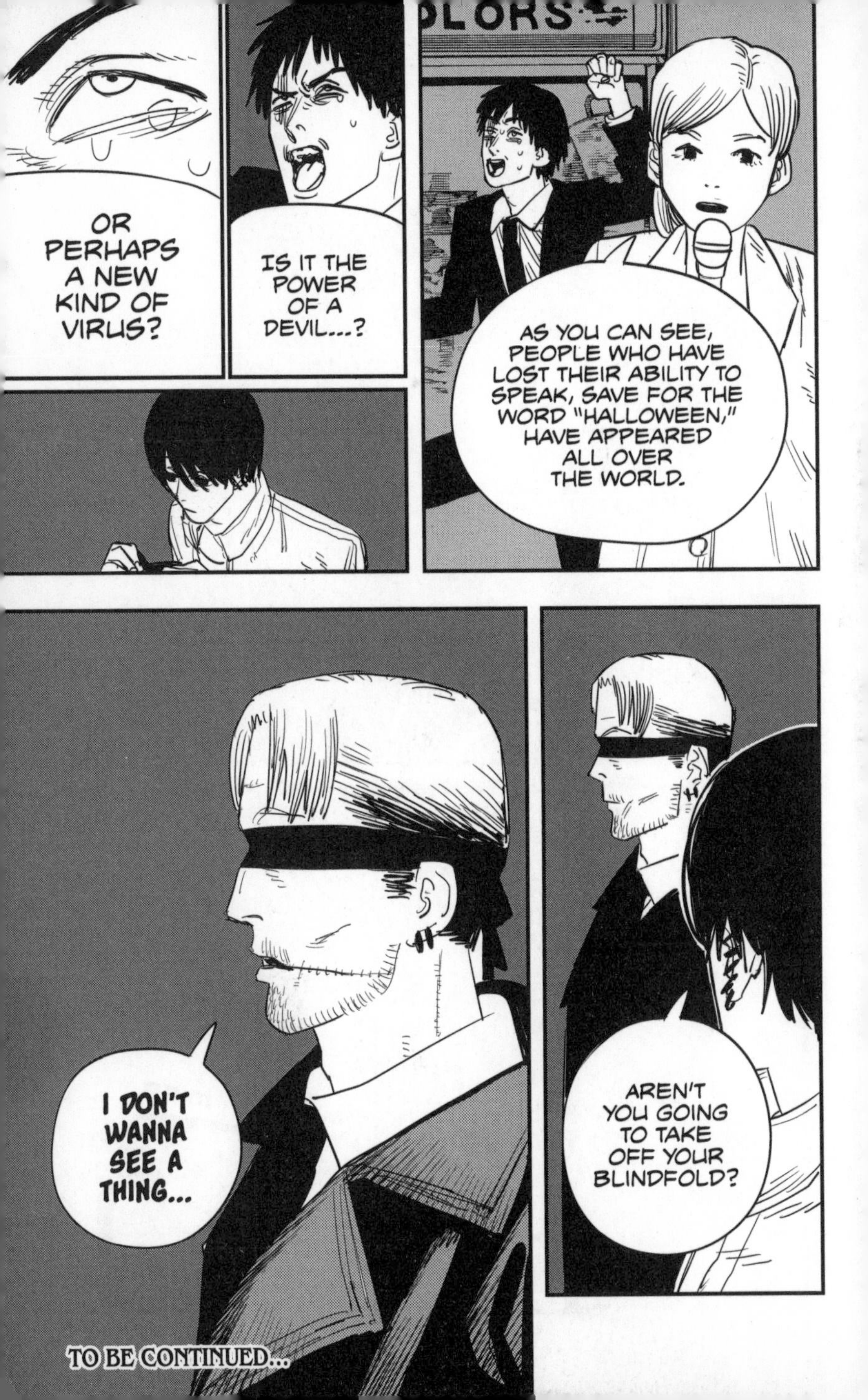
AS YOU CAN SEE, PEOPLE WHO HAVE LOST THEIR ABILITY TO SPEAK, SAVE FOR THE WORD "HALLOWEEN," HAVE APPEARED ALL OVER THE WORLD.
IS IT THE POWER OF A DEVIL...?
OR PERHAPS A NEW KIND OF VIRUS?
AREN'T YOU GOING TO TAKE OFF YOUR BLINDFOLD?
I DON'T WANNA SEE A THING...
TO BE CONTINUED...

saw man
Chain

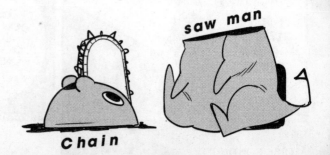

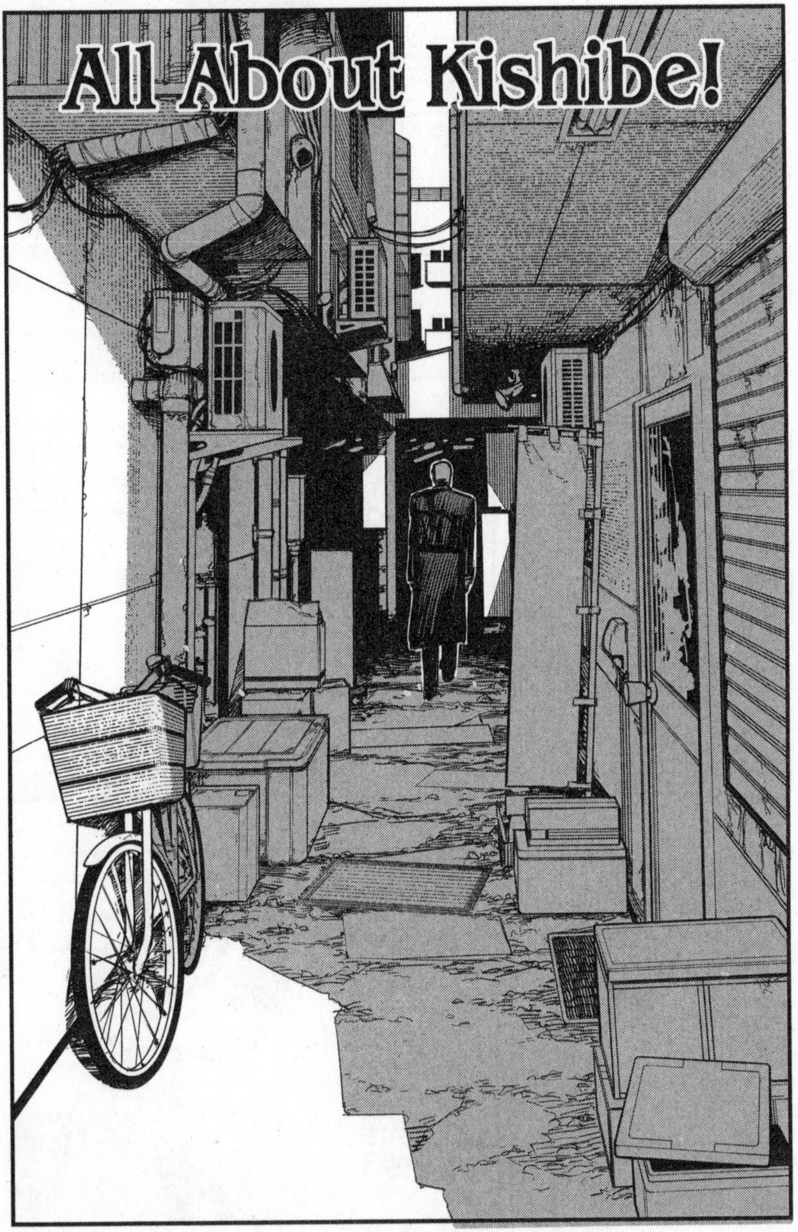
All About Kishibe!

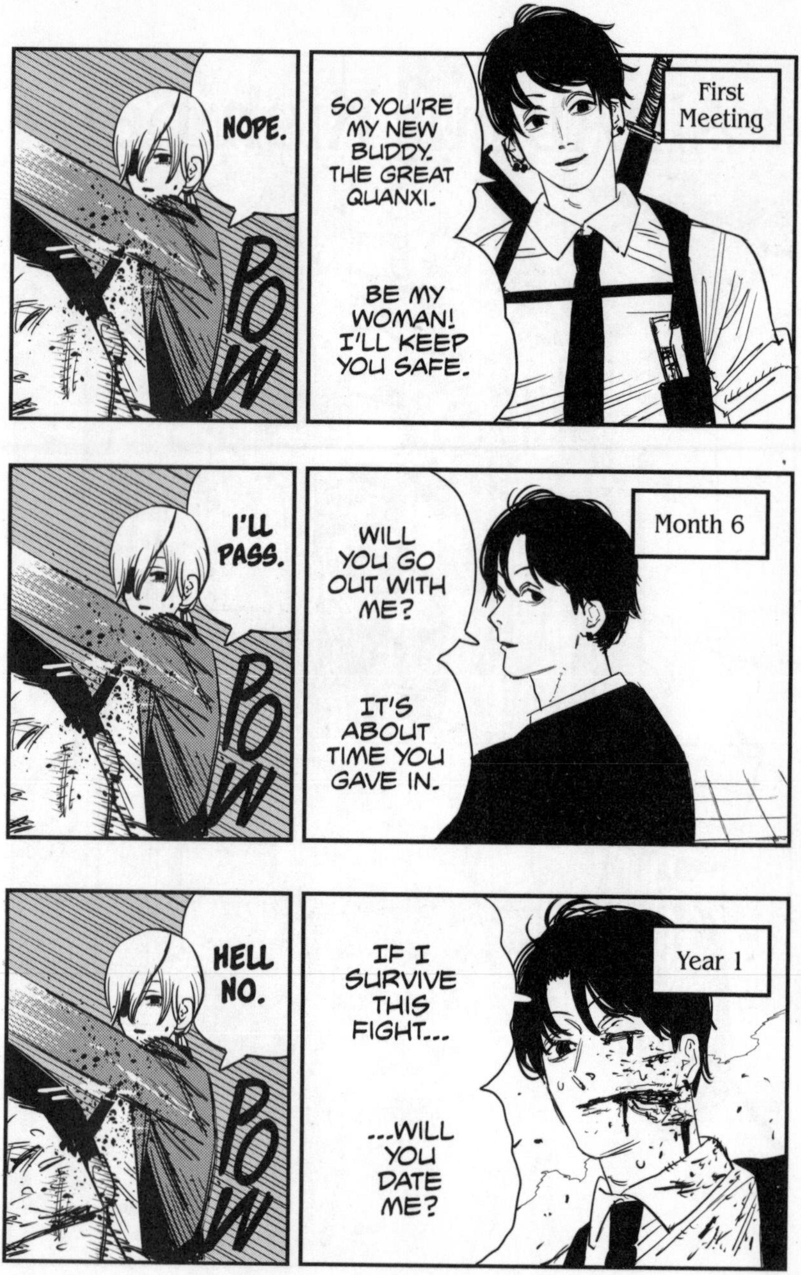
First Meeting
SO YOU'RE MY NEW BUDDY. THE GREAT QUANXI.
BE MY WOMAN! I'LL KEEP YOU SAFE.
NOPE.
POW
Month 6
WILL YOU GO OUT WITH ME?
IT'S ABOUT TIME YOU GAVE IN.
I'LL PASS.
POW
Year 1
IF I SURVIVE THIS FIGHT...
...WILL YOU DATE ME?
HELL NO.
POW

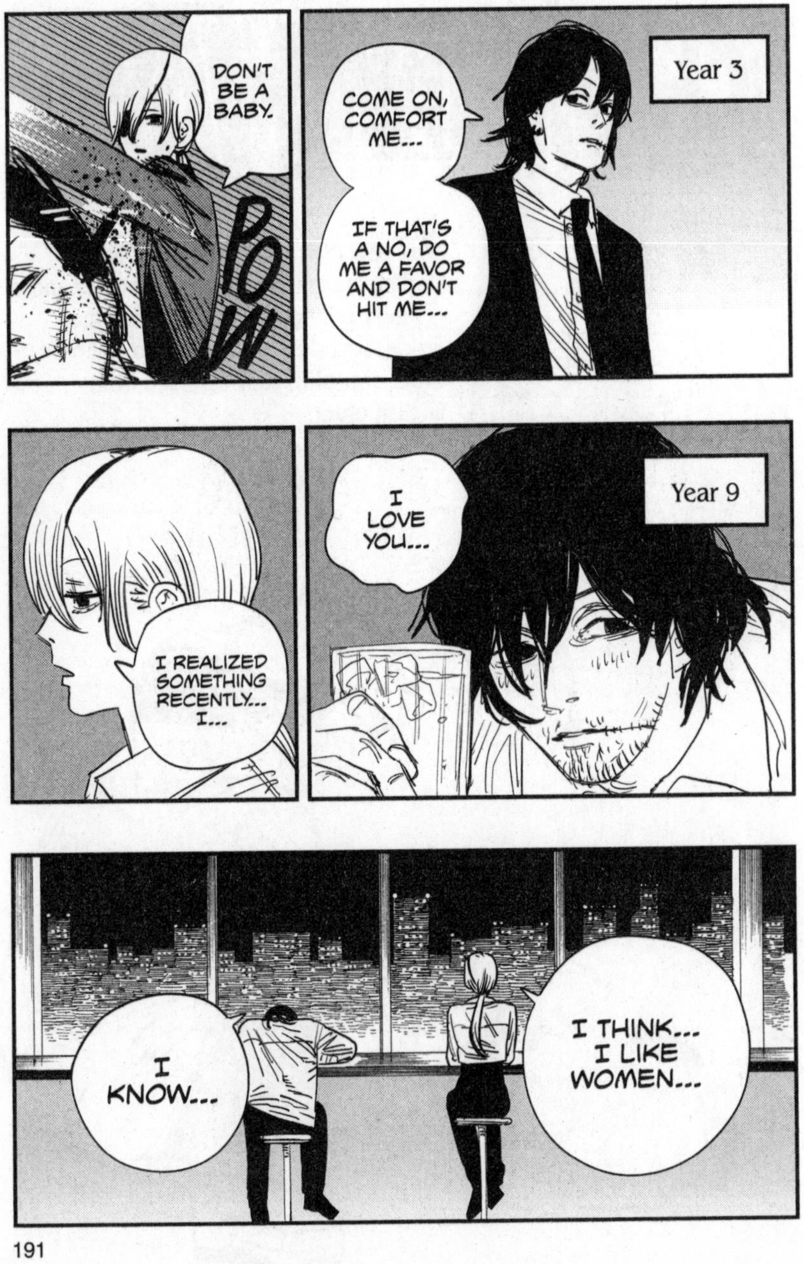
Year 3
COME ON, COMFORT ME...
IF THAT'S A NO, DO ME A FAVOR AND DON'T HIT ME...
DON'T BE A BABY.
POW
Year 9
I LOVE YOU...
I REALIZED SOMETHING RECENTLY... I...
I THINK... I LIKE WOMEN...
I KNOW...

YOU'RE READING THE WRONG WAY!

CHAINSAW MAN

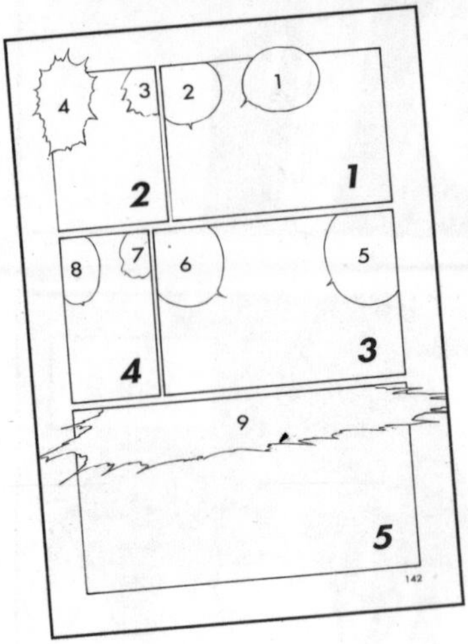

1
1
2
2
3
4
3
5
6
4
7
8
5
9
142

Chainsaw Man reads from right to left, starting in the upper-right corner. Japanese is read from right to left, meaning that action, sound effects, and word-balloon order are completely reversed from English order.

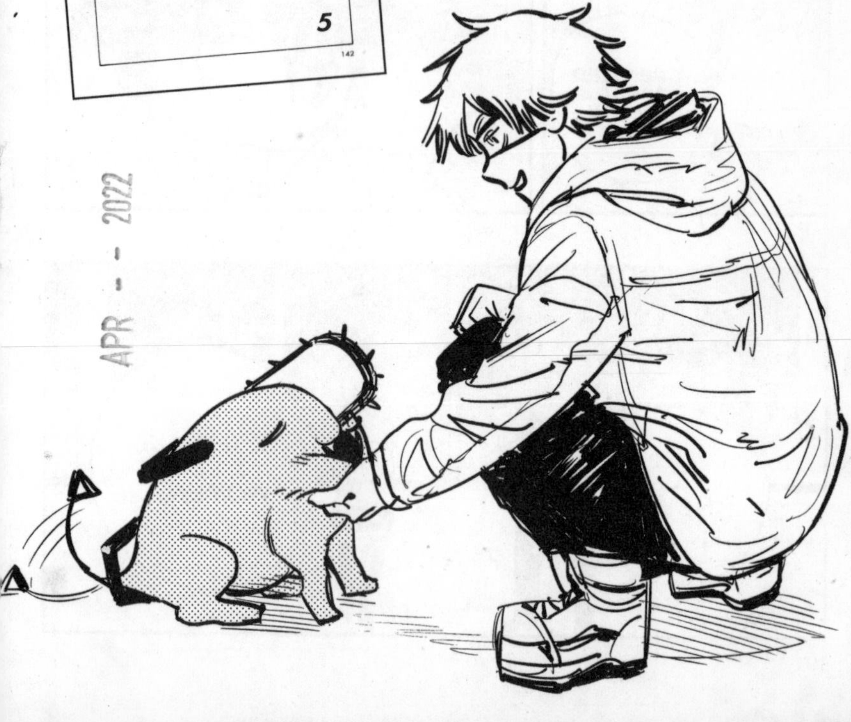